From Foundation to Summit

# From Foundation to Summit

## A Guide to Ngöndro and the Dzogchen Path

ORGYEN CHOWANG

Edited by Charles Goldman

Foreword by Dzongsar Jamyang Khyentse

SHAMBHALA

Shambhala Publications, Inc.
2129 13th Street
Boulder, Colorado 80302
www.shambhala.com

Cover art: irihaLA/Shutterstock and Bro Studio/Shutterstock
Cover design: Erin Seaward-Hiatt

9 8 7 6 5 4 3 2 1

First Edition
Printed in the United States of America

Shambhala Publications makes every effort to print on
acid-free, recycled paper.

Shambhala Publications is distributed worldwide by
Penguin Random House, Inc., and its subsidiaries.

LIBRARY OF CONGRESS CATALOGING-IN-PUBLICATION DATA
Names: Chowang, Orgyen, author. | Goldman, Charles, editor.
Title: From foundation to summit: a guide to Ngöndro and the
    Dzogchen path / Orgyen Chowang; edited by Charles Goldman.
Description: First edition. | Boulder, Colorado: Shambhala
    Publications, Inc., [2024] | Includes index.
Identifiers: LCCN 2023014052 | ISBN 9781645471820 (trade paperback)
Subjects: LCSH: Thinley Norbu. Cascading waterfall of nectar. |
    Bdud-'joms-gliṅ-pa, Gter-ston, 1835–1904. Sṅon 'gro bsdus pa. |
    Spiritual life—Rnying-ma-pa (Sect)
Classification: LCC BQ7662.6.B373 T5633 2024 | DDC 294.3/444—dc23/
    eng/20230508
LC record available at https://lccn.loc.gov/2023014052

# Contents

# Foreword

The Buddha's teachings are perfect and have never needed to be adjusted. Even so, times change, and, as the Buddha's words have spread to people living in all kinds of situations, they have been taught from many different angles. Buddha's disciples, especially the lineage holders of the great vidyadharas of the tantric tradition, found unique ways of expressing these profound teachings that were custom-made for their time and situation. The great Dudjom Lingpa was such a lineage holder, as was his reincarnation, Dudjom Jikdral Yeshe Dorje, as those who had the good fortune to meet him will testify. Thinley Norbu, Dudjom Jikdral Yeshe Dorje's heir in both the physical and spiritual sense, was highly revered during his lifetime for his exquisitely poetic approach to expressing the Buddha's truth. I feel sure that the publication of Orgyen Chowang's commentary on Thinley Norbu's *A Cascading Waterfall of Nectar* will be of immense benefit, and my aspiration is that it will inspire the blessings and fearlessness of the great tertön Dudjom Lingpa to shower down ceaselessly on this earth.

Dzongsar Jamyang Khyentse

# Editor's Preface

Back in 1994, I was asked to organize Thinley Norbu Rinpoche's first publicly announced teaching in many years. On the day of the event, I drove him from his hotel near the Los Angeles airport to the venue a few miles away, where a crowd of five hundred eager followers awaited him. Driving an unfamiliar car with a passenger who evoked so much awe and fear, sneaking looks at him in the rearview mirror, I nervously recited the Vajra Guru mantra under my breath, counting on my *mala*, as I negotiated the congested, unruly Los Angeles traffic.

After a seemingly endless silence that I perceived as a menace, Thinley Norbu Rinpoche suddenly and unshakably said, "Don't do your practice when you're driving, Chuck. See all those cars out there? Driving requires your ordinary mind. Focus on traffic with mindfulness. Do your Guru Yoga practice at home!"

That was one of my early lessons in the practice of Guru Yoga. Orgyen Chowang Rinpoche, the author of this book, gives the same teaching: "When you cook, cook; when you drive, drive; and when you meditate, meditate."

Many years later, Orgyen Chowang Rinpoche asked me to consolidate three months of his teachings, where Guru Yoga played a central role, into a book manuscript. The teachings were based on Thinley Norbu Rinpoche's superlative *A Cascading Waterfall of Nectar*,* which was ostensibly a commentary on the Dudjom

---

*Thinley Norbu, *A Cascading Waterfall of Nectar* (Boulder, CO: Shambhala Publications, 2009).

Tersar Ngöndro (the "foundational practice"), a treasure text of the Dudjom lineage; but when one reads it, it doesn't take long to see that it spans the entire range of the buddhadharma, from the very first teachings of Shakyamuni Buddha, all the way to the pinnacle of Dzogchen, with Guru Yoga as the fulcrum.

Thinley Norbu Rinpoche gave his blessing to Orgyen Chowang Rinpoche to give these teachings. He saw that Orgyen Chowang Rinpoche was quite perceptive, not just well educated (after ten years of intense study and practice, he was granted the *Khenpo* degree by Jigme Phuntsok Rinpoche, one of the greatest Dzogchen masters in modern times). After Thinley Norbu Rinpoche invited Orgyen Chowang Rinpoche to the United States, he was hosted by Lama Tharchin Rinpoche, Thinley Norbu Rinpoche's heart friend and devoted disciple, at Tharchin Rinpoche's beloved retreat center in the Santa Cruz Mountains of California, Pema Osel Ling. There, he gave teachings at the center's comprehensive three-year residential retreat program and at its college of dharma studies, which included the teachings that are the source of this book.

In early 1997, when Orgyen Chowang Rinpoche gave these teachings, his skill in speaking English was still somewhat elementary, but his skill in understanding and dealing with Western ways of thinking (which typically tend toward skepticism and confusion) were already exceptional. His teaching is as fresh and revelatory today as when originally given. Working from the original Tibetan version of *A Cascading Waterfall of Nectar*, he teases out the essential points of Thinley Norbu Rinpoche's text and points out the meaning and purpose of the *ngöndro* practice clearly and simply. He outlines the levels of dharma philosophy and places Dzogchen into the palm of our hand. He tells us why Guru Yoga is indispensable to accomplishment in Dzogchen, explains how to connect with the guru, and reveals a treasure trove of supplemental information.

This book is not intended to be a line-by-line or page-by-page guide to Thinley Norbu Rinpoche's masterwork; rather, it provides a framework for exploring that extraordinary text. Not surprisingly, this book can stand alone. It can be of immense benefit to those engaged in the Dudjom Tersar Ngöndro, to those who have already finished their ngöndro accumulations, and to those engaged in foundational practices from other Nyingma lineages.

Editing the transcripts of many hours of oral teachings to create a book manuscript had its challenges. A large amount of material had to be reduced to a publishable length. In this massive pruning project, I was careful to avoid cutting material that at first glance looked repetitive but in fact contained something novel. Also, the spoken voice is different from the written voice. Words and phrases that help in oral teachings to provide transitions, create pauses for mental breaths, and get points across often need to be eliminated for the reading audience. A series of thoughts that may need two or three sentences to say aloud are often better understood in written form when condensed into a single sentence. Editing also affords the opportunity to maintain consistency in vocabulary and style.

A special challenge arises in using English to render Tibetan thought processes. Although I am most definitely *not* a translator, I understand that the subject-object, actor-action-result structure of English can constrain the meaning of a sentence in Tibetan; as Thinley Norbu Rinpoche says in his introduction to *A Cascading Waterfall of Nectar*, "Nondoer speech does not exist in English." So I have attempted to phrase Orgyen Chowang Rinpoche's expressions in a "nondoing" way when it seemed possible and appropriate. I encourage the reader to read the words of this book as active experiencers, not as passive recipients. In the pursuit of clarity and concision in English, I hope the result does not trap the teachings in a box of intellectualism but helps blow the lid off narrow conceptual thinking.

I have inserted some explanations and observations from Orgyen Chowang Rinpoche's more recent teachings and have also added a few footnotes. Orgyen Chowang Rinpoche is passionate about making all buddhadharma teachings, especially Dzogchen teachings, as accessible to English speakers as they are to native Tibetan speakers. So in his own teachings, he updates some of the standard English translations of many Dzogchen terms.

This book is organized in chapters that follow the order of ngön-dro practice, and so the reader may be interested in starting some-where in the middle; but fair warning—some advanced material, such as Dzogchen terminology, is introduced very early (as it is in *A Cascading Waterfall*), so the experience of Dzogchen may be diluted if earlier chapters are skipped.

I am immensely indebted to Ngawang Zangpo (Hugh Thomp-son) for his amazing skill in translating Orgyen Rinpoche's dif-ficult Golok-accented Tibetan on the fly. Also, this project could not have been even contemplated without the sometimes tedious but ultimately ennobling work of recording and transcribing these teachings, so immense thanks to those who undertook those tasks. I would also like to thank Giovanna Brennan for her encouragement, Joshua Hayes for some helpful commentary, and Jane Ellison for her dakini stimuli and the opportunity to work without distraction. My sincere thanks go to Shambhala Publications and its president, Nikko Odiseos, for accepting this book for publication, and to Sham-bhala's editor Michael Wakoff for his thorough review and insightful commentary.

Although I undertook this project with enthusiasm, I know there are others who would have been much more qualified to complete it. If, in editing the original transcriptions, I have taken too many liberties, created distortions, or misunderstood Orgyen Chowang Rinpoche's meaning or intention, I offer my sincere apologies. I have embraced the opportunity to work on this project to better understand Thinley Norbu Rinpoche's amazing masterwork and to immerse myself in Orgyen Chowang Rinpoche's teachings as part of my practice. I don't know if my own effort will actually benefit others, but if it does, then it is all due to the blessings of Kyabje Dudjom Rinpoche; Kyabje Thinley Norbu Rinpoche;* the great yogi, mentor, and my root guru and companion, Tsawe Lama

*At the time of Orgyen Chowang Rinpoche's teaching in 1997, Thinley Norbu Rin-poche was commonly referred to honorifically as Dungse (family, literally "bone," lineage holder). Since his parinirvana in 2011, he has been increasingly referred to as Kyabje (Lord of Refuge).

Tharchin Rinpoche;* and the great teacher, dharma navigator, and friend Orgyen Chowang Rinpoche, who always keeps our focus on the ultimate meaning, about whom Lama Tharchin Rinpoche said, "Follow him; he will never steer you wrong," and for whom Thinley Norbu Rinpoche declared:

> From the treasury of only the white virtue of holy dharma,
> The evenly pure samsara and enlightenment teaching of
> Mahasandhi [Dzogchen],
> The uncontrived flowing teaching, is revealed by you, our
> Guru.
> By your feet being firm, may your life go from being long to
> the longest.

CHARLES GOLDMAN

---

*One of Lama Tharchin Rinpoche's many amazing qualities was his ability to make every person he taught feel like they were his best friend. I have no monopoly on this feeling.

# Preface

In 1995 I was living in Kathmandu, Nepal, and giving teachings at Ka-Nying Shedrub Ling Monastery. I knew about the great Dudjom lineage, its preeminent Lord of Refuge (*Kyabje*) Dudjom Rinpoche, and his eldest son, the great Kyabje Thinley Norbu Rinpoche. I had immense respect for these remarkable teachers. I wanted to meet Thinley Norbu Rinpoche. He was living in the United States but would visit Nepal from time to time. So I wrote him a letter and had it delivered by one of his students. He responded that he would be happy to meet me on his next visit. We met when he came to Kathmandu. We made an immediate, strong heart connection, and I received precious teachings from him. Then he returned to his home in the United States.

A few months later, Thinley Norbu Rinpoche invited me to visit the United States and stay for a while at his sacred home in upstate New York, in the outskirts of a town called Delhi. I accepted his invitation without the sliver of a moment of hesitation.

I arrived in August when the climate was warm and the land was lush. Then it turned to autumn, with its splendid display of colorful foliage and crisp air. Soon it would turn bitter cold and snowy, and Thinley Norbu Rinpoche would go to his winter home in Palm Springs, California. But Rinpoche in his wisdom knew the perfect place for me—Pema Osel Ling (Lotus Clear Light Land) in the Santa Cruz Mountains of California, where his devoted disciple Lama Tharchin Rinpoche had established a thriving Vajrayana dharma meditation center at the request of Dudjom Rinpoche. I met

Tharchin Rinpoche very briefly in Delhi. He was planning to start a *shedra*, a type of college where devoted students could spend many months learning topics in depth, at Pema Osel Ling.

So, late in 1995, I got on a plane and flew to California. Lama Tharchin Rinpoche was a wonderful person, so welcoming to me, and he was a thoroughly accomplished yogi. We made a deep connection, and I felt so much appreciation. I could not have asked for a better situation.

I spent a year getting settled at Pema Osel Ling. I learned about living in the United States and gave occasional teachings. Then, at the beginning of 1997, the shedra started. Thinley Norbu Rinpoche had recently finished writing (in Tibetan) *A Cascading Waterfall of Nectar*. I had asked him to include Dzogchen teachings in his book, and he agreed to make it part of the section on Guru Yoga. He mentions in his text that it is thanks to Tharchin Rinpoche that he wrote the text for people of future generations, for people of the West, and for Tharchin Rinpoche himself. So Lama Tharchin Rinpoche and I thought it would be perfect as source material for teaching the Dudjom Tersar (New Treasures of Dudjom) foundational practice, the Ngöndro, in depth. We asked Thinley Norbu Rinpoche for permission to give these teachings on his book, and he gave his encouragement, appreciation, and blessing.

The teachings took place most mornings continuously over a three-month period from January through March of 1997. It was intense. It was my first lengthy teaching in the United States. As my English was only rudimentary at the time, I spoke in Tibetan and Ngawang Zangpo (Hugh Thompson), an accomplished translator and devoted practitioner, translated. We had a really enjoyable time, and I was told by many people that he did an excellent job translating.

I could tell that the teachings had a big impact on all the shedra students. Many of them stayed for additional teachings after the completion of the ngöndro course. They became real practitioners.

Fortunately, thanks to all the people who helped, the teachings were recorded and transcribed. Students used the six-hundred-plus-page transcript as a reference in their ngöndro practice. From time to time, people asked if there could be a condensed version published, but other projects had to take precedence. After the English translation of *A Cascading Waterfall of Nectar* was published in 2006, there was again some interest expressed in having the teachings available as a guide to Thinley Norbu Rinpoche's book. Again, the time was not right due to other commitments.

In 2020, in the middle of the first year of the COVID pandemic, I decided that the time was right to start giving teachings based on Dzogchen texts. I had not previously given any extensive Dzogchen teachings in public. However, I felt that the right circumstances had come together to begin to share those teachings. Around the same time, I again received many students' requests to publish the teachings I had given back in 1997. Since the ngöndro course included commentary on the entire path from ngöndro through Dzogchen, it became an appropriate idea to pursue.

I could not spend much time going through the transcript myself to create a consolidated work. But fortunately, I knew that one of my longtime students, Chuck Goldman, could take on the task. Chuck received pith instructions from Thinley Norbu Rinpoche, and he was a student of Lama Tharchin Rinpoche from 1990 until Rinpoche's passing in 2013. He completed the accumulations of the Dudjom Tersar Ngöndro, attended many Dzogchen retreats at Pema Osel Ling, and spent six months in closed retreat under Tharchin Rinpoche's personal guidance. And he had extensive experience helping me with my first book, *Our Pristine Mind: A Practical Guide to Unconditional Happiness*.* So I have given my trust, confidence, and blessings to Chuck to bring this project to fruition.

I have the utmost admiration, respect, appreciation, and gratitude for Thinley Norbu Rinpoche, Dudjom Rinpoche, and the entire Dudjom lineage. I know with 100 percent certainty that this book fulfills Thinley Norbu Rinpoche's wishes and wisdom mind. Hopefully, this commentary will help unlock the keys to his boundless

*Boulder, CO: Shambhala Publications, 2016.

wisdom for the current generation. Students who have no familiarity with any teachings of buddhadharma may feel a little challenged by some of the terminology; in the past, the English vocabulary of Middle Way, Vajrayana, and Dzogchen teachings has been hard to fathom, but it continues to improve. However, readers who have some acquaintance with Vajrayana teachings will find this book to be exceptionally helpful in understanding ngöndro and Dzogchen, not only the Dudjom Tersar Ngöndro but also any other Dzogchen foundational practice, and they will find it to be especially useful in practicing Guru Yoga, the essential groundwork for Dzogchen.

From Foundation to Summit

# Introduction

I would like to express how happy I am to provide a teaching based on Thinley Norbu Rinpoche's exquisite text *A Cascading Waterfall of Nectar*. I'm not making empty praises of Thinley Norbu Rinpoche when I say that this text is very, very wonderful. It makes things extremely easy for me, as if when I read this text, it's being poured into my mind like pure water from a crystal pitcher. It makes me happy to teach; it makes it easy for me to teach. This is due to the blessing of this particular lineage, from Dudjom Lingpa to our refuge Dudjom Rinpoche, to Thinley Norbu Rinpoche. It is a sign of their blessing that this text is so wonderful and so effective.

When I read Thinley Norbu Rinpoche's text, a tremendous number of things arise within my mind—different impressions, different understandings. This is what I will try to share with you. Each word seems to have huge significance. A sense of delight arises. This is what we mean when we say "blessing." We should understand blessing as being this happiness, this joy that arises within our mind. Blessing isn't like a cloud that comes out of space and just dissolves into our head. That isn't blessing.

I would like us to begin teachings the way we begin meditation sessions—with an open mind, relaxed, a sincere sense of appreciation and gratitude for this opportunity, a readiness to be open to the possibility of an extraordinary experience. Listening to, or reading, teachings is itself a form of meditation, as we are focusing and giving our undivided attention to something special. And more than just having this relaxed and open state of mind, we generate incredible power—we cultivate the strength of our desire, our motivation, our intense intention to teach and to listen to the Buddha's teachings not just for ourselves but for the benefit of all beings in all realms, beings who fill the infinity of time and space. For their benefit, we feel an unrelenting need to attain during this very lifetime, right now, unsurpassable enlightenment, the personification of the five wisdoms, the primordial protector Buddha Kuntuzangpo (Tib.), Samantabhadra (Skt.) (Ever Excellent). The stronger our desire to feel the extraordinary, the stronger is the possibility that we will actually experience the extraordinary. Our appreciation, admiration, gratitude, devotion, and love for enlightened qualities give the teaching the power to move us, and our listening or reading, our contemplation and our meditation, make us the really powerful, extraordinary beings that we actually are. That is also what *blessing* means. This transformation from the plain, ordinary mind-set to the exalted, extraordinary mind-set makes recognition of our true nature—enlightenment, what we so much desire to experience—effortless.

The central topic of this teaching is the foundational practice (ngöndro) of the New Treasures of the Dudjom tradition (the Dudjom Tersar) and how this practice leads inexorably to the recognition of our true nature, which is undeniable enlightenment. It is important to talk a little about where this profound ngöndro comes from. We must also talk about the lives of the dharma masters, particularly Guru Rinpoche Padmasambhava. It is said in the tantras (the source texts for Vajrayana, including the Dzogchen tantras) that it is absolutely essential to begin any practice or teaching with an understanding of its particular lineage. Otherwise we will not gain confidence in it. Then we can go into a detailed discussion.

## Samantabhadra

The original, first, primordial buddha is the buddha of the ultimate aspect of enlightenment (*dharmakaya*), Kuntuzangpo (Samantabhadra, Ever Excellent).* Regarding all sentient beings, he noticed that wherever there is space, there are sentient beings, and wherever there are sentient beings, they are pervaded by suffering. Seeing this, immeasurable compassion toward all beings arose in him, and innumerable manifestations of him emanated throughout the universe. Among those manifestations of Samantabhadra, there are 1,002 buddhas manifesting in our particular world system.

## Buddha Shakyamuni

At our particular place and time, the historical buddha is Buddha Shakyamuni. He was an emanation or manifestation of Samantabhadra. In this world, he performed what are called the "twelve acts of the Buddha," and particularly in Bodhgaya, India, on the Vajra Seat, he attained full and complete enlightenment. From that moment on, he taught the buddhadharma.

Like Samantabhadra, Buddha Shakyamuni was faced with sentient beings who had differing desires and capabilities. Some were interested in the Shravakayana teachings—for example, the listeners (shravakas) and the solitary sages (pratyekabuddhas). Some were drawn to Middle Way (Madhyamaka) teachings. Others were attracted to bodhisattva teachings. So Buddha Shakyamuni "turned the wheel of the dharma" on three different occasions, and these are the three distinct cycles of his teachings. For the first audience, he taught the Four Noble Truths in Varanasi, India: (1) all life in samsara (the endless repetition of rebirth in the realms of existence) is suffering, (2) suffering is caused by karma—the universally operative principle of cause and effect—and the negative emotions, (3) it is possible to extract oneself from this cycle of the causes and effects of suffering, and (4) practicing the buddhadharma leads to the cessation of suffering and its causes. The Four Noble Truths are Shravakayana teachings.

*Orgyen Chowang Rinpoche points out that rather than going back in time to a beginningless beginning, the primordial Buddha, like all aspects of enlightenment, lies beyond any concept of time or place and is ever present, never born.

In the second turning of the wheel of dharma, he taught the bodhisattva teachings at Vulture Peak, India, which included the Prajnaparamita (transcendent wisdom) sutras. This particular cycle of the Buddha's teachings is called "without characteristics"—that everything on a relative level is unreal and has no solid reality, like a dream or an illusion.* This is the truth we call "emptiness." He went on to say that the reality of things is beyond our ordinary conceptual mind, beyond our ordinary range of experience.

The third cycle of teachings began, according to Jamgon Mipham Rinpoche, in an area of Sri Lanka known as Lotus Land. In this cycle, the Buddha said that the true nature of all sentient beings, their buddha nature, is enlightenment. This last cycle was given for persons of the highest level of capability.

The Buddha gave all these teachings in order to guide sentient beings. It is simply not possible to satisfy everybody with one particular type of teaching. If you say, "The nature of all beings is enlightenment," some people will not be satisfied. Perhaps you have to start with something a bit more elementary. Thus, the first level of teachings of the Buddha describes the impermanence of all things and the cause of suffering. On the second level, he describes everything as emptiness. On the third and final level, he describes all beings' nature as enlightenment.

All of these teachings fall into the category of the discourses or the sutras of the Buddha. These constitute the first three of the nine levels (*yanas*) of the buddhadharma. The first three levels are called the "causal systems"—to reach enlightenment you create

---

*Orgyen Chowang Rinpoche has replaced the customary use of *phenomena* in Thinley Norbu Rinpoche's text with terms such as *everything, experience, things that appear, all things,* and similar words and phrases that refer to the experiences and the field of experience of sentient beings or those in transcendent states, depending on the context, because (1) *phenomena* carries with it a connotation of something out of the ordinary, an unusual experience, and also has a scent of intellectualism; and (2) *everything* includes whatever is, or may be, within the experience, actual or imagined, mental or physical, material or immaterial, of sentient beings in all realms whatsoever, or within the experience of enlightened ones, again depending on the context.

causes that have the eventual effect of enlightenment. However, during his lifetime the Buddha predicted that in the future there would be teachings that were more direct, that don't rely on cause and effect—that is, the fruition teachings of the tantras, what we call the "Vajrayana."

## Padmasambhava

The systems of the listeners, the solitary sages, and the bodhisatt-vas all teach that enlightenment is attainable only after many life-times of effort. The basic idea in the tantras, however, is that the true nature of the mind and all the mind's experiences are already infinite purity from beginningless time, so that enlightenment can be obtained in three lifetimes, or even one. The Buddha did not stress this teaching during his own lifetime. However, he did predict that twelve years after he passed into nirvana, someone greater than him would be born at Lake Danakosha in the north-west country of Oddiyana. He would not take birth from a womb but from the center of a lotus. This was the prediction of the birth of Guru Rinpoche Padmasambhava, whom we can consider to be an emanation of Buddha Shakyamuni. We can also consider him to be an emanation of the transcendent Buddha Amitabha. In any event, Guru Rinpoche has been considered greater than Buddha Shakyamuni since he came into the world to teach all nine yanas of view, practice, and conduct of the Buddha's path, including the three highest yanas, the Mahayoga, Anuyoga and Atiyoga (Dzogchen) teachings.

Guru Rinpoche taught throughout India, Oddiyana, Nepal, Bhu-tan, and Tibet during the eighth century, and particularly mani-fested in eight distinct embodiments that he revealed throughout these places. The buddhadharma teachings first appeared in Tibet earlier, with a Tibetan king named Lhato Tori Nyantsen. They didn't spread much during his reign, but during the reign of a later king, Songtsen Gompo, the dharma doctrine spread quite a bit. And when King Trisong Deutsen invited the exceptional Khenpo

Shantarakshita and Guru Rinpoche to Tibet, this enabled all the Buddha's teachings to proliferate widely.

Shantarakshita mainly taught the discourses of the Buddha (the sutras), the teachings on monastic discipline (the *vinaya*), and the teachings on knowledge (the *abhidharma*). Guru Rinpoche and Vimalamitra, and many others, mainly taught Vajrayana and Dzogchen. There was also a tremendous amount of translation being done at that time at Samye Monastery by Tibetan translators and the great masters from India. There was a wide-ranging exchange between India and Tibet during this period, so not only the basic teachings but also the teachings of all the yanas came to Tibet and were very well translated and corrected. This made that particular time extremely important.

## Treasure Teachings

Guru Rinpoche himself gave quite a number of teachings in Tibet. After the death of King Trisong Deutsen, his successor and Yeshe Tsogyal, Guru Rinpoche's principal consort, asked Guru Rinpoche, "What is going to become of us? What will our future be?"

Guru Rinpoche made many predictions. Based on his vision of the future, he (or, thanks to her infallible memory, Yeshe Tsogyal) concealed throughout the Tibetan territory a large number of teachings (called "treasure teachings") and other materials. Guru Rinpoche predicted who was going to discover them in the future, where they would be found, and how and when they would be discovered.

Since our central topic is a treasure teaching, it is very important for us to understand what treasure teachings are, in general, and in particular, the treasure history of the Dudjom lineage.

We say that there are one hundred different treasure discoverers or treasure revealers (*tertons*). However, each one is an emanation of one or another of Guru Rinpoche's twenty-five major disciples. Whatever their names might be—for example, Dudjom Lingpa or Dudjom Rinpoche—they all have their source in the inner circle of these twenty-five disciples. For example, Guru Rinpoche would predict that, at a specific place and time, a specific treasure revealer would be born. He explained that, at such place and time, there would be a particular problem, such as a famine, war, flood, and so on, for which particular teachings would prove beneficial. Guru Rinpoche prepared or arranged things so that every one to two hundred years, treasure revealers would appear and reveal treasures that were important for that particular place and time.

## The Dudjom Lineage

The source for our ngöndro comes from one of the translator-disciples of Guru Rinpoche, Kyeuchung Lotsawa. Because this translator was a disciple of Guru Rinpoche during his lifetime, he received entirely the empowerments, transmissions, and instructions of the Dudjom lineage that we now have. They were rediscovered when he was reborn as Dudjom Lingpa.

Dudjom Lingpa was born in 1835 in the province of Kham, which is in eastern Tibet. During his lifetime, he had visions of various deities or individuals such as Tara, Guru Rinpoche, Longchenpa, and Saraha. He also recalled entirely his previous lifetime as a disciple of Guru Rinpoche. This experience overflowed in his mind and became the source of many teachings; he also found many teachings concealed underground. This particular teaching on ngöndro was received in a vision.

Dudjom Lingpa taught many students. He brought them to maturity in dharma, then to liberation. Near the end of his life, he told his students that he was going to be reborn in a very remote area of southwest Tibet called Pemako. He was reborn as Jigdral Yeshe Dorje, Dudjom Rinpoche, in 1904.

The story of Jigdral Yeshe Dorje is extremely well known throughout Tibet and particularly in the Sertar area where Dudjom Lingpa had lived before going to Pemako. Everybody knew that Dudjom Lingpa was going to be reborn in southwest Tibet. When they went to Pemako to see the child who was thought to be the reincarnation, he spoke to them in the dialect of far eastern Tibet (Dudjom Lingpa's dialect), which is very, very different from the dialect of Pemako. That made them completely convinced that this was the right child.

Dudjom Rinpoche was extremely exceptional even from a very young age. He had visions and recollected his past lives. Aside from his many treasure revelations, he wrote extensively—more than forty volumes. He provided both the ngöndro practices and his own commentary to these practices. Now we have a commentary written by his son Thinley Norbu Rinpoche, who is a reincarnation of Tulku Drimed, one of Dudjom Lingpa's eight sons. Dudjom Rinpoche said a number of times that Thinley Norbu Rinpoche had greater realization and erudition than he did.

Dudjom Rinpoche gave the entirety of his teachings, empowerments, reading transmissions, and instructions to Thinley Norbu Rinpoche. It is thanks to this particularly strong connection between the two of them that Thinley Norbu Rinpoche wrote his commentary. So this comes to us with a very strong connection. What is more, I asked Thinley Norbu Rinpoche for permission to give these teachings, and he gave his blessing.

Thinley Norbu Rinpoche's commentary on the ngöndro is unlike any other. Here we find all the thought of the sutras. Here we have all the thought of the Middle Way philosophy. Here we have all the tantras. We have Dzogchen. Thinley Norbu Rinpoche based his book on the teachings of three renowned teachers: Longchenpa, Rongzompa, and Dudjom Rinpoche, and especially on his own experience of the view, meditation, and action, or conduct, of Dzogchen. He has experience of the view, meditation, and action, or conduct, of Dzogchen, so we need not have any doubt whatsoever about the authenticity of his commentary. We can't really say that this is just a commentary on the preliminary practice. This is really the main practice.

# CHAPTER 1

# Introduction to the Foundational Practice

The foundational practice is part of the cycle of teachings from Dudjom Lingpa called "pure vision," the "net" or "web" of wisdom. Dudjom Lingpa revealed particular treasures through pure vision—literally, pure appearance. What do we mean when we say "pure vision"? Usually, sentient beings experience the world as impure vision—that is, as filtered through our karma, thoughts, and negative emotions: anger, desire, ignorance, jealousy, pride, and so on. A person who has done some refinement of their inner experience has half-pure, half-impure vision. For example, someone on the path may have achieved the ability to experience a universe of galaxies as the manifestation of enlightenment but still feels sad and angry about war, hunger, disease, and other realities. Those who have attained enlightenment have only pure vision. Pure vision is to see the nature of things directly as they are—entirely wisdom. Instead of experiencing reality through a lens of thoughts and negative emotions, they see all-accomplishing wisdom, the wisdom of equanimity, and other forms of wisdom that represent the purification of the negative emotions, the end of karma.

Ordinary, impure experience originates from the mind. As ordinary sentient beings, we perceive ourselves as subject and everything else as object.* However much we rely on our experience

---

*Object* is used in its broadest sense. It refers not only to things of matter that we

from karma, negative emotions, and various thoughts and beliefs, that much impurity we experience in the objective world. However, our mind's true nature is pure. All the various thoughts, emotions, beliefs, and results of various causes that arise in our mind give us the impression that the world is an impure mix of good and bad, beautiful and terrible; but there is no actual impurity in the world. Impurity is entirely an experience of our own mind. It is not a thing with any real existence whatsoever.

The best metaphor to understand this is a dream. During a dream, we might see mountains, rivers, beings, or other various things, but in fact we're lying in bed asleep and our dream experience is a projection of our own mind. In the same way, the outer world that we experience every day is a projection of our own mind. Once our own mind is completely pure, once we have experienced the nature of our own mind,* then all these impure appearances simply cease to exist and the world is experienced in its primordial purity. This is what we mean when we say that Dudjom Lingpa had pure vision and that these teachings came from his pure experience. And by meditating on the path of Dzogchen, we, too, can experience pure vision.

This particular practice is a preparatory practice to Dzogchen. The term used in Tibetan is *ngöndro*, which literally means "what goes before." It leads to the main practice of Dzogchen. We have various teachings for the main practice of Dzogchen. However, for these practices to become effective, we must receive "pointing-out" instructions—introduction to the nature of mind, exactly how the

---

perceive but also to processes, systems, structures, patterns, rhythms, and other experiences. Examples include a baby's attraction to its mother's face; the language we use to identify thoughts; the mathematics we use to describe space, time, matter, and energy; and even our penchant for organizing dharma into lots of categories.

*To say "we have experienced the nature of our own mind" reveals the limitation of language, and English in particular, when it's used to describe the experience of nondual awareness. Instead of *we* and *our* the terms *one* and *one's* may be used, as they are in Thinley Norbu Rinpoche's text; but here, in an effort to make the view of Dzogchen accessible, and in keeping with Orgyen Chowang Rinpoche's teaching style, *we* and *our* are used most of the time.

mind is. And without first training the mind, this pointing-out instruction will not be effective. So we do ngöndro to prepare the mind for the pointing-out instructions. When the mind is prepared, we can really see from these pointing-out instructions exactly what the nature of mind is. Then all the Dzogchen teachings and practices will be effective.

The particular form of practice for which this is the commentary is a very abridged form of foundational practice, very simple and direct. Thinley Norbu Rinpoche says he wrote his commentary like a smoothly flowing river. That is to say, it is natural. It is whatever came into his mind, and it allows us to enter into the practice very easily, very directly.

## The Connection between Sentient Beings and Buddhas

We can differentiate two aspects of enlightenment. One is the nature of mind, which is ultimate enlightenment. The other is the appearance aspect, like Guru Rinpoche, Avalokiteshvara, and Tara, who are manifestations or emanations of enlightenment.

How do sentient beings connect with enlightenment? Through the compassion expressed by these appearance aspects. We sentient beings have within us the natural state of enlightenment, the nature of our mind. However, we live in a state of ignorance and delusion. Enlightened ones realize this. They say, "Where there is no self, beings hold to a self; where there is no necessity for suffering, they suffer." So to express their compassion and help us sentient beings wake from our sleep of ignorance, they teach the correct path to enlightenment, in order to free us from suffering. This is the basis of the connection between buddhas and sentient beings.

The remarkable teacher and scholar Jamgon Mipham Rinpoche gave an illustration of this compassionate activity. He said it is like two persons in a room, one of whom is sleeping and having a bad dream, terrified that a tiger is coming to eat him. Now the other person has a higher perception. He knows that this person is having a bad dream. He can tell him in his dream, "Look, you are just dreaming. This is all an appearance of your own confusion. This is not really happening. Wake up." We are like the sleeping person going lifetime after lifetime without knowing that our life experience is a dreamlike appearance that arises from ignorance and confusion. The buddhas come into our world through their compassion and help us to awaken from the sleep of ignorance to our own inner nature. Based on this compassion, there is a relationship between us and enlightenment.

It's important to understand that a buddha's activity and wishes for the benefit of sentient beings is not about "Buddhism." A buddha doesn't think, "I want my doctrine to grow. I want to help my particular tradition spread." This is not a buddha's perspective at all. Whatever people need, a buddha can help them in that respect. If sentient beings need medicine, a buddha can take the form of a doctor or medicine. Shantideva prayed that if sentient beings would be helped by a bridge or a boat, he wanted to be reborn as a bridge or a boat. Of course, specific dharma practices are crucial to us; we see them as what is most essential to benefit ourselves and others. However, a buddha's perspective embraces all space and all the needs of sentient beings through compassion. It has nothing to do with the buddha being "Buddhist" or not.

Also, when we talk about a buddha's activity, it is not like an ordinary person who has thoughts and thinks, "I am going to do this or that." A buddha's activity is effortless and manifests naturally. A buddha's actions are like those of the sun. However many buckets of water you put on the ground, the sun appears in every one of those buckets. It is not that if it appears here, then it can't appear elsewhere at the same time. Also, there is no intentional thought behind the appearance of the sun. The sun doesn't decide to appear here or there. It is effortlessly and naturally manifest. This illustrates how a buddha's activity appears in the world. Before we attain enlightenment, we make different prayers and aspirations— for instance, "I wish to appear in one hundred different forms for one hundred sentient beings." We try to clear away the veils that cover our mind, and we try to develop positive actions. However, our action depends upon our intention. At the point of enlightenment, there is no longer any intention. There is simply effortless, naturally manifest activity.

A buddha's compassion is totally pure. A buddha has no self-clinging, no self-interest, no negative emotions. Through the strength of enlightened compassion, a buddha can work for the benefit of sentient beings. This is very different from our own experience of compassion, which is always mixed with our own emotions, our own self-clinging, even if such emotions and self-clinging are motivated by positive intentions.

In order to benefit and guide sentient beings, a buddha may take any number of forms—peaceful, wrathful, and in between. Some people say, "You people have an awful lot of deities." Well, yes, we do. We've got about as many deities as there are sentient beings! If it were possible for all sentient beings to be guided by a single deity, we would have just one. Buddhas have no need to take many forms; the various buddhadharma deities are emanations of buddhas in response to the myriad needs of sentient beings. Thinley Norbu Rinpoche says it would be just fine with him if there were only one form, only one teaching, and that would be it. That would be very easy.

But people have preferences and desires for variety. Some people will not be guided by peaceful deities. Some cannot be guided by wrathful deities. This range of interests is not only reflected in the range of deities. Shakyamuni Buddha gave elementary teachings for the listeners and the solitary sages. He taught the bodhisattva path. Then he gave teachings in the levels of tantra. Each of these teachings were given only in relation to the persons in front of him. It was what was useful for them to guide them to enlightenment. The Buddha said, "As long as there are various states of mind of sentient beings, different kinds of interests, there will be that diversity of teachings." An inconceivable and infinite number of teachings exist in order to guide us. The Buddha had no wish to make things particularly complicated for us. Simply, this is in relation to our needs.

Buddhas and all the enlightened deities are projections that come from the pure essence of our mind, our buddha nature. In much the same way, when we experience harm or unhappiness, it's not caused by a demon who exists as a separate entity outside of ourselves; it's an appearance that arises from our negative habits. Mipham Rinpoche gave an example. Most people find human corpses very unpleasant; they don't want to be around a corpse. However, a person unaware that a corpse lay inside their pillowcase could nevertheless sleep very soundly. Nothing negative would arise in their mind whatsoever. In the same way, any experience of suffering or feeling of harm is a reflection of our feelings and thoughts.

The reclusive sage Milarepa was once visited by a demoness. She told him, "Look, if you don't understand that demons are simply an expression of the innate energy of your own mind, not only will I visit you but also lots of other demons will come to visit you." In this way, he began to understand the true nature of demons. He realized that demons appear through self-clinging and through the force of getting lost in thought.* In experiencing a devil, that force brings tremendous harm. However, if we understand that this is an appearance of our own mind, it doesn't provoke any sort of inner turmoil and we are liberated from any appearances of demons.

---

*"Lost in thought" is a way of translating the Tibetan term *namtok* and is used in this commentary. An important term, *namtok* has often been translated as "discursive thought," but *discursive* means "meandering," "wandering," or "drifting," whereas *namtok* covers a much broader territory. It can indicate a train of thought, obsessing on thoughts, distorted thoughts, preoccupied thoughts, proliferating thoughts, ordinary thinking, and so on. One way that Orgyen Chowang Rinpoche has explained *namtok* is that due to our karmic propensities, we engage in lots of thinking, fabricating and projecting our sense of self and reality; we get lost in thought because we don't recognize the true nature of self and reality. Being lost in thought, the universe of inner and outer experiences we create through namtok defines our view of ourselves and the world, and continues our experience of samsara by reaffirming and creating karmic propensities. In this text, *namtok* is also sometimes translated as "ordinary thoughts" or "ordinary thinking."

## The Invocation

The Ngöndro text begins, "Namo, lumed tengyi gonpo lama khyen." "Homage! I beseech you to know me, Lama, deceitless, constant protector."* *Namo* is Sanskrit for "homage" or "I pay homage." We pay homage to our dharma master, the lama, who is considered to be inseparable from Guru Rinpoche. It is said here that the lama is infallible ("deceitless") and a constant protector for all sentient beings. And we ask for the lama's attention.

The lama is the person who leads us to temporary happiness in the higher realms of existence. The negative experiences of life in the lower realms—the hell realms, the realm of the starving spirits, and the animal realms—have arisen due to negative karma. The experiences of life in the higher realms—the human realm, the demigod realms, and the god realms—are positive experiences that depend upon the accumulation of positive karma.

The attainment of a life in the three higher realms is what we call "temporary benefit" or "temporary happiness." The dharma master also protects and leads us infallibly to ultimate or complete happiness, the state of enlightenment. The dharma master is the union of all the three jewels: the buddha, the teachings of the buddha (the dharma), and the community of practitioners (the sangha). We take refuge in the lama as our own root teacher from now until we attain enlightenment.

Who is our root teacher? This is the person who has given us empowerments, transmissions, and instructions; Dudjom Rinpoche, for example. His body is the community of practitioners. His speech is the Buddha's teachings. His mind is the Buddha himself.

When we ask the teacher to know us, *lama khyen*, *khyen* is asking for the lama's attention. Thinley Norbu Rinpoche explains this by describing three kinds of faith: (1) clear or inspired faith, (2) enthusiastic faith, and (3) confident faith. When we first hear of the

---

*Translations of the Ngöndro text have changed slightly since the publication of *A Cascading Waterfall of Nectar.*

qualities of the three jewels or the lama and have a special feeling of inspiration or a very clear openness, this is what we call "clear faith."

The second type of faith is the faith of desire or intention, which Thinley Norbu Rinpoche calls "enthusiastic faith." We've been inspired to think about enlightenment, and now we actually wish to attain enlightenment ourselves.

The third type of faith is the faith of confidence. The words Thinley Norbu Rinpoche uses are "request for the dharma master to know me." That is to say, when we really appreciate the extraordinary qualities of enlightenment, we remain completely open, completely confident in the three jewels whether we are sick or suffering, whether we go to the lower realms or the higher realms, whether we are happy or sad; and we think, "I have no other reference point but you." We translate it as "confidence," but as Thinley Norbu expresses it, it means opening one's mind and saying, "Please know me." With whatever level of faith we have, from the depths of our heart, we ask the dharma master, through their compassion and love, to accept us.

At this point in the commentary, Thinley Norbu Rinpoche says, in effect, "We've said so far that the lama is infallible. In order to discern the quality of infallibility, we have to ask, 'Are there objects of refuge that are fallible?'"

He responds, in effect, "Wow! There are a whole lot!" There are many objects of refuge that can deceive us, that can lead us in directions we do not wish to go, that can cause suffering, resulting in our remaining stuck in ordinary, worldly life with ordinary, negative emotions.

This begs the question: What is the source of all this ordinary experience, this ordinary life, these causes and results of suffering, all the various psychological and physical constituents of our experience?

## The Views of Eternalism and Nihilism

Ordinary existence can be explained in different ways—for example, as the creation of God, as something that arises naturally, or as coming from nothing whatsoever.

The view of those who believe the world was created by God is the idea that although the world may be impermanent, it is a creation of God and God is permanent, eternal. Thinley Norbu calls this view "eternalism." From the view of the buddhadharma, the idea of a real, all-powerful, all-knowing, all-good, eternal God is incompatible with an impermanent, ignorant, impure world.

Thinley Norbu Rinpoche also discusses the view called "nihilism," the view that the world has no ultimate cause. Everything just happens, like mushrooms growing in a field: nobody has planted them; they appear to just grow all by themselves. According to nihilists, there is no underlying cause of our having come into being. Also, once this life is over, the mind comes to an end; there is no future life, nor is there any life before this one. And nihilists don't believe in the existence of anything that cannot be experienced (directly or with instruments) through the senses.

However, just because you can't see something doesn't mean it does not exist. Just because a blind person can't see an object doesn't mean it does not exist; a deaf person might think there are no sounds, but there are sounds. In the same way, we can talk about past lives and future lives.

Also, we cannot say with any certainty that there aren't other worlds like our own throughout the infinity of space. Nobody has gone through the infinity of space and determined whether there is life somewhere else in the universe. We simply cannot affirm or deny this statement without such experience. To deny the existence of something that isn't seen or detected is the sign of a very limited viewpoint, like that of a child who simply doesn't understand.

But if the world did not arise from nothing, or from an ultimate creator, then where did it come from? How does the world come into being?

From the very beginning of the Buddha's teachings, from the Shravakayana view that existence arises from permanent, atomic particles, to the highest view of Dzogchen, it has been agreed that there is an underlying causation of the world and links of causation through cause and effect. We do not believe that the world was created by a god or that it has arisen without any cause. If you want to understand a result, you must look at its underlying causes. If you want to understand the future, you must look at the causes being created now. Once a cause has been made, there is no obstruction to its inevitable results. It is just that the different conditions must come together for the results to manifest. It is only a matter of time before all the conditions are collected in order for the result to be produced.

## The Primordial Basis

From the Dzogchen point of view, the root of the links of causation is the dualistic mind. The dualistic mind is the source of the outer universe and of one's own self, all the psychophysical aggregates of one's being.

But if this whole world, everything that we know in the universe as well as ourselves, has arisen through the dualistic mind, where does this mind come from? Obviously, this is a crucial question.

In the Mahayana tradition, the question is sometimes framed as follows: "All life lives on earth. What is the basis of the earth?" "The basis of the earth is a great ocean." "What is the basis of this great ocean?" "The ocean is sitting on air." "What is the air sitting on?" "It is sitting in space." Here we have arrived at the basis of all things: space. Space doesn't rest on anything at all. Space simply is. Similarly, we have our body, with all our different senses and faculties. These arise from our karma, which in turn arises from our emotions, which arise from getting lost in thought, which arises from luminosity, the basic, substanceless luminosity of mind. What is this luminosity of mind? There is nothing besides this luminosity of mind. There is nothing underlying it. It is simply the nature of everything. Just as everything in the outer world, all the elements, everything whatsoever, arises within space and nothing underlies space, so in our own experience, the basis is this fundamental luminosity. There is nothing besides that. This is simply the way things are.

In Dzogchen, the essence of this primordial basis is neither positive nor negative. There is no pure or impure, virtuous or nonvirtuous, samsara or nirvana—they never exist in fundamental reality. Thinley Norbu Rinpoche says the primordial basis is "indefinite" or "empty" because it has none of the characteristics of samsara or transcendence. It goes beyond any of our possibilities of conception or expression. You cannot take our ordinary concepts and try to apply them to the primordial basis.

However, the primordial basis is not void like a vacuum; while its essence is empty or indefinite, its nature is clarity, and its energy is all-pervasive wisdom. At this particular stage, the clarity is inner; there is no outward expression at all. This clarity is often referred to as "inner luminosity" or "inner radiance."

We can try to understand inner radiance through the example of a crystal. The potential for radiating different colored lights exists within the crystal. However, without sunlight striking the crystal, these lights will not appear outside. Yet, we can think of these lights as existing within the crystal whether the sunlight is on it or not. In the same way, the inner radiance and energy of wisdom abide within the primordial basis but are not expressed.

When appearances arise from this primordial basis, at that moment, we can talk about the beginnings of enlightenment or the beginnings of ordinary mind, and we can distinguish between enlightened experience and the experience of ordinary beings. When the wisdom appears outside, like when sunlight hits a crystal, at that first moment, the experience is radiant, primordial basis. If these appearances are immediately recognized as arising from the natural energy of our own true nature, this is awareness (*rigpa*). The recognition of these appearances as being our own appearance indicates enlightenment. We experience accurately the enlightened mind. However, if these appearances are not recognized as being the appearance of our own natural energy, then this is ignorance (*marigpa*), and this is the source of ordinary mind. Everything follows from that immediate recognition or nonrecognition.

Apart from the teachings of Dzogchen, this distinction cannot be easily explained. At the moment when inner wisdom within luminosity appears outside, there are various appearances. If these appearances are seen but not their essence, then this is called "ignorance." We think that there is a self and there are appearances, and there is a difference between "me" and "you." The dualistic mind arises right at that moment. But Buddha Ever Excellent (Samantabhadra), at that very point, is aware that there is neither subject nor object. Appearances simply arise from his own essence. This rigpa, this awareness, perceives all the various forms of enlightenment and all the various wisdoms. This appearance of wisdom on the outside is the manifestation of his awareness. For ordinary persons like ourselves, our ignorance at that point in time creates dualistic experience, and all these various forms of wisdom or the bodies of enlightenment become our various emotions and karma.

This description of Samantabhadra's awareness illustrates the difficulty of describing the nondualistic nature of enlightenment in the conceptual terms of language. Samantabhadra is not a being who "has awareness" of something other or who recognizes anything either within himself or outside; "his awareness" is the nature of nondual awareness, which is inexpressible.

Mipham Rinpoche explained that without having clarity, it is impossible to attain realization. We must accurately identify the essence of what we see with this subjective mind. We might see a multicolored rope on the ground and think it is a snake. We would then have feelings about the snake. But we don't necessarily see the actuality, the essence (that is, the rope). Similarly, we don't understand the true nature of all of these appearances that arise from the primordial basis. Seeing an appearance from the primordial basis as it is, is enlightenment. It is like seeing a rope as a rope.

In Dzogchen, the introduction to rigpa is extremely important. At the moment that we understand the presentation of rigpa, we become aware of the primordial basis, and at that point, our nonawareness dissolves. This is why, in Dzogchen, this introduction to rigpa is essential.

We have two forms of ignorance. The first is called "coemergent ignorance." Ignorance and our ordinary mind arise at the same time. We simply do not recognize the essence of the appearance of the primordial basis at the time it arises. It does not come to mind or we have been distracted. At that particular moment, there is dualistic thought and this is coemergent ignorance.

The second form of ignorance is called "pervasive labeling." Once coemergent ignorance has arisen and we don't recognize our own essence in the appearances before us, dualistic experience solidifies into "I have a self; everything else is other." There is labeling self, labeling this, that, and the other.

These two forms of ignorance are the basis of the confused experience of ordinary sentient beings.

To take a slight step back, the primordial basis is the basis of both buddhas and sentient beings. We share the same nature, the same primordial basis. Upon this basis, if there is awareness, rigpa, this creates the path of the buddhas. Upon this basis, if there is ignorance, this creates the path of sentient beings. However, at the beginning, there is this shared, fundamental, primordial basis.

All the galaxies of this universe have appeared out of space. At a certain point, they are going to disappear. All this change, the big expansion and the big reduction to nothing, appears within the sphere of space.* Similarly, our dualistic experience comes out of the primordial basis and dissolves back into it. There is nothing solid or real about this particular experience of duality.

Clouds come out of the sky, rest in the sky, and dissolve back into the sky. In the same way, all the experiences of ordinary life and transcendent states such as nirvana appear out of this primordial basis. Right now we are the manifestation of the primordial basis, whether or not we are aware of it. We will dissolve back into it. There is no point at which we are separate from the primordial basis. We

---

*The concepts of sphere and circle may be the best approximations we have for a sense of edgelessness. However, while circles and spheres have centers (where we typically place the self) and outer limits, it is taught by all the great masters of Dzogchen that the sphere of space, the sphere of totality (*dharmadhatu*), the sphere of the ultimate body of enlightenment (*dharmakaya*), and the great vital essence (*thigle*) have no centers, no edges, and no other reference points at all, which puts them beyond description, beyond concept, beyond all ordinary experience.

have nowhere else to go. We have never really been separated from this primordial basis.

No matter how large or awesome the clouds may be, they always arise from, and appear only in, the sky. No matter how much we experience pleasure or pain, or whatever lifetime we live through in this world or in any conceivable world, all this appears only within the primordial basis.

Awareness produces enlightenment, and ignorance produces our ordinary mind, ordinary sentient beings. Our confusion many, many lifetimes ago and our confusion right now are exactly the same. Awareness, as well, is exactly the same. It has never changed.

This is a very particular teaching of Dzogchen. It is like enlightenment being given to you in the palm of your hand. Certain types of thoughts characterize you as a sentient being. However, if you are aware of your true nature and recognize your pristine awareness, then you are enlightened. You will be able to understand this directly. It is very, very close. Immediate.

## Primordial Appearance

Now we can say a little bit about the energy within the primordial basis—the inherent, innate energy that manifests as wisdom. There are two Tibetan words that mean "energy" here: *rangtsel* (natural energy) and *yeshe gilung* (wisdom energy). The inner luminosity of the primordial basis manifests naturally. It is like the sun. It has its own inner nature, and it just arises naturally. It is not like the Chinese concept of *qi* (chi). It is not like outer, worldly energy. It is simply the natural manifestation of wisdom—rangtsel.

If this wisdom is recognized when it manifests in the outer world, this is enlightenment and we call it "wisdom energy" (*yeshe gilung*). If it is not recognized, this manifestation becomes dualistic experience. It is at the moment of the manifestation of wisdom that either enlightenment or sentient beings occur.

Thinley Norbu Rinpoche says that the primordial basis is "primordially pure" (*kadag*). *Ka* is the first letter of the Tibetan alphabet, and it also means "first" or "original." *Dag* is pure. The basis is original purity, beyond the conceptual notions of purity and impurity. Its natural display, its natural energy, manifests as the appearance of the basis. We have the basis and the appearance from the basis. If this appearance is recognized as being one's own true appearance, this is enlightenment. If this appearance is not recognized as one's own true appearance, if it is thought of as other, then this is the original experience as a sentient being.

Kadag (primordial purity) relates only to the inner luminosity of the primordial basis. The ultimate body of enlightenment (*dharmakaya*), the body of enlightenment's perfect splendor (*sambhogakaya*), and the manifest body of enlightenment (*nirmanakaya*) all abide within this natural, inner luminosity of the primordial basis, like the way butter is contained in milk. Butter does not manifest from milk until it is churned out; similarly, the three *kayas* are intrinsic to the primordial basis, but they only manifest outside kadag. Kadag is used in the context of inner luminosity but not in the context of outer manifestation.

My root teacher, Dzogchen master Jigme Phuntsok Rinpoche, gave the example of a very sharp sword that has not touched any object. Is it sharp or not? You don't know until the sword has cut something. In the same way, the primordial basis has these three bodies of enlightenment, but until they naturally manifest, their qualities are not evident. The sharp sword and our not being aware of it as sharp until it cuts something is a metaphor for the way that the three kayas abide within the primordial basis. One or more of the three kayas can be experienced only when they manifest. It is important to understand the context of the different metaphors that are presented.

## The Qualities of Samantabhadra

To go into this in a little bit more detail, how does enlightenment occur at that point? We are talking about the original purity of the basis and then the natural manifestation, the moment that enlightenment first manifests. Therefore, we are talking about the original buddha, Samantabhadra, Buddha Ever Excellent.

For the term *original protector*, you can say "first." You can also say "before any other" because Samantabhadra precedes all other buddhas. He is the protector not only of all sentient beings but also of all buddhas.* He is one who first attained enlightenment; but we should not think of his enlightenment as occurring in time.

Because he recognizes awareness, Buddha Ever Excellent is considered more exalted than the primordial basis. This is the first of his six special qualities. The second quality is that at the moment of the display of the appearance of the basis, there was no mistaking this as being dualistic appearance. There was no thought "There is 'I,' and there is 'other.'" There was immediate awareness that this was entirely only manifestation or appearance.

When this appearance from the basis is recognized as being only appearance, all the qualities of the basis, including the three kayas, completely manifest. That is the third quality. For ordinary sentient beings like us, when we do not recognize the appearance as being our own appearance and get confused in dualistic experience, all our inner qualities are obscured, latent. They are innate but covered up within us.

Not only do all the qualities manifest but Buddha Ever Excellent has no clinging whatsoever toward any of this manifestation. Due to this lack of clinging, he experiences complete liberation. That is the fourth quality.

Whatever appears to Buddha Ever Excellent is seen without any obstruction (Tib. *zangtal*). This is the fifth quality. As sentient beings, when we look at things, we think that they either exist or they don't exist. Our perception stops in the face of objects because

---

*In almost all cases in this text, Samantabhadra represents both the male (Samantabhadra) and female (Samantabhadri) aspects of the primordial buddha, Ever Excellent. The use of *he* or other pronouns in reference to Samantabhadra illustrates the shortcomings of describing enlightenment with our limited language: not only does it suggest the idea of gender when gender is symbolic, not ordinary, but it also implies duality between the enlightened one and everything else, whereas there is no subject-object dichotomy in enlightenment. But we use *he* as a convention, following Thinley Norbu Rinpoche and countless others.

we consider that there is an object there. When we've got a thought or feeling in our mind, it becomes a thing within our mind and we are blocked by its presence. Buddha Ever Excellent's perception is without any obstruction at all. The term *zangtal* is used, for instance, if somebody walks through walls; the wall presents no obstruction to passing through it. If we are sitting within the nature of rigpa and a thought of anger arises, we can look into the nature of this anger. It is not outside. It is not inside. There is no place where it exists. It presents no obstruction to our awareness. This is the difference between our ordinary experience, in which we are blocked by the presence of thoughts or emotions, and the presence of rigpa, in which there is no obstruction at all.

This idea of zangtal is one of the most critical points of Dzogchen. When we eat food, we have a thought or feeling about the food; we focus on an object that we are looking at or on what we are doing. We do this and we eat in our ordinary fashion. A buddha eats in exactly the same way. However, neither the food, nor any thought about the food, nor any action in eating the food presents any obstruction to the buddha's pure awareness.

If we look without any judgment about what we see, then everything is seen as enlightened form. If we hear something without any judgment about whether it is pleasant or annoying but simply rest within the empty nature of sound, this is heard as enlightened sound. If we simply allow whatever appears within the mind—negative thoughts, emotions, or other movements—to rest within its own nature, it dissolves into the ultimate body of enlightenment. This perspective toward what we see, hear, and think helps us to realize that, in fact, the Buddha is not just somebody who appeared in India, did his works, attained enlightenment, and passed into nirvana somewhere else, and that all sentient beings are not in his space. The Buddha is not somewhere else at all. The difference between a sentient being and enlightenment is just this recognition of our own awareness.

The sixth quality of Buddha Ever Excellent is his unchanging nature beyond all causes and conditions. Some of us feel that, in order to attain enlightenment, we have to cultivate merit and wisdom. We have to make prostrations and offerings. We have to rely on all sorts of causes and conditions to gather the accumulations to attain enlightenment. This is not how Buddha Ever Excellent attained enlightenment. He simply recognized the nature of his own mind. All qualities of enlightenment were just the natural display of his awareness. They haven't come from any causes and conditions. He remains forever without changing within the state of enlightenment.

What's really important to understand is that Buddha Ever Excellent's moment of liberation came at the same moment as his awareness of his own nature. It is not like an ordinary being who, according to some traditions, must purify anger, desire, and ignorance before attaining liberation. For Buddha Ever Excellent, the moment of awareness and liberation happen at the same time. This is really the most critical thing to retain about the qualities of Buddha Ever Excellent.

The various tantras of Dzogchen have different ways of describing the qualities of Buddha Ever Excellent. The six qualities I've just described is one way. There is a second system: The first three qualities are the same. The fourth is that his enlightenment did not arise through ordinary teaching. In our case, we have to rely on the teachings of the sutras, the tantras, symbolic teachings, and so forth. Buddha Ever Excellent's enlightenment was due entirely to what is called "profound" or "direct" instruction. This profound instruction is the recognition of his own natural awareness. There weren't any extensive teachings. It is just his direct experience of his own nature.

The fifth is that the result of his enlightenment arose without any cause. Often we hear that buddhas first experience the mind of confusion, then they cultivate the causes of enlightenment (merit and wisdom), and eventually they attain the result, enlightenment. This is not the case with Buddha Ever Excellent.

The sixth is that the enlightenment of Buddha Ever Excellent did not arise through his mind. Here we have an extremely important difference between awareness and mind. His enlightenment did not appear from within his mind because he did not have a mind in the way we understand the term *mind*. His awareness was naturally manifest and there was only that. This is called *rangjung yeshe* (self-manifest or self-arising wisdom).

Due to these last three qualities, he attained "the citadel [or fortress] of the primordial sphere." What the Buddha sees and what we see are exactly the same. However, in the Buddha's case, everything is recognized doubtlessly as being entirely an appearance of his own enlightened nature, whereas we see things dualistically. Tilopa said to Naropa, "You are not bound by appearances. You are bound by your attachment to appearances." There is no reason to think that everything has to appear to be empty, to look different from what it looks like to ordinary eyes.

Let's make this a little simpler. An individual who has the view of Dzogchen senses and does things exactly as anyone else senses and does things, but their experience is entirely different. Dudjom Rinpoche said that because he had the view of Dzogchen, he was able to see everything as "naked" or direct awareness. When an ordinary person walks into a house, they look at the walls, the beams, the furniture, and the other parts of the house, and their experience is made up of the consciousness of all these separate parts that we define in the aggregate as a house. Thoughts about it arise, and this in turn creates different positive, negative, or neutral emotions toward its qualities, such as attraction, aversion, or indifference. Now a person who has studied the Shravakayana tradition would say that the essence of the house is impermanent, therefore it has the nature of suffering. A person who practices the Mahayana, or Middle Way, tradition says it appears as a house but its nature is emptiness. Dudjom Rinpoche, or anyone who has the Dzogchen view, sees the house as being the unobstructed nature of awareness. Each is looking at the same appearance but is experiencing it in a different way. Each of these viewpoints is subtler and more direct than the last.

## How Sentient Beings Become Deluded

As we have discussed, the primordial basis is described as primordially pure, and at the same time, it is indefinite. It is great emptiness.* When this primordial basis outwardly displays its inner energy, an inconceivable number of various kinds of appearance-wisdom are produced. Especially, there is an incredible display of the "five wisdom lights." If you don't recognize these appearances as your own display, this awareness remains latent or dormant and they are seen as the five elements, as other and separate from self. This is our first moment as a deluded sentient being.

And without recognition of rigpa, we are left with ordinary mind, with its experiences of happiness and suffering, which Thinley Norbu Rinpoche calls the "fundamental basis" (Skt. *alaya*). Long-chenpa described this fundamental basis, which is also described in the Mahayana sutras, as having two aspects: ripened and unripened. The ripened fundamental basis manifests as our experience at this time—all that we see, all our world, our own body, our own mind. We also have in our mind various habitual tendencies, latent or dormant, that will create our experience in the future. Anything that appears in the future, whether it is during this life or in future lives, is the unripened fundamental basis.

The three higher tantras (Mahayoga, Anuyoga, and Atiyoga) agree that the fundamental basis (often called "primordial basis" in Dzogchen but not to be confused with the primordial basis discussed above) is, in essence, enlightenment. It is primordially pure and unchanging. But it is obscured or veiled by our obscuring emotions, our dualistic experience, and our karma, in the same way that gold might be covered by a tarnish or a jewel might be covered by mud. Nevertheless, it is the primordial, pure essence of enlightenment.

*When "great" is used in this book to modify terms such as *compassion, joy, exaltation, emptiness,* and other attributes or qualities of wisdom or realization, it is not just to emphasize its importance but signifies that the attribute or quality is great beyond any measure or comparison.

The various forms of tarnish that cover the fundamental basis—our different experiences in samsara—can change, but our fundamental nature does not. It is said in a tantra, "It is like a radiant jewel covered by mud. Although covered by mud, its radiance shines up into the sky." For those who can see, the fundamental basis is always brilliant. In brief, all experiences in samsara—happiness, suffering, whatever—come from nonrecognition of our primordial basis and arise from our fundamental basis through our habitual tendencies.

The Mahayana, tantric, and Dzogchen traditions all say, as is said in the *Changeless Nature* (*Uttaratantra*) by Maitreya, that sentient beings are enlightened right now. This is because (1) buddhas emanate from within, not from outside, the minds of sentient beings; (2) there is no difference between the inherent nature, or the nature of reality, of buddhas and the inherent nature, or nature of reality, of sentient beings—our inherent natures are exactly the same; and (3) all sentient beings share this buddha nature as a permanent condition.

For example, in the *Changeless Nature*, a sentient being is described as like an extremely poor person with an enormous treasure of gold hidden from them under their house. They think, "I am incredibly poor." If they understood that they had all that gold, then they could obtain whatever they wanted. In the same way, until we wake up to our inherent nature, we live in the poverty of being an ordinary sentient being. We don't understand that within ourselves we have buddha nature.

The point is that right now, at each stage of Mahayana, tantra, and Dzogchen, the mind is enlightened. However, there are differences in the depth, or directness, of the teachings. Some teachings lead you very quickly to that experience. In the Dzogchen tradition, you can just rely on the direct teachings, or the direct pointing-out that the dharma master gives, of your mind as naturally manifest awareness. This is enough to arrive at enlightenment, at liberation. Some teachings are slower. However, the point is still the same. Awareness doesn't change whatsoever. It is always and forever the same.

## Meditation on the View

To really arrive at the experience of the nature of mind, we must receive the profound instructions from a qualified teacher. From Buddha Samantabhadra down to the present, we have one lineage of mind to mind, one lineage through symbols, and one lineage through words, that have been passed from one sublime master to another, down to the present day. Without direct introduction, Dzogchen teachings seem imprecise, unclear, and it seems impossible for them to produce an understanding of awareness. But when we have received these direct instructions, we will say of the words of the teachings, "Oh yeah, that's what it is." You will see directly into your awareness, rigpa, within your own mind, as have all the others of the lineage since the time of Samantabhadra. Without these words, it would be difficult for us even to approach the teaching. We have to try to deal with what is imprecise. For example, when we say something appears without any cause or condition, or it hasn't been produced by other things but simply is and exists primordially, this is almost impossible for an ordinary person to understand. However, when you have received pointing-out instructions and you see your mind to be exactly like that, you will get it.

It is important to understand the words that give us some indication of the Dzogchen teachings. If you can understand the words, that is great. Then you can go on and get the meaning, to have the direct experience. I might teach you that honey is sweet. You study that, learn it, understand it, but when you taste it, you don't need these words anymore.

For many of us ordinary persons who have had pointing-out instructions, understand rigpa, and have some experience of it, appearances arising from lack of awareness continue to arise as before. Our meditative experience is not powerful enough to change that. Longchenpa said, at that stage, we will be carried away by our enemy, ordinary appearance, like a child wandering onto a battlefield. At one point in his text, Thinley Norbu Rinpoche says, "Until the dualistic experience sets into our fundamental wisdom, all these other experiences will appear." So it is really important to meditate. The more we meditate, the more the appearances arising from lack of awareness will diminish and pure appearances will tend to increase.

With increasing familiarity with the nature of rigpa, gradually the strength of this awareness increases; dualistic experience, like a setting sun, dissolves into pure experience, into the same taste. At that point, there is no more karma, obscuring emotions, desire, anger, or ignorance; no more suffering; and no more dualistic experience. This is the arising of the experience of enlightenment.

If you are a beginner, not only will you find what we are studying difficult to understand but also you will not believe it. It is the same for almost everybody. When I started out, not only did I not understand but also I didn't believe what I was being taught. You gradually, gradually understand and gradually come to some confidence in what is being said. You come to some understanding and then to belief.

It might take several years of diligent meditation until you come to a very strong sense of certainty, a strong sense of power. No matter what appears in the outside world, however great or wonderful, your inner certainty, your inner view will be much stronger. Whatever happens, positive or negative, you will be extremely happy inside because you understand the illusory nature of things. Once it happens, then your inner certainty, your inner view, which is what we are trying to develop, will give you a great amount of comfort and the ability to face anything whatsoever. You will always remain happy and peaceful.

We pay attention to the outside world to make our body happy and comfortable. We get very involved in material progress. But it does not make our mind truly happy. If we want to make our mind happy, we must develop the qualities of mind from within. Understanding the nature of reality will make the mind extremely happy.

At this point in our discussion of Thinley Norbu Rinpoche's text, we are considering the primordial state of all beings. According to the Mahayana tradition, it is buddha nature. According to the tantric tradition, it is coemergent wisdom. According to the Dzogchen tradition, it is manifest awareness. Because they do not recognize this primordial state, sentient beings do not attain enlightenment but remain sentient beings; the wisdom that is the primordial nature of all beings remains hidden, like the sun covered by clouds. We do not recognize our own natural luminosity as our own. We consider it as being other. And due to this habitual tendency, we create dualistic experience.

Here is a really fitting metaphor: The sun heats the earth and causes mist or vapor to rise up into the sky. This collects into clouds. The clouds collect into very large clouds that obscure the sun. The sun is our naturally manifest awareness. When it is not recognized as being our own luminosity, by its own force and energy this light creates obscuration.

Whether we call this "naturally manifest awareness," or the "ultimate body of enlightenment," or "all-pervasive wisdom," it is through its own natural energy that obscurations arise when it is not recognized as being our own appearance.

I have been asked whether there are two moments of recognition: the first, when we recognize our experience as a manifestation of our own mind; and the second, when we recognize all appearances as the manifestation of our innate awareness or of the ultimate body of enlightenment. But even without that second moment of recognition, thinking "This is really an appearance of my own mind" is an incredibly helpful way of seeing things. All of a sudden, there is more space between you and what seems to be happening, and you recognize that this is simply an appearance. At that point, you have freed yourself from an awful lot of unhappiness. Gradually you will be able to recognize that there is no self, and then nothing from the outside will provoke any anger or suffering. How can you be unhappy or angry if you understand the lack of self? How can you have any suffering about things (you yourself, as well as the outside world) that have no self? We are not putting a label on something in order to change it. We are not trying to trick our mind. We're seeing things as they are. But even temporarily, that first recognition is extremely helpful.

If you want to apply this first recognition experience to the Mahayana tradition, in the Mahayana we analyze the outer world. We analyze whether something exists or does not exist. We develop a certain logic or way of looking at things. We come to understand that everything we experience is like a dream or an illusion. Although we may have come to some certainty in this view of the nature of things, it is not enough to simply understand the illusory or dreamlike nature of everything. We must get increasingly familiar with it. The word we use to refer to that process is *meditation*, but in Tibetan it really means "familiarization." We rest single-mindedly within that deep experience or understanding. This direct experience of the nature of things becomes stronger and stronger. We move from view to meditation and then to conduct, or action. We carry our view through life within this experience of everything being nothing but an illusion, or a dream. We don't create any harmful thoughts toward others. We don't harm anyone in any way whatsoever. We simply live within this experience of the nature of things. This is how our immediate recognition enlarges through meditation, or familiarization, into something we carry on the path. It becomes part of our day-to-day existence. This is how, from the Mahayana point of view, we work with this moment of recognition.

## The Nonrecognition of Wisdom Lights

Thinley Norbu Rinpoche describes how we, as sentient beings, experience our mind and the outer world when we fail to recognize naturally manifest awareness as being our own appearance. On the first and coarsest level, the yellow and blue wisdom lights appear in the outer sphere as the elements of earth and water. In an inner way, earth and water are our flesh and blood. On the level of our physical and mental states (called the "aggregates"), the wisdom lights become the aggregates of sensation and consciousness. On the secret level of our obscuring emotions, they are pride and anger. All of this is entirely from the lack of recognition of naturally manifest awareness. Although it is not explicit in Thinley Norbu Rinpoche's text, the first level of wisdom that goes latent is the nirmanakaya, the manifest body of enlightenment.

On the second level, pure sound, the sound of the nature of reality, and the green and red wisdom lights are not recognized as being our own nature. Therefore, the body of enlightenment's perfect splendor, the sambhogakaya, goes latent. Instead, on an outer level, the green and red wisdom lights become the elements of air and fire. Inwardly, in our body, these wisdom lights become breath and body heat. On the level of the aggregates, we have perception and karma (habitual tendencies). On the secret level of our obscuring emotions, these wisdom lights become envy and desire.

The third level of lack of recognition is in relation to the wisdom of emptiness, the ultimate body of enlightenment, the dharmakaya. We do not recognize this as being our own manifestation, so the ultimate body of enlightenment, which is our nature, goes latent. On the outer level, the white wisdom light becomes space, the last of the five elements. On the inner level, we have what is called the "vital essence" of our body. Also we have the aggregate of mental states, which depends upon this vital essence in our body. On the secret level, it is the obscuration called "foolishness" or "ignorance."

In brief, the three bodies of enlightenment, which are our nature, are not recognized, but through their natural energy, all our various experiences are produced.* The metaphor for this that I have described is that when the sun's heat hits the earth, by its own natural energy it creates clouds that obscure its light. In the case of Buddha Ever Excellent, who experienced no confusion or lack of recognition, this same energy of the three bodies of enlightenment became entirely manifest in its pure form. In our case, the pure manifestations of the three bodies of enlightenment remain latent; instead, we have experiences at the outer, inner, and secret levels, as just described. Within the level of the different obscuring emotions we might experience, we have both subtle and coarse

---

*See appendix 1 for a table outlining the consequences of the nonrecognition of the wisdom lights.

obscuring emotions. Desire, anger, envy, pride, and ignorance are the most basic emotions. However, there are many different levels of subtlety or coarseness within these emotions.

There is a self we identify with, and there is an other. Based on this dualistic experience, of course we are going to have attachment to what is favorable to us and aversion, or anger, toward what seems to threaten us. Our beliefs form the basis for the continuation of this dualistic experience and all that that entails, which prevents us from avoiding the creation and ripening of karma, the continuous cycle of birth, death, and rebirth. If we do not avoid karma and taking rebirth, we cannot attain liberation.

The basis of the problem is this attachment to a self. This is the underlying cause, the root of the entire problem of worldly existence. We are naturally going to develop negative emotions and karma. This will send us traveling in samsara. Without this basic, underlying cause, we don't create karma or negative emotions, and samsara will not appear.

## The Three Realms and the Six Classes of Existence

This particular world of ours has its own limits. However, we shouldn't imagine there is no kind of sentient life other than what we now experience. Wherever there is space, there is sentient life, and it can manifest in many different ways. Sentient beings are classified as beings of three realms: the desire realm, the form realm, and the formless realm.

From the collection of extremely subtle obscuring emotions and extremely subtle causes and effects, outer, inner, and secret links of causation produce beings in the formless realm who have minds but no outer form at all.

When the outer, inner, and secret elements that collect together are somewhat coarser, this creates the beings of the form realm. The elements that collect to produce these sentient beings allow them to have minds plus bodies of only light. In the form realm, there are seventeen different kinds of gods.

The beings of the form and formless realms are there due to their cultivation of certain meditative states. Over an extremely long time, they rest within a calm mind, they rest within the impression of nothing whatsoever, or they rest within the idea that their mind pervades all things. However, they do not go beyond dualistic experience, beyond clinging to a self. They do not recognize the nature of mind. Their meditation is merely a state of mind that they've cultivated and can maintain. After the karma of their meditative state is exhausted, they are sent to the desire realm, in the class of humans or below, because their habitual tendencies of negative karma return.

There are many different meditative states we might cultivate without getting to the heart of the matter, without really recognizing the nature of either reality or our mind. When we understand the nature of reality, the nature of mind, then our meditation can lead us beyond worldly experience.

Advanced practitioners recognize the nature of their mind and the nature of reality. With familiarity, everything that appears— including the appearance of gods and demons—comes under their control. No appearance of any kind is any longer threatening; they are entirely in the mind.

When extremely coarse outer, inner, or secret elements come together through various links of causation, this creates the beings of the desire realm. We are beings of the desire realm. On this level, we have bodies of flesh, blood, heat, and breath. We experience the outer, coarse elements in common with the gods of this world, demigods, human beings, animals, starving spirits, and beings of the hell realms—the six classes of existence. All of us share this experience as living with solid bodies.

All beings of these three realms experience various forms of happiness and suffering. Their experience is based on something that does not really exist. We are like a magician who creates appearances but who gets so involved in their own illusion that they feel very happy or sad about what they created and have forgotten that it was simply an illusion. We sentient beings find ourselves in this situation of simply responding to appearances we ourselves have created.

This attachment we experience toward the objects of our senses is deceptive and causes suffering. Examples from nature abound. We are like a moth that flies into a flame; like a deer, distracted by music, that gets shot by an arrow; like a bee, attracted to pollen in a flower, that gets trapped inside. A fish looks for food, bites a hook, and gets caught. An elephant, oppressed by the heat of the sun, wallows in some mud to cool off and gets trapped by quicksand. Without that attachment, all the beings in these cases would not die.

In all six classes of existence, and in all three realms, we consider what is unreal to be real. We develop attachment toward these various appearances, and we develop various thoughts and feelings such as happiness and sorrow. In this way, we continue to involve ourselves in samsara. If we understand all these appearances to be manifestations of our true nature, then we do not experience happiness or suffering because we recognize their nature. We no longer have the necessity to be born, grow old and die, and continue in samsara.

No matter how high up we go up into the formless realms or how low we go down to the lowest hells, our experience is entirely suffering. This is not to say that we don't often have temporary happiness. However, the happiness we experience carries within it the seeds of later suffering, because through our attachment to all our various senses, we continue our lives oriented only toward the appearances of samsara. Nothing lasts a long time in our lives. We might be successful for a couple of years, then die. Or, for a few days, we are really happy with some new clothes we bought, but after a while we get used to them and they lose their freshness. We buy a new car and a few days later—you know what happens—a maddening scratch or dent. All our various attachments do not last a long time, do not give us lasting pleasure. All our things cause more attachment. We experience all of these appearances of samsara as real, and, in this way, we suffer. This is why we consider all of these appearances to be deceptive.

What will not deceive us is the dharma master and the three jewels. We will now discuss the dharma master, the lama. We'll talk about why the lama is not deceptive, why this relationship does not deceive us, and how we will be led to temporary and ultimate happiness through the master's teachings.

## The Dharma Master

We are still explaining the first line of the Dudjom Tersar foundational practice: "Namo, lumed tengyi gonpo lama khyen" (Homage, I beseech you to know me, Lama, deceitless constant protector). In Tibetan, *lama* literally means "unsurpassable." This refers to two characteristics: (1) this person is entirely free from samsara, and (2) this person embodies, or personifies, enlightened body, speech, mind, qualities, and activities. From the time of Guru Rinpoche or even Buddha Shakyamuni, all lamas, in succession, down to our present root teacher, embody these characteristics.

To help understand the qualities of the lama, let's look at the introduction to the nature of mind in the first level of Dzogchen practice, *trekchöd*, which means "cutting through solidity." All the work we do in relation to the view, meditation, and conduct in Dzogchen depends upon the instruction we receive from the dharma master and our recognition of the nature of awareness. We can then proceed in Dzogchen practice. Nothing else apart from the introduction to awareness that we receive from the dharma master allows us to proceed in the practice.

The process of attaining enlightenment in Dzogchen is that we first have the flash of recognition of our basic, fundamental awareness and then, through meditation, the fundamental qualities manifest and we unite in a single taste with, and are completely inseparable from, these qualities that manifest from within.

We have the idea that there are pure lands that we can go to, for instance, the western pure land of the Paradise of Great Bliss (Dewachen) of Buddha Amitabha, or the eastern paradise of Great Joy, and so forth. Our experience of these pure lands depends on the extent to which we have recognized our innate awareness and whether it has stabilized within our experience (or the purity of our faith at the time of death). These paradises are not outside places, but, due to our impure vision, we conceive them as being far away. We might even see hells and starving spirits, as well as animals and humans. But with the recognition of our innate awareness, we see the world, or the universe, in its natural purity; we see the pure lands here and now.

All ordinary beings experience their lives in much the same way. Our lives are collections of happiness and suffering, of regular daily events. We go to sleep at night. We wake up in the morning, take a shower, eat food, do our work. This is our ordinary confused experience that is similar to that of all other sentient beings. Yet, all sentient beings have, within themselves, wisdom. This is our nature. In order for it to manifest, we have to study, reflect upon our study, and meditate. The only reason we study, reflect, and meditate is so that our inner wisdom can manifest.

So how do we take the great journey of recognition, familiarization, and inseparability? We begin by listening to the teachings of a dharma master. For example, we hear that all things are impermanent. Or we hear that all appearances are illusory. Or we hear that our nature is the ultimate body of enlightenment. We listen and try to understand. What is this ultimate body of enlightenment that is our inner nature? The teacher goes on to explain how sentient beings have gotten confused in relation to their inner nature and how they can free themselves from confusion and experience their inner nature.

We gain a certain knowledge from listening. Then we must contemplate what we've heard from the teacher. Having heard about impermanence, we try to come to the conclusion that all things truly are impermanent. Having heard that everything is illusory, we really try to come to a firm conclusion concerning this. Having heard that our nature is the ultimate body of enlightenment, we try to understand this as best we can. In reflecting upon the teachings on the primordial basis of everything, we try our best to understand

and to reflect again and again on this. We try to come to a clear understanding of the primordial basis. Once we have understood, we don't leave it at that; instead we bring our mind again and again to the subject to try to arrive at a very definite conclusion about the teaching.

This leads us to very personal reflections: What is the meaning of my life? Why am I here in this world? Do I have future lifetimes? If so, how must I act in this life in relation to that fact? Have I had past lives? If so, where does this body come from? Where does this mind come from? At this time I have a precious human body—what should I do with this life? Should I be practicing buddhadharma, or some other path? We should try to make sense of both the teachings and our own orientation to what we can understand or accept in the teachings. This is the process of reflection, which is general in relation to the Buddha's teachings and personal in relation to our own life and circumstances.

We must arrive at some definite understanding through our reflection before going on to meditation. It is not effective to jump directly into meditation. That would be like mountain climbing without arms; you will start out and then fall down the cliff. After we have arrived at a definite understanding, we can receive the pointing-out instructions, and then meditation will provide us with the possibility of our inner nature manifesting entirely as the three bodies of enlightenment.

In order for our wish for the manifestation of our inner wisdom to come true, we must from the outset depend upon the guidance of a dharma teacher. If we want to go somewhere and there are no maps, we would have to rely upon someone who had been there. However, there are many different kinds of dharma teachers. If we are interested in complete actualization of the three bodies of enlightenment within ourselves, we must rely upon a genuine, fully qualified dharma master and no one else.

I use the term *dharma teacher* or *dharma master*. Sometimes the equivalent terms *spiritual master* or *spiritual friend* are used. Many of these teachers are emanations of Buddha Shakyamuni.

Just before the Buddha passed away into complete nirvana, his nephew Ananda was overcome by grief. At that time, the Buddha said to him, "Look, Ananda, don't enter into such a state of despair. In the future, I will take the form of the spiritual friend. You and all sentient beings will have a guide to enlightenment." In this way, many persons such as Guru Rinpoche and others have taken form in this world to guide sentient beings, after the passing away of the Buddha.

Especially in this dark time, the Buddha and Guru Rinpoche take many forms as dharma masters in order to guide beings. However, for us it is important that the dharma master's teachings are not their personal invention but are the real teachings that have been passed down through an unbroken lineage. It is not enough for a person to say, "Well, I have attained enlightenment, and I give you these particular teachings."

Many traditional texts, as well as the life story of Guru Rinpoche, state that before the appearance of dharma teachers, even the term *enlightenment* did not appear in this world. All 1,002 buddhas of this aeon have relied on a dharma teacher for their enlightenment. The teachings are effective only because they come to us from Buddha Ever Excellent, in a lineage unbroken from master to disciple, down to the present day. Some lineages were broken when there was no disciple who became enlightened. The lineages we have today are unbroken. One qualification of a dharma master is being a holder of such a lineage. The teachings that have been preserved and passed down allow the master to know the nature of their own mind, manifest the three bodies of enlightenment, understand the confusion of sentient beings, and know how to help sentient beings journey to enlightenment.

By reading about the Buddha's teachings, we can understand something of them. However, although books give us some of what we need to know, what is essential is passed directly from teacher to disciple in an oral transmission.

We have to develop some clarity about what sort of dharma teacher we should rely on. If we shop for a teacher who pleases us from a worldly or even a scientific point of view, they will not be able to help us develop. The quality we need to find in a dharma master is the ability to reveal to us through the pointing-out instructions that our own essence is enlightenment. The master can clear away the "bark," the transitory or incidental obscurations that cover our inner nature, and can make perfectly manifest our innate wisdom.

In the Dzogchen teachings in Tibet, this pointing-out instruction was essential. Sometimes the teacher would give instructions to thirty people and say, "Well, twenty of you got it. The rest of you didn't get it." The teacher would know directly who understood the pointing-out instructions and who didn't. Sometimes over a series of three or five months, the teacher would work with a group of students, gradually leading them to the stage where they could recognize their awareness. The lama would give instructions. The students would then talk to the lama about their experience. The lama would either confirm their experience or not and do this over a period of time so that the student was led to the experience of awareness.

To lead the student to understanding, sometimes the lama would say, "You don't get it yet. You have to do more Guru Yoga practice." Or, "You have to do *rushen*" (a Dzogchen preparatory practice, distinguishing between samsara and transcendence). Or, "You have to do more Vajrasattva practice." When someone understood the nature of mind, the lama would say, "You've got it. You don't need anything else. Now go and meditate. Don't think about anything else."

Thinley Norbu Rinpoche says that to examine the qualifications of a teacher, we should have some familiarity with the buddhadharma to begin with. However, it may not be possible for beginners to be clear enough in their own mind about exactly what is necessary in terms of qualifications. At the very least, when meeting a teacher, it is important for us not to have pride but to have an attitude of humility. With pride, the mind is like a solid ball. If water is poured on the ball, nothing is absorbed. In the same way, if our mind is closed by pride, no qualities of the teacher can enter our mind.

A servant monk by the name of Legskyi Karma (Fortunate Star ) accompanied the Buddha for twenty-four years. At the end of that time, he said to the Buddha, "I have been with you for such a long time. I don't see any difference between us. All the qualities you have, I also have. The only difference I see between us is that you have an awful lot of light surrounding your body." After twenty-four years, he left the Buddha, never having learned anything at all. His mind wasn't open, and none of the qualities of the Buddha entered his mind. In the same way, if we see faults in our teacher and they begin to multiply in our experience, it becomes impossible for us to receive the blessing of the teaching. It is said that for those people who are extremely critical, accomplishment stays very distant. Whereas if you have faith and humility and are open to receive the extraordinary teachings, and if you study and meditate, then you will get extraordinary results in your life.

I will describe in a little more detail the qualifications of a dharma master, but the bottom line is what Patrul Rinpoche said in *Words of My Perfect Teacher*: "At the very least, the master must have the qualification of compassion, the wish for enlightenment for all sentient beings. Even lacking other qualities, with this quality the teachings will be effective in helping others." So, if you are shopping around, the dharma master must at least possess this quality.

The dharma master has the means to allow us to wake up to our enlightened nature. How do we know this awakening process has begun? The first sign is that upon merely hearing teachings of emptiness, teachings of our enlightened nature, or teachings of Dzogchen, we have feelings of joy. We might even cry when we reflect on these teachings. We have strange experiences; we get goose bumps. These indicate that the seed planted in our mind has taken root, that the karmic connections made in previous lifetimes are reawakening. This is not the entire awakening of our enlightened nature, but it has begun. Quoting from a text by Chandrakirti, *Entering the Middle Way*, "At that point, then, teaching, whether on emptiness or Middle Way or Dzogchen, can be given to the person because there is the initial awakening. Then these teachings have the proper field to become effective." This is just a temporary or momentary awakening. But it provides the proper environment for receiving the Middle Way teachings or the direct pointing-out instructions of Dzogchen teachings. We become what we call a "qualified receptacle" for the teachings, especially when we see the teacher without dwelling on their personal faults or shortcomings—ideally, we see the teacher with pure vision and see that the teacher embodies buddha nature. Later, when the pointing-out instructions are given, we will be able to understand and see directly our own enlightened nature.

Now I will describe some of the qualifications of the dharma master. In the Mahayana tradition, the tantras, and Dzogchen, the main characteristic that the teacher must have is the mind of awakening (*bodhichitta*), the pure motivation to attain enlightenment for the sake of all sentient beings. Without this serious wish to help others, however high a person's meditation might be, however high their realization might be, if they enjoy their own state of meditation but do not consider the sufferings of others, they are simply a Shravakayana practitioner. On the other hand, someone may realize that all sentient beings have this buddha nature and sincerely wish for their enlightenment but might not have the means to meditate and make this enlightened nature manifest. Such a person might decide to teach anyway. This is actually the mind of awakening put into action.

In the Mahayana tradition, whenever we do any sort of ritual, we begin by taking refuge and developing the mind of awakening. Also, whenever we do any activity at all, if we begin by developing the wish to help each and every sentient being and orient all our life to that goal, then whatever we do will not be harmful to others. Without this wish to help others, the benefit, if any, will be very limited. We might be helpful or we might be harmful. For example, Tibetans consider that being a doctor is an extremely dangerous profession since it is possible to be of great harm to others. But if a doctor takes this motivation seriously and really makes it part of their experience, then whatever they do for their patients will not harm them.

In matters involving the development of realization, this motivation is even more crucial because one's mind is profoundly affected by the teachings, in this life and succeeding lives. Patrul Rinpoche said, "The single most important quality in any dharma teacher is the mind of awakening. Whenever you meet a master who has this quality, they can be relied upon and it will only be of benefit."

A master of the Nyingma school should have received the "four streams of transmission." The first stream is the transmission of the major source works of the Nyingma tradition, for example, the Seven Treasuries of Longchenpa. The second is the transmissions of the oral lineages of direct teachings on the nature of the mind, and the third is the transmission of the "four levels of empowerment"—the vase empowerment, the secret empowerment, the knowledge/wisdom empowerment, and the precious word empowerment.

The fourth stream of transmission in the Nyingma tradition is that of enlightened activity. This is related to the various protector practices, for example, those of Ekajati, Gesar, and others. The master should have inherited and maintained these practices in their entirety. Inheriting all four streams and keeping their commitments make the master's lineage as pure as gold without any tarnish whatsoever.

The next quality the dharma master must have is to strive to be of service to sentient beings through teachings, empowerments, and transmissions.

In the context of Vajrayana, the teacher must be skilled in the various levels of tantra. In the Nyingma tradition, this means the Mahayoga tantras (the creation stage), the Anuyoga tantras (the completion stage), and the Atiyoga tantras (the direct-instruction stage). It is not just a question of being skillful in the words or in the tantras themselves but in the practice. The master must also be skillful in accomplishing the four enlightened activities: pacifying, or calming; enhancing, or enriching; magnetizing; and overpowering, or wrathful, activity.

Through practice, the master must have arrived at manifesting some of the signs of accomplishment, literally the signs of heat, or intensity, whether on the level of Mahayoga, Anuyoga, or Atiyoga. Otherwise, with only a vague idea of Dzogchen, without having received all the necessary teachings, without having really practiced it to completion, trying to help someone else is exactly like the blind leading the blind. You are going to fall down a cliff.

If we want to learn Dzogchen, then we must go to a Dzogchen teacher who is completely capable in the Dzogchen tradition. A Dzogchen teacher may not have the same level of capability in Mahayoga or other levels of tantra. A teacher of Mahayoga doesn't necessarily understand Dzogchen. So we need to learn the teacher's specialties. All the qualities of all levels were present in great masters of the past, such as Dudjom Rinpoche.

Thinley Norbu Rinpoche comments, "These are the qualities of a properly qualified master. However, it is possible that we will have impure vision or that because of the darkness of these times where emotions and karma are very coarse, it might be very difficult for us to find a teacher who has no faults at all and whose qualifications are complete. In that case, what is important is to find someone whose faults are as few as possible and who has as many of these qualifications as possible, and to rely on that person."

Though the lama might have a lot of faults in relation to worldly circumstances, if this teacher is skillful in guiding students through the paths and stages of enlightenment, then it doesn't really matter if the teacher has such faults. Thinley Norbu Rinpoche comments that this is because we don't go to the dharma teacher for advice about our worldly life. We want to attain enlightenment. So what is important is to see whether the teacher has faults in relation to dharma teaching.

Thinley Norbu Rinpoche says that, at the very least, if you are on the path of cultivation (sometimes called the "path of accumulation"), your teacher should be someone who is on the next level, the path of application. If you have reached the path of application, then your teacher must be someone on the next level, the path of seeing. At the very least, you have to choose a teacher who is more advanced than yourself.

You need to develop some qualities in your own practice to see the signs of the lama's accomplishment. With some inner knowledge arrived at through practice, you will have access to an understanding of the lama's practice. Without that, you can understand only a small fraction of the lama's practice.

It is important for us to be skillful in how we rely on a teacher, because the arising of qualities within our mind depends upon our relationship with the teacher. When we have faith, appreciation, and devotion, this provides the circumstance for the teachings to become effective. We must not act, even inadvertently, as a hunter or predator. Rinpoche says that in Tibet and China, a musk deer's musk is considered extremely valuable medicine. The hunter doesn't care at all about the deer's life; he cares only about the musk. In the same way, it's not helpful if we don't care at all about our relationship to the teacher or our commitments but just want the teachings. The teacher has something valuable. We lie in wait for the teachings. We take the teachings and run away. This is not how we should consider our relationship with the master. This metaphor is in the *Treasury of Enlightened Qualities* by Jigme Lingpa.

We should remind ourselves that our basic condition is we are sick with the suffering of samsara. We experience birth, old age, sickness, and death. Then we must regard the teachings as being medicine that gradually cures us of these maladies. We should ask the advice of our master as we would ask a skillful doctor. We should put that advice into practice as if we were taking the medicine that the doctor prescribed for us.

As we develop more of our own qualities in dharma practice, we will see more and more of the qualities of the master. For instance, when our vision is still limited, we may see the teacher as subject to karma by getting ill or dying. One way of explaining this is that buddhas and bodhisattvas may experience much illness because all their karma ripens in this very lifetime. We, as ordinary sentient beings, have lots of time in future lifetimes to experience all our negative karma. Buddhas and bodhisattvas attain enlightenment in this lifetime, so there is no necessity to be reborn.

The great Indian master Nagarjuna provides an example of this. He had a karmic connection with a king such that both of their lives were expected to be the same length. However, Nagarjuna attained the level of awareness holder of infinite life, so he was deathless. That was fine for the king, but his son, the prince, got very upset that he would never inherit the kingdom. So he went to Nagarjuna and said, "I want to take over. Please give me your head. Give me your life." Nagarjuna said, "Well, try and take it." The prince tried to sever Nagarjuna's head, but even though he struck him many times with his sword, he could not cut off his head. "That," Nagarjuna said, "is because I made no karma in the past of harming people with a sword or knife. However, in another lifetime, I inadvertently cut an insect's head with a blade of grass. So you can cut my head off with a blade of grass." That is exactly what the prince did.

It is also possible that buddhas and bodhisattvas appear to be sick in the experience of sentient beings, but in fact they are not sick.

All of these explanations point to the fact that in our current state, we don't have pure vision with regard to the teacher. Because of all our habitual tendencies, we experience the world and all beings, including our teacher, as imperfect. But from the Dzogchen point of view, the whole universe—all our experience—is primordially pure. We need to consider the teacher as being equal to a buddha, so with meditation, we train in seeing the master as the Buddha himself. We train to extend this to our companions on the path. Gradually, we extend this to all appearances. As a result, we see directly the primordial purity of the entire universe.

In a famous quote from a sutra that describes the pure land of Manjushri, the advice is this: "Remain in your best intention." Remain in your development of the mind of awakening, the wish to attain enlightenment for the benefit of all sentient beings. If you remain within that best intention, then you will be successful in your practice. This sutra goes on to say that whatever prayer of aspiration you make with this good intention will produce results. Even though because of your negative habits, you may experience negative activity, if you maintain pure intention, even this negative activity can be a positive action.

# CHAPTER 2

# The Outer Foundational Practices

We have come to the "outer" foundational practices, which are common to all buddhadharma traditions. In fact, in any spiritual tradition, a person should reflect on these considerations. The special, inner foundational practice, which starts with refuge and the development of the mind of awakening, is specifically a part of the buddhadharma. However, the outer preliminaries are for everyone.

The outer preliminaries are called the "four thoughts," "four facts," or "four contemplations" that turn the mind to a meaningful life. They are the considerations of (1) the preciousness of human birth, (2) the impermanence of life and the inevitability of death, (3) karma (causes and effects), and (4) the sufferings of samsara.

These reflections are concerned with the outside world, with how things actually are for sentient beings. Having said that, we have to stress that these outer foundational practices are really important. Without a proper basis in these foundational practices, the main practice of Dzogchen will not go well. The mind must be placed in the proper environment for the teachings of Dzogchen and understand the "big picture" view of the way things are. This provides the foundation for our later practice. In building a house, if the foundation isn't stable, then anything constructed on this unstable foundation will also be unstable.

The purpose of the four thoughts is to help reduce our attachment to what we experience as the outside world. For example, when we think about this precious human body, we can understand what the idea is, but this is not enough. We must really familiarize ourselves with this thought. Then we will begin to understand how really precious this life, this body, is. We will begin to really value it and put our best into every act we do, and thereby choose very carefully what we do with our lives. Similarly, when we think about death and impermanence, it is not enough to just understand the idea that we are going to die. We have to familiarize ourselves with this in order to recall that each and every day of our lives is extremely important.

For each of these four thoughts, we try to develop energy for our path to awakening. We think about each thought and conclude, "I must practice." If we do this, we will practice very diligently, but we will also be happy that we are dedicating ourselves to our goal. Otherwise, without this good basis in the foundational practices, even though we might concentrate on Dzogchen, receive all the teachings, and practice them a little, in the end we will have nothing to show for our practice because we haven't really transformed our mind. These thoughts, as simple and easy as they are to understand, will lead us to make good use of our lives and benefit from the teachings.

## This Precious Human Birth

The first thought, in brief, is as follows: "The eases and obtainments of this precious human rebirth are extremely difficult to find."* There are eight kinds of eases or freedoms, and ten obtainments, or favorable conditions, that we can enjoy when we are born as a human. They are discussed at length in Patrul Rinpoche's *Words of My Perfect Teacher*, so I won't go into detail here but will merely list them.

There are eight ways we can be free to practice teachings that will lead us to enlightenment:

1. We have not been born in the hot or the cold hells.
2. We have not been born in the starving spirit realm, where beings

*This is from the Dudjom Tersar Ngöndro.

experience intense hunger and thirst. The emphasis on the hell realm and the starving spirit realm is on the body; beings' bodies have such intense, overpowering experiences that they cannot consider anything else, to say nothing of dharma.

3. We have not been born as animals. In the Tibetan cultural tradition, we think that the greatest number of animals live in the ocean. (But insects may well outnumber sea creatures.) The large eat the small. Many small eat the large. They harm one another and have extremely limited mental scope.

4. We have not been born in a place where positive teachings are present but are rejected. In such a place, there is no consideration of karma and its effects, past or future lives, giving up negative acts and performing positive actions. We call this "wrong view."

5. We have not been born as a "savage." Unlike a culture where dharma is rejected, such a culture does not recognize what is positive and negative, what is extraordinary or just ordinary. Someone in it is like someone who is blind in the middle of a great plain who wanders everywhere but has no idea where they are going.

6. We are not so seriously mentally handicapped that we can't understand any teachings at all.

7. We were not born during a time when there is no teaching of enlightenment at all.

8. We have not been born as long-lived gods, who live for many aeons entirely distracted by pleasure. When all their pleasure ends at death, they take rebirth in lower worlds and have no opportunity to realize their true nature.

Of the ten endowments, or favorable conditions, the first five depend upon ourselves, our own good karma:

1. Our own previous actions have resulted in this human rebirth.

2. Among human beings, we have been reborn in a "central country." Traditionally, the central country was considered to be India

and the center of the central country was Bodhgaya, where the Buddha attained enlightenment. However, we now understand a central country to be anywhere the buddhadharma has spread.

3. All our senses are intact, with similar experiences to other human beings.

4. We experience revulsion toward negative acts—we take no pleasure in the sufferings of others or in seeing others create negative acts. When we ourselves do something negative, we feel badly about it.

5. We feel some level of faith in relation to the Buddha's teachings.

There are five endowments that depend upon others:

1. The Buddha appeared in this world.

2. The Buddha taught. Some buddhas appear in this world but do not teach.

3. The Buddha's teachings still remain in the world.

4. Persons other than ourselves have entered into these teachings; we are not alone.

5. Among those who have entered into the teachings, there are those who accept us and guide us in our practice.

When we have the eight freedoms and the ten endowments, we have a "precious human body" (Tib. *milu rinpoche*), because based on this body, we can overcome the enemies of birth, old age, sickness, and death; we can realize that our mind is the ultimate body of enlightenment.

The great Indian master Shantideva said, "Right now, with this precious human body, I can attain enlightenment and get rid of every suffering. If I don't use this opportunity, how in the world am I ever going to get it again?" The circumstances that have given us this precious human body are a collection of an incredible number of causes and conditions. How can we ever imagine that these causes and conditions will come again?

Thinley Norbu Rinpoche says that if we plant a needle standing up and drop a multitude of seeds on this needle, perhaps one of them will stay on the top of the needle. The attainment of this precious human body is even more difficult than that. Compared to the number of fish in the sea and the number of insects on the earth, human beings are very few. Among human beings, the number of persons who are wise, who understand the nature of mind, and who have the intention to practice positive teachings are extremely rare.

In his commentary on the foundational practices, Dudjom Rinpoche stated that the sufferings we experience come from having wasted our human life. In one of the sutras of the Buddha (translated by Thomas Cleary as *Entering the Realm of Reality*), the Buddha says, "The cause of all samsara is not having thought of the qualities of one's precious human life, the freedoms and endowments. In this way, one has followed nonspiritual friends. One has been led into the suffering of samsara." The Buddha continued, "For my part, I have become freed from all [samsaric] existence by my thoughts of my own precious human birth." There are an infinite number of benefits we receive from these freedoms and favorable conditions when we put them into practice for their best use.

We can get familiar with the thought of this precious human birth by observation. We can go into town, see lots of people, and try to understand what they are doing with their lives. So many of them are just trying to entertain themselves. They have no idea that their own human life is incredibly valuable. This is not a question of arrogance, thinking we are better than others. It is simply very sad that they don't use their human life to its best advantage and that they have no access to an understanding of their own lives, no access to teachings that lead them to pure vision. That way, we develop happiness, in relation to ourselves, and compassion, in relation to others.

## Impermanence and Death

We come now to the second fundamental fact: "Whoever is born possesses the phenomena of impermanence and death."* We think

---

*This is from the Dudjom Tersar Ngöndro.

about the impermanence of life because even when we've developed the wisdom to practice the teachings, we sometimes believe that there is something solid or reliable in our precious human birth, that we are going to live for a long time, so we put off our practice for another day. Acknowledging the impossibility of living forever, or of predicting when we will die, forces us to bring all our attention to practice right now.

Whatever existence we consider, in this or in any other world, is there even one example of somebody once born who has not died? Thinley Norbu Rinpoche says that our life is like a candle in the wind. Who knows when our life force will be extinguished? Many different things can cause death, and very few things nurture our life force.

Impermanence applies not only to all the living beings we might imagine but also to the entire outer world. Anything that has come into being remains for a certain time but eventually changes into something else or is destroyed. It is said in the sutras that this entire world has come into being, will remain for a certain amount of time, and will eventually return to the emptiness of space.

In the discourse the Buddha gave just before he passed away, he said that just as like when you have a field, the best thing to do with it is to produce a harvest, so the best thing to do with the teachings of the Buddha is to meditate upon death and impermanence because such thoughts prevent attachment to any of the three realms of existence. What did he mean by that? In the Shravakayana tradition, meditating on death and impermanence creates cessation of the ordinary experience of our body; we realize nonself of the individual, and this realization ensures that there is no further creation of karma or the various aggregates. This is the state of an arhat, literally "someone who has defeated the enemy," the enemy being our ordinary sense of self.

In causal Mahayana, meditating on death and impermanence rids us of the veils of obscuring emotions and ignorance, allowing us to attain enlightenment. In resultant Mahayana, in this case, Dzogchen, we meditate directly on the result of enlightenment. What's written at this point in Thinley Norbu Rinpoche's text is very, very beautiful in Tibetan—very brief, succinct, and precise. Here is the best English translation we have:

Dharmakaya is the permanence of the essential nature as it is,
Sambhogakaya is constant permanence.
Nirmanakaya is uninterrupted permanence.

If we don't explain it, it's very difficult to understand.

First, the mind of the desire realm is exhausted in the wisdom mind of the manifest body of enlightenment (nirmanakaya); this mind is realized as being of the nature of the fundamental wisdom of mind that embraces all sentient beings—all-penetrating energy (sometimes translated as "all-penetrating compassion," but we can't really say *compassion* right here; it's energy or the comprehension of all sentient beings and things). It is called "bliss-emptiness" and is the nature of our mind.

Second, the mind of the form realm is exhausted in the wisdom mind of the body of enlightenment's perfect splendor (sambhogakaya). The mind dissolves into emptiness and spontaneous clarity—not luminosity or clarity like light but that there's no obstruction whatsoever to our experience and emptiness. We've come up one level, from the nature of our mind as bliss-emptiness to spontaneously manifest clarity and emptiness. This is also the nature of our mind.

Third, the mind of the formless realm is exhausted in the sphere of the wisdom mind of the empty awareness of the ultimate body of enlightenment (dharmakaya). When we realize the nature of our mind, we experience all the elements of the nature of our mind: bliss-emptiness, clarity-emptiness, and awareness-emptiness; they are all interchangeable. And when we say "emptiness," in Dzogchen, we mean the mind beyond all limits of our conceptual mind.

The mind's essence is emptiness; its nature is clarity, or unobstructedness; and its energy is all penetrating. Through the process of considering birth, old age, sickness, and death, this meditation allows us to experience the cessation, or dissolution, of our ordinary consciousness into what is, in fact, eternal, or permanent, the three sacred bodies of enlightenment.

It is said in the sutras that the three bodies of enlightenment are permanent, or eternal. The ultimate body of enlightenment is eternal because of its essence. It exists primordially; there is no particular moment when it came into existence. The body of enlightenment's perfect splendor is eternal because of its continuity; that is to say, in the pure lands there is no moment when it ceases to exist. And the manifest body of enlightenment is eternal because it appears for as long as there are sentient beings to be guided. How is this different from the idea of there being a god, as in an eternalist philosophy, where an eternal, or permanent, god exists separately from ordinary sentient beings, who are impermanent? It's this: the three bodies of enlightenment are the nature of all sentient beings; they are not separate from us. And when we reflect upon permanence and impermanence, we consider things in the outside world, but the three bodies of enlightenment go beyond any consideration of permanence and impermanence; we call them eternal because they transcend all concepts, any labeling whatsoever.

It is said in one of the basic texts of the Mahayana, the *Changeless Nature* (*Uttaratantra*), that the Buddha has defeated the lord of death. As ordinary beings, we have different aggregates—form, perception, feeling, and so on—so we are subject to death. Because the Buddha has transcended, or exhausted, his aggregates, there is nothing to die within his being. At the level of the ultimate body of enlightenment, because the essence of the Buddha is empty, he is eternal, or permanent.

*Entering the Middle Way* states that, at the level of enlightenment's perfect splendor, the ultimate body of enlightenment unobstructedly appears as if it were a wish-fulfilling tree. This is a symbol of the forms of the Buddha that appear to sentient beings. A wish-fulfilling tree is not responsive to our ordinary thoughts but to our sincere prayers. When we pray to a wish-fulfilling tree, if we wish for food, food appears. If we wish for jewels, jewels appear. In the same way, the body of enlightenment's perfect splendor responds in forms appropriate to our aspirations. As in the metaphors of a wish-fulfilling tree or a wish-fulfilling jewel, the sambhogakaya will take the form appropriate to the minds of sentient beings for as long as it takes for all sentient beings to attain liberation. Because of this quality of continuity, these forms are considered to be eternal.

At the level of the manifest body of enlightenment, forms appear to sentient beings in relation to their minds. The metaphor for this is vessels of water that reflect the moon in the sky. The moon doesn't descend into the vessels of water. It simply appears wherever they are. We say that the manifest body of enlightenment in its nature goes beyond permanence and impermanence. It is simply part of the nature of reality that these manifest bodies of enlightenment appear uninterruptedly for as long as there are beings to be guided to enlightenment. Therefore, we consider them eternal.

Thanks to meditating on death and impermanence we can transcend birth, old age, sickness, and death. We don't attain some separate existent state that is eternal. Instead, we realize the empty and continually appearing nature of mind that transcends the ordinary impermanent nature of things.

Milarepa said that he went into the mountains to meditate due to fear of death and impermanence. There he meditated on the unpredictable nature of death. Thanks to that, he arrived at a state beyond death, beyond birth. He forgot entirely about his fear of death.

It is difficult to be really diligent in our practice. To cultivate diligence, we have to recall that death and impermanence are exactly the way things are. There is nothing we can do to prevent death. By remembering death, we will be happy in our dharma practice and we will become diligent. There's no other reason to meditate on death and impermanence except to recognize the nature of reality and allow it to encourage our practice.

## Karma: Cause and Effect

The third fundamental fact is "the cause and result of virtuous and nonvirtuous actions cannot be denied."* Simply put, the relationship between cause and effect is infallible. It's in the nature of things that virtuous causes will lead to happiness and negative acts will lead to unhappiness, or suffering. The opposite is never the case. Positive acts will never lead ultimately to suffering. Negative acts will never lead ultimately to happiness.

We might think it doesn't really matter if we die—death is like a fire going out, leaving only lifeless ashes and nothing that continues beyond. This is a nihilist view of only paying attention to events as they appear right now. Buddhists don't accept this misleading and erroneous view. We believe that the mind† continues unobstructedly whether there is birth or death. The body has a birthday and a death day; it is created anew at conception, and its development depends on what happens during gestation. Although it is said that the mind enters the mother's body at the same time as conception,‡ the mind comes from a previous lifetime, bringing whatever mental habits or habitual tendencies it created or continued in its previous lifetime. Similarly, when the body dies, the mind continues and takes rebirth once again. There is a continuity of mind regardless of what physical form we take.

Everything in the outside world depends upon its individual causes, be it a human being, an animal, trees, grass, flowers, or rocks—everything depends on its own causes. Nothing is created

*This is from the Dudjom Tersar Ngöndro.

†Orgyen Chowang Rinpoche does not delve deeply into the distinction between the mind-stream that goes through successive lifetimes—the cumulative, karmic propensities and mental-emotional habits—and specific personalities. But we use the term *mind* for convenience.

‡Orgyen Chowang Rinpoche explains that conception does not mark the creation of a sentient being; rather, sentience develops gradually during gestation. Also, he says, the Mahayana and Vajrayana view on terminating pregnancy always takes into account all the facts and circumstances, not only the issue of whether there is sentience.

outside this relationship of cause and effect. In our past lives, we created different forms of karma. These became part of the fundamental basis of mind. Because we have this fundamental basis, we have consciousness that moves from our past life into this lifetime. During this life, we create karma and habitual tendencies that in turn create the impulse, or energy, toward a future life.

As sentient beings, we are powerless to change this relationship between our actions and their results. For instance, nobody wants to get sick. Even when we get sick, we say to ourselves, "I don't want to get sick." If that wish were enough, nobody would ever get sick. Sickness is related to a particular habitual tendency, to our acts in the past or to conditions in the present. The result: we get sick.

Dreaming provides an example of our karma. After the experiences of daytime, we fall asleep and dream. We might dream of many different worlds or places. We haven't left our bed or our body and gone to see these different worlds. These worlds don't come and fit themselves into the space of our room or our bed. Rather, our habitual tendencies determine what we see in our dream. In the same way, what we have kept in our heart from one lifetime to another produces our experience in our future lifetimes. In order to attain liberation, we need pointing-out instructions of the nature of mind and we need to meditate on these instructions. This is the only way that we can undo these habitual tendencies that propel us from one lifetime to another.

Shantideva said in his *Guide to the Bodhisattva's Way of Life* that all sentient beings' sufferings appear through, and are created by, the mind's habitual tendencies. Shantideva continued by saying that the Buddha correctly explained exactly how it is that everything has arisen from mind: everything we experience is simply the display of the natural manifestation of mind, through both impure habitual tendencies of mind as ordinary beings in terms of suffering and pure experience of the outer world as a pure land filled with buddhas or bodhisattvas.

We can deal with our inner suffering by understanding the nature of mind. We cannot eradicate all suffering by trying to deal with each form of suffering as it appears; but if we understand the nature of mind, this will eradicate the root of all suffering because the negative mental habitual tendencies that created suffering are eliminated. Shantideva said that if there is a large area of land covered with thorns and stones, you can't cover it completely with a carpet to make it more comfortable to walk on. Instead, you should simply cover your feet with proper shoes. In the same way, if you want to experience the outer world in its primordial purity, your mind must be purified. You cannot purify the outside world. The root of all is your own mind.

In the *Thirty-Seven Practices of the Bodhisattva*, by the Tibetan author Tokmay, it is said that if you don't defeat the enemy of anger within yourself, your enemies outside will multiply; but if you totally defeat the anger within yourself, you suddenly don't have any enemies at all.

Shantideva remarked that if we tame our obscuring emotions and all our inner negative habits, the outside world becomes tame and calm. He asked, for beings in hell, who sharpened those cutting weapons? Who lit the fires arising from the ground? Who created all the suffering? He explained that the Buddha said that nobody sharpened those weapons, nobody lit the fires. The experience of hell was created by the negative habits of mind of the person experiencing that hell. Without negative habitual tendencies, we cannot experience hell or life as a starving spirit. In the same way, all our happiness in this world is the result of positive acts that ripen as agreeable experiences.

In the Buddha's discourse called the *Descent to Lanka* (*Lankavatara* sutra), it is said that what we experience is the mind, and if we think that there is actually something outside of ourselves that exists, this is a misguided impression. What does exist is the result of the turmoil of these habitual tendencies that create the impression of something solid and real in the outside world.

In another of the Buddha's discourses, two disciples of the Buddha discussed whether this world and everything within it is the Buddha's pure land because he dedicated himself to this world.

Shariputra, one of the main disciples of the Buddha (always pictured to the left of the Buddha), remarked that the world doesn't seem very pure at all—there are both pure and impure inhabitants, high mountains and deep ravines, some pleasures and many dangers. Another disciple of the Buddha, a god from another universe, said to Shariputra, "No, you're wrong. It's your mind that has all these highs and lows and various kinds of experience. In fact, this land is a pure land."

As these two disciples were having their little debate, the Buddha made the pure land to the east of this world appear to them. He asked Shariputra, while presenting this pure land, "If a blind person cannot see the sun and the moon, is it that the sun and moon do not appear or is it that the blind person can't see them?" Shariputra said, "Of course, the sun and the moon always appear, but the blind person can't see them." The Buddha said, "In the same way, this pure land always exists, but because of your habitual tendencies and ignorance, you are unable to see it."

As long as we continue to experience our world in terms of subject and object, we will follow our karma and habitual tendencies. We act. Our actions plant habitual tendencies in our fundamental consciousness, which then result in our experiences of pleasure and suffering. In turn, we act in relation to those experiences, which creates more habitual tendencies, which ripen in turn. We continue this process of actions, which lead to habitual tendencies, which lead to results, actions, habitual tendencies, and so forth, until our dualistic minds dissolve into the wisdom of the ultimate body of enlightenment. For this to happen, in Dzogchen, we must receive direct instructions on the nature of mind, at the level of trekchöd, cutting through solidity. Then our dualistic experience begins to fade, and eventually it dissolves entirely into the sphere of totality (dharmadhatu).

The basic point of the Buddha's teaching is the importance of mastering the mind. There are nine yanas and many teachings in them, the eighty-four thousand teachings of the Buddha. The Buddha gave a succinct synopsis of his teaching. He said we must not do anything harmful to others, no negative acts whatsoever. We must perform perfect virtue—that is, do whatever is excellent. And we must entirely master our mind. These three points encapsulate the eighty-four thousand teachings of the Buddha.

Thinley Norbu Rinpoche remarks that there are some people who do their best to practice virtue and not harm others but who suffer badly during this lifetime and that there are some people who have no consciousness, or thought, of virtue or nonvirtue, who do things to harm others, and yet who are sometimes extremely happy during this lifetime. So we might think that there is no relationship between action and cause and effect. This is not really the case. Sometimes people suffer during this lifetime because their negative habitual tendencies from past lives have ripened during this lifetime. Once they have finished that specific suffering, if they practice virtue during this lifetime, their life (whether this life or future lives) will be extremely happy. In the other case, people who are extremely happy during this lifetime but who harm others are experiencing the result of positive habitual tendencies from the past. But eventually the harmful acts they do during this lifetime will result in suffering, either during this life or in the future. We have to consider the order in which things occur. We might create good karma, but the result of these acts will be experienced later. What we experience now is the result of previous acts.

Maudgalyayana, another very close disciple of the Buddha, was murdered by some nonbelievers because he had said something horrible to his mother in a past life. He had miraculous powers and could have avoided that sort of situation, but at the moment of his murder, he had a momentary lack of awareness, became subject to these persons' blows, and died. It was the completely ripened result of his previous action. Even a highly evolved person experiences the result of previous acts.

Our acts can produce results that situate them within the continuum of time in three ways. First, if we do something in this life and it ripens in this life, this is karma that we experience and can see. For example, the first part of my life was spent in Tibet and the result was my coming here to the United States. I may see more results very soon. For now, I don't know. Time will tell.

Second, it's possible that positive or negative acts taken during this lifetime do not ripen until the next lifetime.

Third, it's possible that the actions we take during this lifetime, positive or negative, don't ripen even in our next life but are stored for any number of lifetimes in the future until conditions allow them to ripen. One basic buddhadharma text says that for sentient beings with a body, an act lasts for one hundred aeons. And when conditions and causes are conducive (it can even be after one hundred aeons), the result will ripen.

Jigme Lingpa said that an eagle flying high in the sky doesn't see its own shadow until it descends and approaches the ground. In the same way, we create causes, but we don't see the effects of our particular acts until conditions come together, through the links of interdependent causation. Then we can see directly the effects of our acts.

We should look at the life stories of Milarepa, Longchenpa, or Jigme Lingpa, who all arrived at enlightenment during their lifetimes, to see how karma can be purified. What were their early lives like? At what point did they come in contact with the teachings? How did they rely upon their teacher? How did they practice and what accomplishment did they arrive at? We should look at these not as fables or legends but as facts. If we study these lives, we can understand that in the Vajrayana there are methods, such as Vajrasattva meditation practice, that can purify all the karma we have accumulated since time without beginning. The most effective purification of karma is when dualistic experience dissolves into nondual wisdom. Until we have purified entirely both positive and negative habitual tendencies, we must maintain extreme vigilance in renouncing even the subtlest forms of negative acts and in accomplishing even the subtlest forms of positive ones.

There are two aspects to self-clinging when we experience the world in a dualistic way. We cling to the "self of self" when we believe that, as individuals, we have a self. And we cling to the "self of things" when we believe that everything in the outer world has a self (not a sentient self but a separate existence).

As for clinging to the self of self: We have the five aggregates, the five psychophysical constituents of our experience. Based on the aggregates' experience, we imagine that there is a self that exists. We experience it as very solid and real. This is basic delusion in relation to our nature. However, from the perspective of awareness (*rigpa*), there is no self.

One area where we find attachment to self quite acute is our attachment to our body, especially when we feel physical pain. The true way to overcome attachment to pain is to understand the nature of our mind, not just to have an understanding but to get really familiar with it. Gradually, we begin to see that there is no self. As this belief, or fixation, on the self diminishes, our attachment in relation to our body, or any physical suffering that we might experience, will diminish.

The approach of trying to get rid of fixation on pain is sort of one-sided. If we dwell only within the correct view of nonself, this lacks compassion. At the same time that we develop the view of non-self, we should also develop compassion toward all sentient beings. These two together produce a balanced approach to realization.

The second aspect of self-clinging is clinging to the self of things. To a certain extent, it is based on our experience of the self of self, because this clinging to a self reflects what we experience as other. When we look at any sort of outer experience, although it manifests from emptiness and it has no existence, we consider what we sense to be real and to possess the same solid existence that we posit for ourselves.

Based on these experiences of self-self and other-self, emotions arise. We experience aversion or anger toward what seems harmful and happiness or attraction toward what seems helpful. Or we experience neither attraction nor aversion but remain in a deluded state of ignorance. Our experiences of anger, desire, and ignorance, and all the variations of these emotions, create positive or negative karma. Our positive or negative karma propels our lives within samsara. However, once we have understood the nature of our mind and reality as being appearances that arise out of emptiness, that is, once we recognize the lack of self-self and other-self, these experiences of attraction, aversion, and ignorance have no way to arise.

## Virtuous and Nonvirtuous Acts

There are many kinds of virtuous and nonvirtuous acts. We condense all of these acts done physically, verbally, or mentally into ten virtuous acts and ten nonvirtuous acts.

There are three physical nonvirtuous acts:

1. Killing any kind of sentient being. The corresponding virtuous act is to strive to protect the life of all living beings.
2. Taking what hasn't been given—that is, to steal. Stealing can arise from anger, desire, or ignorance. The corresponding virtuous act is to renounce stealing and to be as generous as possible.
3. Impure sexual conduct—for example, committing adultery with somebody else's wife. Does that also mean a woman shouldn't sleep with somebody else's husband? Of course. You must apply it to your specific situation. The corresponding virtuous act is to maintain pure, respectful sexual conduct.

There are four verbal nonvirtuous acts:

1. Lying and deceiving others. The corresponding virtue is to renounce lying and deceiving others, and to speak honestly, with a good motivation.
2. Creating disharmony between people. This can be between friends, persons who are simply acquaintances, or between teacher and student. On the positive side, one should try to make peace between persons.
3. Speaking argumentative words, words that strike somebody else, or words that hurt. Harsh words. Patrul Rinpoche comments that even though words are not sharp swords, they can

be more destructive than swords in terms of their effect on a person's mind. Instead of speaking harshly or aggressively, the virtuous practice is to always speak pleasantly.

4. Using frivolous speech. If what moves us to speak is desire, anger, or ignorance, then whatever we say will be frivolous speech. Instead, we should try to recite prayers or mantras or say meaningful things.

There are three mental nonvirtuous acts:

1. Acquisitiveness—coveting things that belong to other persons, thinking, "How can I get this? How can I possibly have something similar for myself?" The opposite of acquisitiveness is cultivating the intention, or wish, to give gifts and being generous to others.
2. Malice—holding a negative attitude toward somebody, wishing to say or do something to harm somebody, or wishing that somebody not be successful or have bad luck or misfortune. That attitude is based in anger. Instead we should rejoice in the merits of others and wish good fortune for others.
3. Holding misleading views. If we have an outlook on life, or a belief, that does not correspond to the nature of reality, that is a misleading view. If we think that there is no relationship between our acts and their results; if we think that there are no past or future lives—that we begin with our birth and end with our death; if we do not believe in enlightenment beyond this ordinary life; if we don't believe in the Buddha, the teachings, and the dharma community—these are all misleading views. The opposite of this, the corresponding virtuous mental act, is to develop faith, or belief, in the three jewels.

These descriptions of virtue and nonvirtue may sound moralistic. But virtue is not some kind of moral imperative that is right or correct because an outside authority says so. Rather, virtue is a practical method for our happiness. We don't necessarily expect some particular special effect to take place in our lives because we're practicing virtue. We just become happy. The people around us also become happy. Virtue is like medicine. Virtue is extremely helpful for us on an individual and a community level. However, nonvirtuous, or harmful, acts are like poison. They poison our individual lives, and if communities or countries act nonvirtuously, they poison our social life.

These descriptions of virtue and nonvirtue may also seem arbitrary and too strict. The foundation of the Mahayana path is to see everything as an illusion, as a dream. With this view, we do not consider at all whether an act benefits us. We just think of the benefit to others. If a person truly has this view of reality, with no thought of benefiting themselves, then it might be appropriate, depending on the circumstances, to do one of the seven nonvirtuous acts of the body and mind, because, in the Mahayana view, the basis of what makes an act positive or negative is one's intention, one's motivation. The Shravakayana does not accept this viewpoint, because in the Shravakayana view, things are seen as material, as substantial, so it matters exactly how things appear in the outside world.

An example of how it is possible for a person to perform beneficial negative acts is found in a story about the Buddha. In a past life, he was born as the captain of a ship. He learned that a certain individual wanted to sink his ship on which five hundred bodhisattvas were traveling. He thought to himself, "If this person succeeds in sinking this ship, he will kill those five hundred bodhisattvas, and the effect will be that he will suffer many lifetimes in miserable existences. He will have created a lot of bad karma." So he killed him. Because of his compassion, his totally pure, positive intention, and with no thought of his own benefit, he saved this person from life in the lower realms and saved the lives of five hundred bodhisattvas but suffered no negative karma from a nonvirtuous act. Without all of those elements, a nonvirtuous act is just a nonvirtuous act.

In the case of committing murder, this is a major nonvirtuous act that perhaps only a bodhisattva is capable of doing without negative karmic consequences. Sometimes a small nonvirtuous act doesn't require such a high level of realization. Let's say that you meet a hunter on the road, and he asks, "Have you seen any deer around?" If you know the deer are south but you say, "Yeah, I saw some. They were headed north. Go that way," that sort of lie won't yield negative consequences. You've saved lives.

So in looking at our own intentions, it is important to work with vigilance and mindfulness. We must bring our attention to our mind to notice our various thoughts and work with our mind intentionally. One teacher's advice to beginning students was to examine their thoughts one at a time for the entire day. When they had a good thought, they put a white stone in front of themselves. For a bad thought, they put down a black stone. At first, it is natural for everybody to have a nice big pile of black stones by the end of the day. After some time of working with pure intention, there will be an equal number of black and white stones. Eventually, the mind can remain within its positive pure intention, leaving only a pile of white stones. This sort of work is good for beginners. Later, after you have received pointing-out instructions and you remain in the nature of mind, there is no longer necessary any control of, or work on, motivation. Whatever you do within that state, physically or verbally, accomplishes virtue.

## The Dissolution of Dualistic Experience

As discussed above, the dissolution of dualistic experience into nondual wisdom is enlightenment. Where, in fact, does dualistic experience dissolve? Thinley Norbu Rinpoche uses the expression "into the great circle of awareness (*rigpa*)." The word translated as "circle" is *thigle*. In Tibetan, *thigle* can mean different things, such as "zero," or "circle." In this case, it refers to the all-embracing, all-pervasive sphere of totality without any center, sides, corners, or edges. All our dualistic experience, positive and negative, all the aspects of our ordinary mind, dissolve into the sphere of totality of awareness. One rests still, without moving, within this sphere of totality.

Right now, our mind has a center and many corners and edges. We experience self and other, I and you. Based on this, we experience desire, anger, and ignorance. We experience things as high and low. In enlightenment, where there is no sense of self and other, all separateness and difference has dissolved into complete equanimity in this great sphere of totality, this thigle, where there is no dualistic experience.

This is not the case only "after enlightenment." This is also the nature of our mind at this point, at any point. We've got to understand it, then realize it. Once we realize it, we remain stably within this nature of mind. It's like a king who gains the citadel, his palace, the place where he is completely secure. Similarly, we have to grasp and remain in this nature of our mind.

Thinley Norbu Rinpoche quotes the following passage in Longchenpa's *Treasury of the Sphere of Totality*:

> Never moving from the basis of present awareness,
> With this experience, existence will be emptied.
> Free from the habit and karma of returning to existence,
> The even nature of cause and result is called the "equality of
>     samsara and enlightenment."
> Without remaining in existence or enlightenment, one arrives
>     at the essence of enlightenment.

Longchenpa's *Treasury of the Sphere of Totality* has that name because it contains many treasures, many jewels from the sphere of totality. The sphere of totality is where all things and all sentient beings come into existence. They remain within the sphere of totality and they cease within the sphere of totality. Even though Longchenpa's Seven Treasuries are all written from the Dzogchen perspective, this work describes almost entirely the view of Dzogchen. It explains how sentient beings come into existence, how they become confused, how they remain within the sphere of totality, and most particularly, how they attain liberation within the sphere of totality. We call it a "treasury" because it is completely full of precious things. Just as you put only gold, silver, and precious jewels in a vault, not rocks or ordinary earth, there is nothing ordinary about this text. Patrul Rinpoche said in a long, profound, and enjoyable praise of the *Treasury of the Sphere of Totality* that this treasury subdues pride. If one has any suffering, this treasury is one's best friend.

We have, at this moment, the nature of our mind, which is enlightenment. All Dzogchen and tantric texts tell us not to look outside the mind for enlightenment, not to look in the past, present, or future, but to look within our own mind. So, in the first line, Longchenpa says, "Never moving from the basis of present awareness."

The first half of the next line is "With this experience." This means that by remaining within this present awareness (it may take a year; it may take two or more), the mind gets clearer and clearer, like water in which all impurities settle until it becomes completely clear. All the myriad thoughts that come from dualistic experience, which don't come from awareness, clear within the mind.

The second half of the second line is "existence will be emptied." In other words, by remaining within this present awareness, ordinary thought gradually decreases. Obscuring emotions decrease. Karma and the habitual tendencies that would have created the conditions for future lifetimes decrease.

Without the recognition of awareness, we continue as ordinary persons getting lost in thought, which leads to emotions, karma, and continuation in samsara. Dzogchen practitioners experience liberation through the recognition of awareness and becoming familiar with it and more stable within that awareness.

The next lines state that when we reach certitude about cause and effect, we arrive at equanimity in relation to both samsara and its transcendence, or nirvana. This certitude about cause and effect is not ordinary certainty or decision; instead we cut through cause and effect into the sphere of totality; cause and effect dissolve. Within this state, there is no difference between samsara and its transcendence. The essence, or heart, of awakening is reached, in which, through compassion, other sentient beings are not left behind; samsara is transcended while compassion for others remains.

The last line is "Without remaining in existence or enlightenment, one arrives at the essence of enlightenment." Having reached this stable citadel, the palace of this particular state, one is no longer subject to the appearances of confusion within samsara or nirvana.

## The Sufferings of Samsara

We've arrived at the fourth of the four thoughts that turn the mind to dharma: the consideration of why, in light of the faults of samsara, we should enter a path to awakening. If life were one great, happy event, there wouldn't be any reason to search for liberation. However, when we consider birth, old age, sickness, and death in the human realm and the tremendous sufferings in other realms, we give ourselves encouragement to enter into meaningful practice. We need to consider the sufferings of samsara in order to set the stage for our determination to attain liberation.

The foundational practice states, "The continuous character of the three realms of samsara is an ocean of suffering." Then comes the last line: "By remembering this, may my mind turn toward the holy dharma."* The final line goes with each of the four thoughts: when remembering precious human birth, may my mind turn toward the dharma; remembering death and impermanence, may my mind turn toward the dharma, and so forth.

As humans in samsara, we have four great rivers of suffering: birth, old age, sickness, and death. We also have the sufferings of meeting our enemies, of separation from those we love, of not getting what we've wished for, of getting what we've wished to avoid, and of suffering heaped upon suffering, in which we haven't finished one trial and tribulation when another one visits us.

Then there is the potential for suffering that pervades all life. We have moments in our lives when there is no current suffering, but our thoughts and actions will cause future suffering. We naturally develop negative thoughts, negative habitual tendencies, which later will lead us to the experience of suffering. We may not experience

---

*These two lines are from the Dudjom Tersar Ngöndro.

this at the moment, but it lies in the nature of life. That is the cosmic heaviness of things. Thinley Norbu Rinpoche asks us to reflect upon the fact that there is no place in samsara free from suffering. It's like an ocean of suffering. We should recall this and give our mind over to the idea of being liberated from this cycle of birth and death, and with this motivation, enter into the practice of dharma.

Another form of suffering is the potential for suffering within change. An example from a Tibetan master is that, if you have a child to whom you are very attached, there is the potential for suffering within your love for your child if the situation were to change—for example, if your child were to die.

As ordinary human beings, we don't often recognize or consider suffering in quite the same way as it is considered in the dharma context. We say we've got a headache; then we're suffering. With more contemplation, we can look a bit closer at things, perhaps in a darker light. Patrul Rinpoche talks in detail about all the different sufferings that a child experiences during gestation and the sufferings that a mother and her child experience at birth. He goes into horrific detail in all of this. He does the same with the sufferings of sickness, old age, death, and dying.

## View, Meditation, and Conduct

Thinley Norbu Rinpoche quotes from the *Prayer to Buddha Ever Excellent* (*Kunzang monlam*), which says, in effect, that the fundamental basis (which is named *kunzhi* (*alaya*) in the prayer—but in this case is meant to mean the primordial basis, *yezhi*) is not composite. It is naturally manifest, a vast, inexpressible expanse. Within this fundamental basis, there is not even the name of samsara or its transcendence. And if one is aware (using the word *rig* as in *rigpa*) of this fundamental basis, this is enlightenment, Buddha Samantabhadra. If this is not recognized, it is what we call a sentient being. Until we have recognized and stabilized within this nature, we must perfect the view, meditation, and conduct of Dzogchen. We must recall and be mindful of karma, our acts, and causes and effects.

We must consider and recall the sufferings of samsara. However, once we have gained stability within this fundamental basis, it is no longer necessary to consider view, meditation, and conduct, to consider action and causes and results, or to consider the sufferings of samsara, because that is the moment of enlightenment.

On this subject, Guru Rinpoche gave some advice to King Trisong Deutsen: "Great King, the critical point, the most important point, is the view. Within the view, there is no realm of samsara, no transcendent state, no positive or negative acts, no bad karma or good karma. But remember, within the view, don't lose hold of conduct." In other words, we mustn't imagine that in our conduct there is no positive or negative karma because of our view. If we lose our conduct within the view, we become like a demon.

There is a story about a man who mixed up his view and his conduct. Because there was no sense of positive or negative acts in his view, he thought that it was just fine to kill a sheep. Guru Rinpoche warned against this. Have the view, but don't mix it up with conduct. In the context of conduct, we retain a sense of ourselves and others, we have a sense of ethical behavior, of positive and negative acts. Guru Rinpoche said, "Don't lose the view within the time of conduct. Don't let the view become part of your attachment or your sight of things as having characteristics. Don't make it part of your realm of dualistic experience. If you lose the view within conduct, you lose the opportunity to reach liberation."

Guru Rinpoche also said that his view was wider than all space but his attention to conduct was finer than highly refined flour. His attention to positive and negative acts, to ethical conduct, was extremely precise even though he maintained an inconceivably wide and open view.

For us, the view must precede meditation and conduct. We must first come to some conclusion about the view. Our meditation and conduct can follow. If we join our view to conduct, we will lose sight of the view.

In the *Treasury of the Sphere of Totality*, Longchenpa states that the entire outer universe appears within space and will eventually dissolve back into space. There is nowhere else to go but this open space. In the same way, all sentient beings have appeared from the sphere of totality and eventually will return to this sphere of totality. There is nowhere else for us to go.

Within luminous awareness, or luminous wisdom, a presence of clinging provokes dualistic thought. This in turn leads to emotions, which lead to acts, which lead to suffering and happiness. This is who we are as sentient beings. When we recognize luminous wisdom, clinging ceases and none of the rest of the series of events occurs. Wisdom is our nature, but we have a circumstantial, transitory, incidental experience of being a sentient being, of clinging, of not recognizing our nature. However, even this occurs within this luminous wisdom, and when we recognize wisdom, we will no longer be sentient beings. There is no difference between an enlightened being and a sentient being at the level of luminous wisdom. There is simply the difference between the presence of clinging or not. As soon as there is no clinging, that is enlightenment.

The moment of the appearance of either samsara or its transcendence is the spontaneous manifestation of the sphere of totality. There is nothing at all that exists in reality. An example of this is our dreams, which arise through the natural energy of our sleep. When we're dreaming, if we don't recognize that we're dreaming (if we do recognize this, then we are dreaming lucidly), then we take whatever appears to be real, and we have various experiences of suffering or fear in relation to what we experience. We might experience ourselves being carried away by a great river or we might be attacked by tigers. These appearances that arise from the natural energy of sleep are like all the appearances that arise from the natural energy of the sphere of totality.

If we are dreaming lucidly, we understand that what we are seeing are simply appearances and we have no fear or anxiety about what we are dreaming. Similarly, during our waking life, when we recognize these appearances as the primordial appearances of confusion from the basis of the sphere of totality, at that moment, we have no fear or anxiety about our waking experience.

However, until our experience within the nature of mind is stable, we have to rely upon momentary vigilance or mindfulness to recall the nature of mind, the basis of the sphere of totality, which is ultimate wisdom. We must understand this to be the ultimate body of enlightenment. Without such mindfulness or vigilance, not only will we be unable to reach our goals in our dharma practice but even our worldly work will not meet with success. Nagarjuna commented that if vigilance, or mindfulness, is abandoned, all dharma (by this he meant both worldly and dharma practice) falls to ruin.

Padampa Sangye was a great Indian yogi who visited Tibet. He said that the ultimate purification of vigilance is wisdom. Thinley Norbu Rinpoche says this means that when the object of vigilance—that is, virtue or the view of Dzogchen (whatever it is that one is being vigilant or mindful of)—and the person who is being mindful dissolve inseparably into one another, that is wisdom. When you begin to see the Dzogchen view, at the beginning, you must have mindfulness, vigilance in relation to this view. Eventually, this vigilance through habit dissolves directly into the view, and there is no difference between what you have kept in mind and your self. The result is wisdom.

## The Importance of Training Our Mind in the Four Thoughts

Thinley Norbu Rinpoche finishes his discussion of the outer foundational practices by emphasizing how important it is for us to train our mind in these four thoughts. When we do so, we will understand that we already have within ourselves habitual tendencies accumulated in our past lives, and these tendencies produce experiences of fear, anxiety, depression, and other forms of suffering. These accumulated habitual tendencies are higher than the highest mountain. They feel very, very solid. When we reflect upon these four thoughts to turn the mind to dharma, we think to ourselves, "If I continue to live in the way that I have until now, I will continue to add to these habitual tendencies, and in both this life and future lives I'm going to continually experience suffering and dissatisfaction."

Thinley Norbu Rinpoche says, "I haven't presented all these thoughts for you to reflect like this and then just sit and cry." Instead, he says, "I hope you reflect upon the nature of samsara and then use this precious human birth that you have in order to attain liberation."

It's important not to get carried away by reflecting on past, present, or future suffering. Instead, reflection on suffering should motivate us to enter into practice and to cross all the paths and stages of awakening.

Through these four thoughts that turn the mind, we've reflected on the characteristics of samsara exactly the way they are. However, at the end of these four thoughts, we must really return to the first one, that we have this precious human birth and that this wonderful opportunity can be used effectively to attain enlightenment. These reflections and the appreciation of this precious human birth are really to inspire our mind, to give us confidence in the practice of attaining enlightenment.

If you really think about your precious human birth, you'll be the kindest person to yourself that you'll ever meet. On the other hand, if you think only about this life and don't think about others or future lives, this is the greatest waste, the greatest loss anyone could ever inflict upon you.

To be more specific, when you're practicing dharma, the basis of your practice is compassion, development of the mind of awakening, and the experience of the correct view. These three things are essential for you, for your own benefit, but developing them, strengthening them, will also be of great benefit for those around you.

Putting off practice to some later time is not a skillful use of your time. The Buddha said, "I've taught the path to enlightenment. However, traveling that path depends on you. Liberation depends on you." The Buddha opened the path of enlightenment for all persons. However, the Buddha could do no more than that. The rest is up to those of us who have heard the Buddha's teachings: to attain enlightenment by following his instructions.

These thoughts are the foundation of our practice. On this strong foundation we can discuss refuge and the development of the mind of awakening. After we've got a firm understanding of refuge and the development of the mind of awakening, we can discuss Guru Yoga. When we have practiced Guru Yoga effectively, then the teachings and practice of Dzogchen, trekchöd and thögal, will go very well.

These foundational practices, along with refuge and development of the mind of awakening, are preparatory practices for Dzogchen because through them our mind is pacified, our harmful thoughts recede, and we appear to ourselves and other people to be happy and not so lost in thought. This is a little like preparing a field. When you cast your seeds on a field, if it's been prepared, things will grow. If, on the other hand, the field is hard or rocky, you cast your seeds for naught.

The wildness of our mind is the effect of countless past lives of lack of mental training. With training in calming the mind, with training in these four thoughts that turn the mind, with refuge, and with the development of the mind of awakening, our mind calms down and is tamed. At that point, if we wish to practice Mahamudra or Dzogchen or whatever teachings, it is said that many wondrous signs of accomplishment will arise.*

*Mahamudra (Great Seal or Great Symbol) is the highest teaching of the Kagyu school. It has been said that according to the great master Jamgon Kongtrul, Mahamudra corresponds to the mind class teachings of Dzogchen.

# CHAPTER 3

# Refuge

We have come to the teachings on the special inner foundational practices—taking refuge, developing the mind of awakening, mandala offering, meditation on Vajrasattva, and Guru Yoga.

What does it really mean to take refuge? In an ordinary sense, whenever we have suffering or sickness, we search for a solution to our state of suffering. If we contract a serious disease, for example, we need someone who knows what is making us sick and what we need to do to get cured. When we go for that help, we are taking refuge in that person and their skills. In the context of dharma, we begin with an understanding of our situation in the ocean of samsara. We expect that old age, sickness, and, particularly, death await us. By reflecting on these sufferings of samsara, we realize that we need a solution to this problem of suffering, and we need help in finding and utilizing that solution; and that's what it means to seek refuge. However, we cannot thoughtlessly take refuge in anything that might protect us; we must bring intelligence to bear on our choice of refuge, to choose a genuine object of refuge that can actually protect us and relieve us from suffering. Once we have made the right choice, then we can take refuge with genuine appreciation, devotion, and gratitude; and even when we have no expectation of reward, we are rewarded with limitless blessings.

In whom can we take refuge to attain freedom? It is not sufficient for us to take refuge in a god, for example, who is unable to give us the ability to be freed from samsara. Nor should we to take refuge in somebody who does not have compassion for sentient beings.

However, the three jewels have the capability and the compassion for refuge in them to be effective.

In the sutras, it's said that most people seek refuge in an average or inferior object of refuge, such as a particular place, like a mountain, a forest, a garden. Or they go for refuge in persons who are powerful in this world: a ruler, a government minister, a wealthy person. Or they go for refuge in worldly deities who dwell within this world. But these sorts of refuges are average or inferior; they cannot provide solutions to all the suffering and unhappiness in this world. It's like when somebody falls into a very strong river and the person who jumps in to help them isn't a strong swimmer. Both persons get carried away by the river and drown. Wealthy or powerful persons, even gods within this world, are not free from ordinary thoughts, emotions, and habitual tendencies, and therefore they are not free from suffering. They're not free from this world. They are unable to give us permanent refuge.

Our best object of refuge has three main qualities: wisdom, love, and capability. As for wisdom, the one who gives us refuge should thoroughly understand the states of samsara and nirvana; where suffering comes from; the nature of the minds of all beings; how suffering arises physically, verbally, and mentally; and the path to freedom from all suffering. If the Buddha had a tremendous amount of love for each and every sentient being but not enough wisdom, he wouldn't be a proper refuge. It would be like if we wanted to go to New York from California; however enthusiastic we were about the journey, however ready we felt, if we didn't know the path or where the road was, it wouldn't be wise for us to set out on the journey. However, the Buddha does have all the necessary wisdom, especially about the path to enlightenment.

This first quality of wisdom allows the Buddha to put his second quality, boundless love for all beings, into action. If the Buddha had the quality of wisdom without love for others, he would stay within the sphere of totality and not act in relation to sentient beings. His love is many times greater, hundreds, thousands, millions, trillions of times greater than that of sentient beings. The Buddha's love is overwhelming, overpowering, without any partiality, grasping, or aversion. Thanks to this love, his wisdom activates into deeds of service for the benefit of all sentient beings.

The third quality is capability. The example given in the sutras is of a mother who has no arms seeing her child fall into a river. The mother sees what is happening and understands what needs to be done (she has wisdom). She has immense love for the child and longs to help, but she can't help because she is incapable. Similarly, if the Buddha had only wisdom and love but no capability, then he would not be a proper refuge for sentient beings. However, the Buddha does have the capability to help others.

So these three qualities—wisdom, love, and capability—are fundamental qualities of our object of refuge.

To truly take refuge, it's important to understand the importance of these qualities. If somebody were to ask you, "Why did you take refuge? What are you seeing about this place of refuge?" It's not enough to say, "Well, I don't know. I like the three jewels. I like the lamas." It's not enough. You need to be able to say, "I know the qualities of those in whom I've taken refuge. I do not take refuge in others because they don't have these essential qualities."

If we know the qualities of refuge and we have taken refuge, this fosters within us a very deep confidence, a happiness both in an ultimate sense and even temporarily in relation to very ordinary circumstances. For example, when you take an airplane, you may worry when you feel turbulence. If you remember at that point, "I have my refuge, both in this life and every life," then you calm down. This brings comfort and relaxation in a relatively minor circumstance.

Whenever we feel any sort of insecurity, it's important for us to remember our refuge. It's not enough to simply say, "I've taken refuge." It is the reminder of the qualities of the object of refuge that develops confidence, or belief. For example, when you're in an airplane and everyone's getting nervous amid the turbulence, saying the Vajra Guru mantra should be the trigger for you to recall the qualities of Guru Rinpoche. By recalling his qualities, your mind will relax. You will think, "Whatever happens, it's okay. I have the refuge of Guru Rinpoche, and I know who he is. I know his qualities." For refuge to be effective for you, you must have an understanding of the qualities that bring confidence and belief.

This is a very temporary benefit of refuge. There is also the ultimate benefit of refuge. If we have taken refuge in Guru Rinpoche, then thanks to his teachings of Dzogchen, following his practices through to realization can be an ultimate refuge for us, taking us from this life to liberation.

That was a short introduction to the idea of refuge. To understand the authentic object of refuge, I will now go into detail about the three jewels as described by Thinley Norbu Rinpoche—specifically, the four bodies of enlightenment and the five wisdoms.

## Buddha and the Bodies of Enlightenment

The buddha in the context of the three jewels is the embodiment of the three aspects, or bodies, of enlightenment: the ultimate body of enlightenment (dharmakaya), the body of enlightenment's perfect splendor (sambhogakaya), and the manifest body of enlightenment (nirmanakaya).

The ultimate body of enlightenment is the essence of the buddha, the part of his experience that never had any impurity. The buddha has two forms of purity. The first is primordial purity. The buddha's primordial purity is no different from that of any sentient being. The buddha's second form of purity is that all "incidental" obscurations—those that arise, abide, and ultimately end—have been completely cleared away. This distinguishes the buddha from ordinary sentient beings, who have "incidental" or "transient" obscurations such as anger, desire, and ignorance. These obscurations are like clouds that cover our view of the sky. The sky is the primordial purity that we share with all buddhas. However, for an ordinary sentient being, clouds of incidental obscurations hide the sky of primordial purity. Purification of these transient obscurations is the body of enlightenment's perfect splendor.

Both the ultimate body of enlightenment and the body of enlightenment's perfect splendor emanate as the manifest body of enlightenment. Infinite manifestations of enlightenment can appear anywhere in this world or any other world. For example, Buddha Shakyamuni was the manifest body of enlightenment who came into our world. Any form of the manifest body of enlightenment is an emanation of this pure nature of the ultimate body of enlightenment and of the purification of transient obscurations that results in the body of enlightenment's perfect splendor.

So the three bodies of enlightenment's qualities are (1) natural purity, (2) the purification of all the incidental obscurations, and (3) the manifestation of enlightenment within the world. Ultimately, in fact, they are inseparable. This inseparability is called the essential body or vajra body of enlightenment (svabhavikakaya). This is the fourth body of enlightenment.

For sentient beings, the qualities of the body of enlightenment's perfect splendor do not manifest. Through the purification of the incidental obscurations, the five certainties or the thirty-two major and eighty minor marks of physical perfection actually manifest. Although they are innate qualities of the ultimate body of enlightenment, they do not manifest without the incidental obscurations being purified.

As sentient beings, we have natural, innate, primordial purity, which includes wisdom, love, and capability. The attainment of both innate purification and the purification of incidental obscurations have already taken place in the buddha. However, we don't have the aspects of wisdom, love, and capability that come as a result of the purification process. So we must meditate on love and compassion, engage in training in wisdom, and practice in relation to capability. Eventually, through this purification process, our practice and our innate qualities will unite inseparably; there will be a meeting of what we have innately and what we've developed through our training. When our practice and our innate qualities join, we won't be any different from the Buddha.

In Thinley Norbu Rinpoche's text, he provides only the briefest reference to this subject. In the *Do Gyud Dzod* (*Treasury of Sutra and Tantra*), by Choying Tobden Dorje, this subject is dealt with in great detail.

The particular way of expressing the first three bodies of enlightenment that Thinley Norbu Rinpoche has given, in which the ultimate body of enlightenment is that from which the body of enlightenment's perfect splendor appears (and from which, in turn, the manifest body of enlightenment emanates), is a way of expressing the three bodies of enlightenment that is not shared by everybody but is found in both the sutras and the tantras. However, there are other ways of explaining these three bodies in the sutras and there are other ways of explaining them in the tantras.

With four bodies of enlightenment, we're talking tantric language. There is also a fifth body of enlightenment, sometimes called the "unchanging" or the "infinite vajra body." It's spoken about in tantra, but that's fairly rare.

The important lesson to take from this description of the bodies of enlightenment, as well as from the following descriptions of the wisdoms of the ultimate body of enlightenment, the aspects of the body of enlightenment's perfect splendor, and the aspects of the manifest body of enlightenment is that the buddha exemplifies the qualities of all the kayas, and if we follow the path given to us, we will know that we ourselves personify the same qualities and thereby will be free from suffering.

## The Five Wisdoms

The buddha also embodies the five wisdoms. Wisdom is primordial understanding, or mind, or awareness. In Dzogchen terminology, the word for "wisdom" is *yeshe. Ye* is "primordial" and *she* is "mind." *Yeshe* is not defined this way elsewhere (although the term is used elsewhere). Each of the five wisdoms is a form of yeshe.

This wisdom is not created by different causes and conditions; all sentient beings have yeshe as the nature of their mind. Whether a sentient being is born in the three lower realms or in the heavens, the nature of mind remains entirely the same. It is not changed or affected by outer experiences of happiness or suffering. It is the primordial nature of mind, primordial awareness. It is, in the Dzogchen tradition, what is pointed out by the teacher. The teacher doesn't give it to you; the teacher points out wisdom that already exists in your mind. In an enlightened being, this primordial awareness is completely manifest, and the recognition of it is stabilized. For the rest of us, it is not manifest until it is pointed out to us, and typically it is not stabilized without practice.

The first of the five wisdoms is the wisdom of the sphere of totality, dharmadhatu wisdom (*choying yeshe*). This means that all things in both samsara and transcendent states are seen exactly as they are. To the buddha, their nature is manifest and recognized— there is no obscuration by the negative emotions; nor is there any obscuration to knowledge. There is no subject, object, or relation between them. As an analogy, if we consider the act of generosity, there is one who gives, one who receives, and the thing passed between the two. When we see those three things as separate, that is the obscuration to knowledge. In actuality, there is no mistake, no impurity, and no separability in those three things; it is all just generosity. Because the totality of everything is seen in its purity, this is the wisdom of the sphere of totality.

Another way of depicting the purity of the sphere of totality is to use the sun. We can say that the sun in its essence is its potentiality, and its nature is radiance, or luminosity. We might experience the sun as being covered by clouds, but in its own essence, it has never been covered by anything.

The second of the five wisdoms is mirrorlike wisdom, or mirror wisdom (*melong yeshe*). In the same way that what appears before a mirror is perfectly reflected in the mirror, the qualities of both samsara and transcendence arise exactly from the natural energy of mirror wisdom. An example is given in Longchenpa's *Treasury of the Sphere of Totality*: whether you have a positive appearance or a negative appearance, the appearance of an enemy or of a friend, in the reflection of a mirror, they are exactly the same.

The third wisdom is the wisdom of equanimity (*nyamnyid yeshe*). Within this appearance of wisdom, there is nothing positive or negative; there is nothing that truly exists. All appearance is simply appearance without an underlying reality. So every appearance, regardless of whether it is of samsara or nirvana, exists within great equanimity.

The idea of the wisdom of equanimity is based in emptiness. All experiences, or things of ordinary existence, are empty at the moment they appear. As well, all pure appearances of transcendent states are empty at the moment they appear. There is no difference between the emptiness of one and the emptiness of the other; they are both equally empty. The wisdom of equanimity is the experience of the fundamental sameness between these two appearances.

Omniscient Longchenpa said that everything appears as the display of the energy of wisdom, but at the very moment things appear, nothing whatsoever exists. No matter what kind of dream we might dream, nothing in the dream actually exists; there is an appearance without an underlying reality. Like a dream, all appearances of samsara and nirvana are the appearances of the energy of wisdom, but at the same moment that everything appears, it appears within emptiness. This is the wisdom of equanimity.

The fourth wisdom is discerning wisdom (*sosor togpai yeshe*). This wisdom sees each and every thing in both ordinary existence and nirvana, each of the beings in the six realms and all the phenomena of nirvana, and each and every detail of these configurations without them being mixed up. It sees each separately and at the same moment. Ordinarily, we give our attention to one thing and then we turn our attention to something else. The buddha, on the other hand, sees everything both distinctly and simultaneously. This is the wisdom of discernment. Literally in Tibetan, it is the "discernment of each detail."

The fifth wisdom is all-accomplishing wisdom, literally "the wisdom of the accomplishment of acts" (*yagrub yeshe*). Typically we must purify obscurations and cultivate merit and wisdom over a period of time in order to attain enlightenment, and all-accomplishing wisdom appears as the result. It is effortless, all-pervasive, impartial, and spontaneous, unlike when we act for the benefit of just one person, where we must act willfully and with effort, and we must ignore others. It is like the difference between doing an ordinary calculation in our mind and using a computer, which can do a tremendous amount of work at one time. The buddha's mastery in accomplishment comes with enlightenment because it is part of primordial awareness.

All-accomplishing wisdom is like the sun, which is reflected in however many containers of water are placed on the ground—one hundred, one thousand, or one million. As long as the container has water, a reflection appears. In the same way, the buddha's activity appears wherever sentient beings have merit for this appearance. However, we mustn't think that the buddha's activity is limited to specific teachings. If it is appropriate for the buddha to appear in the form of a lama, a king, a political leader, a doctor, a teacher, or a poor laborer, he will do so. Whatever form is necessary or useful for sentient beings, the buddha will appear in that form.

The activity of the buddha for the benefit of sentient beings is the result of his cultivation of compassion on the path to enlightenment. If the buddha had cultivated anger, the result would be the creation of wars or of sufferings for sentient beings. However, on the path of training, he cultivated a great amount of compassion. The result is his compassionate activity for others.

## The Seven Aspects of the Sambhogakaya

There are seven aspects ("seven branches of union" in Thinley Norbu Rinpoche's text) of the body of enlightenment's perfect splendor. The first aspect consists of the five certain qualities, or the five certainties. You may recognize these from the *Treasury of Sutra and Tantra*. The first of these is the certainty of the teacher. This is represented by the chief, or the lord, of the five families of enlightenment, Buddha Vajradhara. This is the certainty of the teacher of the body of enlightenment's perfect splendor.

The second of the five certainties is the certainty of the entourage, those who appear around Buddha Vajradhara. Although these individuals appear to be separate, in fact, they are not; their minds and his mind are completely inseparable. These figures are the male and female buddhas of the five buddha families and the eight male and female bodhisattvas, including the bodhisattvas Manjushri and Chenrezig. These male and female bodhisattvas are what we call "result," or "ultimate," bodhisattvas. They are beyond even tenth-level bodhisattvas, who are still called "causal" bodhisattvas. Although they still appear as bodhisattvas, they are in fact completely enlightened buddhas.

The third certainty is the certainty of the instructions. The certain instructions are the Vajrayana instructions. On this level, there is no teaching related to the Shravakayana, or even to the lower levels of the Mahayana (the way of characteristics, the way of the listeners, and the way of the solitary sages).

The fourth certainty is the certainty of the time, or the sphere of equanimity of the fourth time. Ordinarily, we have an idea of the three times—past, present, and future. However, although we have created an impression of time based on appearances, in the nature of things there is only the primordial, or original, moment. There has never been a moment besides the primordial moment. In that primordial moment, the body of enlightenment's perfect splendor appears and teaches. Or we can say that the three times take on one flavor, one taste, within the sphere of equanimity.

The fifth certainty is the certainty of the place. For the appearance of the body of enlightenment's perfect splendor, this is the highest pure land, Akanishta (Tib. Ogmin). Literally, Ogmin means "below nothing." There is nothing above it. In traditional cosmology (even Hindu traditional cosmology), we are in the desire realm, where the heavens appear. Then there is the form realm, where different heavens appear, the highest of which is Ogmin (Highest Realm), within the manifest body of enlightenment. However, here we are talking about the body of enlightenment's perfect splendor, the pure nature of everything. It is called the "highest pure realm," but it is beyond any idea of it being above or below anything, because it is the nature of all reality. It is not localized anywhere in particular. In the *Secret Essence Tantra*, it is said that without understanding the nature of everything, a pure land can be experienced as hell. However, with the understanding of the nature of everything, even hell can appear as a pure land.

These five certainties appear only within the experience of buddhas. Not only do they not appear for ordinary beings, but even tenth-level bodhisattvas do not experience these five certainties. The five certainties as explained in Dzogchen or in the *Secret Essence Tantra* (but, I underline, this is the experience of enlightened beings only) are somewhat different from the five certainties you may have heard about in the Mahayana.

The second aspect of the body of enlightenment's perfect splendor is the primordial union of male and female buddhas. The male buddhas represent the arising of all appearances. The female buddhas represent that these appearances from the beginning have no point of creation, abiding, or cessation. She represents the great emptiness called "the supreme of all appearances." These male and female aspects of enlightenment, appearance and emptiness, were not joined at a certain point in time. Despite how they may appear in images, they arise primordially in union, inseparable, indivisible.

The third aspect of the body of enlightenment's perfect splendor is that even as small a part of the body as a pore is entirely pervaded by pure great bliss. "Pure" means it is untainted by desire, anger, or ignorance.

The fourth aspect is that the body of enlightenment, at this level, does not appear in a solid, material form of flesh, blood, and so forth. It appears as the union of the male and female buddhas, appearance and emptiness, but it has no fundamental reality.

The fifth aspect is that these male and female buddhas' experience is the energy of the display of wisdom, which is compassion. This wisdom is completely filled with compassion for all sentient beings.

The sixth aspect is that this body of enlightenment is endowed with inexhaustible enlightened activity of the bodies and wisdoms of enlightenment. Whether past, present, or future, there is no point when this enlightened activity ceases.

The last of the seven aspects is the unceasing activity that appears for the benefit of others in any way appropriate. Arising unceasingly and without any effort, it appears in whatever way is appropriate for sentient beings.

The ultimate body of enlightenment and the body of enlightenment's perfect splendor are the experience of buddhas. Bodhisattvas and sentient beings do not have this experience. In contrast, the manifest body of enlightenment is the experience that can be seen by bodhisattvas and ordinary sentient beings. We see differences in time and space.

## The Five Uncertainties of the Nirmanakaya

The manifest body of enlightenment is characterized by the five uncertainties, which are the opposite of the five certainties of the body of enlightenment's perfect splendor. The first is the uncertainty of the teacher. For the body of enlightenment's perfect splendor, the teacher is certain—Buddha Vajradhara, surrounded by other buddhas and bodhisattvas. In the case of the manifest body of enlightenment, the teacher is uncertain. It can take any form in relation to those being guided—a teacher, a buddha, a bodhisattva, a man or a woman, an animal, a dakini, a yogini, or some other kind of being.

The second uncertainty is the entourage. In the sambhogakaya, Buddha Vajradhara is surrounded by buddhas and bodhisattvas who are, in fact, his own appearance, inseparable from him. In the nirmanakaya, the entourage, or the retinue, is uncertain; those being taught can be humans, gods, *nagas* (serpentine water spirits), or any other sort of spirit. They can be at any level of capacity: very astute, average, or inferior, and they can be interested in any level of teaching.

The third uncertainty is the teaching. In the body of enlightenment's perfect splendor, the teaching is only Vajrayana. In the manifest body of enlightenment, the teaching depends on who is receiving the teaching. Teachings of any yana are possible, depending on the interests and capacities of those being taught. There are endless numbers of teachings the manifest body of enlightenment can give.

The fourth uncertainty is the place. In the body of enlightenment's perfect splendor, the place is always the highest pure land. For the manifest body of enlightenment, wherever sentient beings are to be guided to enlightenment, the teacher appears at that place. This can be not only in the human realm but also in any other realm, including the hell realm. The tantric tradition talks about each of the six forms of buddha (*munis*) appearing in one of the six realms of beings. Shakyamuni is the name of one buddha in the human realm.

The last of the five uncertainties is the uncertain time. The forms of the manifest body of enlightenment can appear anytime in the past, present, or future.

The main point of the manifest body of enlightenment is that these forms appear for sentient beings, within their experience. This is very different from the first two bodies of enlightenment. The three bodies of enlightenment can also be amalgamated into two. The ultimate body of enlightenment is the body of enlightenment without form, and the body of enlightenment's perfect splendor and the manifest body of enlightenment together are the bodies of form (*rupakaya*). The body of enlightenment's perfect splendor represents the ultimate purity of form. The manifest body of enlightenment is the natural appearance, or emanation, of the body of enlightenment's perfect splendor. It appears in the world in forms that are appropriate to guide sentient beings.

In some systems, the ultimate body of enlightenment appears only to buddhas, the body of enlightenment's perfect splendor appears only to bodhisattvas, and the manifest body of enlightenment appears to sentient beings. However, as explained by Thinley Norbu Rinpoche, the ultimate body of enlightenment and the body of enlightenment's perfect splendor appear only to buddhas, whereas the manifest body of enlightenment appears to bodhisattvas and ordinary sentient beings.

## The Essence, Nature, and Display
## of the Three Kayas

From the perspective of Dzogchen, each of the three bodies of enlightenment has the special characteristics called essence, nature, and display (or energy). We say that the essence of mind is emptiness, its nature is clarity, and its energy is all-pervasive compassion. But these terms mean something different in each of the three bodies of enlightenment. Thinley Norbu Rinpoche quotes Omniscient Longchenpa: "The ultimate body of enlightenment's essence is called 'emptiness,' but it is described as unimpeded awareness (*zangtalgi rigpa*), and its energy, or display, is called 'the ocean of nonconceptual wisdom.'"

Continuing, the essence of the body of enlightenment's perfect splendor is described as self-occurring, inconceivable natural light, and its display is the form of the five buddha families of enlightenment. This includes Vajrasattva, Vajradhara, and so on, all of whom have the signs and marks of physical perfection.

The essence of the manifest body of enlightenment is the basis of all-pervasive wisdom energy. Its display is that all-pervasive wisdom energy that appears in various forms to guide sentient beings.

Again quoting Longchenpa, it's important to distinguish between the essence and the display of each of the three bodies of enlightenment. This is because although the essence of the three bodies is the same and indivisible, there is a difference between their essence and their outer appearance. Fundamental, or basic, wisdom is the essence of the three bodies of enlightenment. The essence is described as like the primordial, or the fundamental, basis without appearance. The display, or manifestation, of each kaya, however, is different. Thinley Norbu Rinpoche says that if the essence and the manifestation are not distinguished, two faults arise. First, if these two bodies of enlightenment are one in essence, and if the manifest body of enlightenment and the body of enlightenment's perfect splendor appear when they guide others, then the ultimate body of enlightenment would also appear; but it does not. Second, since the ultimate body of enlightenment does not appear, then the form bodies of enlightenment would also not appear; but they do.*

## Dharma and Sangha

The second of the three jewels is the dharma, the treasured instructions. Dharma has two divisions. The first is the actual content: all the words of the teachings that have been expressed, either verbally or in writing. It's the oral and written words of the Buddha, as well as those of the great sages such as Padmasambhava, Longchenpa, Mipham, and others, and the written and oral teachings of other lamas, yogis, and yoginis who carry on their lineages. This is what we call "scriptural dharma."

The second division is the dharma of realization. Based on scriptural dharma, compassion, faith, correct view, experience, and realization are developed. These developments are what we call the "dharma of realization."

Those who turn their minds entirely to the scriptural dharma and the dharma of realization are called "the sangha" (Tib. *gendun*). The first part of *gendun* is *gewa* (virtue). *Dun* means "to like," "to enjoy," "to yearn for," or "to be intent upon." So "to be intent upon virtue" is how Tibetans have translated the Sanskrit term *sangha*. Here Thinley Norbu Rinpoche defines *virtue* as the specific virtue that they incline toward, the virtue of the dharma of scripture and realization.

Those are the three jewels, or, as Thinley Norbu Rinpoche says, the triple gem—the buddha, the dharma, and the sangha.

In the *Changeless Nature* by the bodhisattva Maitreya, it's said that the ultimate refuge is the buddha alone, not the dharma or the sangha, which are considered temporary refuges. Maitreya says that when an individual sees the truth of reality, that person naturally abandons scriptural dharma because it is no longer needed. Likewise, since realizations change as progress is made on the path, each

---

*See appendix 2 for an outline of certain aspects of the three kayas.

stage of previous experience and realization is naturally abandoned, particularly when the stage of enlightenment is reached. Therefore, Maitreya says, the dharma of realization proves to be temporary as well. In the sangha, Maitreya says, those who have not yet arrived at enlightenment have habitual tendencies that remain in their mind-streams. Therefore, because they still need guidance to eliminate all their negative emotions and obscurations, they cannot act as an ultimate refuge.

## Lama, Yidam, and Dakini

Maitreya's explanation is from the point of view of the sutras. From the point of view of the tantras, however, the dharma and the sangha are considered to be inseparable from the buddha. How is this possible? In the tantras, we consider the three jewels to be the three roots, or the three sources. Instead of the buddha, dharma, and sangha, we call them the lama, the *yidam* (a male meditation deity), and the assembly of *dakinis* (female meditation deities).

In the tantras, we consider the lama to be the union of the essence of the three jewels. Therefore, the lama is the ultimate body of enlightenment, the buddha. The appearance of the qualities of the ultimate body of enlightenment is the lama's speech, the sacred instructions, the dharma. The yidam deities are the body of enlightenment's perfect splendor. The enlightened mind that is always intent upon this pure virtue is the sangha, or the dakinis. Therefore, the three jewels are, in fact, the three roots.

Thinley Norbu Rinpoche's text includes a quote from the great master Vimalamitra. He explains why the Tibetan word *sangye* is used to translate the Sanskrit term *buddha*. *Sang* means to "purify" or to "clean away." In the buddha, dualistic experience has been cleared away. *Gye* (*je* in the Khampa dialect) means "blossom," "enhance," or "increase." In the buddha, not only has dualistic experience been completely cleared away but nondual wisdom has also completely blossomed, completely flourished, completely increased. This nondual wisdom is completely manifest.

What are the yidams, the meditation deities? The first part of this word *yidam* is *yi*, short for "mind," and *dam* means to "fix," to "bind." In deity meditation, we fix our mind one-pointedly on this object in order to practice and accomplish the deities in stages. One way to understand how the yidam fits into buddhadharma practice is that they are not separate entities from the lama or the dakinis. We can practice a meditation deity because the lama has given us a prophecy or has told us which yidam to practice in order to arrive at enlightenment. Or sometimes during an empowerment ceremony, we are given a flower to throw onto a mandala. If it falls in the east, then we do a deity that corresponds to the vajra buddha family, in the south to the jewel (or *ratna*) buddha family, in the west to the lotus (or *padma*) buddha family, in the north to the karma buddha family, and in the center to the buddha buddha family. Where the flower lands shows us what karmic connection we have to a specific deity. Then we practice a deity of that buddha family. When we practice, we imagine that all deities are gathered within that single deity. Because of our connection and our attitude toward this deity, our practice will give quick results. Until we've arrived at awakening, we don't give up this yidam. We practice with the idea that this deity is in fact the lama and the dakinis.

The various forms of meditation deities can be peaceful or wrathful. For example, in relation to the lama, the peaceful form can be different forms of Guru Rinpoche. The wrathful form could be Dorje Drolod. In relation to the dakinis, the peaceful form could be Yeshe Tsogyal, and the wrathful form Senge Dongma or Tröma Nagmo.

For example, if we imagine the lama as Vajrasattva, then this is our yidam. In the same way, if we imagine the lama as Vajrakilaya, this is the lama or this is the yidam. The dakinis can be Vajravarahi or the yidam can be Vajravarahi. The lama can be Yeshe Tsogyal or Dechen Gyalmo, or this can be our yidam, or this can be the dakini. This is simply to say that the yidam is not different from the lama or the dakini.

Whatever the case, you consider that deity to be the union of all lamas, yidams, and dakinis, in that one form, and then you don't have to consider any other practice. You simply do that practice as the union of all of them.

When you do a yidam practice, it's important to keep secret the different signs you receive, and any special higher perceptions you have, of accomplishment of your practice. It is best even to keep the name of your deity secret from others. It's entirely a personal practice.

## The Three Jewels and the Qualities of Enlightenment

To summarize our description of the three jewels: Outwardly, the three jewels are the buddha, the dharma, and the sangha. Inwardly, they are the lama, the yidam, and the dakini. Secretly, they are the ultimate body of enlightenment, the body of enlightenment's perfect splendor, and the manifest body of enlightenment.

From the perspective of Vajrayana teachings, the three jewels and the three roots are gathered within the dharma master, who embodies all the attributes (body, speech, mind, qualities, and activities) of the buddhas of the five buddha families, both completely and distinctly. The five buddha families illustrate this. There is an inconceivable number of buddhas, as many buddhas as there are sentient beings. However, they can all be grouped into the five buddha families, and the attributes of each buddha family are contained in every other buddha family. For example, the attributes of all the buddha families are gathered in each of the buddhas of the vajra buddha family. The attributes of the buddha family, the vajra family, the jewel family, the lotus family, and the karma family are gathered in the vajra family. All attributes of all buddhas can be gathered into one.

Furthermore, each attribute of each buddha of the five buddha families has all the other attributes of all the other buddhas. For example, Vairochana's body contains the body, speech, mind, qualities, and activities of enlightenment; and his speech contains the body, speech, mind, qualities, and activities of enlightenment. In this way, one buddha has at least twenty-five different aspects. These are called "the twenty-five qualities of the result."

All the buddha families of enlightenment can be multiplied into hundreds, thousands, millions, or an incalculable number. From one aspect of enlightenment, we can experience millions of aspects of enlightenment. In the *Secret Essence Tantra*, we have the idea that in one form of Samantabhadra, for example, we can imagine within his body a countless number of forms of buddhas. Each and every deity can represent hundreds, thousands, millions, or an inconceivable number of aspects of enlightenment. Thinley Norbu Rinpoche includes a quote from the *Flower Ornament Sutra*. The last pages, the grand finale of the *Flower Ornament Sutra* (which is about one thousand pages long), end in the *Prayer for Excellent Conduct*, which we often recite in the Tibetan tradition: On each atom, there are realms equal to the number of all atoms. In each of these realms, there are an inconceivable number of buddhas. Each buddha sits in the midst of an equally inconceivable number of bodhisattvas. Reciting the prayer, we wish to have the experience of witnessing this. It is very difficult for us to imagine, but, at least, we have to try to understand it. Gradually, as we practice, we will be able to experience what is now inconceivable to us.

The forms of buddhas, lamas, yidams, and dakinis appear in various ways: in various physical forms, realms, and celestial palaces. Although lamas, yidams, and dakinis appear in distinct ways, there is no difference between them, no higher or lower, good or not so good, in relation to these appearances. There is nothing that distinguishes their nature at all. They are all part of the appearance of the attributes of enlightenment.

Omniscient Rongzompa, the great Tibetan master, in defining what we call a "god" (whether a worldly deity or transcendent wisdom deity), said that a god is infinite, or does not die, is particularly stable, bestows blessings or answers our prayers, is peaceful, is beneficial to us as we experience our own body now, and is venerable (worthy of being worshipped). Rongzompa's definition comes from the "outer" buddhadharma sciences, which include astrology, divination, and so forth. In tantra and Dzogchen, however, we understand gods, or deities, as being the emanations, or manifestations, of nondual, natural, self-arising, self-manifest wisdom, which is the enlightenment of the two purities; regardless of their color, form, gender, or realm, they are entirely the play of the wisdom of enlightenment. So, any yidam in the Dzogchen or tantric tradition is only the play of the wisdom of enlightenment. It is not separate from the wisdom of enlightenment.

In the Nyingma tradition, there are six levels of tantra, three outer and three inner. The three outer tantras are *kriya* (action) tantra, *charya* (activity) tantra, and yoga (union) tantra. In action tantra, we call the deities "deities of the nature of reality" or "deities of the pure sphere." The higher levels of tantra, and specifically the highest level of tantra, remark that this is a partial view and that the nature of reality should include all forms of reality as well. For example, a table, a house, any of the elements of mountains and trees—everything has the nature of reality and should also be understood to be the deity. If the essence of every single thing in its ultimate purity is enlightenment, then the thing itself in its form should also be considered to have this enlightened nature. So, in the highest level of tantra, all things, both the essence and the form, are considered to partake of this same enlightened nature.

When we do creation-phase practice, we think to ourselves, "All things are pure." It is just a thought that accompanies our meditation practice. Further on, when we understand the view of the *Secret Essence Tantra*, we can arrive at some decisiveness concerning that. We begin to see that directly. It is not just a thought in our mind accompanying our meditation. A piece of candy is sweet because its essence is sweetness. Everything is pure because its essence is pure. This is a very important point.

So far, we have considered the three bodies of enlightenment. There are two more, making a total of five bodies of enlightenment.

The fourth body of enlightenment is the fact that all the qualities of the three bodies are not mixed together. They are all distinct within awakening, and that quality is called "the body of manifest

awakening." To be clear, in this system of description, the fourth
body of enlightenment is not what is often referred to as the svabhavikakaya; that's from a different system of description.

The fact that these four bodies of enlightenment are in essence
inseparable is the fifth body of enlightenment, called "the vajra body
of enlightenment." So we have the five bodies of enlightenment, the
five buddha families, the five wisdoms, and so on. No matter how
many aspects of enlightenment that can be described, all of these
are the lama, our supreme object of refuge.

When we take refuge, it's best to have studied these qualities of
enlightenment, the qualities of the buddha, of the master, and so
forth, and to keep them in mind. Retain them in your mind, and take
refuge in the qualities you recall. If we're beginners and are unable
to recall all of these qualities, it is essential to develop faith and
positive intention in taking refuge. We can take refuge thinking that
the buddha is a particular form (for example, a painting, a drawing,
or a statue). We can think of the teaching as being embodied in a
text. In this way, we begin by developing faith and positive intention
in relation to our object of refuge.

In relation to the community of practitioners, even though we
may not think of anyone as other than an ordinary human being,
if we cannot conceive of anything else, we can appreciate someone
(for example, a novice, a fully ordained monk, a yogi, or a yogini)
whom we admire for their commitment to dharma. In any case,
whether we are thinking about a painting, a statue, a text, or an
ordinary individual, we really think that these are the three jewels
and we take refuge in them. This is how we begin taking refuge.

## The Three Levels of Refuge

We can take refuge with three different perspectives depending on
the capacity of our mind. A person of the most limited view takes
refuge for their own benefit only, in order not to be reborn in the
lower realms and with the idea that taking refuge will ensure that
this life and the next will be happy.

A person of middling capacity considers that even being reborn in a higher realm is ultimately pointless, because eventually a person who remains in samsara can be reborn in the lower realms. This person decides to attain enlightenment in order to attain freedom from any rebirth in the six realms. Enlightenment for one's own benefit leads to the states of enlightenment of the Shravakayana tradition—the states of the listener and the solitary sage.

The great teacher Vimalamitra said that we take refuge thinking of both fear and the qualities of enlightenment. We take refuge with the thought of fear of the lower realms, of nirvana without compassion, and of lesser paths such as the Shravakayana, in which there are still obscurations to understanding. So we take refuge in fear of samsara and in aspiration toward transcendent states, remembering the qualities of enlightenment.

A person who is particularly courageous, who has the highest perspective, decides that enlightenment for one's own benefit is not sufficient. This person reflects that even though enlightenment may be obtainable, in the six realms we have connections to all other sentient beings through family, friends, and beyond, and they all can be enlightened. Through compassion, this person doesn't remain in a stagnant state of personal peace, and through discriminating awareness, they don't stay in the six realms. This is how refuge is taken in the Mahayana tradition.

In the tantric tradition, we take refuge (as in the Mahayana tradition) for the benefit of all sentient beings. However, we do so with the idea that we take refuge only until our experience of the infinite purity of everything as it is right now is full, complete, and unwavering.

We take refuge vows. We can receive refuge either during the course of an empowerment (because refuge is given at the beginning of each empowerment) or we can take refuge in a separate ceremony. In either case, we should take refuge from a qualified master. Once we have taken refuge, we should recite refuge prayers three times during the day and three times at night (six times during a twenty-four-hour period) or, at the very least, three times. We

should remember the qualities of enlightenment and recite whatever formula of refuge we wish.

## Training in What to Abandon and What to Practice

Once we have taken refuge, we train in both what to abandon and
what to practice. This isn't a question of attachment or aversion,
rejecting something and thinking that we are doing better than
anyone else: we enter this training in order to focus on attaining
enlightenment. There are three points I want to make about each
of these two aspects of training.

As for what to abandon: First, once we have taken refuge in the
buddha, who is capable of leading us to both uplifted states within
samsara (birth as a human or a god) and true happiness (enlightenment), we abandon refuge in those worldly deities, or gods, who
cannot lead us beyond samsara. Second, once we have taken refuge
in the dharma, we do not accept any practice that teaches that one
can or should harm other beings. In some traditions, it's considered to be an offering to the gods to cut the neck of an animal. We
renounce causing harm to any sentient being. And third, once we
have taken refuge in the sangha, we don't befriend persons whose
view is aggressively against the dharma view. If we befriend those
whose perspective on life is contrary to the dharma perspective, as
beginners, we fall under the influence of such people and our own
practice suffers because of it. If they won't have any bad influence
on you, you can befriend them as you want. If befriending someone
causes obstacles to your view, meditation, or action, then don't
befriend them. This is not to judge them negatively; it is just that
their influence on you is negative. Otherwise this sort of advice
appears to be very sectarian.

As for what to practice: First, once we have taken refuge in the
buddha, we should consider any form of the buddha (whether a
painting or a statue) to be the buddha, and we should make offerings or express devotion to that form. Thinley Norbu Rinpoche
quotes Nagarjuna as saying that wise persons revere even statues

of a buddha made of wood (a very ordinary material). These statues shouldn't be disrespected but should be offered our homage.

Second, we should develop reverence for every dharma text. Even if it isn't complete or is in poor condition, it is a form of the buddha himself. Thinley Norbu Rinpoche quotes from an old text where Buddha Shakyamuni said that, during the time of degeneration (our time), he would take the form of letters and words and, at that time, persons should honor the written word and the scriptures.

And third, no matter how members of the sangha might appear—novice monks, fully ordained monks, novice nuns, fully ordained nuns, ordained laypersons, white-robed, long-haired yogis, yoginis in diverse apparels, other laypersons—we should think of them as embodiments of the three jewels, part of the community of awareness holders (*rigdzins* or *vidyadharas*). We should never criticize or look down upon them. Thinley Norbu Rinpoche quotes a sutra saying that pride is the source of all faults and mistakes and that one should not disrespect even the least among the monks. We should develop appreciation for each and every one. Among all of these, those who have realization or a high level of practice are chiefs. Yet each and every one is a member of that community.

Part of the practice of taking refuge is doing prostrations. Prostrations are the antidote to pride. In the foundational practices, we have what are called the five "hundred thousands": five different practices that we repeat one hundred thousand times each. Generally speaking, we do prostrations during the offering of the Seven-Branch Prayer that is part of the Guru Yoga practice, but in the Dudjom Tersar Ngöndro, we do prostrations as we repeat the refuge prayer. Thinley Norbu Rinpoche suggests reciting the prayer for developing the mind of awakening at the same time as you do prostrations, so you end up doing the one hundred thousand repetitions of refuge, bodhichitta, and prostrations all at once.

It's important to know the benefits of taking refuge. By taking refuge, we will not fall into the lower realms, because by truly taking refuge in the three jewels, we will cease to create negative karma. Once we've taken refuge, we often have the opportunity for protection from physical or mental suffering and eventually refuge from all forms of suffering. Refuge provides the foundation, or basis, for all vows, be they the vows of Shravakayana, the commitments of the bodhisattva, or the commitments of the tantras. Ultimately, the refuge vows lead us to the attainment of enlightenment. So there are limitless benefits to taking refuge.

It is said in some texts that if the merit of taking refuge had form, the whole of the three realms would be too small to hold it. It is said in a sutra that no being who has taken refuge in the buddha will be harmed by any form of demonic negative forces. Even a person who breaks their vows (monastic vows or others) or gets upset mentally, thanks to their refuge vows, will continue to take a positive rebirth in samsara and will eventually transcend samsara.

## Visualizing the Objects of Refuge

Why do we use the technique of visualization in our practice? To answer that, first we must recognize that as beings in the desire realm, we visualize all the time. We imagine our loved one and have vivid dreams of being together. We think about what we want for dinner and bring to mind a delicious meal. We are especially impacted by negative images; we pay rapt attention to images and scenes that shock, disturb, or disgust us. It's our habit, developed and sealed over uncountable lifetimes, of protecting our sense of self from outside threats. If only we paid as much attention to positive, extraordinary images as we do to negative, repulsive, or troublesome ones! Because if we make a habit of focusing on the extraordinary, then we become extraordinary. To break our habit of focusing on negativity, we need to inspire ourselves to pay attention to extraordinary manifestations of enlightenment. The more we are inspired—the more time and energy we invest in understanding and appreciating enlightened qualities—the more transformative will be our experience, until our visualization completely takes over our mind, overwhelming all ordinary sights, sounds, thoughts, and feelings.

There are different ways of visualizing the objects of refuge. The Longchen Nyingtik (Innermost Essence of Longchenpa) uses the "marketplace style." There is an image of Guru Rinpoche with a huge crowd around him. Above are the lamas of the lineage. Below are the protectors. To the right, left, and in front are the buddhas, yidams, dakinis, and the sangha.

Another style is called "gathered into one jewel." You imagine Guru Rinpoche in front of you in the sky. He represents all meditation deities, all lamas, all protectors, the buddha, the dharma, and sangha, all united in his single form. This instruction is found in the Khandro Nyingtik (Innermost Essence of the Dakinis), a text written by Thinley Norbu Rinpoche's father, Dudjom Rinpoche.

We begin by sitting in an isolated place—either a retreat place far away from everyone or just in our own home but in isolation from any other activity. We sit comfortably without putting any strain on the body, because that makes it difficult to visualize. What's most important in our physical posture is for our body to be straight—not tense, just straight, so our inner channels will be straight. When our inner channels are straight, the energy moves properly within the channels, which helps make the mind open, or clear. On the other hand, when our posture is not correct and our channels are not straight, our energy does not move properly, and we have many feelings of discomfort, or our mind simply isn't as clear as it should be.

Mentally, relax. Thinley Norbu Rinpoche says to let the mind rest and relax in its natural state. This means that we aren't following thoughts of anger, desire, or ignorance, thoughts of activity in the world. Relaxing may feel forced; to avoid that, it helps to remind ourselves that being relaxed is compassionate, because kindness to ourselves enables compassion for others, which is our essential motivation for effective practice.

To begin, we imagine that where we are is not an ordinary place but a pure land. We imagine that we are sitting in a great open, soft, and level field. The ground is spongy, poofy. There are rivers of nectar, beautiful fruit trees, and many types of flowers. The grass is very new and green. Wild animals like deer abound. They are very tame and not at all afraid, and we are not afraid of them. We don't see any impure appearances.

In the midst of this pure land, we imagine a lake such as Lake Danakosha, where Guru Rinpoche was born. This lake is filled with water of eight qualities (crystal clarity, coolness, sweetness, lightness, softness, being soothing to the stomach, being free of impurities, and being able to clear the throat). It is the purest water imaginable. Around the lake, imagine wonderful birds singing sweetly. The lake is surrounded by jewels and sand made of particles of gold.

In the center of the lake appears a grand lotus made of jewels of many different colors. From a single stem, it rises and fills all space. This flower bears heavy fruit. Around its sides, the lotus is edged in gold. From the lotus appear five-colored silk banners, either as part of the lotus or part of the gold, however you want to imagine it.

The lotus has jeweled ornaments and bells of gold and silver (like the little bells that, in Tibet, we put on dogs or children). When the wind moves, the bells ring with the sound of the dharma. In the center of the lotus is a jeweled throne supported by eight lions. On top of that is a thousand-petaled lotus, in whose center is a seat of a sun disk, upon which there is a moon disk.

On top of this seat appears our root teacher, the union of all buddhas, in the form of Guru Rinpoche.

The following description of Guru Rinpoche is used in the Dudjom Tersar Ngöndro. Other lineages describe Guru Rinpoche differently, such as in union with a consort; but in essence, all the lineages describe the same essential source of refuge. Here, Guru Rinpoche is called "he who overpowers all that appears" (*nangsi zilnen*). There are different ways that Guru Rinpoche holds his five-pointed golden vajra, depending on the particular practice. It can be out in the sky, at his heart, or down at his right knee. In this case, he holds the vajra in his right hand, at the level of his right knee. In his left hand, he holds in his lap a skull-cup containing a long-life vase filled with sublime nectar.

We imagine Guru Rinpoche as being our kind root teacher. If our root teacher is Dudjom Rinpoche, we imagine that Dudjom Rinpoche appears before us in the form of Guru Rinpoche. It is said that if we visualize Dudjom Rinpoche, or whoever our root lama is, in this form, we can receive very quickly his blessing and accomplishment. Imagine Guru Rinpoche being white with a red glow.*

Guru Rinpoche's eyes are somewhat wrathful, but he is smiling. With his eyes, he has a wrathful regard toward negative forces, but he is smiling, as if he is laughing.

Guru Rinpoche wears several layers of clothes. The clothes closest to his body are white. Over that is a dark blue shirt. On top of that is the robe of a fully ordained monk, a yellow robe made of square pieces. Covering all is a great red cape. His crown has a vulture feather at the top. At his left shoulder, he holds a trident staff (*katvanga*), which is the symbolic form of his consort, Mandarava. His right leg is slightly extended, and his left leg is drawn in, the position of royal ease. He is surrounded by rainbows and light. We imagine that Guru Rinpoche is looking at us and all sentient beings with overwhelming love.

Thinley Norbu Rinpoche has taken the description, up to this point, from Dudjom Rinpoche's instructions in the Khandro Nyingtik. In this description, we have just one lotus upon which Guru Rinpoche sits. In other traditions, from the single, solid lotus stem, there are more lotuses in different directions that hold deities or buddhas in whom we take refuge. Thinley Norbu Rinpoche says that we have only one lotus, upon which Guru Rinpoche sits, not because it is somebody's invention, and not because something is missing or because it is a meditation for beginners, but because this is a very easy meditation and it allows us to receive the blessings of Guru Rinpoche very quickly.

Perhaps the most important thing to remember about our visualization, especially for Western practitioners, is that the way Guru

---

*We can think of a painting with a translucent red glaze over a white base. Orgyen Chowang Rinpoche describes Guru Rinpoche as having a white face glowing with pink light.

Rinpoche looks is not a cultural or historical style, or affectation. We should not think of Guru Rinpoche as wearing Tibetan garments; rather, each component of the visualization, each article of clothing, each implement, is symbolic of the many qualities and aspects of enlightenment, the reasons we take refuge in the three jewels. If we keep that in mind, then our mind will not be blocked by these unusual aspects of his appearance.

As explained above, we consider the lama to be the union of the three jewels. His body is the sangha, his speech is the dharma, his mind is the buddha. Or we can consider that the lama is the three roots: his body is the lama, his speech is the yidam, and his mind is the dakini. We can consider as well that the lama is the three bodies of enlightenment. At the same time, we can imagine that among these bodies of enlightenment, the two form bodies of enlightenment can be gathered into the single, ultimate body of enlightenment.

When we describe Guru Rinpoche as having a five-pointed vajra at his knee, a skull-cup in his left hand, and a staff at his left arm, this is simply Guru Rinpoche as the manifest body of enlightenment. This is not always how we should imagine Guru Rinpoche. For example, Guru Rinpoche as the ultimate body of enlightenment is emptiness, clarity, and all-pervasive wisdom. When we experience the infinite purity of the nature of all things, this is Guru Rinpoche as the ultimate body of enlightenment. We can also imagine Guru Rinpoche in the highest pure land (Ogmin), one of the five certainties of the body of enlightenment's perfect splendor, where he appears as Guru Vajradhara, the teacher of Ogmin. Guru Rinpoche also takes various forms for the benefit of others in the manifest body of enlightenment such as his eight manifestations (*tsen gyad*). These are the manifest body of enlightenment appearing in the world for the benefit of others. Guru Rinpoche is thus all three bodies of enlightenment.

The ultimate, or absolute, certain meaning of Guru Rinpoche is the ultimate body of enlightenment. The ultimate form of Guru Rinpoche appears from the nature of mind. From the nature of mind, the eight manifestations of Guru Rinpoche appear in the outside world. These outward forms of Guru Rinpoche give us pointing-out instructions to help us understand the nature of mind, the absolute form of Guru Rinpoche.

When we imagine Guru Rinpoche as the ultimate body of enlightenment, we say that this is "the great vital essence" or "the great sphere" of the ultimate body of enlightenment; it is completely beyond everything of the subjective or objective world. It is beyond any dualistic experience. From this great sphere arise an inconceivable number of form bodies of enlightenment. When we have sincerely developed faith and confidence from our heart in this single form of Guru Rinpoche, then, as was said by the great masters of the past, when we accomplish one deity, we accomplish one hundred—Chenrezig, Amitabha, Vajrasattva, all deities—because Guru Rinpoche in this form represents the union of the three bodies of enlightenment and the union of all deities.

In our visualization of Guru Rinpoche before us in the manifest form of enlightenment, we imagine, also facing Guru Rinpoche, our father of this life to our right, our mother to our left, our friends and family behind us, and all around us our enemies, friends, and those to whom we are indifferent. We imagine all sentient beings with us. We lead all sentient beings toward enlightenment, toward Guru Rinpoche. Physically, we join our hands, palms together, at the forehead, throat, and heart. When we join our hands, it is like a lotus bud, not with the palms flat together but with the thumbs resting between the forefingers. Verbally, we repeat the refuge prayer, thinking of its meaning and reciting it in a pleasant voice. Mentally, we think that whatever happens in this life and until we attain enlightenment, we wish that Guru Rinpoche knows us, pays attention to us. Whether we are happy or unhappy, no matter what happens, not only in this life but in our future lives, until we attain enlightenment, we ask for Guru Rinpoche's attention and we take refuge in Guru Rinpoche.

Thinley Norbu Rinpoche explains what you should be thinking when you recite the refuge prayer "From this moment until attaining the essence of enlightenment, I take refuge in the lama, who is the three jewels." The heart of enlightenment, he says, is the complete and perfect enlightenment of the buddha according to the unsurpassable Mahayana tradition (that is, the enlightenment of the two purities—the intrinsic nature of awareness and the recognition of everything as the display of intrinsic awareness).

When Thinley Norbu Rinpoche mentions Mahayana here, he refers to both the causal Mahayana of the sutras and the resultant Mahayana of tantra (Vajrayana). Sometimes we refer to Mahayana as exclusive to the sutra tradition, but, in this case (and often), it refers to both branches of the Mahayana tradition.

We take refuge until we attain the heart of enlightenment. Right now, we don't understand the nature of reality. We experience the sufferings of the three realms (desire, form, and formless realms); the sufferings of the six classes of beings; the sufferings of birth, old age, sickness, and death. Once we understand the nature of reality and are free from suffering, once we have attained the heart of enlightenment, we no longer have to go for refuge. At that point, we've united with the essence of all enlightenment, with the essence of the buddhas, with Guru Rinpoche. At that point, we are no longer a person who takes refuge. We are an enlightened being who gives refuge to all sentient beings.

We recite the refuge prayer verbally, but it is not enough merely to recite the refuge prayer and count the prayers we have been reciting. We must also develop faith and belief by recalling the qualities of the three jewels and the three roots, the teacher, and taking refuge fully conscious of these qualities.

At the end of your session of recitation, imagine that, from Guru Rinpoche's heart, an inconceivable amount of light streams forth and touches both you and all sentient beings. This relieves the obscurations and bad karma of the body, speech, and mind of yourself and all sentient beings. Your body turns into a sphere of light. You and all sentient beings dissolve into light and are absorbed into the heart of Guru Rinpoche. Then Guru Rinpoche (inseparable from yourself and all sentient beings) dissolves like a rainbow into space, into the sky.* If you understand the view of Dzogchen or the Middle Way, then remain within that view without any mental activity whatsoever. Even without an understanding of Dzogchen, at this point, remain sitting without any mental activity.

At the beginning of this practice, we took refuge in Guru Rinpoche in a visualized form of enlightenment. Now, after our own form has dissolved into Guru Rinpoche and Guru Rinpoche has dissolved into space, we rest our mind in our natural awareness of clarity and emptiness inseparable; this resting of the mind is taking refuge in the absolute, certain, true form of Guru Rinpoche. The meditation of taking refuge in the visualized form of Guru Rinpoche is called "causal refuge." Resting in natural awareness is called "resultant refuge," which is experiencing the primordial purity of our own enlightened mind.

Because we have a mind, because we have dualistic experience, we must meditate on the visualized form of Guru Rinpoche. This is our method of ridding ourselves of dualistic experience. Until then, we've got to believe in certain things—that fire is hot, that our actions have results, and so on. We also have to take refuge in the form of refuge that appears before us. We have got to rely on this support within our dualistic experience in order to do away with our dualistic experience. When we no longer have dualistic experience, when we are no longer lost in thought, then we don't need to meditate on the visualized form of Guru Rinpoche. We experience the essence of our own mind that is primordially pure enlightenment. From this meditation, the blessings of our dharma master make manifest the qualities of primordially pure enlightenment. All appearances arise as the display of Guru Rinpoche. The pure land of Guru Rinpoche is everywhere. Everything appears as divine form.

When we have been introduced to the nature of our mind as Guru Rinpoche and we recognize the inseparability of the Guru Rinpoche that we imagine before us and the nature of our own

*In some forms of practice, Guru Rinpoche (with his retinue) dissolves into light, which then dissolves into the center of your heart. In any case, the essence of Guru Rinpoche and your own essence merge inseparably.

mind, at that point all appearances arise as the display of the nature of our own mind as Guru Rinpoche. This is not created anew, or by different causes and conditions. This is called "great noncomposite appearance." This has not come from our renunciation and is not something we have attained. It is the primordial nature of our own mind that we experience. So we experience all appearances as our own mind, blissful and peaceful.

That we recognize that the inseparability of Guru Rinpoche and the nature of our own mind, without any renunciation, without any attainment, is the primordial nature of our mind, is the buddha. That the qualities we see are without change and are the nature of all things (spontaneous, automatic appearance) is the dharma. That we experience the appearances of pure virtue as nondual is the sangha. As I explained above, the Sanskrit term *sangha* is translated into Tibetan as *gendun*, meaning "intention toward virtue." Intention toward virtue as a dualistic experience (that is, a positive intention that renounces or avoids negative intentions) is one kind of intention toward virtue. But here the intention toward virtue is the nondual experience. The experience of the nondual qualities of enlightenment is the sangha.

In brief, we take refuge in Guru Rinpoche as the manifest body of enlightenment. (As explained above, in some lineages, we take refuge in Guru Rinpoche with a consort in the form of the body of enlightenment's perfect splendor.) Refuge protects us from all obstacles; from suffering during this life; from the sufferings of birth, old age, sickness, and death; and from suffering in future lives. The ultimate refuge is taking refuge in Guru Rinpoche as the ultimate body of enlightenment, in the nature of our own mind. This protects us from desire, anger, ignorance, jealousy, and pride. This protects us from dualistic experience. This creates the experience of wisdom. This is the ultimate refuge. Thus taking refuge protects us from fear and suffering in a temporary form when we take refuge in the manifest body of enlightenment, and protects us ultimately when we take refuge in Guru Rinpoche as the ultimate body of enlightenment.

Consider whether Guru Rinpoche can give you refuge. Taking refuge in the ultimate Guru Rinpoche as the ultimate body of enlightenment diminishes our ordinary habit of getting lost in thought, our troubling emotions, our dualistic experience. Taking refuge in this way leads us to the understanding of the nature of mind. This makes our mind peaceful and happy. In the same way, taking refuge in Guru Rinpoche in the sky before us clears away our obstacles during this life, including all manner of sickness, sufferings, demons, negative thoughts and emotions, and our unknowingness.

Understanding that the ultimate form of Guru Rinpoche, the form of Guru Rinpoche in the form of enlightenment's perfect splendor, and the manifest form of Guru Rinpoche are all inseparable from the nature of our mind, and taking refuge in this way, protects us both ultimately and temporarily, in our daily circumstances. That we can take refuge in this way is a sign of great merit on our parts.

CHAPTER 4

# The Mind of Awakening

Refuge, as we have explained, is the special gateway to all buddha-dharma practice. The development of the mind of awakening (*bodhichitta*) is the gateway to the practice of the Mahayana, the "Great Way," that includes Vajrayana and Dzogchen as well.

The essence of the mind of awakening is the wish to attain full and complete enlightenment for the benefit of all sentient beings. Keeping this essence in mind, we will discuss the mind of awakening from the point of view of the causal Mahayana, from the point of view of the *Secret Essence Tantra*, and from the point of view of Dzogchen. We will describe it in relation to both the fundamental basis and the meditation of tranquillity. All of this will be related to the mind of awakening.

We begin with the intention to cultivate great compassion for all beings. The cultivation of this intention is the aspiration aspect of the mind of awakening. Once we have formed this aspiration, we apply ourselves to the six transcendent perfections to accomplish our awakening. This is the application aspect of the mind of awakening.

The mind of awakening is stressed in the Mahayana scriptures. Even the Buddha himself said that if one wishes to attain enlightenment, it is not necessary to study a lot of subjects, such as how to paint or construct stupas, or how to understand logic or medicine. Many subjects are extraneous. He said that there's only one subject that you really need to study: great compassion. With an understanding of great compassion, all the teachings of the Buddha are as if placed in the palm in your hand.

Everybody expresses compassion to some extent. All sentient beings, even the most vicious, ruthless animals, have some amount of compassion; almost without exception, they protect or nurture their offspring, or at least provide the circumstances for reproduction. But in the context of the mind of awakening, we speak of "great compassion," the all-pervasive, or all-embracing, compassion expressed by buddhas and bodhisattvas. When we develop great all-embracing compassion, this universal compassion, which is not easy, we have access to the rewards of all the teachings of the Buddha. We can attain awakening for ourselves and benefit others.

When we develop great compassion, we develop it toward each and every sentient being without feeling close to some and distant from others, without attachment to some or aversion toward others; our compassion embraces all sentient beings equally.

The great Indian master and scholar Shantideva said that just as adding an alchemical substance to metal changes it to gold, when we add the mind of awakening to our own experience, then our desire, anger, ignorance, jealousy, and pride transform into the mind of the buddha. Eventually, even our bodies transform into the presence of the thirty-two major and eighty minor marks of the physical perfection of the buddhas.

The development of the mind of awakening is the root, or source, of all teachings of the Mahayana. In the Mahayana context, arriving at enlightenment ends all time spent in samsara. What happens when a person arrives at enlightenment can be explained in terms of the conventional or provisional meaning as follows: Our experience of samsara is both individual—that is, different from everybody else's—and in common with other beings. Individually, each of us has an individual experience of self and the world. When I slept last night, I had dreams; nobody else had my dreams. When you went to sleep, you had your own dreams; that's your experience. As we develop the mind of awakening, our relationship to the objects of our experience gets more and more gentle, or relaxed. There is less cause for distracting thought, negative emotions, karma, and suffering. At the level of enlightenment, we give up clinging entirely;

there is no longer any cause for the development of any negative emotion, any karma, any suffering. Our dualistic experience has come to an end in enlightenment. However, at the moment of one individual's enlightenment, other sentient beings continue to have dualistic experience.

Aside from our individual experiences, as sentient beings, we have similar habitual tendencies in common. We are all related; we have common experiences through interdependent causal links that have come into being. The Mind Only school says that our collective experience appears from having awakened similar habitual tendencies. So for human beings, water is for drinking and washing; for fish, water is their living environment; and for hell beings, water burns like fire. So we have our individual experience, and we have our collective experience.

By developing the mind of awakening, we are not trying to change the basic nature of beings, as if they were colored red and we want to make them yellow. That would be an impossible task. However, since for all sentient beings everything that appears is nothing more than illusion or confusion, their experience is thus subject to change. For example, I lie in my bed and dream about meeting friends in Tibet. I haven't gone back to Tibet; it was only an appearance of illusion or confusion. In the same way, in our ordinary waking life, we all experience unreal things as real. The reality of our situation, our basic nature, is enlightenment. We can shed our mind of unreal appearances; so we dedicate ourselves to the path of awakening so that all sentient beings may reach enlightenment (because we share this same enlightened nature). Otherwise, it would be impossible.

One of the scriptures says that the buddha, all sentient beings, and the path to awakening are all appearances of our mind. The appearance of the buddha is our pure vision; the appearance of sentient beings is our impure vision; and the appearance of the path to awakening is the process of transforming impure vision into pure vision. When we practice on the path, we work with our mind; physically there's not a lot to do. When we understand the essence of our mind, we purify our habitual tendencies, and all our negative emotions and habitual tendencies completely end. At that point, there will no longer be any experience of confusion or the objective experience of samsara. Everything will end with no remainder.

Mipham Rinpoche said that as much as we purify our subjective experience, our objective experience is purified the same amount. A buddha has pure experience because their mind is completely pure. It is not possible for our mind to be pure and our experience to be impure. We sometimes use the example of a cup or a bell. There is space within the cup and space within the bell that is separate from all other space. At the point where our dualistic experience ends, it's as if the space within the bell or the space within the cup completely unites with all space, without any distinction between them. There's no longer any barrier separating them from all space.

Give it a try. Recognize the nature of your mind, and watch what happens at that point. Your ordinary thoughts will diminish. Negative emotions will diminish. The wisdom of mind will increase. You'll begin to have experience and realization. Just give it a try. You'll see for yourself.

There have been many great masters in the past who did exactly this. They studied the very same ideas that we're studying now.

Thinley Norbu Rinpoche quotes from the *Prayer to Buddha Ever Excellent* (*Kunzang monlam*), "May all parent sentient beings of the six realms without exception, simultaneously arrive at the state of original purity." All our mental events arising from getting lost in thought, all our experience of what is unreal that we take to be real, dissolves at the same time.

At this time, when we know that we're sentient beings and that we have impure experience, we can recognize the view. From that moment on, we can begin to familiarize ourselves with the view— that is to say, we can begin to meditate. We can put our understanding into practice and engage in conduct. We have view, meditation, and conduct. We are on the path; there is a mixture in our experience of both impure experience and pure experience. Our ordinary impure experience diminishes, and our pure experience increases.

Bodhisattvas have ten stages of awakening. Those stages are degrees of this mixture of purity and impurity. As a bodhisattva rises through the stages of awakening, pure experience increases and impure experience decreases. One hundred percent pure is enlightenment. One has gone beyond the stages of awakening to full and complete enlightenment, buddhahood.

## The Development of the Mind of Awakening

In the foundational practice text, we have the lines, "From now until samsara becomes empty, I will strive for the benefit and happiness of all sentient beings, who have all been my mother." This raises the question of how we work for others' benefit and happiness.

We can start, as Thinley Norbu Rinpoche does, with examining how buddhas and bodhisattvas work for beings' benefit and happiness from the causal Mahayana perspective. Bodhisattvas are still on the path of training. Because they still have habitual tendencies and the two obscurations—obscuring emotions and ignorance of the true nature of reality—they have a mixture of pure and impure vision in their experience. Until they reach full and complete enlightenment, this mixture of pure and impure vision remains, and they continue on the path of developing the perfection of discriminating awareness of emptiness.

As bodhisattvas arrive at the unerring and unchanging realization of emptiness, they simultaneously develop compassion for all sentient beings. They make prayers for the benefit of all sentient beings equal to the limits of space (which is limitless), equal to the limits of sentient beings (which exceeds all calculations), equal to the limits of beings' obscuring emotions, karma, and suffering (which is boundless). Thinley Norbu Rinpoche says that until the sickness of sentient beings' obscuring emotions is cured, bodhisattvas vow not to be cured of the "sickness" of compassion.

Based on this motivation and these aspirations, bodhisattvas cultivate oceans of merit and wisdom. They cultivate merit by being generous, keeping vows, being patient, being diligent, teaching, and other actions. Myriads of outer acts are done for others. And bodhisattvas develop inner wisdom by realizing emptiness.

Bodhisattvas also make aspirations to purify oceans of worlds. Buddha Shakyamuni came into this world because this was a world that he had aspired to purify. Through his teaching, he purifies this world. Bodhisattvas make such aspirations. When they are fully enlightened, they actually realize their aspirations. Buddha Amitabha created the pure land called Great Bliss (Dewachen). This is an example of a buddha creating a pure land for the benefit of others.

While bodhisattvas' experience is both pure and impure, buddhas' experience is entirely pure. This difference is evident when we understand that bodhisattva activity involves effort and movement on the part of their body, speech, and mind, whereas buddha activity is effortless; without any effort, motivation, or aspiration, when the conditions for helping those they have previously vowed to help come together, buddhas appear, in different forms—a wish-fulfilling jewel, a wish-fulfilling tree, a human, an animal, or some other form.

Thinley Norbu Rinpoche then explains the Vajrayana perspective, particularly that of the *Secret Essence Tantra*, which differs from the causal Mahayana. According to this view, buddhas and sentient beings are related through their inner nature. The relationship doesn't depend upon outer, impure conditions because the primordial nature of all beings is emptiness, clarity, and all-pervasive wisdom. The Tibetan word translated as "all-pervasive wisdom" in this context is *thugje*. Often, the English translation of it is "energy."* The "inner energy" of beings is all-pervasive wisdom; we do not say merely "compassion" (although it means compassion or kindness in other contexts). Like sentient beings, a buddha's nature as well is emptiness, clarity, and this energy of all-pervasive wisdom. The compassion (*thugje*) of buddhas and the inner energy of sentient beings is the same. This is how buddhas and sentient beings are

*Thinley Norbu Rinpoche often translates *thugje* as "compassion," and translators have more recently been translating *thugje* as "responsiveness." The appropriate meaning depends on the context, but, in this text, "energy" is used with the intention that it be understood as wisdom energy that includes great compassion.

directly related, not through outer causes and conditions that need to come together for buddhas to appear. The connection of the inner essence of buddhas with the identical inner energy of sentient beings permits the outer appearance of the buddhas' compassion.

There are three different ways the mind of awakening is developed, depending on the strength of a person's mind, literally, "how strong the heart is." At the lowest level, a person who wishes to attain enlightenment for the benefit of others by leading them there and being the first to get there, develops "the mind of awakening like a king." The middle level is the wish to attain enlightenment at the same time as others, like a boatman; we're all in the same boat and we travel together across the ocean of samsara to the island of enlightenment. The highest form of courage of the mind of awakening is as a shepherd. A shepherd's flock, or herd, goes before the shepherd; the person with this attitude wishes to help all sentient beings attain enlightenment first, and only then will they attain enlightenment.

The bodhisattva vows are a commitment to be a bodhisattva and to practice both the aspiration aspect and the application aspect of the development of the mind of awakening. To do so, according to the main tradition of the Mahayana, we need to find a qualified teacher, one who is familiar with the ritual of the Mahayana (how to give the vows), has taken and keeps bodhisattva vows, has compassion for others, and agrees to pass on the bodhisattva vows to others. If you meet this type of teacher, you can ask for and receive the bodhisattva vows. If for some reason you don't meet face to face with this sort of teacher, you can take the bodhisattva vows by imagining that the buddhas and bodhisattvas or Guru Rinpoche or other enlightened ones are sitting in the sky before you. Or you can take vows in the presence of a painting or a statue of Buddha Shakyamuni or Guru Rinpoche, or even a text, anything that represents the three jewels. The really important thing to keep in mind, the thing that makes the vows meaningful and impactful, is to take the vows, to take refuge, or to make any aspiration or prayer wholeheartedly and sincerely. Hesitation and doubt are enemies of enlightened experience. If you are willing to admit that enlightened qualities are positive and worth striving for, even selfishly, then why bother doubting? In taking refuge and generating the mind of enlightenment, express your intention, your undiluted willingness, to experience extraordinary enlightened blessings.

## The Four Immeasurables

We have had a countless number of lives in the past. In each of those lives, we've had parents. We must be conscious of the kindness of all our parents and try to return that kindness. Even if our own parents in this life have been lacking in their kindness toward us, we can still have compassion for them, for their actions were caused by their own karma, and aspire for their enlightenment.

The aspirational aspect of developing the mind of awakening starts with our wish to bring all sentient beings to both temporary and permanent happiness. This wish is what we call "love"—the first of four boundless attitudes commonly called the "four immeasurables." Love is the wish that all sentient beings have happiness and the causes of happiness, both temporarily, in daily life and in future lifetimes, and permanently, in enlightenment. We must cultivate love from the bottom of our heart.

Next, we develop compassion, the second boundless attitude—the wish that all beings be free from temporary suffering, ultimate suffering, and the causes of suffering. We cultivate a sense of urgency about the need to relieve all beings from their suffering, to spur us toward taking the proper actions for beings' benefit.

Third, we develop sympathetic joy. We cultivate a sense of joy for those who have good situations or find success or contentment. We wish for them to maintain and increase their level of happiness, wealth, and enjoyment of life. We wish for all sentient beings to reach the same level of happiness.

And fourth, we develop equanimity, impartiality; we wish to extend our love, compassion, and sympathetic joy to humans, animals, insects, and all other sentient beings in all realms, without any partiality. At present, we feel love for some but not for others, more compassion for some and less compassion for others. This is partiality, which is not what we mean by "immeasurable." We aim for immeasurable love, immeasurable compassion, immeasurable joy, and immeasurable equanimity. It might seem impossible, with our ordinary mind, to accomplish the four immeasurables by going step by step from those closest to us, to those further away, to those at the furthest extent of the universe. But by taking the path of pure awareness, we develop all four immeasurables naturally.

## The Six Transcendent Perfections

Having started our mind training with the aspirations of the four immeasurables, we continue by practicing the six transcendent perfections (Skt. *paramitas*). This is the training of a bodhisattva.

The idea behind all six perfections is that, in acting for the benefit of others, we accomplish our own aims. Taking the commitments of the mind of awakening for the benefit of others helps to do away with our own negative emotions and lack of understanding. Eventually, just the thought of helping others leads us to the state where we can help others effortlessly.

The first transcendent perfection is generosity, which has three aspects: giving teachings (dharma instructions), giving material objects, and giving security (refuge both in the ultimate sense and in the temporary sense of protecting the current life of a sentient being).

The second transcendent perfection is ethical conduct, which also has three components: restraining from negative conduct; gathering positive qualities through (among other methods) meditation on the path (view, meditation, and action); and actually working for the benefit of others.

The third transcendent perfection is patience, which also has three components: endurance (not falling under the influence of events); patience (open-mindedness about the teachings and tolerance of those with lower views and those who disagree with us);

and working for the benefit of others without consideration of our pain or inconvenience, thinking only of the sufferings of others.

The fourth transcendent perfection is often translated as "diligence," which again is composed of three aspects: determination (the "armor of diligence"), avoiding negative emotions (the "diligence of application"), and avoiding laziness or pride about past efforts ("diligence without contentment"). We maintain our focus on helping others until the attainment of full and complete enlightenment.

The fifth transcendent perfection is meditation. Meditation can be described in both worldly and transcendent forms; for our purposes it has two aspects: tranquillity and insight. Tranquillity (Skt. shamatha, Tib. shinay) is resting in mental calm, and insight (Skt. vipassana, Tib. lhagtong) is comprehension of the nature of mind.

The sixth transcendent perfection is transcendent knowledge (Skt. prajna, Tib. sherab). Sometimes sherab is translated as "wisdom," but we also translate yeshe (Skt. jnana) as "wisdom," so we'll use "transcendent knowledge" (which means understanding the nonself of everything and the nonself of self). The other aspect that is important to join with transcendent knowledge is meditative absorption (Skt. samadhi), which is the ability to remain within that transcendent knowledge.

## Tranquillity Meditation

There are nine stages of meditation on tranquillity. The goal is to calm the mind. Ordinarily, many mental events flash through our mind like lightning or like a piece of paper caught by the breeze, going in every direction. Until we are not so lost in thought, our attempts to work with the view, meditation, and action will not be successful. We must come to some basic calm in our mind. This is why we do tranquillity meditation.

We try to train our mind in tranquillity because when we receive pointing-out instructions in the nature of mind, of reality, we need the habit of resting in a calm, relaxed state so we can remain within this nature. Otherwise, even though we have received the teachings, our mental events continue, our attention goes back and forth, and the teachings lack effectiveness.

The first of the nine stages of tranquillity practice is to place an object before us and allow the mind to rest on it without moving. The object can be an ordinary piece of wood, a stone, a bell, or something pure, like a statue or an image of Buddha Shakyamuni. It doesn't matter because the action is the same. When the mind begins to wander, we bring our attention back to the object.

We can also, as a basis for our meditation, pay attention to the expiration and inspiration of our breath. It is said that typically we take twenty-one thousand breaths during the course of one day. But when we do this practice, gradually we take fewer breaths, not because we force the breath to slow but because breath is related to thoughts; as our level of mental activity decreases, our breathing rate decreases. Longchenpa gave many teachings on using the breath for meditation.

The second stage is "placement"—bringing the mind back from distractions. The third stage is "continual placing." The fourth is "intense placing of the mind." The fifth is to have "tamed the mind." The sixth is "to calm." The seventh is "to completely calm the mind." The eighth is "to rest single-mindedly in tranquillity." The ninth is "to rest within equanimity." Each stage could be described in detail. For example, in the first stage, there are five different experiences as one gets familiar with merely placing the mind. There are also different ways the five experiences relate to one's increased familiarity with placing the mind. Each stage has different experiences related to it.

When we begin to meditate, we find our mind to be extremely fast and busy. This is similar to a waterfall in a high mountain. The water falls extremely hard and fast. We think, "My goodness, my thoughts are churning hard and fast!" When the mind calms a little bit, our mental energy moves like water through a narrow, high valley, slightly calmer or gentler than a waterfall. It is still moving very fast, but at least it's on the ground. With more time, our mental energy moves like a vulture flying above a corpse. The vulture doesn't go straight to the point but takes its own sweet time circling the corpse down below. In the same way, we don't go right to the point of our object of meditation; our mind circles around. Further in our practice, we come down to the subject of our meditation; inside there is still a lot of movement, but we can grasp the object of our meditation. We begin to calm down. The metaphor for this is an ocean that looks fairly calm from a distance, but in fact there is movement underneath and the rising and falling of the waves. We appear to be meditating, but our mind has a lot of subconscious gossip.

The eventual meditative state of tranquillity meditation is like a mountain; whatever happens, the mountain doesn't move. Whatever thoughts arise, however our breathing moves, or whatever events happen outside, our mind stays on the object of meditation. Of course, we will still have thoughts. Until we have arrived at the level of the view, it is impossible to have the mind rest on a chosen object without having thoughts; but we are not affected by those thoughts.

Great teachers of the past such as Mipham and others taught tranquillity meditation and had their students develop it very strongly, because even though we might receive teachings on the view and we might understand it intellectually, we can still lose the view if we haven't calmed our mind. Without tranquillity meditation, our view, meditation, and action tend to get lost in the waves of our mental movement.

You can be introduced to the view and to tranquillity meditation at the same time; you can first do tranquillity meditation and then do insight meditation; or you can do tranquillity meditation and insight meditation together, followed by introduction to the view. It depends on the person, how the mind is able to develop. Later on, in Dzogchen, when we have transcendent meditation, there is no difference between tranquillity and insight meditation. At that point, you can't say this is tranquillity and that is insight. They become inseparable.

It has been said that the longest that a person can rest the mind on an object and not be moved by any thought whatsoever is one week. To go beyond that, you would have to go to the form realm or the formless realm where beings can rest within different meditative states for years or centuries.

In the process of developing this sort of meditative concentration, you may experience effects on your sense consciousness. The primary change is a reduction in your focus on attachment or aversion to what you see, hear, smell, taste, and touch, and your inner thoughts. Through meditative concentration, our attraction and aversion diminish. When we meditate, everything calms down. Thinley Norbu Rinpoche says that instead of spending twenty-four hours a day in the experience of happiness or suffering, in sensitivity and the obscuring emotions, these types of distraction weaken and our body and mind get happier.

We've been wandering in samsara for many lifetimes, so our thoughts and feelings are out of control. They're wild. We've been feeding off our attraction and aversion. No matter what happens, we immediately have a reaction to it. Our mind goes out toward appearances. If we hear something agreeable, we are happy. If we hear something disagreeable or unpleasant, we are unhappy. When we follow our thoughts, they fuel our emotions. This leads to various forms of sickness or suffering or tightness in our body.

When we begin to meditate, the various thoughts that fuel our negative emotions, which in turn fuel our karma, begin to be calmed. The first effect is that our body gets more comfortable. Our backbone straightens naturally. Our body feels suppler. Our mind also calms down and feels suppler. We no longer follow exactly what we see, hear, taste, smell, touch, or think. With more and more meditation, our mind is less affected by these outer stimuli. It's as if the stream that started with a waterfall high in the mountains has finally arrived at the valley.

To conclude, tranquillity meditation calms the mind. However, the root of thoughts or the root of samsara—that is to say, the mind—remains intact. It hasn't really changed. In the higher realms, for example, in the gods' realms, a god might spend one hundred years, one thousand years, or an aeon resting in this state of complete tranquillity. However, this is just a rest period because the habitual tendencies of mind remain. Once their meditative state is finished, they return to one of the six classes of the desire realm. To do away with the basis of habitual tendencies that return us to samsara, we have to meditate on insight, the seed and nature of mind. This is the second type of meditation, insight meditation (*lhagtong*). *Lhag* means "higher" or "superior," and *tong* means "to see."

## Insight Meditation

Tranquillity meditation is not really enough to allow us to arrive at the experience of the nature of mind. We are aiming to see nakedly, directly, the awareness and emptiness that is the essence of our mind. That is the goal of insight meditation.

Insight meditation has two techniques of looking into the mind and seeing its nature. The first is called "the analytical meditation of the *pandits* (scholars)." This type of meditation is common to the Middle Way and even the Shravakayana. It is also found in Dzogchen; for example, there is the preparatory practice called "destroying the little 'hut' of mind." To give an example of this analytical meditation, take each of the five aggregates and ask yourself, "Where does this aggregate exist? Outside? Inside? In my body? In my mind?" This search leads you to insight.

You begin with an analysis of all appearances. You aim to realize that all appearances are projections of the mind. You keep on examining and analyzing, and you try to come to the conclusion (not just an intellectual conclusion but the insight) that all appearances are mental projections. Then you look at the mind itself. Again, through analysis and examination, you arrive at the conclusion that the nature of mind is emptiness. Then you examine, or analyze, this emptiness and arrive at the conclusion that the nature of emptiness is luminosity, or clear light. Your dharma master guides you on this path.

The second style of insight meditation is called "placing meditation," or what we might call "direct meditation." You don't analyze at all; you don't try to understand the mind through the intellect or analysis. You simply place the mind in its own nature. You find mind's natural rest. It is called *kusali* in Sanskrit, which means "the beggar's tradition."

Analytical meditation should be used by those who develop gradually. Those who can arrive at immediate understanding based on the pointing-out instruction can use the second style. For example, when Guru Rinpoche received pointing-out instructions, Shri Singha made a gesture, pointing to the sky, and said, "Whatever arises, have no attachment to it." The idea was simply to look at the inner nature of mind. Based on that simple gesture and instruction, Guru Rinpoche arrived immediately at understanding the nature of mind.

Analytical meditation is very busy. We go through many stages of analysis, trying to understand our mind. We ask, "Is there form? Is there color? Is there sound? What is the nature of outward appearances? What is the nature of our mind?" On the other hand, if we try to put our mind directly into its own natural state, we may fail. Our mind doesn't rest. Our mind doesn't stay. The second style of insight meditation is for those of higher levels of capability. Most people like us have to begin with analytical meditation. We use the busyness of mind to arrive at some understanding of its nature, and then we rest our mind. If somebody told us, "Well, just look into the nature of mind and rest there," it wouldn't really be useful to us at this point.

Mipham Rinpoche, in his book the *Jewel Lamp of Certainty*, explains that we have to begin with analytical meditation. If we do this well, our certainty increases until we arrive at firm certainty. Then we no longer need analytical meditation. When you see your mother, you don't have to think, "Is this my mother or not?" You know immediately. At a certain point, we alternate analytical meditation and direct meditation. Finally, once we've arrived at full certainty, we give up any analysis, and we simply do direct meditation.

## Faults in Tranquillity Meditation

There are five faults in tranquillity meditation, mental obstacles that can impede our progress.

The first is laziness—not considering either the teachings of the Buddha or the direct teachings of our instructor.

The second is forgetfulness—even though we have considered the teachings of the Buddha or the direct instructions of our teacher, we don't continually bring them to mind.

The third is having extremes of depression or excitation. With depression, our mind gathers inside itself; we fall asleep, our mind isn't clear, or there's no energy in our mind. With excitation, our mind diffuses entirely to the objects of our senses. Both of these extremes block our meditative state.

The fourth is, when we are meditating on both tranquillity and insight together and the mind wanders, to follow the distraction and not gather our attention back or not use that distraction as part of our meditation.

The fifth is the opposite of the fourth—to gather our attention too tightly when we are meditating. We keep trying to get it "just right." The mind gets tied up in a little ball. This is as much an obstacle to our meditation as any of the others.

Fortunately, there are remedies for these five faults. Laziness is remedied through the development of faith, good intention, diligence, and interest in the training (that is, to try to "bring the mind to virtue," or "intense training"). Forgetfulness is remedied by mindfulness—try to keep in mind the teachings you have received.

Depression and excitation are removed by remaining conscious of what is going on in your mind. When your mind begins to sink into inactivity, spot that. If the mind is too excited, recognize that as well. Distractions are remedied by uplifting your mind. Try to inspire yourself.

Getting too tight in meditation is remedied through developing equanimity. It's enough to be mindful one time. You don't have to insist. Be mindful, then let it go. Don't keep on repeating that within your meditation.

Machig Labdron, who originated *chöd* practice, gave a short bit of advice for meditation. She said, "Be attentive or tight when you need to be. Be relaxed when you need to be." This is one of the vital points of meditation. When your attention has wandered, that's when you need to tighten things up a bit. But when your mind is resting too firmly, that's when you need to relax. You need to find some balance between tightness and relaxation within your meditation.

These five faults and their remedies are really essential for whatever meditation you do. If you can remedy these five faults, any meditation you do will be effective.

## Obstacles to Insight Meditation

Just as we must overcome faults in tranquillity meditation, we must surmount obstacles to insight meditation. The first obscuration to insight meditation is that when we don't understand the lack of self of everything, that nothing has any objective reality, then whatever we meditate upon becomes an object of attachment. We cling to the object of our practice. This obstructs liberation. This first obscuration relates to the ultimate nature of things.

The second obscuration to insight meditation is to believe that things either are or are not. On a relative level, everything arises through interdependent links of causation. If we do not recognize this, we believe that things either exist or do not exist. We fall into the extremes of eternalism and nihilism. This undermines wisdom and thus obscures insight. This second obscuration relates to the relative nature of things.

The third obscuration is to remain in samsara due to insufficient understanding through lack of study and reflection. When we sit down to meditate, we don't know what we're doing. We don't know how to place the mind. Thinley Norbu Rinpoche uses the example of a daytime bird flying at night that crashes into things.

The explanation of the faults of tranquillity meditation and the obscurations to insight meditation, as well as what is coming next, collectively called "the nine obscurations of the path," are taken from the Buddha's discourses. Each of these faults impedes our progress in meditation.

## The Nine Obscurations of the Path

Of the nine obscurations of the path, the first three are considered "obscurations to effort" and are described as ways we fail (to move). The first fault is that we don't make any progress but remain fixed in a particular practice, comfortable in a certain practice or level. We don't move on. The image used is a bird who stays in its own nest. The second fault is "to dissolve into the path." The image is an arrow stuck inside something solid. The third fault is called "clarity," which means giving too much attention to where we are. For example, if I look only at the color of an object in front of me, that color gets very clear, but everything else disappears; I see only that one color. This extreme form of attention or this intensity in looking at something fixes the mind.

The second set of three obscurations on the path are classified as obscurations to true, or correct, meditation: the wish to develop many meditative experiences, the wish to develop psychic powers, and the wish to develop miraculous powers. First, if we focus on a wish to develop the experiences of bliss, clarity, or emptiness, or a wish to develop some sort of knowledge or understanding, these distract us from correct meditation. Second, the wish to develop various kinds of psychic powers, or third, the wish to develop miraculous powers (for example—leaving one's handprint or footprint in stone, or flying through space), obscure true meditation. The example Thinley Norbu Rinpoche gives is of a person who has a lot of cows but lets his children drink all the milk and yogurt so he can't make any butter.

The third set of three faults are self-contentment, pride, and arrogance, which are obscurations to correct recollection. The first of this third set of obscurations is to think to yourself, "I have gained the best or the highest teaching." The second is pride; you are convinced that your view is the best. The third is to look down on, or denigrate, the views of others; the example given is the son of a powerful king or government minister who, due to his parent's position, is full of himself and won't listen to any advice. To do away with the obscurations to correct recollection, we must guard in our mind the meaning of the discourses that teach the correct or true meaning. We must remember the teachings of our master.

Apart from these nine, there are "natural obscurations," that is, any of the ten practices (such as copying texts, reciting prayers, doing prostrations, reciting mantras, and so on). When we meditate on the view of Dzogchen, we have to put aside all physical and verbal forms of positive practice, because they obscure our meditation. The example given is wood in which you carve a design on top of the design you carved before.

We are distinguishing here between lesser and greater virtue. Positive acts done physically or verbally are wonderful, but they are not as beneficial as remaining in meditation or in the view of the Middle Way or Dzogchen, when we must put aside study, malas, prostrations, offerings, and any form of physical and verbal activity, and remain concentrated on the task at hand. These physical or verbal actions are not wrong or negative; they simply eat up our time. When we do away with the nine obscurations to the path and these natural obscurations, we enter the real path to awakening.

## Beyond Worldly Meditation

Thanks to our meditation on the union of tranquillity and insight, we can arrive at meditation that goes beyond the desire realm, and even beyond the worldly meditative states of the form and formless realms. I will describe those worldly meditative states to show what we are going beyond.

There are four meditative states of the formless realm, where a person can remain for aeons, nearly indefinitely. The first is a state thinking that everything is the infinity of nothing whatsoever anywhere. All objects of the senses, including consciousness of self, are blocked. The meditator has no insight into the nature of mind.

The second is the infinity of consciousness. Here the meditator remains within the clarity of consciousness, but without any appearance at all. The appearance side of consciousness is blocked.

The third is the state of nothing whatsoever. This is compared to deep sleep, in that there is no experience outside or inside. There is no feeling or sensation. The meditator is not even within consciousness at this point; no dream, nothing.

The fourth is called literally "not something, not nothing." There is a slight sensation of bliss or happiness, but nothing at all appears. This is the highest level of formless worldly meditation. It is somewhat like the state of nothing whatsoever, but here there is a slight experience of bliss within the state of nothingness.

These four levels of meditative states in the formless realm are very advanced states of tranquillity meditation, but they are without any experience of the nature of mind. They resemble rest or sleep. The habitual tendencies in the mind just remain latent. It is like sleeping without having any ordinary thoughts. There is no special state of freedom from thought. That kind of freedom requires realization of the nature of mind. It is only through insight meditation, seeing the nature of mind, that we go beyond the limits of the five aggregates.

The root of samsara is our clinging to a self. These meditative states that appear to give us some freedom are merely suppressing the thoughts that are the root of our clinging to a self. Even if we go to sleep for a very long time, of course we wouldn't have ordinary mental events, but as soon as we wake, our mind would be exactly as it was before. Insight meditation, on the other hand, cuts the root of our habitual tendencies and our clinging to self. It is the effective remedy for our continual experience in samsara.

When we do tranquillity and insight meditation together, our experience gets bright, luminous, and clear. By "bright" I mean we don't get lost in thought or experience negative emotions. "Clarity" or "brightness" is the opposite of that foggy feeling you may feel in meditation. When you have fog in your meditation, your mind is not at all clear. Your consciousness dims and almost dissolves in this lack of clarity. When we see the nature of mind and have the experience of wisdom, then clarity, brightness, and great joy arise in our meditation, and we don't get lost in thought.

Regardless of the type of insight meditation that we are doing (Middle Way, Dzogchen, and so on), these four characteristics of clarity, brilliance, joy, and not getting lost in thought will be part of our meditative experience. We are then free of the five aggregates.

How do we free ourselves of the five aggregates? When we have insight that within the essence of mind there are no distinctions of color or shape, this is freedom from the aggregate of form. When the essence of our meditation is free from attachment to any experience (happiness, suffering, and so on), this is freedom from the aggregate of sensation. When we are free from any reference point, this is freedom from the aggregate of perception. When we are free from any specific intention, virtuous or nonvirtuous, this is freedom from the aggregate of karmic formations. When we are free from clinging to the appearance of any subject and object, we are free from the aggregate of consciousness. Resting within this kind of meditation, we are set free from any ordinary mental formation in the three realms.

At the beginning of Dzogchen practice, we must recognize the nature of mind as free from the five aggregates. When we eventually perfect the display, or energy, of this recognition, this is enlightenment, buddhahood.

If we can rest in awareness in meditation, we can be aware of samsara or nirvana but our awareness is not stolen by any object of experience. To remain in meditation without losing awareness is freedom from the mind of the desire realm. In the desire realm, when any form appears, we reflect on it: this is attractive, that is not attractive. Our attention gets stolen from our awareness. In Dzogchen meditation, appearances do not provoke lots of ordinary thinking. We remain within awareness.

With meditation, we can be freed from the desire realm, the form realm, and the formless realm—all three realms of samsara. The first level is freedom from the ordinary mind of the realm of desire, as I just explained.

The mind of the form realm clings to the clarity aspect of the mind's nature. Without fixation or clinging to this luminosity of mind, we are freed from the mind of the form realm.

In the formless realm, the mind remains in the nonconceptual state; there is nothing whatsoever (neither "is" nor "is not"), only limitless space. But all appearances are blocked. In Dzogchen meditation, we rest within the nonconceptual state but nothing is blocked, repressed, or suppressed. In Dzogchen meditation, we continue to hear, see, taste, touch, and smell, but we stay within rigpa, awareness. Our awareness does not block the play of the senses, so we can continue to sleep, eat, walk, play, and remain within awareness. This is a special quality of Dzogchen practice. Thinley Norbu Rinpoche says that this teaching of how to be liberated from the various levels of mind in the three realms was given by the great masters of the past: Guru Rinpoche, Longchenpa, Jigme Lingpa, and Dudjom Rinpoche. All the great masters of the past taught this way.

In Dzogchen meditation, because we remain in awareness, gradually our thoughts about appearances are provoked less and less. Our clinging diminishes. Eventually we arrive at a state of "doing as one wishes," with complete control over our mind.

But this may take time. It's like learning how to drive a car. There are many things that you have to study, such as the rules of the road and what to look out for. There is some danger trying to drive without learning those things well before you get your driver's license and get out on the road by yourself. Similarly, in the buddhadharma tradition, we have study, reflection, and meditation. "Study" means that we have to learn all of these "rules of the road" in terms of meditation. We have to learn what to watch for, so that it is all clear in our mind. We have to reflect on all of this and put it in some kind of order related to ourselves. Then we have to meditate.

When we meditate, we don't have to keep all of this in the forefront of our mind; just like when we drive, we don't have to think of everything in the driving manual. All these subjects (avoiding laziness, forgetfulness, and so forth) are fairly easy to understand. We try to remember them. If we have questions, we ask our teacher.

These are things we must have under our belt when we meditate. Gradually, with experience, we build confidence. If we haven't done this basic study, it's not that we won't be able to meditate but that we won't be able to meditate effectively.

## The Ultimate Middle Way

Ordinarily, we talk about the mind of awakening on a relative level—to develop the wish for enlightenment for the benefit of all sentient beings. Now we are going to a deeper level. *Jangchub kyisem* is the Tibetan word for "mind of awakening." It is called *bodhichitta* in Sanskrit, but in Tibetan it takes on a more exalted meaning. The first syllable is *jang*, which literally means "cleaned" or "pure." In this case, it means that in the nature of mind, within the sphere of totality, there are no obscuring emotions, no impurities. *Chub*, the second syllable, means that within the nature of mind, all qualities of enlightenment are spontaneously present. Both syllables together, *jangchub* (Skt. *bodhi*), are translated as "awakening." *Sem* is mind—but here, not the same as ordinary mind but the mind beyond dualistic experience. So we combine these syllables to mean "buddha nature" or "ultimate mind of awakening." Getting familiar with the expanse of this mind of awakening brings us confidence. Once we develop familiarity and confidence with the mind of awakening, we gain control of all aspects of mind.

A text says that as long as your ordinary intellectual mind continues to move, it is in the domain of demons. If you think emptiness either exists or does not exist, if anything is one way or another way—as long as there is some movement of the mind, you remain in the realm of demons; not demons who appear in the outside world with big heads, fangs, and claws but the inner demons of the mind, such as anger, desire, or ignorance, any part of our dualistic experience.

Guru Rinpoche said that all obstacles come from our own mind, that the devil is our clinging to our self, because the obstacles are our own thoughts. They make us unhappy, discontent, or unaware.

When the primordial nature of mind is recognized, there are no more obstacles because there is no more ordinary, dualistic experience, or clinging. The subtle path is not resting either in movement or nonmovement, not resting in any mental activity, no matter how it is labeled. We don't rest and we don't not rest, though it is called "not resting." This is "the middle way without appearances." This is the mind of awakening.

There is no difference in the way emptiness is explained by the Middle Way and Dzogchen. The difference is, in the Middle Way philosophy, we understand emptiness, but in Dzogchen, we also experience emptiness. There is no other real difference between these two.

Any thought a sentient being might have falls into one of four categories, called the "four extremes" or the "four limits." They are part of the labeling process of our mind, the ways we understand reality. In the context of ordinary mind, everything is experienced in one of these four ways of processing our world. When we understand each of the four, we will understand what goes beyond them; the nature of reality. It's transcendent; it's wisdom.

The first way of apprehending ordinary reality is the affirmation that things exist. It covers everything, not only things before us but everything that we can imagine existing anywhere. The second category covers everything that doesn't exist—anything that can be negated, that can be said not to exist, like horns on a human being. These are two huge categories.

The third category covers both affirmation and negation together; for example, if I say, "I exist, but I don't have horns on my head," then I am making both an affirmation and a negation—both "exist" and "not exist" together, but the combination of the two is itself a kind of affirmation.

The fourth category is when we negate both an affirmation and a negation together. For example, I can say, "I don't exist, nor are there no horns on my head." In that case, I am negating both myself as an affirmation and the horns on my head that do not exist.

The four extremes are ways we have of reflecting on things: affirmation, negation, affirmation and negation together, and negating both. Understanding what exists outside of those extremes is wisdom. Within the subject of insight meditation, it's called the "non-appearing Middle Way." Some say that the Middle Way means not falling into extremes but staying in the middle. However, if there are no limits, there's no middle. That's really how the ultimate Middle Way is defined; there is no center and no limit. With no center and no limit, the ultimate Middle Way means that the nature of reality (or the nature of mind) is free from these four extremes. Our experience at the moment is like a veil, or a cloud, made up of these four thoughts of existence, nonexistence, both, and neither. When the veils, or clouds, are cleared away, when all these thoughts cease to capture our attention, we see the nature of appearing reality and the nature of the mind. We see the ultimate Middle Way.

Although the ultimate Middle Way is beyond description, we need words that try to describe it or we won't arrive at an understanding of the meaning. By seriously studying Thinley Norbu Rinpoche's text, Nagarjuna's work, or the works of many other authors on this subject, we can eventually come to a direct realization of the Middle Way.

The Middle Way relates to meditative states and to our realization, in that when outer appearances or thoughts arise, we don't repress or suppress them. This is called "self-manifest" or "self-arising," the natural state of mind. Neither appearances nor our mental activities are blocked; we allow them to arise, but we do not follow or get distracted by them. That way, without effort, we remain in our true nature, in great equanimity. When we can develop some capability in that style of meditation and can remain within that state for an extended period, even though appearances and thoughts continually arise, we have no clinging, or attachment, to them.

In the *Precious Treasury of Immortality*, the master Nagarjuna says that when emptiness has been pointed out to you in the style of the Middle Way, you no longer need to analyze. Until then, you always analyze. For example, if you think that your book really exists, then you analyze over and over until you realize that it is emptiness. In the same way, all material things can be analyzed and seen as emptiness. You can use a single support and then realize that everything is empty. At that point, since you have achieved the purpose of analysis, you no longer need to use it, so you put it aside. You remain in the natural state without any artificial effort. This is the treasury of immortality, the path of all buddhas. This is an example of the Middle Way meditation.

A metaphor for the effect of this meditation is that if a dream is experienced as unreal as you dream it, then even if you don't wake up until later, the dream still has far less effect on you. It is finer, lighter. In the same way, if you understand that everything is empty and you can remain in the state of emptiness, even though all appearances don't disappear, your attachment to things as real, your "clinging to characteristics," will get finer and finer. Not only that, your tendency to take rebirth in the six realms will diminish.

The expression translated as "clinging to characteristics" has a special meaning in Tibetan. In English, we think of clinging as a kind of attachment, holding on to something; but here it means identifying a thing as a thing. When any of our ordinary experience is put into thoughts such as "this is a flower" or "this is a house," we call this "clinging to characteristics." When we engage in any of the four extremes of existence, nonexistence, both, or neither, it is also an experience of things being existent or nonexistent and so on—"clinging to characteristics."

If you talk while clinging to characteristics, it is sentient beings' talk. If you have some not-clinging and some clinging, you can still talk, but it is bodhisattvas' talk. If you talk with no clinging, it is buddhas' talk. There's no difference in the object itself, but there is in your experience, your level of clinging. In the example of "this is a flower," the difference is that an ordinary being sees a flower that exists, while a buddha sees a flower that is beyond all four extremes. A buddha understands the reality of the flower.

When we gain some mastery of transcendent knowledge and the ability to remain within it, we go beyond thinking, not thinking, both, and neither. We go beyond any ordinary mental activity. At that stage, it's not a matter of whether we experience or we don't experience something. We go beyond the level of experience, sensation, and appearance. This is why it's called the "nonappearing Middle Way."

## Meditative Experience of Emptiness

You might ask, "What sort of experience is this? How does this feel in the mind? What is happening when we experience emptiness?" There is no experience in the ordinary sense. Right now, we experience subject and object, "I" and "it." But at the stage of transcendent knowledge, we go beyond habitual experience. There is no "experience" of emptiness in that respect. If we have an "experience" of the sphere of totality, we don't consider this to be quite the correct view because there is still an experience and one who experiences. But if the sphere of totality and our natural awareness have fused inseparably, there is neither experiencer nor experience.

The sutras distinguish between the experience of emptiness during meditation and after meditation. In the sutra tradition, we have a period of meditation and then a period of postmeditation, called "subsequent attainment." Consider the sky's reflection in water. The sky continuously appears in the water but only until the water evaporates. Likewise, we have dualistic experience only until our ordinary consciousness disappears. This points to the experience of nondual wisdom; once our ordinary consciousness disappears, we are left with nondual wisdom.

During our meditation on emptiness, we rest within a state beyond all extremes of existence, nonexistence, both, and neither. We rest within ultimate emptiness, or ultimate luminosity. After meditation, there has to be some effect from having meditated in this way; we see everything as like a dream or an illusion. During meditation, we do not think of dreams, illusions, or that things do not exist. We rest our mind in a state beyond that. In the sutra tradition, the meditative state is within ultimate luminosity and in the postmeditative state we rest within the example of luminosity.

This ultimate luminosity is our experience during meditation. It's as if the water of our ordinary consciousness has completely evaporated and been absorbed into the sky. Or we can say that the cup has been broken and the space inside the cup and the space outside have been unified. We call this "ultimate wisdom" or "ultimate luminosity." It is the experience of the great sphere, literally without any corners. The great pervasive sphere, the "great zero," is the experience of ultimate wisdom or ultimate luminosity in meditation. We meditate within that great sphere, resting our mind without any corners or edges.

So to summarize, during meditation, we rest without clinging to any thought, reflection, or mental activity, in the nature of mind. Then afterward, in our daily life, we view everything as being without fundamental reality, as an illusion or a dream. Until we gain stability in this practice, we use continual vigilance to question, "How is our mind? What is happening in our mind?"

Regardless of the type of meditation we do, tranquillity or insight, and even if we have received pointing-out instructions in Dzogchen, we must always remain vigilant, like a guard in a watchtower looking over a crowd of people. Is there anyone with a gun? Is anyone starting a fight? Regardless of the type of meditation we do, we must be continually vigilant of our own mind. Even if we have received pointing-out instructions and understood them, even if we have seen the nature of mind, it is possible to get distracted and lose that view. We must bring our mind back to the view. This is a continual process. We remain within the view as long as possible. After it is gone, we realize it is gone. Then we bring the mind back to that point in our meditation. This is the practice of vigilance.

Any mental activity can be considered getting lost in thought. We have coarse mental events, our strong emotions; we are usually quite aware of these experiences, although sometimes we "lose it"—we get into a blind rage or develop an infatuation without being aware. Then there are very subtle mental events; anger may predominate but we can feel desire or passion below the surface; we call this in Tibetan "subconscious gossip" or "subconscious movement." If you throw a lot of straw, or chaff, into a calm lake, it floats on the surface without moving. But beneath the surface there is movement, either the water itself or fish swimming. In the same way, the surface of the mind may seem stable but, in fact, some subconscious movement is always taking place underneath. The mind is always in movement. Another example is a campfire that looks like it has gone out. We see only a thick layer of ashes, but when we stack more wood on top, the hot coals beneath the ashes make the wood burst into flames. Similarly, we may not be angry right now, but later today or tomorrow, when we hear somebody talk about us in a negative way, our latent anger bursts into flames; the hot coals of our habitual tendencies are ready. So what should we do? We must remain within the awareness pointed out in the Dzogchen instructions. Remaining within awareness continually with vigilance will clear away both coarse and subtle thoughts and their habitual tendencies.

When we meditate, we may not have any surface thoughts but, in fact, a tremendous amount of mental activity is going on just below the surface. Our early experience in meditation is often, "Oh, my goodness! Before I meditated, I didn't have these thoughts. I've got a tremendous amount of mental activity. My meditation is not going very well." No; it was just that you weren't aware of the way the mind has always been. The subconscious gossip has always been taking place. You just haven't given yourself an opportunity to spot it. One of the goals of meditation is to recognize your subconscious mental activity. As discouraging as it may be for you, recognizing subconscious gossip is actually a positive sign, a sign of progress.

When you look into your mind and see all these thoughts, don't give up. Don't think to yourself, "This is really an impossible situation. I can't meditate. Meditation isn't for me. I have no talent. It's not possible for a person like me to meditate." Don't let yourself get overwhelmed by this experience. That's one wrong move. The other wrong move is to try to force yourself not to think, to tighten, to try to stop all of these thoughts, to look at them as enemies. What you should do, instead, is to let the mind rest naturally. Keep as open and wide a mind as possible within this natural relaxation. Right when your mind is very upset and meditation seems impossible, just relax.

Don't bring all your thoughts or any mental agitation to your meditation session. Begin your meditation session with relaxation. Then rest within that relaxation. And at the end of your period of meditation, don't jump back into activity, but make a slow, easy transition. Do whatever you have to do, but do it mindfully and remain physically collected. Verbally, don't let a dam burst, saying anything at all to anybody at all; be careful with your speech. Try to maintain the same relaxed vigilance, or mindfulness, that you had during your meditation in your daily life. The point is to blend your periods of meditation with the periods between meditation, so eventually you have a single state of mind.

Beginners are strongly advised to keep periods of meditation brief. Do many brief periods of meditation rather than meditating for a long time all at once. Take short breaks. If you meditate for a long time without a break, you may get very depressed, lose confidence in yourself, feel dissatisfied with your lack of progress, and think it is impossible to continue. The best approach is to do short periods several times a day.

Our meditation begins with tranquillity meditation, using any of the techniques available. At first, we may feel very happy with ourselves when the mind slows down and rests, or we may feel unhappy when we see the mind in continual movement. The problem is with neither our resting nor our movement; it is with our judgment. We don't aim for 100 percent stillness but to diminish the sense of attraction and aversion to our states of mind. Our attachment to resting and our aversion to movement is just more movement. We need to let go of this judgment. At that point, the mind moves along very slowly and calmly, like a wide river in a valley.

As we get used to resting the mind in equanimity toward movement and stillness, we can relax and extend the natural state. Gradually, our coarse and subtle thoughts diminish and our ability to rest within the natural state of mind increases. This is the "experience of mind like an ocean." Even though there is a slight movement in the ocean, there is less obvious surface movement than in a river.

Thinking about resting and movement is relevant in the context of tranquillity meditation, but it is an error within the view of Dzogchen. In Dzogchen, our practice is to recognize the essence of the resting of mind and liberate it and, equally, to recognize the movement of mind and liberate it as well. We do not judge the resting of mind as positive and the movement of mind as negative. Neither has more value than the other. The important thing is to recognize their essence and to liberate them. If we are content with merely resting our mind when it calms down, it is only tranquillity meditation. If we meditate with the view, it is Dzogchen.

We must try to help our mind arrive at liberation. The only means to reach it is to recognize and remain within our present awareness. Present awareness is direct, without any reference point. It is completely natural, direct, unimpeded, present awareness. If we recognize and remain within present awareness, then regardless of what subtle or coarse thoughts arise, they will not enter our meditation. Nothing can overcome or undermine the state of present awareness.

## Dzogchen Practice of Insight Meditation

In the Mahayana tradition, when we discuss mind, wisdom, and thoughts, generally we think that when we have a particular problem, we should find a solution to it. We have antidotes. If my teacup keeps tipping over, I take a hammer and smash it and replace it with one that stays upright. This is the Mahayana way of dealing with problems. In Dzogchen practice, however, although we still have both coarse and subtle thoughts, they liberate naturally, without any thinking, analysis, practice, or antidote, like a snake tied in a knot that naturally unties itself. When we remain in present awareness, then thoughts, whether subtle or coarse, naturally, directly, and unobstructedly are freed because we recognize their nature.

When we talk about present awareness, it is really important to understand that we are not saying that there is past, present, and future and that we remain in the present, or that there is a present awareness that we try to create in our mind, or that we try to remain only within the present moment. I will now say exactly what I mean.

To define awareness (*rigpa*): We do not analyze, or concern ourselves with, past experience. Also, we do not anticipate, or speculate about, our future experience. And we don't simply remain in the present. Instead, we recognize the nature of our mind, which is beyond ordinary thought—beyond existence, nonexistence, both, and neither. We must remain within the nature of mind, which goes beyond all extremes and all ordinary thinking, including the idea of past, present, and future. We remain in that awareness. At that point, no ordinary thought enters or overcomes our awareness. How to recognize this awareness is something we must receive individually from our teacher; this is the pointing-out instruction in the first level of Dzogchen trekchöd. We receive the pointing-out instruction, and then we remain in that awareness.

All sentient beings have rigpa, and all buddhas have rigpa. There is no difference in this awareness whether it is in sentient beings or in buddhas. Buddhas experience this awareness, and they always rest in it; they are one with it. Every sentient being in the six realms of existence also has this awareness, but the great majority of them do not know how to recognize it or be in it.

Awareness is primordially present. In Dzogchen, we say that we are primordially liberated. When we recognize the nature of our mind, thanks to this awareness, we see that, within our nature, there are no ordinary thoughts, no negative emotions, and no habitual tendencies. In Dzogchen practice, the lama can say to us, "What is your original mind? I don't mean your mind right now, your mind these days. I mean what is your original mind?" This is what is introduced when awareness is pointed out. It is always there. It is always the same. It has never changed. When we say "present awareness," we mean the present, or primordial, awareness that has no ordinary thoughts, negative emotions, or habitual tendencies.

This wisdom of enlightenment is pointed out in our mind through this introduction to awareness—this pointing-out instruction is a special quality of Dzogchen. Here we are, absolutely ordinary individuals, ordinary sentient beings. There is nothing special about us whatsoever. Yet we can have the wisdom of enlightenment within us pointed out. We can have this experience! This is not possible in any other way of development in buddhadharma. Even if we talk about the highest tantras (the *Secret Essence Tantra*, the *Kalachakra Tantra*, or any other practice), in those traditions, you can meditate for an extremely long time. When you arrive at the first level of awakening, they talk about the wisdom of enlightenment being part of your mind, that you can have access to the wisdom of enlightenment. But in Dzogchen, in the pointing-out instruction, even extremely ordinary beings like ourselves can have access to the wisdom of enlightenment.

In trekchöd, sometimes the wisdom of Dzogchen is pointed out by saying, "Subtract three-quarters of your mental activity." What does that mean? It means that you take four parts of your mind: one part concerned with the past, another part concerned with the future, and a third part concerned with the present. If you subtract your attention from all those thoughts, the remaining quarter is your naked awareness.

It is important to understand that your awareness is not separate from your mind. When the pointing-out instruction is given, it does not make something separate or bring something into existence. It does not make it into a material object within a fourth aspect of time. This extra quarter is beyond any extreme of permanence or emptiness. It transcends any finality. It is originally pure equanimity awareness. It is inexpressible and inconceivable. We don't make it separate from any part of our mind.

Once we have had awareness pointed out, we must practice to remain in awareness. By remaining in awareness, all subtle and coarse thoughts, habitual tendencies, and confusions are exhausted. By remaining in awareness, all the other parts of mind are exhausted. What remains is called the "mind of enlightenment."

Until we gain stability within the mind of enlightenment, we have to remain as much as possible in awareness. By remaining in awareness, thoughts and negative emotions continue to occur, but they dissolve into awareness. Anger, desire, ignorance, good thoughts, bad thoughts, happiness, sadness, and so forth all dissolve into awareness, and awareness gets stronger and stronger.

Mipham Rinpoche said that a person who has received pointing-out instructions and can rest in awareness gets more and more relaxed, more and more peaceful. He said that if you spend one week resting in awareness, then the machine of your ordinary thoughts and emotions falls apart. It is like a very powerful car. We can go anywhere in it. But if the engine breaks, the entire car slows down and eventually falls apart. In the same way, when we rest in awareness, our ordinary negative emotions, the machine that feeds on getting lost in coarse and subtle thoughts, falls apart. That begins to happen after one week. If we spend three years resting in awareness and only in awareness, then we arrive at the state of the luminous, or rainbow, body.

We have been discussing rigpa. In the context of Dzogchen, the terms *rigpa* (awareness), *yeshe* (wisdom, literally "primordial consciousness"), and *dharmakaya* (ultimate body of enlightenment) are often used interchangeably. Rigpa is awareness of the nature of mind, the primordial nature of mind. In the word *yeshe*, the syllable *ye* is literally "primordial"; it means the primordial sphere of totality, the primordial nature. To know this primordial nature is yeshe: consciousness of the primordial state. Dharmakaya, the ultimate body of enlightenment, is the fundamental, or primordial, essence, nature, and energy of the mind. Being aware of that, being aware of rigpa, and being aware of yeshe are all the same.

There is no real difference between rigpa and yeshe. However, if you look at just the words, rigpa might be said to be closer to the mind's nature, and yeshe is a little further away. If you refine your understanding, you approach it through refining your understanding of wisdom. But just looking at the words, *awareness* is closer to the real point. With the idea of "wisdom," we have to look at the two parts of yeshe, "primordial" and "consciousness." We may not understand that this is pointing to the nature of mind. But when we speak about our own awareness, our own rigpa, we go straight to the point.

This description of rigpa, since it uses words and sentences, is not itself a pointing-out instruction; it is merely a story about pointing-out instructions. The student must do the foundational practices. It is not necessary to do lots of complicated creation-stage or completion-stage practices. What is really necessary is your ngöndro. The Guru Yoga section is especially critical. Do your Guru Yoga practice well. Develop faith and confidence in the Guru Yoga practice. Once you have done your foundational practices well, then you can understand awareness and receive these pointing-out instructions from a qualified teacher, and the instructions will be effective, like a sponge that absorbs water. It depends on your good practice and meeting a qualified teacher. If you have done your work, then the qualified teacher can do their work; you can receive pointing-out instructions and you can experience the nature of mind, the nature of awareness.

If you think it is impossible for you to maintain present awareness over a long period of time, either by being terrorized by the idea or by just feeling that it is impossible for you to do, or if you get far too tight within your mind, these are faults in your meditation. Instead, you should try to simply rest naturally within the mindfulness of awareness. This is all that is necessary.

There are two forms of mindfulness: intentional mindfulness and natural mindfulness. Intentional mindfulness is resting within the sphere of totality, or in the clarity and emptiness of awareness, with vigilance. We don't allow ourselves to fall into confusion or a mistake. We intentionally guard our mind within the sphere of totality, or awareness, and we remain within a very clear mind in relation to it.

Vigilance in Dzogchen practice is simply, at the moment that we are distracted, to spot the distraction and to rest the mind within its own clarity of awareness. When the mind goes wild or gets excited, sinks, is too focused on the inside, is too tight or too loose, we recognize this and return to the basic, clear, empty awareness.

Intentional mindfulness is useful for your practice, but you are not meant to maintain it forever. At first, you need intentional mindfulness to check up on your mind, to notice if the mind is getting too tight, too loose, too excited, or too dull. You need it to tune up your awareness. Later, you must let it go so it can turn into natural mindfulness, which, once we are used to awareness, is maintained regardless of the situation.

The basic definition of natural mindfulness is that, within the essence of everything, nothing exists—there is no experience of subject, object, oneself, or other; no clinging to self or to anything. These experiences merely reflect the thoughts of confusion. This experience of natural mindfulness is direct insight into the nature of things. At that point, intentional mindfulness no longer exists. There is only direct, natural mindfulness.

Starting from the first experience of the Dzogchen view, it is absolutely necessary to develop intentional mindfulness. As familiarity with the view increases, it gradually becomes less necessary to bring intention to mindfulness. It becomes more and more natural; natural mindfulness begins to take place more often than mentally constructed mindfulness. In natural mindfulness, there is nothing to see and there is no viewer. There is no distinction between the object of sight and the seer. There is no person who is distracted nor is there any object of distraction. These dualistic experiences pass away into a completely pure nondual state. This is natural mindfulness.

A person who has become really familiar with the Dzogchen view is said to have entered into the sphere, or expanse, of Dzogchen, where all objects of distraction dissolve into the nature of reality. This sort of language indicates that their view has had an effect on their experience. In the chöd practice, Dudjom Lingpa wrote, "As a yogi of the Middle Way, I see everything as emptiness." That is to say, with familiarity with the idea of emptiness, all sights, sounds, tastes, touches, and smells, all experiences, are seen as a dream or illusion, as emptiness. He went on to state, "As a yogi of Dzogchen, I see everything as naked awareness." With understanding of the Dzogchen view, all sights, sounds, tastes, touches, and smells, all experiences, are seen not only as emptiness but also as the play of naked awareness. An ordinary sentient being sees subjective and objective experiences as real and solid. However, familiarity with recognition of the view has an effect on one's experience of everything. That view overcomes habitual tendencies. Thus when one enters into the expanse of the Dzogchen view, objects of distraction dissolve into the nature of reality.

Is this experience nihilistic? Is there something that once existed that is now no longer existent? Are we negating something in order to have this experience? No, this is not the case. Nagarjuna wrote that it is not that once there was something and now it has been annihilated. That would be a nihilistic view. Instead, the objects of distraction dissolve into the nature of reality. The nature of things is seen. It is simply seeing things as they are.

By remaining continually within the experience of self-manifest, or natural, awareness, we separate from the very basis of our confusion as sentient beings, so all objects of distraction dissolve into the nature of reality. In the Dzogchen experience, our reflective consciousness purifies and any distraction dissolves. Even the basis, or root, of distraction dissolves into the nature of reality, because within the Dzogchen view, we go beyond all limits or extremes, beyond the experience of subject and object, beyond ourselves and our experience. We say that the root of distraction dissolves. Our experience becomes like space, totally even and unimaginably wide. The experience of equanimity and infinity makes any distraction dissolve into the nature of reality. By remaining in the Dzogchen view, even the distinction between night and day dissolves. All our distractions dissolve into the nature of reality. And all distinctions between meditation and nonmeditation disappear as well.

This state of natural awareness transcends any sign, symbol, or expression. Nothing can point at it. Everything appears as the ultimate body of enlightenment. There is no place to go to attain enlightenment, so there is no longer any hope of attaining enlightenment. And there is no place to go to wander in samsara, so there is no longer any fear of being a sentient being. All ordinary thoughts have completely dissolved into the nature of reality. This is the state of a person with high realization, a high level of familiarity with the Dzogchen view. This person has given up making any distinction between view, meditation, or action. There is no concept of these being separate from exactly the way things are.

For a person of a high level of realization in Dzogchen, resting within the view, meditating, or being involved with conduct appear to be unnecessary work. For example, we don't bother washing our clothes by hand if we have a good washing machine. In the same way, when we rest within the view or meditate, we feel that it is very beneficial for our mind. But for a person of high level, it's all outer activity, unnecessary. Once you've realized everything to be the nature of reality, why involve yourself with the view? Why meditate? Why engage in intentional conduct? When all distraction has dissolved into the nature of reality, there is no point. We recognize awareness as primordially present. There is nothing extra, nothing more than that.

## Bliss, Clarity, and Nonconceptual Mind

Three experiences typically occur in meditation: bliss, clarity, and nonconceptual mind. In relation to tranquillity meditation, bliss (*exaltation* is the term used by Thinley Norbu Rinpoche) is the feeling of pleasure. Our mind is extremely happy. We experience pleasure just sitting there. Even physically we are very happy. We really enjoy meditation. In insight and Dzogchen meditation, bliss is an increased and heightened sense of well-being.

Concerning clarity: In our ordinary mental state, our senses are a little dull. As we gain experience in meditation, sounds, sights, and other sensory experiences become far clearer to us. During tranquillity meditation, an experienced practitioner might have psychic experience, higher perception, or direct perception. In general, our experience becomes more and more vibrant, brilliant, and vivid.

The nonconceptual experience in tranquillity meditation is simply resting without extraneous thought for moments, minutes, hours, or even days at a time. The more experience we gain in tranquillity, insight, and Dzogchen meditation, the more we attain freedom from thoughts; thoughts arise but clinging to thoughts fades.

When you meditate, it is important that these three experiences are in balance. For example, if bliss is much stronger than the other two and you don't know how to relate your bliss to the view, then your interest in outer objects of desire will increase and your meditation practice will burn like dry wood thrown on a blazing fire. For monks and nuns, we know where that leads! It becomes the cause of their losing their vows. For beginners in tantric practice, this creates very strong ordinary desire for outer objects, a further cause for returning to samsara.

A person who doesn't have much bliss or clarity in meditation but has mainly nonconceptual experience (very few thoughts happening) may gain confidence in the practice of tranquillity but also may enter a state in which all ordinary thoughts are blocked, consciousness sinks, and awareness doesn't arise. This is like the higher god realms, where one rests in the state of nonconceptual experience for many aeons, which unfortunately doesn't lead to liberation.

If clarity and the lack of thoughts are equal and balanced but bliss is faint, then you will lose interest in meditation; it won't be an attractive experience for you.

If bliss and the lack of conceptual thoughts are balanced but your clarity is faint, your awareness, rigpa, gets blocked or goes latent within your mind. The image for this is clouds covering the sun. It's very peaceful and blissful but without awareness.

If your experience of bliss and clarity are balanced but your non-conceptual experience is faint—you get lost in thought without recognition or control—then you will fall into the extreme of holding things as real. The state of nonthought means that objects don't provoke our thoughts; we don't think about the outer objects of our perception. In this case, we rest within meditation but can't stay still. We might go into retreat for a month and then immediately go back into the marketplace. Or we meditate for an hour and then immediately go back to what we were doing with no change in the way we relate to things; we go back to ordinary experience after a period of so-called meditation.

In summary, if bliss, clarity, or nonconceptual experience are too faint or not in balance, these are faults in meditation, so the meditation will not lead to liberation. It is very important to pay attention to your experience and do what you can to balance these three.

In insight meditation, the experiences of bliss, clarity, and non-conceptuality continue the same. The difference is that we recognize or hold them with the view. In insight meditation, the nonconceptual part of mind is neither tranquillity nor nontranquillity; it is free from both extremes. The mind maintains the view whether it is resting in nonthought or not. Whether the mind is in clarity or nonclarity, when the inseparable essence of both is recognized by our awareness, that is the clarity part. Whether the mind is in bliss or in nonbliss, we are freed from both when we see that the mind is not empty, not not-empty, not both, and not neither. When we rest within the essence of that awareness, then the natural, spontaneous nature of awareness is recognized.

If you have had awareness pointed out but are unable to rest in awareness, then when thoughts arise, as they will continue to do, they won't be naturally liberated. This is called "knowing how to meditate but not knowing how to gain liberation." It is not different in any way from the higher levels of the gods who rest within meditative states. They know how to meditate, but they can't gain liberation.

Sometimes the imbalance of experiences in meditation can be resolved by very simple techniques. In Tibet, when we have the problem that our mind is so dense that we can't do anything, we go up to the top of a hill where there is a fair amount of breeze. That will sometimes do it. Or we go where there is very clear water, splash water on our face, and then lie down on the grass and take a rest.

Sometimes this thick state of mind is related to eating, sometimes it's due to the behavior or work that we're doing, sometimes it's just from sleeping too much. As long as you can identify the cause, you can change your diet or activity. If you eat a lot of meat, your mind is never going to get clear.

The main point of tranquillity meditation is to have the mind rest. Within that, different experiences arise. For example, there are people with higher perception; they meet somebody, and just by seeing the person, they not only know something about what happened in their past life but also something about their future. That sort of capability, or power, comes from the clarity of tranquillity meditation. It is fairly common. However, whether it's nonconceptuality, clarity, or bliss, it is just tranquillity. It's not insight. Insight is looking into the mind and, no matter what arises, seeing its nature.

The Shravakayana attitude is to push all these experiences away for fear of harming our meditation. The Mahayana approaches these experiences as a kind of illness, poison, or malady that requires an antidote to transform them into enlightened experiences. In Dzogchen, no matter what arises—bliss, clarity, or nonconceptuality—we don't regard it with either attachment or renunciation; we don't crave these experiences but neither do we try to get rid of them or apply an antidote to them. Instead, we regard them within awareness, within their essence, and they are liberated. Allowing these experiences to arise without awareness increases their force; they cause confusion in the sense that they put us into ordinary states of mind.

If we don't recognize these experiences as having the nature of awareness, then we get attached to them. But we don't need to push them away or find a way to transform them. Just see them as having the nature of awareness. In this way, they form part of the path of liberation. They are liberated in themselves through recognition of their nature as awareness.

Every meditator has experiences of bliss, clarity, and nonconceptuality in both tranquillity and insight modes. However, if you start making the maintenance of those experiences the motivation, or motor, for your meditation, then it will turn into a worldly activity. For example, you meditate and think, "My mind is so happy." If your desire to maintain that state of happiness continues and expands, it makes your meditation worldly. Similarly, if you have an experience of clarity and sense higher perceptions, psychic abilities, and so on, if your meditation extends and increases that, it also makes it worldly. Or your mind rests for a long time and you think, "Wow, I want to continue to push the limits of mind, resting without any thought." Such attitudes about these three experiences won't bring you to liberation but will instead trap you in a worldly activity. Not having these attitudes is nonattachment to meditation.

We should have the same sort of attitude toward outer experiences. Whatever we experience with our five senses lacks intrinsic reality. We can notice everything that appears but without attachment. Then our attention is liberated. A hawk flies down very quickly, takes its prey, and doesn't even touch the ground before flying up again. Our attention should be like that. There is barely a moment of contact, but we don't stay on it, clinging to experience.

Whether it's pleasure or pain, the same principle applies. When pain arises, return again and again to the view. If you are new to this practice, your view is not going to have very strong effects. Take medicine, get help to relieve the pain, be practical, take a break. With sufficient experience, the pain diminishes; you can be sick but by meditating on the view, it's almost as if you've forgotten the sickness. It overcomes everything. That's the best medicine. For a person who is more advanced, pain just doesn't have the same quality at all. Pain is not experienced the way an ordinary person experiences it. So remain in the view. In the beginning, we must constantly return to the view.

## View, Meditation, and Conduct

Between Shravakayana practice and Dzogchen practice, there are nine levels of development, the nine yanas, each of which is wider, larger, and more open than the previous one. This has an impact on practice, meditation, and conduct. When we examine the different meditations and deities at these nine stages of development, we see this distinction in the view. On the Shravakayana level, the only visualized figure is Buddha Shakyamuni and some of the highest members of the sangha of monks and nuns. They don't accept even the eight great bodhisattvas, the eight closest disciples of the Buddha.

At the Mahayana level, we have the presence of great bodhisattvas. We imagine them, but we don't go much further. In the three outer levels of tantra—action (Skt. *kriya*), conduct (Skt. *acharya*), and yoga tantras—we imagine the buddhas, bodhisattvas, and deities, but we imagine them singly or in a mandala. For example, we meditate on Vajrasattva alone, not with consort, or we meditate on the buddhas of the five buddha families but without consorts. The view isn't wide enough, or open-minded enough, to accept or be able to do these meditations on deities in union.

It's only when we get to the stages of Mahayoga, Anuyoga, and Atiyoga that we have deities like Vajrakilaya, Samantabhadra, and others, buddhas and bodhisattvas in sexual union. We can meditate on deities in sexual union at the higher levels of tantra because we have the view of infinite purity, the primordial, or natural, purity of absolutely everything. Also, at the highest levels of the highest yoga tantras, we use thighbone trumpets (Tib. *kangling*), human skull-cups, bone ornaments, the five meats, the five nectars, and so forth. All these things reflect the higher view at this level of tantra, in which everything is accepted. This is impossible at the lower levels. Mipham Rinpoche said, "The basic difference between all the various levels of practice is the view. The view increases as you progress."

We can see the relationship between a person's view of practice and the relative openness or closedness of their mind. On the Shravakayana level, a monk or nun is not even allowed to look at someone of the opposite sex for fear of causing negative karma. From a higher view, there is nothing inherently harmful in that act. As one progresses in dharma practice, the mind grows more and more open as the view gets larger or more inclusive. When the view is really open and inclusive, we see everything, all appearances, as being part of the mandala, the configuration of infinite purity. We see purity and equanimity in all things. For a person who doesn't have this view, things like thighbone trumpets and deities in sexual union are very confusing and threatening.

Our meditation and conduct should follow our view, so for a person practicing Dzogchen who has the view of infinite purity, there is nothing that is pure or impure. Nothing is either allowed or not allowed. There is no sense of limit to our meditation or conduct. First, we must have the view of infinite purity at the level of the mind; then verbal and physical acts follow (that is—meditation and conduct). However, if we have the view of Shravakayana, for instance, but the conduct of Dzogchen (or Mahayoga, Anuyoga, or Atiyoga), then we're going to go crazy. "Crazy" here means that we create negative, or nonvirtuous, acts—there is a dysfunctional relationship between our view and our conduct. In the inner tantras, there are practices of union and liberation; if our view doesn't correspond to that, then we're in big trouble.

Mipham Rinpoche, remarking that our meditation and conduct must follow our view, uses the metaphor of a person's sight: when you see where you are going (the view), then your legs (meditation and conduct) allow you to walk on the path toward what you have seen. In this same way, our view, or sight, of the nature of reality must come before our meditation and conduct. Depending on what we see and if we can see clearly, then if we have good legs, we can go anywhere we want. When we recognize that our primordially existent, ultimate body of enlightenment has always been there, then whatever thoughts arise are naturally liberated because we see their primordial nature.

## The Three Stages of Liberation through the Dzogchen View

The Dzogchen practitioner who maintains the view ascends through stages of liberation. First, we recognize the primordial nature of all

THE MIND OF AWAKENING | 157

inner and outer experiences and are liberated from them. This is likened to meeting an old friend whom we know very well, in the midst of a crowd of many people. Second, as we get more familiar with this nature, there is no first or second moment. The thoughts are autoliberated, liberated in themselves. A snake in a knot unties itself without effort or intention. Thoughts arise, but they are liberated naturally, without even a second moment of recognition. There is no effort involved because of our familiarity with our basic nature. Third, no matter what thoughts arise, they neither benefit nor harm our mind. If thoughts arise, they are liberated into awareness. If no thoughts arise, we rest within awareness. There is no harm or benefit from any mental event. The metaphor for this is a thief entering a completely empty house. The thief doesn't harm anything because there is nothing to take, and they don't help anything either. This thief represents our thoughts. This is the highest level of liberation.

In Dzogchen practice, any thoughts can be liberated through these stages of liberation. Ordinarily, we think of buddhadharma as the way of liberation—an ordinary person enters practice and finds the way to liberation. However, often a person enters dharma practice, reaches a certain level, and stays bound to that level due to being stuck in ordinary thoughts. Without practicing at a sophisticated enough level, practice turns into a way of being bound. That's not right. We need to be liberated from both the bonds of worldly existence and the bonds of practice. This is possible in the context of Dzogchen.

Fortunately, the Tibetan tradition of debate has not taken too strong a hold in the West, because practicing debate all the time limits the expansion of the mind. Also, spending all our time doing nothing but rituals and recitations can be a way of limiting our mind. We can't say that these practices are entirely negative; there is an inconceivable amount of merit and positive energy in ritual practice and recitation, and it will have very good effects in future lives. But the real point is to be liberated from thoughts to arrive at enlightenment. Our view, our meditation, and our practice must correspond to the real point so that our practice doesn't devolve into yet another way of binding us.

Building stupas, making mandalas of deities for empowerments, giving teachings to large numbers of people, despite the immense positive benefit that they provide, are auxiliary, supporting activities. The root of the buddhadharma is exactly what I just said: the gradual liberation of thoughts, looking at mental activity and finding liberation within the mind. If we can conceive of making an offering of the entire world to Buddha Shakyamuni or to Guru Rinpoche, or if we can conceive of many very wonderful, positive acts, it might create an inconceivable amount of merit. However, the Buddha himself said that the simple practice of finding liberation within the mind, realizing freedom from the bonds of ordinary conceptual thought, is even more wonderful than any conceivable meritorious act, because at that point we have realized the Buddha or Guru Rinpoche. I'm not inventing this. I'm just repeating the words of the Buddha and of Guru Rinpoche.

If we have understood and experienced the Dzogchen view but develop attachment toward it, then we are in danger of establishing a form of clinging that Thinley Norbu Rinpoche calls "the entrance for demons." Whatever we experience, we mustn't have attachment to the experience. Whatever your view, clinging to it is a negative act. Whatever your experience, thinking that you have attained something is simply the movement of mind, more thoughts. Thinking that you have achieved realization is just a form of pride. None of this movement of mind is the true realization; it's the creation of negative, or demonic, karma. "Demons" in this context are ordinary thoughts, clinging, or attachment, to experience of the characteristics of things as having intrinsic existence; demons are not the bogeyman.

"Thinking that you have attained something" is the attitude of thinking you have finished, or completely realized, either the view or the result. If without fully realizing the view or the result you feel that you have done so, this is said in the sutras to be the activity of demons, extraordinary pride. This is not "vajra pride"; it is extraordinary negative pride. It's said in another sutra that if an arhat thinks to themselves, "I have renounced all negative emotions," then that person is not an arhat.

The *Meditation on the Mind of Awakening*, a Dzogchen tantra, says that if our positive activity is not held by the female Buddha Ever Excellent, then any act by the male Buddha Ever Excellent becomes the activity of demons. The female aspect of Ever Excellent is emptiness; so any act done without the emptiness aspect is a negative act. The male Buddha Ever Excellent represents the appearance aspect of any positive act; so if positive conduct is done without the female Buddha, the emptiness aspect, then it comes within the realm of characteristics, wherein things are considered to be existent or real, and it doesn't go beyond the realm of our ordinary thoughts. The male and female aspects of enlightenment are inseparable and maintained together. With the presence of the female Buddha, the aspect of emptiness, then even the acts of demons become the conduct of awakening.

## The Six Transcendent Perfections in Dzogchen Meditation

In Dzogchen, the transcendent perfection of generosity is to have no clinging to anything that may appear to exist, whether material or nonmaterial.

The transcendent perfection of ethical conduct is to have no thought of purity or impurity. If you think, "I have pure ethical conduct and this other person is doing negative acts or hasn't got pure ethical conduct," then you are clinging to a concept of pure or impure ethical conduct.

The transcendent perfection of patience is not to identify the object of patience or the bodhisattva who has to be patient. Realizing that all sentient beings appear as an illusion, that there is no inherent reality to any appearance, and resting within the lack of self beyond all dualistic thought, clinging, and subject-object experience, is the perfection of patience.

The transcendent perfection of diligence is to find enlightenment within and to have realized that there is no need for any hope, for any energetic activity that looks for enlightenment outside. There is no need to think that you must practice over long periods of time, perhaps many aeons, in order to attain enlightenment. Finding enlightenment within your own inner nature is the perfection of diligence.

The transcendent perfection of meditation is to rest without thinking that something exists or does not exist, that something is pure or impure, to not fall into any of these extremes. The transcendent perfection of knowledge is to rest in the great wisdom of equanimity and the purity of both samsara and the transcendence of it. Resting in the great wisdom of equanimity and the purity of these two and not finding any reference points, foci, things to know, or things to accept or reject is the perfection of knowledge. Dualistic knowledge is not transcendent knowledge. One of the Prajnaparamita sutras says that transcendent knowledge is "seeing without seeing anything at all." The meditator sees, with eyes open, but without seeing any object in particular, without falling into any of the four extremes of existence, nonexistence, both, or neither. There's no distinction between the seer and the object of sight, so there is nothing seen. Dualistic experience ends. In the context of Dzogchen, this is called "emptiness." It is also called "the ultimate body of enlightenment." When we consider this emptiness, this ultimate body of enlightenment, it has no form. It has no material or existent characteristics. It has no label, and it has no language. But it is not the extreme of nonexistence.

When you look into empty space, you are seeing, but you aren't really seeing anything at all. You say you've "seen" it, but actually you haven't seen anything at all. When you look into a clear glass of water, you can see the clarity, but except for water there is nothing really there. These are examples of seeing by not seeing, which merely point to understanding. When you are able to see this non-seeing, this is to have "seen" your nature. We are seeing something, but there is nothing there at all.

The Dzogchen view is to see without seeing anything at all. This is a rather difficult point but also an essential one. This comes up repeatedly in Dzogchen. We can look at a bell or a glass and know that there is a space that it encloses, but we don't see the space because there is nothing to see. We see without seeing anything. This is what we see, but by not seeing this, we continue in samsara, because we remain within the subject-object split. We always see some thing; we don't see nothing.

This seeing relates to the nature of mind, what we see without seeing. It is not related to the eyes or any of the other senses. When we say that we see in the manner of not seeing, it means that when we look at the nature of mind, we don't see anything. There is nothing there, but, at the same time, it is not nonexistent. We can say "seeing without getting lost in thought" or "seeing in the way of not seeing" or "seeing what cannot be seen." Whatever way we say it, it relates to the nature of mind. It has nothing to do with the senses.

Mipham Rinpoche said that the seeing of nothing whatsoever is the highest form of seeing if there is no falling into any of the extremes of existence, nonexistence, both, or neither. This experience is completely indescribable and inexpressible, like a mute person who can taste the sweetness of a candy but can't describe it to anyone. Mipham Rinpoche said that practitioners who have confidence in this should practice it.

The sphere of totality, the ultimate body of enlightenment, emptiness, no matter what name is given to it, is primordially present and not created by any causes and conditions. It is not part of anything that appears to either exist or not. We can't think, "It's like this. It's like that. I've got it. I haven't got it." It is not approachable by our ordinary consciousness, because ordinary thinking always falls into the categories of either existence, nonexistence, both, or neither.

When we meditate, we can have very clear experiences of emptiness, of the empty nature of mind. Or we can have very strong experiences of lucidity, or clarity, of mind. Or we can have the experience of both emptiness and clarity together. Regardless of our experience in meditation or our access to the nature of mind, the nature of our mind never moves from one place to another, and it never changes. The Prajnaparamita says that regardless of the number of thoughts, obscuring emotions, or other events that happen in the mind, the pure nature of mind is not at all diminished.

There are no new qualities that can be developed to make the pure nature any greater. It cannot diminish and it cannot get any fuller than it already is.

Even though we might have some understanding and think, "Yes, the nature of reality is enlightenment and this is the buddha" (and it is important to understand this), if we then think, "But my ordinary mind is not like that," then this is a mistake. We have to understand that our dualistic experience has no inherent reality and that the nature of our mind is the same as the nature of mind of all buddhas. We have to develop certainty, uplift our mind, and give ourselves confidence. Feeling bad about ourselves and thinking, "I'm just a little person; I have no relationship to enlightenment; it's all out there" is not how to approach our meditation practice. We should inspire ourselves, feel great about ourselves. There is no point in being overly humble at that level.

When we recognize the primordial purity of the nature of our own mind or the nature of reality, we can realize that there is no basis for confusion. Any confusion is transitory or incidental, so it does not have to be purified; it is naturally, automatically purified without our having to apply antidotes such as renunciation or transformation. If we rest within the single meditation of either Dzogchen or the Middle Way, then all the qualities of the stages and paths of the six transcendent perfections in the Mahayana are accomplished without any effort, spontaneously.

## The Individual as a Support for Enlightenment

*Gangzag* is the Tibetan word for an individual, in dharma terminology. Thinley Norbu Rinpoche says that when you rest within the great sphere of awareness, there is no self, no clinging to self, no individual. *Gang* means "full." *Zag* means "to spill." Guess what we're full of. Guess what we're spilling. We're filled with obscuring emotions. We're spilling them all over samsara. So *gangzag*, an individual, means "filled with obscuring emotions spilling all over the place."

Thinley Norbu Rinpoche continues, however, by saying that while this is generally true, this negative connotation does not mean that it's absolutely certain that an individual is necessarily the basis of obscuring emotions spilling all over samsara. In the Shravakayana, by renouncing the obscuring emotions, an individual can attain, or develop, wisdom; but without the support of the individual, there is no renunciation or any development of wisdom. In the bodhisattva path, when all appearances are recognized as unreal, the individual is the support for the transformation of negative emotions for the benefit of others. It depends upon the "individual." Clinging to self is a negative emotion, but, in the Mahayana, negative emotions like passion can be transformed into compassion on the path to awakening.

As ordinary beings, all our virtuous and nonvirtuous activity share the same root in negative emotions. Even things we consider to be positive qualities or acts, such as having faith, compassion, and the desire to attain enlightenment, are in a sense negative emotions. They are extremely positive and useful and are rare and wonderful in this world, but they fall into the category of impure virtuous activity because they are based on clinging to self, ordinary thought, and desire. However, we must use them to continue on the path. On arrival at enlightenment, these subtle negative emotions are given up because we have attained great compassion, great faith, which are transcendent and not impure.

It is essential to have pointing-out instructions to experience this wisdom. The "engine" of all eighty-four thousand teachings of the Buddha is the view. Without the view, with only understanding, we can perhaps practice accumulating merit. We can achieve rebirth as a god or a human in future lives. It is very positive, but we don't really arrive at the point. We must understand the view. Once we have the pointing-out instructions, we have the central key to all the teachings. It is like the inner life force of all samsara and nirvana.

Now we will look at the individual's negative emotions from the perspective of tantric practice. In the Nyingma tradition, the highest levels of tantra are Mahayoga, Anuyoga, and Atiyoga. In the tantras of the New Translation schools, the father tantras correspond to Mahayoga, the mother tantras to Anuyoga, and the nondual tantras to Atiyoga. An example of a father tantra is *Guhyasamaja* (*Gathering of Secrets*), an example of a mother tantra is *Chakrasamvara* (*Wheel of Supreme Bliss*), and an example of a nondual tantra is *Kalachakra* (*Wheel of Time*). Within the concealed meaning, the inner essence of these tantras are the tantric commitments, both root and secondary. In the secondary commitments, one must maintain the five negative emotions. How does that lead us to wisdom?

The first is desire: The commitment is to have desire, or passion, toward sentient beings through compassion. You don't reject or abandon sentient beings to their lives in samsara, but you are passionate for their release from samsara.

The second is anger: The tantric commitment says your anger must be oriented toward all misguided thoughts related to your natural, innate wisdom of awareness. With the wisdom of this "vajra anger," you overcome, or defeat, all misguided thoughts.

The third is ignorance: The commitment to develop ignorance means that you see everything without any idea of good or bad, positive or negative. You see the equanimity in everything. "Dharma" experiences are not embraced and "worldly" experiences are not rejected. This is the ignorance you develop, "vajra ignorance." Ordinarily, we think we should renounce nonvirtuous activity and cultivate virtuous activity. But in tantra, within this recognition of the view and the equanimity of all things, no choices of action are necessary.

The fourth is pride: The commitment is to remain uplifted. Through the realization of the view of equanimity, you don't fall into a lower state. This is pride at the level of the buddha, the wisdom of enlightenment.

Last is jealousy: On an ordinary level, the experience of jealousy is when we see someone with a quality or a possession and somehow can't accept that fact; it doesn't fit within our mind, so we resist. On the level of the buddha's wisdom, in the space of equanimity, none of the thoughts or appearances of dualistic experience fit within our mind. Any dualistic thought or experience remains on the outside.

For those who have realization of the view, these five negative emotions are thus transformed into the five wisdoms. At that stage, we can call them "negative emotions," with the names of desire, anger, ignorance, pride, and jealousy, or we can call them the "five wisdoms." There is no difference between them.

As ordinary sentient beings, we have these five negative emotions. But no dualistic thought or experience can enter a buddha's mind. In a way, a buddha's mind is not big enough to hold dualistic experience! It is only wisdom.

We are still on the subject of gangzag, the individual. For an individual whose realization is higher than an ordinary individual, we still use the term gangzag, but we modify it with exalted, higher, or more noble. That state of being is defined as a person free of obscuring and nonobscuring emotions, of self and of clinging to self—any of those sorts of thoughts. The exalted individual completely transcends any experience related to ordinary thoughts. The "great noncomposite state" refers to an exalted individual. It is called "noncomposite" because it is not a result of causes and conditions having come together. All composite things are impermanent because things that have come together will also separate.

We can think of empty space as not created by any causes or conditions. Anything that doesn't exist, like horns on my head, has not been created by causes or conditions. When we speak of the noncomposite as being like space or horns on my head, this is using the term noncomposite in a very limited context. It is nonexistence. But the great noncomposite state is beyond all clinging; beyond existence, nonexistence, both, and neither; beyond any thought or nonthought. It is important to say that much at this point; Thinley Norbu Rinpoche says more on this subject later on in his text.

We experience composite things and this is the limit of our experience, so we are ordinary individuals. Exalted individuals are exalted because they have entered the great noncomposite state.

## Meditation and Postmeditation

After quoting from the *Garland of Jewels*, "If something is really important, then you can repeat yourself," Thinley Norbu Rinpoche returns to the subject of meditative and postmeditative states because it is essential.

The true meditative state is not polluted by dualistic experiences of clinging to any object of one's senses, any of the facets of one's subjective experience, or any of the different aspects of one's consciousness. There is no trace of this dualistic experience.

Meditation is recognition of, and resting in, our self-manifest, or self-arising, wisdom; it is primordially part of our experience, always a part of who we are. We have awareness, rigpa, from the very beginning of our experience. Just as space doesn't come into being at a certain time, remain for a time, and then cease, awareness that is primordially part of who we are doesn't come into being at a certain time, remain for a time, and then cease. We remain in "the great sphere," the great thigle.

Having defined meditation and the period of meditation, we define subsequent attainment, or the postmeditative state, as when the mind begins to move. At that time, we experience appearances from our six forms of consciousness, but we don't let our attention go to the objects of experience as does an ordinary person. An ordinary person experiences the play of the six senses but believes that the objects, or appearances, exist. A meditator, on the other hand, experiences the same play of appearances but sees them as being like a dream or like magic. In that state, as was explained before, the meditator cultivates merit and wisdom and clears away obscurations. This is called "the union of the two cultivations."

We find the notion that all appearances are like magic in the teachings of the Buddha himself, the teachings of great masters such as Nagarjuna or others in India, and particularly in the teachings of Longchenpa, in Tibet. For example, Longchenpa's third volume of *Kindly Bent to Ease Us* is called *Resting in Illusion*. He gives eight examples of illusion. One of these is magic. Thinley Norbu Rinpoche explains in detail what is meant by the idea of magic; this is one of the critical points of buddhadharma.

The basic characteristic of magic is that something appears to us, but it's unreal. It doesn't exist. A magician might recite a mantra like "Abracadabra" and produce different appearances out of thin air—temporary appearances resulting from the coming together of a number of causes and conditions. From the very beginning, there has been no fundamental reality in these appearances. We might watch a magician cut off somebody's head. No matter how vivid, or clear, these appearances seem, they have no true existence whatsoever.

At the end of this magic show, the magician might gather together all the created appearances. Though, as spectators, we experience all the illusions being gathered together, in fact, that's only our experience. From the beginning, they didn't exist. They didn't exist while they appeared. And at the end, they are just a display for us. We see something that has only an apparent existence. In fact, from the beginning to the end, there was nothing whatsoever.

The metaphor of a magical display applies to all appearances experienced by us as sentient beings. We experience everything through our sight, hearing, taste, touch, and smell. At the very moment they appear, they are nonexistent, but we have invested them with reality.

Thinley Norbu Rinpoche says we may think this is not a good metaphor for our experience because in a magic show we know that the appearances last only a little while, but our lives in samsara take place over a long time. Also, when we see a magical display, the appearances have no mind in themselves. But in our experience of samsara, in our experience of everything, there is a mind—our mind—which we also believe is real.

To begin answering the first objection, remember that what we call time (past, present, and future) is just an example of being lost in thought; it is created by our thinking. If one person dreams of an experience of one hundred years and another person dreams of a very short moment, the dream of one hundred years would not be more real than the dream of a short time. We can't say that the length of time determines the relative reality of something.

The fact that, in our ordinary experience, beings have mind but in a magic show they do not doesn't matter, in a way. If we say that all appearances are like magic and don't truly exist, then whether a sentient being has mind or not is irrelevant. The appearances of a magic show appear, yet they don't truly exist. They have no ultimate reality. In the same way, even in our ordinary experience, there is appearance without true existence. It doesn't depend on whether there is a mind present within these appearances or not.

Sentient beings take illusory appearance to have true existence. They see a self where there is no self. We call this "appearances of delusion." Based on clinging to what is not real as real, beings continue to wander within the appearances of delusion.

Rongzompa said, "When we discuss the appearances of delusion, we have to ask ourselves, Where do these illusory appearances exist? Since when have we been having this problem? How long have we been within the appearances of delusion? Months? Years? Aeons? Where are we deluded and for how long has this been going on?"

We say confused beings are the beings of the three realms (the desire, form, and formless realms). This is a worldly designation of who is deluded. To continue in our ordinary way (this isn't the real answer), we say that this has been going on from time without beginning. Although this is said in texts and is explained that way, it is just a way of talking. It doesn't reflect the truth. In fact, it's not true; it's not like that at all. The time and place where confusion is happening and the persons who are deluded are all the appearances of delusion. When we imagine to ourselves that we have been confused or deluded from time without beginning, this is simply an appearance of delusion. The place where we have been deluded is also an appearance of delusion, as is the individual.

We can use the metaphor of a dream to explain how it really is. While dreaming, we have a self and appearances, and we see a particular environment and other individuals. Based on these appearances, we have experiences of pleasure and pain and we feel time passing. But no matter the length of time and the places that appear, the people or animals that we see do not exist. Whatever happiness or suffering we experience also does not exist. Nothing existed although it all appeared.

I can go to sleep in my bedroom and dream for an hour. During this dream, I can leave the United States, go back as far as Chengdu in China, and from there travel up to my home in eastern Tibet. Many things can happen during that time. I can meet my root teacher, my dharma friends, my family. I can see everything very clearly. I can have a lot of fun. I can be sad. But this all takes place during one hour of sleep. I have not gone anywhere at all. I was still in my bedroom. Perhaps all our experience, all that we've experienced during our lifetime, happens in an instant.

This is the same as our experience as sentient beings. We say, "We've been experiencing delusion since beginningless time." When we dream, we have very distinct, vivid experiences of self and other, time and place. In the same way, all our experience, from the very beginning, of time and place, self and other, and the objects of our senses are entirely delusion. Although our mind has these various experiences of delusion, in fact we have never left the basic enlightened nature that never changes. The true nature of the mind of sentient beings is luminosity.

During the one-hour dream when I experienced a month's time and travel, did this month actually exist or not? Did I actually go to Tibet or was I still in my bed dreaming? Of course, they were entirely illusion.

Now we come to the meaning of the dream metaphor. Our ignorance, or lack of awareness, is like sleep. Just as we dream when we are asleep, in our lack of awareness, we experience illusory appearances. Within our lack of awareness, we experience ourselves as sentient beings, we experience time without beginning, and we experience samsara. However, in our essence, this is an instantaneous appearance from our fundamental consciousness (kunzhi). Fundamental consciousness produces self, time, and an infinite number of worlds in one instant.

Here are two more ways to understand our delusion. When we look in a mirror, we see reflections of things that seem to be very deep within the mirror, very far away, maybe as far as another valley or country. However, everything in the mirror is on the surface; the mirror has no depth whatsoever. In the same way, we have the impression that things are distinct—that we are here and the hells, the heavens, and the hungry and thirsty ghosts are elsewhere. But these are just reflections we experience from our fundamental consciousness.

In a theater, a movie plays on the surface of a large screen: we see birth, death, time, distance, things coming toward us, and things going away from us. The screen is like our fundamental consciousness, from which all appearances arise (please ignore the film projector for this depiction) that give us the impression of time, space, movement, birth, death, and all the dramas conceivable in life. What appears on the screen appears only on the screen; there is no time, space, characters, or anything, yet we react as if there is. This is a way of understanding how, on the basis of our fundamental consciousness, we have ordinary consciousness. All of these appearances, from the very moment that they appear, have no fundamental reality. They are simply appearances of confusion, or delusion. In the same way that we can dream for one hour of living for a whole aeon, we can experience ourselves as having existed from time without beginning. In fact, this is entirely an appearance of confusion, or delusion.

It is said that bodhisattvas can transform a week into an aeon, and an aeon into a week. However, an aeon of time and a week of time are just creations of mind. It is not that an aeon, or a long time, has actually been gathered into a short amount of time. Even though we say that bodhisattvas can do this, in reality, it is no different from the time we can experience in a dream. Although we dream of one hundred years, it isn't as if those one hundred years were concentrated into a moment. It's rather that they never existed.

Similarly, we might experience an aeon during a week. If we have a very tight, solid experience of time, thinking that past is past, present is present, and future is future, all in definite categories that exist, then it is very difficult for us to appreciate the nature of reality. When we contemplate a dream, a reflection in a mirror, or the experience of time in movies, then we can come to a better understanding of what these appearances of confusion are and the fact that time doesn't have any true existence.

First, you have to read, or listen, to these teachings, and then you have to reflect and meditate on them. Eventually, you will be led to a very clear understanding of the nature of time, space, reality, and the nature of illusory appearances. Though it's not easy at the beginning, when you can view the world in this way, you'll laugh. You'll go out and look at what's happening, and it will all seem fairly absurd.

When you've reflected on these ideas and have come to a very definite understanding, then when you meet people who hold very solid ideas of past, present, and future, or when you see people talking to one another who have a very solid experience of reality, you will either laugh or think, "This is really strange." There are a lot of strange things in this world. But the strangeness is not in the appearance but in the clinging to the solidity, or the reality, of things.

When the mind arrives at an understanding of these subjects, it feels very happy from the inside. From then on, we are no longer obsessed with ambitious projects of achieving fame, wealth, or extraordinary comfort in the outside world. We may enjoy these things, but they don't have the same attraction because we are already very happy within. We experience the way others are living like a sightseer on vacation. To come to an understanding of these subjects has a tremendous benefit even in our ordinary lives. Later on, it has even greater benefits by leading us to enlightenment.

Of course, we don't need only the understanding. We also need direct instruction in practice. As we continue in this text, we will go more and more into both the benefits of the teaching and direct instructions in practice. Right now, we're developing an understanding, from which some sort of feeling comes up in our mind. This slight experience that comes from our understanding can be very useful in overcoming whatever ordinary happiness or suffering arises within our mind.

Exalted individuals with the realization of the nature of mind understand appearances as a magical display. Appearances are not seen as real. Because there is no clinging to appearances as reality, there is no clinging to self. Without clinging to self, there is no basis for anger, desire, or ignorance to arise without their being liberated upon arising. Without negative emotions, there is no karma and no suffering. Instead of appearances being the basis for confusion, they are the basis for liberation.

On the other hand, sentient beings create, from the basis of liberation, their confusion, or delusion. If we are confused about the destination of our journey, thinking that we are going to San Francisco but instead ending up in New York City, this is confusion. Sentient beings do not see things as they are. Instead of seeing appearances as the basis for liberation, they form, through confusion or delusion, the basis for more confusion and suffering.

Sentient beings see what is illusory or magic as real. Exalted individuals see illusion or magic for what it is; they understand its nature. Buddhas have no thought toward either illusion or non-illusion, truth or falsehood. They have no ordinary thought at all in relation to appearances. They rest within deep, relaxed peace from which great compassion manifests. They rest within great equanimity without any movement—that is, thought—in relation to appearances.

When we see things as existent, this is a thought. When we see illusory appearances as nonexistent, as merely illusion or magic, this is also a thought. The latter thought is a step in the right direction; we're approaching the nature of reality. However, on the level of enlightenment, a buddha rests within the equanimity of primordial purity, where there is no thought whatsoever, either of things as existent or nonexistent.

For those of us on the path to awakening, in relation to our clinging, or our impression that illusory appearances exist, we develop the experience and understanding that things do not exist, that appearances are illusory or magic. This is a stepping-stone along the path to nondual wisdom.

When we say that a buddha has no dualistic experience, it is not that a buddha has no perception of appearances whatsoever. The awareness, or wisdom, aspect of a buddha's mind is unimpeded. In the same way that light flows effortlessly from the sun, the awareness, or wisdom, aspect of enlightenment appears unobstructedly. The awareness aspect of a buddha's mind creates inconceivable, miraculous appearances of wisdom.

Our meditation is vast, like space. We rest our mind in emptiness, like space. This is our period of meditation. We rest without moving from this state. This develops the qualities of the ultimate body of enlightenment. In the postmeditative state, we experience everything as like a dream or an illusion; we cultivate merit and purify obscurations. These are the two facets of our path to enlightenment.

The Tibetan word for a buddha is *sangye. Sang* means "purified" and *gye* means "to unfold" or "to blossom." A buddha has purified dualistic experience, like a sun setting, and what has blossomed in its place is nondual wisdom. With full and complete enlightenment, nondual wisdom blossoms and unimpeded great compassion for all sentient beings fills all worlds with emanations, miraculous appearances. There is no comparison between the emanations of a buddha and the creations of bodhisattvas, magicians, or anybody who has the power of emanation, or creation.

## The Ten Stages of Awakening in Sutra

I have given a lengthy description of the idea that everything we experience is a magical display, although Thinley Norbu Rinpoche says this is only a very brief discussion of this subject. Now I will describe how the cultivation of merit and wisdom as an illusion, or like magic, is related to the ten stages of a bodhisattva's awakening until enlightenment.

From the perspective of meditation, there is no difference in the wisdom of emptiness at any of these ten stages. It is like seeing the moon. You might approach the moon, and it would appear clearer or larger, but it is not a different moon; when you have seen the moon, that's it. However, in the context of the postmeditative state, there is a division into these ten stages. The difference is the level of certainty, or clarity. As the impurities, or the obscuring emotions, diminish and wisdom increases, we mark divisions between the various stages. As the sunshine gets brighter, more and more darkness is cleared away. This is the distinction between the different levels.

The first stage of awakening is the first moment of directly seeing the truth of the transcendent nature of reality. Until then, we have some understanding, but we haven't directly seen it. This seeing is like a poor person who finds a wish-fulfilling jewel. It is "perfect joy" because the body and mind are filled with great joy at seeing the nature of reality. At this stage, we can work in a much greater way than before for our own and others' benefit. It is a very satisfying experience, since we now see what we haven't seen before. This first stage of awakening is related to the transcendent perfection of generosity, including the generosity of giving things, teaching, and giving security or comfort to others.

The second stage of awakening is related to ethical conduct. At that stage, thanks to our meditation, view, and conduct, we no longer create any faults in ethical conduct. Because our ethical conduct—of restraint, gathering qualities, and aiding others (the three forms of ethical conduct)—is pure, this stage is "immaculate."

At the third stage of awakening, we can dedicate our time to purifying our mind without thought of our body or our life. We are entirely dedicated to the training. We develop forbearance in relation to deep subjects in the teachings. This stage is related to the transcendent perfection of patience. Because with patience we can illuminate our own and others' darkness of misunderstanding, this stage of awakening is "illuminating."

At the fourth stage of awakening, we develop even stronger joy, or enthusiasm, than we had at the first stage of awakening. This tremendous energy, or enthusiasm, creates a fire of wisdom so intense that Thinley Norbu Rinpoche says it is like "the fire at the end of time." It burns away all our habitual tendencies of clinging. So this stage of awakening, which is related to the transcendent perfection of diligence, is "radiant."

At the fifth stage of awakening, through the force of meditative absorption without any excitation or sinking, we can overcome obstacles that were difficult to overcome in the past, so this stage is "hard to conquer" or "hard to overcome." This stage is related to the transcendent perfection of meditation.

At the sixth stage of awakening, we directly realize that everything, whether of samsara or of all transcendent states, is without a moment of origin, abiding, or cessation. This is the transcendent perfection of knowledge. This sixth stage of awakening is "manifest" because we manifestly, or directly, see the meaning of the nature of things.

At the seventh stage of awakening, we have distanced ourselves from lower ways of practice such as the Shravakayana and we employ the great skillful means of compassion or meditation on emptiness, so the name of this stage is "far-reaching." This is the transcendent perfection of skillful means. (As you may have noticed, in this particular framework, there are ten rather than the usual six transcendent perfections.)

At the eighth stage of awakening, our aspirations made in the past come to fruition. We no longer fall into any of the results of the lower paths of practice, and we remain on the bodhisattva path. Our meditation is no longer moved by ordinary thought, no longer moved by our concept that things actually exist as real. Negative emotion or thought no longer moves us, just as a mountain is not moved no matter how hard the wind blows, so this stage of awakening is "unmoving." Although in the *Treasury of Discourses and Tantras* the eighth perfection is said to be "force," in Thinley Norbu Rinpoche's text, it is related to the transcendent perfection of aspiration.

The ninth stage of awakening is "excellent intelligence" and is related to the transcendent perfection of force, or strength. We have developed mastery of "the four modes of individual genuine awareness." The first mode is awareness of all the subjects of the Buddha's teaching—monastic discipline (the vinaya), the discourses (the sutras) and knowledge (the abhidharma). The second is the awareness of meaning—basis, path, and result; view, meditation, and action. The third is awareness of definitions, anything to do with language; how words are put together, composition, and the science of grammar. The fourth is the genuine awareness of confidence that we have deeply understood and mastered the Buddha's teaching; we can unimpededly give the right answer to any question, correct any mistakes in other's views, and compose whatever is necessary.

The tenth stage of awakening is "cloud of the teachings." A symbol of this stage is space filling with clouds. From the clouds rain falls and produces harvests. In the mind of the bodhisattva, wisdom is as wide as space, from which clouds of compassion form and various ways of aiding beings fall among them like rain. At this final stage of awakening, it is mainly the action of wisdom.

In the fully awakened state, the illumination of the buddha's compassion fills all space and touches each and every being unobstructedly. The buddha roots out all the ignorance of beings through his teaching. For this reason, the stage of full enlightenment is "all-illuminating."

## Meditation and Postmeditation in the Three Inner Tantras

We have discussed the meaning of the meditative and postmeditative states from the sutra perspective. When practicing the sutras, it is said that we must spend many aeons cultivating merit and wisdom and purifying obscurations. Now we will discuss meditative and postmeditative states from the perspective of tantra.

*Tantra* is a Sanskrit term; it is translated in Tibetan as *gyud*, which literally means "continuity." It refers to the continuity of the nature of mind, our changeless nature, which we can recognize right now as ordinary sentient beings and follow until enlightenment.

Tantra falls under the classification of Vajrayana. Vajrayana is said to be profound and very efficient, a very quick and direct path. We usually conceive of enlightenment as very distant, something that we must train in for a very long time to achieve. In Vajrayana, it is always said that we can attain enlightenment during this lifetime or during a series of three, seven, or up to eleven lifetimes. In tantric practice, there are a multitude of skillful means, far more means of practice than in sutra. And in tantra it is not necessary to do very difficult ascetic practices in order to attain enlightenment.

The Mahayana path usually requires that we spend many aeons cultivating merit and wisdom and purifying obscurations through the six transcendent perfections. In tantra, we work with meditations on different deities, and we work with the yoga practices of the channels, energy-winds, and vital essence of the body. For example, in the Kalachakra practice, the series of completion-stage practices is very wonderful, but it takes years of very difficult practice to work with the inner energies. It is said that work with inner energies leads to wisdom.

In Dzogchen, all this very difficult and long-term practice is not necessary. What is necessary is to meet a qualified teacher who has experience of Dzogchen and great compassion. The student who meets this teacher must have faith. Then the teacher can give direct pointing-out instructions to the nature of mind as the primordial, ultimate body of enlightenment. This is given directly, overtly, not concealed or hidden. It is just like giving someone a piece of apple. You give it to them, and they taste it and think it is good. It does not require many years of practice; some people have attained enlightenment within six months. It depends upon the qualifications of the teacher and the faith of the student.

Meditating even for one week after having received pointing-out instructions is equal to many aeons of other forms of meditation. As I have quoted Mipham Rinpoche, one week of correct Dzogchen practice breaks the engine of ordinary thought and negative emotions. After a week's time, we have a sense of relaxation, where thoughts and emotions no longer trouble us to the same extent.

After maybe three years of Dzogchen practice, one can arrive at enlightenment.

Vajrayana practice involves the stages of creation and completion. There are two aspects of the stage of completion: with form and without form, or in technical language, "with characteristics" and "without characteristics." "With characteristics" means meditation on channels, the energy-winds, and the vital essence of the body. We must energetically apply ourselves to this somewhat busy practice. In contrast, the stage of completion "without characteristics" is the effortless practice of radiant Dzogchen, placing the mind directly in its own nature.

From the perspective of Shravakayana, we are asked to renounce, abandon, or avoid all desire and anger. In Mahayana, and more specifically in Vajrayana, since enlightenment appears in relation to the needs of sentient beings, there is a lot more space for enlightenment to appear directly according to those needs. All the deities of the two phases of the completion stage can be gathered into two groups: peaceful and wrathful transcendent deities. They have gone beyond ordinary desire, anger, and ignorance into the sphere of totality that is their nature. For those who have great desire in their mind, enlightenment appears in the form of desire, through the compassion of the buddhas, in order to lead sentient beings to enlightenment. For those persons who are wild and untamable by peaceful means, enlightenment appears in wrathful forms.

If a buddha appeared in a very peaceful form and tried to teach the dharma very kindly, gently, and softly to violent, aggressive people, they wouldn't be able to accept his teaching. So the buddha appears in a form as wrathful as they are. If a buddha taught renunciation of all desire to those whose predominant view is desire, then it would not be an effective way of teaching. Within the sphere of totality, there is no such thing as peaceful or wrathful forms. There is no desire or anger, or the appearance of desire or anger. Yet in relation to the needs of beings, enlightenment appears in the world in these various forms.

When we meditate, from the beginning, we must understand

that the peaceful and wrathful deities don't appear from another place. They are part of our very nature. They appear from our heart, or our mind. Westerners say that emotions are in our heart and thoughts are in our brain. It is a little bit like that. When we talk of the forty-two peaceful deities resting in our heart, it is not as if inside our heart are all the deities with all their arms, legs, ornaments, and implements. Rather, the love, affection, yearning, and other emotions that we hold in our heart are the basis for the arising of the forty-two peaceful deities. Similarly, our brain is very powerful, with many different thoughts represented by the fifty-eight wrathful deities. If we open our body and look into the brain, we are not going to find anything that corresponds to these fifty-eight deities. These deities are the nature of our thoughts. All of the deities represent the nature of our mind. Like a crystal that has not yet been illumined by sunlight, right now we don't have the appearance, the natural display, of these forty-two deities at our heart and the fifty-eight wrathful deities at our brain.

However, for the sake of brevity, we say that all the peaceful and wrathful deities are naturally in the body. We have not created them through our karma; they are naturally part of our makeup. At this time, as sentient beings, we have impure experience, so we experience emotions and thoughts, whether in our heart or in our brain. But with a pointing-out of our nature as the ultimate body of enlightenment, we can experience the nature of all emotions and thoughts as the configuration, the mandala, of the peaceful and wrathful deities.

This is explained only in the Dzogchen tradition; it is not found in the Mahayana or even the tantras. We consider the brain to be extremely important because there is a channel from the heart that rises up to the brain and then splits into five separate channels that go to the eyes, the ears, and the other sense organs. This creates our consciousness. It is not that the mind is in the brain. However, the mind functions through these inner channels. This relationship between heart and brain through the channels is well defined in Dzogchen texts, and the explanation of it is a teaching exclusive to Dzogchen. Generally, Tibetans believe that the mind is in the heart, and Westerners believe that the mind is in the brain. Dzogchen believes both.

The forty-two peaceful deities and the fifty-eight wrathful deities remain in the body in the various channels, or meridians. They naturally form part of our psychological and physical makeup called "the fundamental vajra sphere." "Fundamental" here means "existing naturally in our body." It is not created. It is part of the basis of who we are. The vajra sphere is the basis of our makeup.

Because the vajra sphere is our basic nature, we can practice according to the Mahayoga tantra, the seventh of the nine ways of development in the Nyingma tradition, where we practice the creation phase. We imagine appearing as all the deities, which are our nature. We meditate on them using many different styles of meditative absorption. We begin our meditation practice by dissolving all appearances into emptiness. Out of emptiness appears a seed syllable. From the seed syllable appears a particular form. For example, for Manjushri, we have the syllable *di*. The *di* then appears as Manjushri, orange in color, holding a book and a sword. Or after dissolving everything into emptiness, a syllable *hung* appears, and the *hung* then appears in whatever form of Guru Rinpoche we are meditating on. Then we imagine light radiating and clearing away all the bad karma and obscurations of all sentient beings and helping them to cultivate merit and wisdom. Again light radiates, making offerings to all buddhas and bodhisattvas. In this way, whatever meditation we do in the Mahayoga style, the creation phase, relates to the deities that are part of our basic nature. We are meditating on the manifest appearance of these fundamental deities.

We have seen very briefly how we meditate on the primordially existent configuration that is naturally part of our body, the fundamental nature of both mind and body. This is the Mahayoga level. In Anuyoga, we work with the inner channels, the inner meridians. Although there are a countless number of them, there are three main channels in the body. We work with the main channels and the energy-winds. Based on control of the channels and energy-winds, we gain control of the vital essence of the body. Based on the vital essence, we try to undo all the knots in the channels through-out the body. Ordinarily, thoughts follow our inner energy. As our inner energy circulates, so do our thoughts. When our energy is blocked, or stagnant, we call it "karmic energy," and it creates our ordinary state, being lost in thought. When the channels in our body are untied, our energy transforms from karmic energy to wis-dom energy. Gradually, we gain pure appearance, because impure appearance is based on karmic energy. Based on wisdom energy, our mind is more refined. We are able to see more of the pure nature of the primordial configuration. On the level of Anuyoga, working with the channels, energy-winds, and vital essence of the body is the completion phase "with form," or "with characteristics."

Whether on the level of Mahayoga or Anuyoga, the view is of pure equanimity and the inseparable two truths (relative and absolute). When meditating in Mahayoga (the creation phase) or Anuyoga (the completion phase), we rest the mind without moving within the complete purity of great emptiness, the ultimate body of enlighten-ment. After the period of meditation, in the postmeditative state, we imagine everything, ourselves and all appearances, as having a divine nature. We imagine all beings as deities. We imagine all environments as celestial palaces or pure lands. We recognize, or understand, the view, get more and more familiar with it, and at the end, at the point of realization, we no longer have the experi-ence of subject and object, of oneself and the deity. We see all of this as having not the slightest bit of solid existence. We enter into great emptiness. This is called "the ultimate body of enlightenment without a body." *Chanting the Names of Manjushri* says that the supreme body is no body at all. This refers to the realization of the equanimity and purity of the inseparable two truths, the view of Mahayoga and Anuyoga.

The ultimate body of enlightenment without a body results from Mahayoga or Anuyoga practice. From within the ultimate body of enlightenment without a body, there appears its natural display, the body of enlightenment's perfect splendor. Once the body of enlightenment's perfect splendor arises from the ultimate body of enlightenment, it produces emanations both in pure and impure situations for the benefit of all sentient beings, which we identify as "the manifest body of enlightenment."

We've discussed the paths of Mahayoga and Anuyoga. Now we come to Atiyoga, the summit of all dharma paths, Dzogchen. It is the source of all transmissions, and the supreme stage of all the stages of development. It is far superior to both Mahayoga and Anuyoga. Atiyoga is also the direct, or close, path of all buddhas of the three times.

Practitioners of Dzogchen can be very acute and have the highest level of capability, but they can also be extremely lazy. This is not the case in a practice like Kalachakra, where you have to do many yoga exercises and meditations on energy-winds, which is very demanding. Very lazy people who have faith can receive the pointing-out instructions. For such a person, there is nothing whatsoever to meditate upon because the nature of mind, our natural enlightenment, has been pointed out directly. It is like displaying a bell and saying, "This is a bell." We see directly the nature of mind, and we reach some decision, or certainty, "There it is." Mipham Rinpoche says that it is just like somebody putting a finger right on this nature of mind and saying, "There it is." Pointing out the originally pure ultimate body of enlightenment is the heart of trekchöd practice. Thanks to these instructions, even a very ordinary person can gain the level of an awareness holder.

At this point in the text, we are still at the stage of developing the mind of awakening. Later we will go into the subject of Dzogchen in more detail.

Mahayoga, Anuyoga, and Atiyoga don't use the terminology of the five paths of awakening in Mahayana (cultivation, application, seeing, meditation, and the path beyond training). In the context of the higher tantras, we talk of the four levels of awareness holder. This is how we describe our progress through various stages. In the end, of course, we arrive at the state of the ultimate body of enlightenment: Vajradhara, or Samantabhadra. Whatever the name, it's the same ultimate body of enlightenment, the result of all of these stages.

We have briefly gone through the basis and paths of the three inner tantras. Now we come to describing the result, as explained in the context of the three inner tantras.

Rongzompa said that the essence of enlightenment is always the same. On the level of enlightenment, the only distinction, or enumeration, that we can make is in relation to the different qualities of enlightenment.

This stage, or level, of enlightenment has many names. The supreme level can be called "the level of the awareness holder." This refers to being free of any extreme. Holding the supreme awareness can be called "the holding of the vajra," which refers to nonduality. Or we can call it "the stage of supreme skillful means and transcendent knowledge," where skillful means is compassion and transcendent knowledge is emptiness. We can also call it the thirteenth stage of awakening, the stage of enlightenment.

The *Ornament of the Vajra Essence Tantra* talks about twelve stages of enlightenment. However, there isn't a hierarchy among the different stages; it's all one essence, but it's related to different qualities. There are twelve different aspects: emptiness is one, compassion another, the five wisdoms are five more, and the five families of enlightenment five more—twelve in all. There's no high or low. It's not like the bodhisattva paths.

Stages of enlightenment that are said to go beyond the final stage of enlightenment are called "all-illuminating" or "radiant." But these stages do not transcend the final stage of enlightenment. Without moving from the stage of the ultimate body of enlightenment, there is a compassionate blessing in the form of the different bodies and wisdoms of enlightenment. We're not departing from that enlightenment to go beyond it.

This point is important not only for persons reading texts in English; Tibetans reading books in Tibetan misunderstand talk about the twelfth, thirteenth, or fourteenth stages of enlightenment, that somehow they go beyond enlightenment; but they do not. Tibetans don't necessarily understand the dharma any better than Westerners. The stage of Buddha Samantabhadra, the Ever Excellent, is the primordial nature of mind. There are, in fact, no differences or distinctions in that primordial nature. It is one thing in itself. It is the primordial nature. To say that there is some hierarchy at the level of enlightenment is contrary to the teachings and logic.

Up to this point, I have described the basis, path, and result of the three inner tantras. To review: the basis of Mahayoga is inseparable purity and equanimity. The path is the phase of creation and the phase of completion. And the result is the state of Buddha Vajradhara.

The basis of Anuyoga is that all appearance is the configuration, or mandala, of Buddha Ever Excellent, Samantabhadra. Emptiness is the configuration, or mandala, of the female Buddha Ever Excellent, Samantabhadri. And the two as nondual are the configuration of their children, as it were, the male and female bodhisattvas. Although one says "children" (this is literally what the tantra says) and it may sound very strange, we have to understand that "nonduality" in this case is the mind of awakening.

The path of Anuyoga, like that of Mahayoga, has phases of creation and completion. Mahayoga emphasizes the phase of creation, and Anuyoga emphasizes the phase of completion. Both Mahayoga and Anuyoga lead to the result of the state of Buddha Vajradhara.

The basis of Atiyoga is original purity and spontaneous presence. The path is both trekchöd and thögal. The result of trekchöd is literally "freedom from atoms," or beyond atoms. The result of thögal is "the great transference."

We have been describing how to work with the ordinary mind, by calming the mind and practicing insight meditation, both during the period of meditation, when we see the nature of mind as like space, and in postmeditation, when we see every experience as like a dream, or a magical display. With practice and realization, we enter a very deep familiarity, or relaxation, within meditation. Finally, we gain control of "enlightenment that doesn't appear from the mind." We are not saying that the mind is a cause that later results in enlightenment. Rather, we recognize directly that the nature of mind is enlightenment. Enlightenment does not come from the mind, but we experience enlightenment directly in the expanse of the mind.

If we see enlightenment as being a product of the mind, the mind is lost in thought. If we think that the mind will create, or produce, enlightenment, that is also the mind lost in thought. If we see the nature of mind, which has no point of creation, no abiding, and no point of cessation, then this is enlightenment that has not come from the mind and has not been produced by the mind. When we see its ultimate nature, then we see enlightenment.

When we find the wisdom of natural awareness, when we get it, then we are free from clinging. Freedom from clinging is called "the self-manifest wisdom-body," or "natural wisdom-body." When we recognize the wisdom of natural awareness and are free from clinging, we have found "enlightenment that does not come from the mind."

Up to this point, and for quite some time now, we have talked about meditation and transcendent knowledge together, in the context of meditation. Thinley Norbu Rinpoche explains that this teaching is like medicine. It is a very important teaching because the Buddha's discourses say that it is more important to meditate on the meaning of the teachings for a day than to study and reflect upon them for an aeon. Why is this so? Because through meditation we go beyond, or transcend, the path of birth and death. We go beyond physical and mental suffering. Thinley Norbu Rinpoche asks us to keep that in mind.

We haven't finished the chapter on developing the mind of awakening. We are about to discuss transcendent knowledge, the sixth transcendent perfection.

## Transcendent Knowledge

Up to this point, we've discussed transcendent knowledge in the context of the fifth perfection, meditation. Now we will discuss it just by itself as the sixth perfection. When we talk about ordinary knowledge, we talk about knowing something precisely and applying that same knowledge to different situations. Transcendent knowledge goes beyond the extremes of ordinary reality to the noncomposite sphere. In the context of the six transcendent perfections, transcendent knowledge (Tib. *sherab*, literally the "most excellent consciousness") is a very fine, very astute mind.

In the *Guide to the Bodhisattva's Way of Life*, Shantideva said that transcendent knowledge is the main subject of the Buddha's teaching and that the other five transcendent perfections are just aids to the development of transcendent knowledge; as rivers flow and add to the ocean, the other five transcendent perfections flow into transcendent knowledge and wisdom. Shantideva stressed that all one's study and practice, including the first five transcendent perfections, are to be focused on the development of transcendent knowledge.

The great master Nagarjuna remarked that all the teachings of the Buddha fall into one of two categories: worldly relative truth and ultimate truth. I will first define these two categories. In *kundzop denpa* (relative truth), the first syllable *kun* means "all" and *dzop* means "artificial" or "unreal"—anything false, unreal, impermanent, or deceptive. In this context, *denpa* means "truth." Here, relative truth refers to any appearance that a sentient being perceives. Whatever appears directly to a god, that is the god's truth. Whatever appears to a hell being, that is the hell being's truth. My table, my teacup, and my glass of water are not necessarily true ultimately, but I experience them, so they are truths in the context of relative truths. Also, last night I had a dream; you can say that the dream is not true, but since it appeared to me, at least it is true in the context of relative truth. It is just how things appear to a sentient being. It can be called "temporary truth" or "truth within a certain circumstance" or "what appears real directly before a person." Any appearance to any sentient being or a bodhisattva, anything we consider to be the world, samsara, falls into the category of relative truth.

Now we come to the definition of *dondam denpa* (ultimate truth). In this case, *ultimate* means "unmistaken knowledge of the nature of reality." For example, if I identify my teacup as being emptiness, then I have identified its ultimate truth, or ultimate reality. We can say that knowledge is ultimate truth, or the nature of reality, and is what those who strive for liberation have in their sights, what they are aiming for. The nature of reality is what we call "ultimate truth." When we identify the nature of something unmistakably with nothing deceptive in that nature, then we have identified the ultimate nature. In this case, we define *truth* as the incontrovertible knowledge of the essence of the nature of reality. We see directly, precisely, and unmistakably the essence of the nature of reality.

It is traditional to first give a literal definition, then a classification, and finally the meaning. The classification of relative truth has two categories: genuine and misleading relative truths. Things that are true in the context of their appearance are "genuine," or "authentic," relative truth. For example, when it is dark outside and the moon rises, bringing some light, that is relative truth. It is a true appearance. The moon brings some light to the world during the night. If the moon only appears reflected in water, that is misleading; it looks like the moon, but it isn't the moon itself. So the reflection of the moon on water is a "misleading" relative truth. The distinction between genuine and misleading relative truths is based on how things appear in the world, whether they are as they appear, whether their relative reality corresponds or does not correspond to their appearance.

This discussion of transcendent knowledge is based on the texts of the Middle Way where we find four different characteristics of relative truth. However, the subjects of ultimate and relative truth are not just related to the Middle Way; understanding the Middle Way can also help us identify what we are doing in Dzogchen.

The first characteristic of relative truth is that the outer world appears in the same way to both the very smartest individual in this world and the most deluded fool who understands nothing at all. A mountain, a house, a teacup, or whatever—everything appears the same. This is our collective relative truth.

Second, relative truth is "workable." For example, the earth is solid. Water is wet. Fire is hot. Wind moves. Depending on the circumstances, fire will always behave in a certain way, water will always flow a certain way. Things act in ways that correspond to their own nature.

Third, relative truth arises through a collection of causes and conditions, based on things such as our senses, the way our aggregates work, the way things appear in the world, and the four elements.

Fourth, when any part of relative truth is examined, it proves to have no inherent existence, or nature. For example, saying that all experiences are like a dream, or a magical display, is relative truth. Even saying that everything is empty of inherent nature is relative truth, because it fits into one the four extremes, here the category of nonexistence, and thus is still within the conceptual domain of the mind. Any concepts that fall within the four propositions of existence, nonexistence, both, and neither are relative truth.

In the highest level of the Middle Way, "the Middle Way teachings of certain meaning," it is believed that every view, from those without an articulated belief system up to, and including, the Mind Only school, is misguided. At the lowest level, everything is believed to be real, permanent, with solid characteristics. People understand very gross impermanence, such as the fact that a person changes from birth to death, but not subtle impermanence—things change moment to moment. For instance, what a river was yesterday has completely changed from what it is today. The candle burning now will be different a moment later; its flame will pass on to something else.

The second level of misguided view is nihilism, which we've discussed. Nihilists don't believe that karma, negative emotions, or one's mind-stream will pass from the end of this life to another life. The opposite view, as we mentioned early on, is the eternalist view that posits the idea of God the Creator. Although there is no direct connection between humanity and God, there is still some way that a permanent, or eternal, god or creator exists. We consider this, as well, to be misguided relative truth.

Materialists, such as those of the Vaibashika school of Shravakayana, recognize the moment-to-moment experience of mind.

Our experience ceases in a moment and another takes its place. They understand that gross objects do not have ultimate existence, are just relative reality, but they attribute ultimate reality to indivisible atoms of matter and units of time, without which coarse experience could not exist. The meeting of the indivisible moment of mind, which is the basis of our subjective experience, and the atom, which is the basis of our objective experience, creates our sense of reality. This belief of the Vaibashika school is shared as well by the Sautrantika, the Traditionalist school of Shravakayana.

One step away from those philosophical schools is the Mind Only school. Followers of this school say that the indivisible atom and the indivisible moment of time do not exist. That view is a misguided relative reality because there is a basic contradiction in the idea of an atom being indivisible. They say, "You posit an indivisible atom, and you say that there are no parts to this atom. But if you have an atom, a particle of any sort, it must have sides. It must have a north, south, east, and west side. It must have corners. And if it has different corners, or parts, it must not be indivisible. Or if it is absolutely indivisible, how can other atoms be joined to it? How can they fit together if they are indivisible and completely separate from one another?" One way or another, the idea that an atom exists and that it is also indivisible, or without parts, is contradictory. These ideas are mutually exclusive.

The Mind Only school says that atomic things are not the basic building blocks of reality; they lack ultimate existence. This is a misguided relative truth. Instead, what we experience as reality has no fundamental nature but has arisen from the creation of our habitual tendencies within fundamental consciousness; that is, all appearances come from mind. It says that all our experience is a creation of our ordinary mind, which is a mind of delusion and confusion found within the boundaries of dualistic clinging, or dualistic experience. However, it posits a pure, natural clarity of mind beyond our dualistic experience that exists and is permanent. The Mind Only school says that this naturally clear mind beyond dualistic experience is the ultimate truth.

Then there is the Middle Way, the highest among all the views, up to and including causal Mahayana. The Middle Way view is that anything considered to have true, or real, existence reflects a misguided view or a misguided relative truth. In the Middle Way tradition, the nature of reality is all-pervasive emptiness, beyond either one or many.

We progress from the stage of an ordinary individual who doesn't reflect at all on the nature of reality and simply takes things as they are (to be existent and permanent) by questioning the nature of reality. As we go from that unreflective conclusion through the philosophies of the Shravakayana schools, then to the Mind Only school, and through different levels of the Middle Way, our intellect develops and gets subtler and subtler, until we come to the highest level of Middle Way philosophy, which does describe things as they are.

The Mind Only perspective is that the only thing that exists is the single mind that goes beyond dualistic experience, that everything else is misguided relative truth, and that this mind is the point of our investigation. There is nothing wrong with this view as long as we add the idea that the mind is empty. Then that view does not contradict the Middle Way view; in fact, it is the Middle Way view.

The Mind Only school posits a mind that exists beyond the range and limits of our ordinary dualistic experience. The Middle Way replies, "Show me this one thing." If the Mind Only school posits this mind as having real existence, then it must somehow exist. Or else it doesn't exist. One or the other. Can it be shown? If so, how? If it somehow has an existence, then like any other material form, it must have some parts. It must be approachable, if it exists as this school posits it. It must have some way of being classified or understood. Otherwise, if it cannot be shown, if there is nothing, then it doesn't exist. The Middle Way says, "The idea that the mind really exists is just an ordinary thought." Either it exists or it doesn't, or it's both or neither. The Mind Only school, positively, has recognized that the nature of mind goes beyond dualistic experience, but because it invests it with reality, or existence, it falls within the four extremes.

When one goes beyond the categories of existence, nonexistence, both, and neither, one is approaching the nature of mind.

From the perspective of the Middle Way, in all those philosophies, up to and including the Mind Only school, it is impossible to renounce samsara and it's impossible to reach liberation; they are all misguided relative truths because a person who believes these philosophies still clings to something as really existent.

What does the Middle Way believe? In the context of the nature of reality, or ultimate truth, this is the period of one's meditation experience. It is the inexpressible, inconceivable nature of reality. But first we will identify the postmeditative experience, which is considered to be genuine relative truth.

For a practitioner of the Middle Way school, at the time of postmeditation, all things are seen as appearing but unimpeded, like a magical display. All experiences, although they appear to have been born, or created, are in fact uncreated (like a dream). All the appearances of life, although they are without any fundamental existence, still appear. It is not nihilist to see things are nonexistent; things continue to appear even though they don't have fundamental existence, like the reflection of the moon on water.

Further, the Middle Way sees things as impermanent. Although there is an appearance, it doesn't last because it doesn't have a fundamental nature. It's always changing. An example of this is an echo. You say "ah" and "ah" comes back.

The Middle Way practitioner also sees things as not departing, literally, "not going." It's like an optical illusion. For example, if I am looking at a person's face and press my eyeball, I see two faces, neither of which is coming or going. It's an optical illusion, something to do with my eyes. In the same way, in their basic lack of fundamental reality, things do not change (do not "go").

All of these examples have to do with the lack of fundamental reality, or the lack of fundamental nature, of appearances. All things appear to cease, but they do not cease. Although they appear to have been created, they are not created. Although they appear to be permanent, they are not. Although they appear to come or to go, they don't. All of these examples are pointing to the same lack of fundamental nature.

There are eight examples of illusion: a magic display, a dream, the moon seen on water, an echo, an optical illusion, a mirage, a mirror, and a city of spirits. Reflect upon these eight examples and try to arrive at an understanding. They are extremely useful examples that permit us to arrive at a great understanding of our experience as sentient beings. If we see everything, all appearances, as being like an illusion or a magical display, then it is possible for us to let go of the attachment to the reality of things, to attain liberation. We have gone through other philosophies that don't permit us to abandon the idea of things being real or to attain liberation. But through these eight examples, we can.

These eight examples describe relative truth and provide the path for us to approach emptiness. If we see something that seems to exist, then we can recall, "Oh, this is like a magical display, like a dream, like the reflection of the moon on water." Understanding these examples and gradually applying them to our experience provide a path to the approach of great emptiness. When we arrive at the experience of great emptiness, we no longer need these examples.

When Lord Atisha went to Tibet, he thought, "My goodness! I've come to a country where there are no magicians. How can I explain emptiness and the illusory nature of all things to people who have never seen a magic show?" His Tibetan disciple Dromtonpa suggested that he teach that all things were like a dream. Dromtonpa said, "Even if we don't have magicians, at least we all have dreams. You can use that as the main example in your teaching rather than magic."

This subject is quite critical for us. Reflect upon it. If you don't get it at the beginning, reflect upon the examples. In the modern world, there are many examples of the illusory nature of things. You can think about movies or television. There are lots of opportunities to see, or experience, something that is an appearance without an underlying nature. As we reflect upon these examples and apply them to our experience, we can come to an understanding that will be very useful in a temporary way for our happiness and suffering, and ultimately it will lead us to abandon all karma and negative emotions. This is a really critical teaching.

Also remember that realizing the illusory nature of everything is still within the category of relative truth, not ultimate truth. Ultimate truth is the state beyond any thought, or concept, of existence or nonexistence. We don't think of things as being like or unlike a magic show. We go beyond all concepts.

One step beyond the Middle Way is tantra. In tantric philosophy, misguided relative truth is mainly the attachment that ordinary persons have to appearances and beings as impure. They believe that these exist. The genuine relative truth is to see all outer experience as being pure lands or celestial palaces and all sentient beings as having the pure nature of gods and goddesses.

Whether from the perspective of the sutras or the tantras, the two truths have three ways of appearing regardless of the level of philosophy. Misguided relative truth is the idea that something exists and is real exactly as it appears. Genuine relative truth is the idea that appearances are untrue, or false, like a dream or a magical display, but with clinging to that truth. When one transcends thoughts of both appearance and nonappearance, attachment and nonattachment, when there is no calculation at all in relation to the appearance of past, present, and future, this is the experience of the ultimate truth of the nature of reality—enlightenment.

Maitreya's *Changeless Nature (Uttaratantra)* says that completely impure experience is the experience of a sentient being, which is the misguided relative truth. A mixture of both pure and impure experience is the experience of a bodhisattva, which is the genuine relative truth. Completely pure experience is the experience of enlightenment, which is ultimate truth.

We have come now to the subject of ultimate truth, which is known by several terms, including the "sphere of totality" and the "state beyond any elaboration." There are different ways of getting to ultimate truth. One way is to approach the subject of emptiness.

Emptiness can be approached in a temporary way, as circumstantial emptiness—that is, to see, or experience, everything as if in a dream; to see that nothing has any substantial nature. This is the emptiness of nonexistence that we call either "temporary" or "circumstantial" emptiness, or "temporary" or "circumstantial" ultimate truth.

Ultimate truth beyond this temporary experience is beyond any concept of emptiness or nonemptiness, presence or lack of presence of ultimate nature. When we think to ourselves that all appearances arise but have no substantial reality, it is merely a concept, a thought. Going beyond the thought of emptiness, nonemptiness, both, or neither is ultimate truth.

One way to arrive at ultimate truth is through the process of study, reflection, and meditation. We begin by listening to, or studying, these subjects. We reflect upon them, and then we meditate on them. Gradually, through this process, we cut through our misunderstandings in relation to emptiness and ultimate truth.

A second way of approaching ultimate truth is through meditation practice but without study or reflection. During the state of meditation, we enter into ultimate truth beyond any of the extremes of existence, nonexistence, both, or neither. Then, in the postmeditative state, we see everything as like a dream, like a magical display.

Another approach to ultimate truth is through inference, or reasoning, without meditation. An ordinary individual hears a teaching, considers it, reflects on it, and through reasoning comes to certainty in relation to ultimate truth.

Then there are those who can see ultimate truth directly, not through inference or even through meditation. Everything is seen exactly as it is without any mental activity at all, like the taste of honey. One who is much more developed sees ultimate truth directly.

We have partial ways of approaching emptiness, or ultimate truth, through inference or through the temporary experience of emptiness, or ultimate truth, in different circumstances. The experience of emptiness, or ultimate truth, that goes beyond any limits or extremes is either "lesser emptiness" (ultimate truth with enumerations) or "great emptiness" (completely undifferentiated). Whatever the case, we must approach great emptiness, the experience beyond all limits or extremes, in stages through temporary, or limited, experience.

Nagarjuna explains that there is both appearance and emptiness: appearance is relative and emptiness is ultimate. Everyone begins in somewhat the same way by trying to superimpose the concept of emptiness on appearances. However, as we continue with the practice of trying to understand appearances and emptiness, they merge inseparably so that we see all appearances as empty instantly when they appear.

In the beginning, we think of emptiness as like empty space. However, Longchenpa said that understanding emptiness as like empty space is not very useful when you get angry at your enemies. Emptiness must come down to earth to be useful in our ordinary context of living. We don't have to change appearances or impose emptiness on top of them. That all appearances are emptiness inseparably is their primordial nature. There is an inseparable union of appearance and emptiness, which is also the inseparable union of relative and ultimate truth. We must not fall into the trap of seeing appearance as negative and emptiness as positive. There is equanimity in relation to appearance and emptiness. The essence of appearance is emptiness; and at the moment of appearance, there is emptiness as well. Emptiness appears as appearance. There is no moment of distinction between appearance and emptiness. At the very moment of appearance, the nature of this appearance is great emptiness. Even at the moment of emptiness, there is an appearance. Without the appearance diminishing, there is emptiness. Without the emptiness diminishing, there is appearance.

Absolute emptiness is the sphere of totality, beyond any extremes or limits, beyond the range of the conceptual mind, or intellect. To approach absolute emptiness, we work with an emptiness that we can relate to, or meditate on, emptiness related to particular circumstances or examples. We begin by identifying emptiness in various ways. For example, emptiness as the lack of a fundamental nature can be approached with an analytical mind. We analyze what we believe to exist, and we come to some conclusion about its existence or nonexistence as emptiness.

Our first impression is that everything we experience fundamentally exists. When we bring analysis to that first impression, we come to the conclusion that nothing fundamentally exists. When we see that there is no substantial reality, we see a negation of the first impression. To identify the lack of substance in something we experience is not to have identified its nature. We have negated our impression of existence. What we thought was solid and real we have seen as not solid or real. This is a negation of substantial existence and is as much a label, or a product, of conceptual mind as our first impression of existence. Since each impression of nonexistence is dependent upon an impression of existence, an appearance has neither existence nor nonexistence.

When we negate existence by nonexistence, these two are dependent upon one another in the same way that an insect's death depends on its first having been born. From there, we look at both existence and nonexistence. Both (1) the thought that things are both existent and nonexistent, and (2) the thought that things are neither existent nor nonexistent are attempts at finding the proper label to give to the nature of something. However, they both fall within the realm of mental fabrication, or thoughts related to the nature of reality. Mipham Rinpoche said that when we go beyond belief in existence, nonexistence, both, or neither, there is no other attitude, or mental construct, possible. Once we've gone beyond these four, our mind has no way left to approach the nature of reality of any object. Being free from these four, going beyond these four, is the sphere of totality, buddha nature, the nature of reality.

In the Middle Way, this analytical exercise is followed by meditating gradually on these four impressions—existence, nonexistence, both, and neither—and after progressing through these stages, the nature of reality is perceived directly. This is equivalent to the first level of awakening.

In tantra, and particularly in Dzogchen practice, although it's not wrong to go through these stages, generally speaking, that is not how the nature of reality is presented. We go straight to the point. The pointing-out instructions point out the nature of mind, the nature of reality.

How is the experience of meditation at this level explained? Shantideva said that when neither any material reality (the word *material* refers to all the objects of our senses, as well as the mind and all aspects of our consciousness) nor any nonmaterial reality (for example, space, or whatever is considered to be nonexistent or immaterial), neither existence nor nonexistence, is in the mind, at that moment, because there is no other possibility, the mind is not focused in dualistic experience and we enter into perfect, or profound, peace. When we say that "the mind is not focused in dualistic experience," it means that, within the sphere of totality, there is neither existence nor nonexistence. There is no concept. There is neither any object of experience nor any subject of experience. Because there is neither a subject nor object of experience, there is no existence or nonexistence, so the mind enters into perfect, or profound, peace because there is nothing to get lost in thought.

We can call this state "the sphere of totality," "the nature of reality," "the meditation of the exalted." It is difficult for us ordinary persons to approach the sphere of totality directly, so we begin by developing certainty in relation to the lack of inherent reality in our field of experience. We approach emptiness gradually through its different aspects, and in this way, gradually developing certainty at each stage, we can approach the sphere of totality.

It is ideal if our understanding, which we have gained through analytic Middle Way meditation, and our experience, which we have gained through pointing-out instruction in Dzogchen, meet and come together. Through Middle Way study and analysis, we feel very much like we are approaching the nature of reality—we haven't quite gotten it, but we have a strong impression that we're almost there. At that point, if we receive the Dzogchen pointing-out instruction, we go straight to the experience of mind and we realize that we've gone beyond what we were approaching through Middle Way analysis.

Atisha remarked that the supreme form of transcendent knowledge is not to have any attachment to reality or truth, be it relative or ultimate. The heart of transcendent knowledge is not to be obstructed by any consciousness or object of consciousness. Within the heart of transcendent knowledge, we arrive at the precise, or exact, realization of emptiness.

Those who are not able to approach this view of emptiness make a distinction between emptiness and appearance. They think they are two different things. They think emptiness is like empty space. In this way, the belief can form that there is no such thing as karma, cause and effect, the three jewels, or the ultimate body of enlightenment. This is the extreme of emptiness. Those at this level of intellect defeat their own purpose when they are unable to understand the union of emptiness and appearance.

If emptiness is understood as being emptiness at the moment of appearance—that is, that a thing appears but is empty of fundamental substance—that is not the absolute view, but it is not a fault. But thinking that, in order for something to be empty, it has to disappear, is not a correct view. For example, if a person who is really attached to eating lamb, killed a lamb and said, "This lamb doesn't really exist, and I as the killer of the lamb don't really exist," this would be a nihilistic view due to attachment.

The warning that a person who doesn't understand emptiness correctly causes their own downfall was given by Nagarjuna to point out that the basis of the path is the union of the two truths, relative truth and ultimate truth. Our path is the union of the cultivation of merit and wisdom, and they are cultivated together. The result of the path is the union of the two bodies of enlightenment, the formless body and the form body. Nagarjuna was pointing out that persons who do not understand emptiness miss the basis, the path, and the result.

The correct view in relation to transcendent knowledge is that it is inexpressible and inconceivable. Transcendent knowledge goes beyond the bounds of our ability to conceive or express such a thing. An image of the nature of everything is the essence of space, which has never come into being and will never cease. How can we know the nature of everything? It is not within the bounds of our ordinary consciousness. All of our sensory consciousnesses are tuned to subjective and objective experience. We experience objects only with our senses or our mind. The nature of everything is the experiential domain of our natural wisdom of awareness (which does not split experience into subjective and objective). Our ordinary awareness is turned toward other, but awareness of our own nature is not exteriorized. We're struggling for the opposite of externally oriented awareness. It is awareness aware of itself, perhaps. It is self-aware. But it is awareness without an object. We call it "natural awareness." This is the problem we have in trying to describe transcendent knowledge with the language of ordinary mind.

When we describe the sphere of totality and its nature, we don't fall into the extreme of either emptiness or appearance. It's not more one than the other. We say that the sphere of totality is like space, beyond all limits, beyond all extremes, without fundamental nature. This prevents us from falling into the extreme of appearance only. This is the emptiness aspect. From the side of appearances, emptiness is not an empty emptiness that cannot be experienced or is of no benefit to anyone. It is the domain of self-aware wisdom (or the wisdom of self-awareness). This means that we do not fall into the extreme of emptiness. There is the possibility of wisdom-awareness. We do not fall into either extreme of appearance or emptiness; the two are inseparable.

The wisdom of nondual great equanimity of appearance and emptiness is beyond any object, substance, or place. It is not partial. Therefore we call great emptiness "the supreme element of all circumstances." We have many ways of approaching great emptiness, many partial ways of understanding it. But at this point, wisdom goes beyond any localization or partiality within emptiness. It is the primordial nature of everything. It is not an intellectual conclusion. This wisdom is seen in the primordial nature of all things. Emptiness relieves all fear and suffering in samsara. Because emptiness reveals wisdom and clears away suffering and fear, we call it "the vajra of wisdom."

How is it that emptiness can be beneficial to us? How is it that clinging prevents us from reaching liberation? For example, on the Shravakayana path, the arhats of the listener level are liberated because they realize nonself. However, they don't arrive at total liberation because they have the dualistic clinging of belief in indivisible atomic particles and indivisible moments of consciousness. The arhats of the solitary sages are liberated because they have no clinging to objective experience, but they do not attain complete liberation because they cling to the reality of mind; they believe mind to be real, or existent. On the next level, those of the Mind Only school are liberated since they achieve freedom from all dualistic experience. But they do not attain total liberation to the extent that they still believe in an existent mind beyond dualistic experience. The lower level of those in the Middle Way are liberated in that they realize that ultimately nothing exists, but they remain without complete liberation because they believe on a relative level that things do exist.

Rongzompa pointed out that, at each level, the understanding of emptiness leads to some level of liberation, but what prevents the attainment of complete liberation is the presence of some clinging to materiality. Some part of clinging has not yet been released. He identified both the understanding of emptiness that leads to liberation and the clinging that prevents reaching liberation.

On the other hand, if we have no attachment to material reality whatsoever, but we also have no skillful conduct (that is, compassion), then what? It might be thought that if we don't have clinging to material objects, then we will stop having compassion and the skillful means that come from compassion. But if we have only the transcendent knowledge without compassion, then it's not possible to attain enlightenment, to reach freedom. Perhaps, at this point, this is what you may be thinking.

The answer is, yes, compassion must be developed toward sentient beings. However, it is not necessary to think of sentient beings as really existent. It is possible to develop illusory, or magical, compassion toward beings who are like a magical display and help free them from samsara, which is also like a magical display. So it's not necessary to fall into the extreme of feeling that sentient beings really exist.

The mind of a bodhisattva who develops compassion toward sentient beings with the thought that they really exist is impure because of this thought. For sentient beings, whose existence is as an illusion, a bodhisattva develops illusory compassion toward their illusory happiness and suffering, develops illusory aspirations, and works tirelessly for their benefit. Even though sentient beings do not have inherent existence and the appearances of their happiness and suffering are like a magical display, a bodhisattva develops compassion, tireless compassion, for them without attachment. This is great compassion. Rongzompa finishes by saying how emptiness relieves us of all fear and suffering. You don't have to be afraid of it, he said.

## Benefits of the Mind of Awakening

Shantideva said that when an individual develops the mind of awakening (relative or ultimate) through practicing the four immeasurables and the six transcendent perfections, resolving, "I will attain enlightenment for the benefit of all sentient beings," this person who had been a prisoner in samsara becomes known as a "child of the buddhas," an "heir of the buddhas," venerated by gods, humans, and all sentient beings.

That is a very brief explanation of the benefits of the mind of awakening. Shantideva's *Guide to the Bodhisattva's Way of Life* contains this quote and many others on the benefits of the mind of awakening. The *Flower Ornament Sutra* says that from the time a person develops the mind of awakening and for as long as they maintain it, their physical, verbal, and mental acts become meaningful and entirely virtuous.

This precious mind of awakening, wherever it is developed and maintained, is the basis of benefit for oneself and others, the basis of our life, and it creates the possibility of happiness in a temporary way. But more important, as we maintain the mind of awakening, it becomes more and more profound, more and more noble, leading us through all the paths and stages of awakening until full enlightenment. The maintenance of this mind of awakening has limitless, infinite benefits.

# CHAPTER 5

# Mandala Offering

In our Ngöndro text, we next read the declaration, "My bodies, wealth, and glories of all my lives I offer to the three jewels in order to complete the two accumulations [merit and wisdom]." This "offering of mandalas" is done in order to clear away the two obscurations: our obscuring emotions and our ignorance of the true nature of reality. We offer mandalas to very special recipients: the three jewels. Offering mandalas to the three jewels has both temporary and ultimate benefits. The ultimate benefit is that we manifest the nature of our mind, our buddha nature. At this time, our inner nature, the nature of enlightenment, is covered by transient, or incidental, obscurations. By making mandala offerings to the three jewels, we cultivate merit and wisdom in order to make this enlightened nature manifest.

In mandala practice, we use two physical mandalas. One is the offering mandala, which we hold in our hands, and the other is (literally) the practice mandala, which is placed on our shrine. The practice mandala symbolizes the recipient's field in which we cultivate merit and wisdom. In this case, the field is the unsurpassable three jewels.

We call the field for the cultivation of merit and wisdom the three jewels, but, in fact, we imagine the whole sphere of totality filled with an unimaginable number of different forms of buddhas and pure lands. All the buddhas and pure lands, the number of which is inconceivable, can be grouped into the five families of enlightenment. To represent all the buddhas of the five families, we make five piles of rice on the practice mandala that we place on our shrine, or we can use just one pile of rice to represent Guru Rinpoche. We put this object on our shrine to symbolize the recipient of our offerings. There is no contradiction between putting five piles of rice or just one. They both represent all buddhas, either as the five buddha families or as Guru Rinpoche. We make mandala offerings to the buddhas or Guru Rinpoche, feeling convinced that they are seated before us. There are many different families of enlightenment: three, five, twenty-five, or one hundred. Whatever the case, the number of buddhas in our visualization is inconceivable. However, if we wish to join them into a single form, it is the form of Guru Rinpoche, "joined into a single jewel."

Guru Rinpoche's body, speech, mind, qualities, and activities represent the union of all the families of enlightenment, every buddha without exception. His body represents the buddha family; the chief buddha of the buddha family is Vairochana, "The Illuminator." Guru Rinpoche's speech represents the lotus family of enlightenment; the main buddha of that family is Amitabha, "Infinite Light." His heart, or mind, represents the vajra family of enlightenment, here called the "unmoving" family of enlightenment, whose main buddha is Vajrasattva. His qualities represent the jewel (Skt. *ratna*) family of enlightenment, whose chief buddha is Ratnasambhava, "Source of Jewels." Guru Rinpoche's activity represents the karma, or action, family of enlightenment, whose main buddha is Amoghasiddhi, "Accomplisher of Aims."

If you don't have a second mandala to use as the practice mandala, then you can make offerings before a picture or *thangka* of Guru Rinpoche, a representation of his speech, or a representation of his form, like a statue. You can place that on the shrine to use as a support.

For the offering mandala, the very best material is gold, silver, or any other precious metal. It can be made of bronze or a nonprecious metal, and at the very least, you can even use a flat, smooth piece of wood.

When I go into town looking in the shops, I see lots of very wonderful plates or things that can be used as a support for mandala offering. You can be imaginative in what you use as an offering mandala, as long as you have very pure intention; you are looking for a support for your offerings. If, with this intention, you find something very beautiful and precious that you can actually afford, buy it and use it. If you can't afford something precious or particularly attractive, you can use stone, or wood, or anything at all. It really depends on your mind; with good intention, you can use anything as a support for your offerings.

The best mandala to offer is a supermarket. It has everything inside: food, drink—everything that you can imagine offering. Or you can go to a beautiful meadow with lots of flowers; or a place with lots of fruit trees, grapes, or grains; or the sight of the beauty of nature; or the beauty of any rich environment—any of these can be used as the support for your offering. When you go there, remember the lines in English or Tibetan, and say in effect, "I offer to the three jewels all my bodies and possessions, everything I hold precious or cling to, in this and every lifetime, in order to perfect the accumulation of merit and wisdom." This offering with a pure intention is the true mandala offering.

Whatever you are using, the surface should be wiped clean. The best offerings are gold, silver, turquoise, coral, pearls, diamonds, rubies, emeralds, or any other jewels. Next best are different forms of medicines or herbs. At least you can offer grains: rice, wheat, barley, and so forth, or whatever you want to offer with a pure mind, even chocolate, ice cream, or candies. Even if you have no money, don't feel that you can't make mandala offerings. Thinley Norbu Rinpoche says to remember that if you have nothing else, you can take earth or rocks or sand, clean them, and offer them to the three jewels. The idea is to make offerings to the buddha; it doesn't matter what you offer. Most important is your pure intention and your wish to make offerings to the buddha regardless of what you use as the support for mandala offerings. That intention, that wish to offer, perfects your cultivation of merit and wisdom; whereas, whatever you offer without pure intention, even gold, will have no effect.

In the *Guide to a Bodhisattva's Way of Life*, Shantideva said, "Even though I have no merit and I am very poor and I have nothing else to offer, for the benefit of others, I can offer myself to the three jewels. I can offer my own body and, mentally, all my possessions to the three jewels."

In *Words of My Perfect Teacher*, Patrul Rinpoche said that whenever you see a beautiful place, a beautiful woman, or anything attractive, you can mentally offer this to the three jewels. (It wasn't me who said this! It was Patrul Rinpoche.)

When the mandala prayer in the Ngöndro text says that we offer our bodies and possessions from all our past lives, it refers to our circling in samsara since beginningless time. We have had many lifetimes of wealth and splendor among the gods or human beings. We have created a lot of merit or done much virtuous activity during that time. We gather all the wealth, all the splendor, and all the merit and virtue from our past and present lives, everything we consider precious, valuable, or cherished, and offer it to the three jewels.

We offer the mandala thinking that, from this moment, when we have the freedoms and the acquisition of a precious human birth, until we attain full and complete enlightenment, we will offer all our bodies, possessions, wealth, and splendor to the three jewels in order to perfect the accumulations of merit and wisdom for ourselves and all sentient beings. Regardless of what kind of life we take in the future, whether on the Shravakayana, bodhisattva, tantric, or awareness-holders path, we wish always to continue to make this offering to the three jewels, until we attain enlightenment.

## The Two Obscurations

By making offerings, we cultivate merit and wisdom, and we clear away the two obscurations that we and all other sentient beings possess. The first obscuration is our negative emotions: mainly greed, anger, ignorance, pride, and jealousy—thoughts or feelings provoked by attraction toward the pleasing domain of our senses and rejection of what we consider to be threatening—that is, things that provoke our anger, fear, or some other separating emotional reaction.

The source of the obscuration of negative emotions is clinging to a self, feeling that a self exists. Our negative emotions spring from our perception of "me," "my hand," "my possessions," "my good qualities," and so on, as separate from everything else.

The second obscuration is the obscuration to knowledge. This refers to the thoughts connected to the "three spheres"—the three aspects of any act: the actor (the agent of activity), the act, and the object, or the domain, of that act. When you have thoughts, or concepts, about yourself as the agent, the thing you do, and the recipient of your act, this is the obscuration to knowledge. For example, when you perform an act of generosity, if you think, "I am giving a particular object to somebody else," there is either a gross or subtle clinging to self or other; it does not really fall into the category of a bodhisattva's conduct.

And when we consider anything that appears in the world to be existent, nonexistent, both, or neither; when we consider our aggregates to be a self; when we have any concepts or thoughts related to existence, nonexistence, both, or neither; when anything impedes, or prevents, our mind from seeing clearly and exactly the nature of reality, that is considered to be the obscuration to knowledge.

In Tibetan, the term for the obscuration to the objects of knowledge is literally "the mind is obstructed." When we consider things, we get stopped by the thought of their existence, nonexistence, both, or neither. This impedes our mind. We purify this obscuration by realizing the lack of a self of things. When the nature of reality is seen, the mind is completely unobstructed. Sometimes we may hear the phrase "passing through walls." This means that there is no obstruction for the mind. The two obscurations are, in short, our dualistic experience; the first obscuration is a misperception about self, and the second obscuration is a misperception about the field of experience. So the first obscuration is cleared by realizing the lack of a self of self. The second obscuration is cleared by realizing the lack of a self of things.

When we make vast offerings to cultivate merit, it allows us to attain the manifest body of enlightenment, with its thirty-two major and eighty minor marks of perfection—for example, the body of Buddha Shakyamuni. Or we will realize the body of enlightenment's perfect splendor. Through the cultivation of merit, these form bodies manifest. We cultivate wisdom when our cultivation of merit is guided by transcendent knowledge, in which there is no attachment to the agent, the object of offering, or the recipient of offering. Through the cultivation of wisdom, we attain the ultimate body of enlightenment.

Because our language can be deceptive, it is important to remember that we are not attaining the ultimate body of enlightenment as if our cultivation of wisdom were a cause and our attainment a result. Rather, through the cultivation of merit and wisdom and clearing away the two obscurations, we see our beginningless, primordial enlightened nature. The primordial ultimate body of enlightenment manifests to us. The sun is always in the sky; when the clouds disperse, the sun, which is always there, appears. So, too, our own inner nature fully manifests through the cultivation of wisdom.

Patrul Rinpoche said that it is impossible for us, as ordinary individuals, to have the experience of bodhisattvas who are completely unconcerned with themselves, the offering, and the recipient of the offering. We set up that goal, or ideal, but it is not possible for us to have that experience until we attain the first stage of awakening. Patrul Rinpoche said, and it is true, that what is important at this stage is to have positive intention. We aim in that direction, and we hit that target when we've arrived at the stages of awakening.

## Offering Technique

To make the offering, we take our offering plate in the left hand. It has to be clean to begin with. With the heel of the right hand (where the hand meets the wrist), we wipe off the surface, reciting either the one-hundred- or six-syllable mantra of Vajrasattva. To symbolize the surface being the golden foundation of the universe, we can put saffron water or perfume, anything with a pleasant smell, on the top of the base. It will be the support for our visualization of offering the whole universe to the three jewels. The universe has a golden foundation, so the surface of the offering plate symbolizes this golden foundation.

When we offer rice, or whatever, on top of the offering plate, we are not offering rice; we are offering all the worlds of the universe, including all the wealth, splendor, and glory of gods and human beings. The piles of rice are just symbols for the different aspects of the world.

We make the first pile of rice but we don't think of it as a pile of rice. We think that we are offering, at that moment, the supreme mountain at the center of the world. Then, making four piles of rice in the cardinal directions around the central pile of rice, we think that we are offering the four continents that circle the central mountain. Patrul Rinpoche said that you can consider the eastern direction toward yourself or toward the recipient of the offering. Either is okay. After placing the first five piles of rice, we make two more piles, one in the east and one in the west, representing the sun and the moon. This is the seven-point mandala. We make seven piles of rice representing the world, and we imagine it is filled with riches and anything worthy of offering. We imagine that we offer the world, multiplied hundreds of millions of billions of times, our body, and all our possessions of this and every lifetime to the three jewels, to Guru Rinpoche.

There is also a thirty-seven-point mandala in which we offer the central mountain, the four continents, and also their adjacent continents (eight others). Many other offerings are mentioned in the thirty-seven points. But they are also all gathered in the seven-point mandala offering. When we offer the seven-point mandala, we think that all the extensive offerings are gathered in the offering of the central mountain, the four continents, and the sun and moon. There is no real difference; just the list of offerings differs.

Regardless of what we offer—rice, gold, earth, grains, anything— they are just symbols of our offering. We gather everything wonderful, everything that can be made an offering, everything in the entire universe that we wish to offer into the mandala offering, and we multiply it hundreds of millions of times and make our offering. By focusing our consciousness on Guru Rinpoche with all the enlightened qualities he represents, we accumulate merit from expressing positive energy. By offering the magnificence of everything imaginable, our entire experience takes on extraordinary meaning.

When putting our offerings on the plate, we should think, "I am offering the central mountain to Guru Rinpoche." Putting offerings in the east, think, "I am offering the continent called Noble Body and all its wealth and splendor to Guru Rinpoche." Putting offerings in the south, think, "I am offering this world of Jambu and all its wealth and splendor to Guru Rinpoche." At each point, remember the essence, the point, of what we are doing. We are not just offering grains of rice or whatever.

Everything that we could possibly offer is offered by the mandala offering. Right now, at our own stage of development, we should be doing mandala offerings as a form of generosity, with no expectation of return. We can think that the whole world is gathered in the offering. For example, we can offer the Himalayas at the center, Japan in the east, Australia in the south, Canada or the United States in the west, and Europe in the north. We have no experience of the other continents described in traditional cosmology, the continent Bountiful Cattle and so on; however, we do understand this world and so we can imagine offering the parts of this world that we know. To offer the rich and wonderful places in this world is just fine. It has the same meaning as offering the grandiose continents of ancient cosmology. It is a little bit smaller in scale than the cosmic mandala offering, but we can relate to it. Understand that when you offer Japan or continents or places, they are just symbols of all the wealth and splendor of gods and human beings that it is possible to offer.

In some other foundational practices, taking refuge and the development of the mind of awakening are followed by Vajrasattva practice. However, in the Dudjom Tersar lineage, the mandala offering precedes Vajrasattva practice. We begin by visualizing Guru Rinpoche as our refuge. Then thinking of him as our witness, we develop the mind of awakening, the wish to attain enlightenment for the benefit of all sentient beings, and we dedicate ourselves to that. Next, we consider Guru Rinpoche as the recipient of our mandala offerings. Throughout these stages, we consider Guru Rinpoche as sitting before us, being our refuge, our witness, and the recipient of our offerings. In the mandala practice, we either try to accumulate one hundred thousand mandala offerings or, at the very least, we recite the prayer for the mandala offering three or more times a day.

At the end of our recitation, we imagine an infinite amount of light radiating from Guru Rinpoche's body, which touches us and all sentient beings. This light clears away our two obscurations and perfects our cultivation of merit and wisdom, and then we imagine that we, the offerors of the mandala, and all sentient beings dissolve together into the mandala being offered. The offering mandala dissolves into light and is absorbed into Guru Rinpoche, and we let our mind rest without any thought of offeror, offering, or recipient of offering. We rest our mind without any thought of subject or object. We relax for as long as possible in that state.

If you are doing just the accumulation of mandala offerings, you finish with prayers and the dedication of merit. If not, after you have finished the period of meditation, you go on to the practices of Vajrasattva and Guru Yoga, and so on.

## The Benefits of Making Offerings

We make both real offerings of what we put on our mandala plate and, particularly, mental offerings. Whether the offerings are on our shrine, on our mandala plate, or made with our mind, the temporary benefit of making such offerings to the three jewels is that we gather an inconceivable amount of merit. We also plant a seed of positive tendencies in our mind, which results later in the attainment of wealth and splendor in the worlds of gods and human beings. This is the temporary benefit of making mandala offerings.

Ultimately, mandala offerings allow the body of enlightenment's perfect splendor to manifest.

It is said in the *Secret Essence Tantra* that no wish-fulfilling tree, no wish-fulfilling jewel, and no desirable object is substantial. They come into being thanks to the merit in our own mind. None of the amazing,* miraculous displays of anything that appears nor any of the qualities of the different bodies of enlightenment come from outside of ourselves. These amazing qualities depend upon skillful means and transcendent knowledge for their manifestation. The benefits of mandala offerings are thus inconceivable.

Mandala offerings are a practice shared by both sutra and tantra. In the tantric tradition exclusively, mandala offerings are included in the practice of *tsok* offerings. There are many different levels of tsok offerings: outer, inner, and secret. Mandala offerings form part of that practice.

Outer tsok offerings appear very much like mandala offerings. The inner tsok offering is connected to the channels, energy-winds, and vital essence of the body. The secret tsok offerings are awareness and ultimate wisdom. The mandala offering falls into those categories as well. We can also make mandala offerings of the ultimate body of enlightenment, the body of enlightenment's perfect splendor, and the manifest body of enlightenment.

---

*Orgyen Chowang Rinpoche has explained what *amazing* means when used in a dharma context as follows: First, the amazing thing startles us with the recognition of its significance. Second, finally understanding the true nature of the mind and reality is a marvelous event. Third, the amazing thing is beyond description or conceptualization, so *amazing* (or a similar exclamation) is the only way to verbalize our reaction.

# CHAPTER 6

# Vajrasattva

The Dudjom Tersar Ngöndro text next says, "Above the crown of my head is Vajrasattva, who is inseparable from the lama. From Vajrasattva's body flows a continuous stream of crystal moonbeam nectar, and all obscurations are purified."

Now you might think, "So far, we've taken refuge, developed the mind of awakening, and offered mandalas to the lama in the form of the embodiment, or the epitome, of all buddhas of the past, present, and future as Guru Rinpoche. Why do we have to change the practice now, visualizing a different buddha?" In essence, all the different forms of enlightenment are the same. They are inseparable from one another. Guru Rinpoche, Vajrasattva, and especially our root lama can represent any form of enlightenment. The various, inconceivable number of forms represents the specific qualities of the enlightened mind, or our teacher.

Our precious teacher isn't an ordinary individual. An ordinary individual has a mind-stream separate from somebody else's. Our dharma teacher has a job, an appearance, a personality, and other characteristics, and ordinary individuals have their own jobs, appearances, personalities, and other qualities; but there is a difference between these two persons. For beings such as Guru Rinpoche, Vajrasattva, and our dharma teacher, we do not consider one form to contradict any other form. The essence of the enlightened mind is the same regardless of the form. There's no difference between the Guru Rinpoche whom we imagine at the time of taking refuge and the Vajrasattva, who is permitting and enabling us to purify karma and obscurations, whom we now imagine at the crown of our head. The qualities they emphasize differ only in our perception.

## Aspiration

We may think that buddhas and bodhisattvas are just ordinary sentient beings who began their path of seeking truth, developed the mind of awakening, and worked for the benefit of others, but this relates only to appearances in the domain of ordinary beings. There are stories about buddhas and bodhisattvas—how they developed the mind of awakening, the aspirations that they made, how they accomplished those aspirations, and the results they produced. In fact, however, these buddhas and bodhisattvas are primordially pure. There is no path in their own appearance.

Each of the eight forms of Guru Rinpoche appeared to go through a process of enlightenment. As Lodon Chokse, he learned how to read and write, studied teachings, learned different levels of tantra and Dzogchen, and attained enlightenment. In the form of Padmasambhava, he gradually learned all the teachings and arrived at realization. As Sakya Senge, he first studied the dharma, received pointing-out instructions, recognized the view, and traveled the path to enlightenment. However, Guru Rinpoche himself had no need to study and practice; he presented himself in these ways for the benefit of others. He was able to guide beings by showing up in outer forms that conformed to the ways of the world. There was, in fact, no need for these forms of Guru Rinpoche to follow that progression.

Similarly, when Vajrasattva appeared as a bodhisattva (he was a great bodhisattva), he made the aspiration that when he attained enlightenment, he would have the power to relieve the negative karma of any beings who envisioned him above their heads and prayed to him. Thanks to this aspiration, later, at the time of the Buddha, he manifested this power. Although all buddhas have the capability of purifying negative karma and obscurations, due to his aspirations, Vajrasattva is the specialist in that process. So this is the practice to purify obscurations.

Another example of how bodhisattvas' aspirations differ concerns Tara. When Tara first developed the mind of awakening, she remarked that most bodhisattvas appeared in the form of men: Chenrezig (Avalokiteshvara), Manjushri, and many, many others. She determined that during the path to enlightenment and after attaining buddhahood, she would always be born as a woman.

The bodhisattva Chenrezig made the aspiration never to pass into full and complete enlightenment until all samsara was emptied. The bodhisattva Manjushri made the aspiration to relieve the ignorance of all sentient beings through knowledge, worldly and transcendent. The bodhisattva Vajrapani made the aspiration to powerfully overcome all impediments and obstacles to sentient beings' attaining enlightenment. But there's no difference at the level of enlightenment between one bodhisattva and another. It's in their activity for the benefit of others that we see differences. The activity of Chenrezig and his emanations is in the form of compassion. The emanations of Manjushri enlighten others through their teaching of the development of knowledge, or wisdom. Vajrapani teachings have the effect of subduing all obstacles and impediments on the path to enlightenment.

We can understand the nature of some bodhisattvas by looking at their symbols and at how they are represented. Chenrezig holds a white lotus in his hand as a symbol of purity, that his mind has no faults; his eyes look directly with compassion toward all sentient beings. Manjushri holds a sword as a symbol of clearing away the darkness of sentient beings' ignorance. The sword is not a symbol of battle; he's not going to strike anybody with his sword. It's a symbol of his transcendent knowledge. Vajrapani holds a vajra in his hand as a symbol of his ability to overcome all obstacles and impediments on the path to enlightenment.

Consider Buddha Shakyamuni. Many of the 1,002 buddhas of this aeon made their aspirations to be a buddha during times on earth when people were fairly evolved, lived a long time, had minds fairly free of negative karma and obscurations, and life was fairly comfortable. On the other hand, when Buddha Shakyamuni developed the aspiration to be a buddha, he decided to come at the time of the five degenerations, when life expectancy shortened to one hundred years and very great negative emotions predominated. As a bodhisattva, he made five hundred different prayers, or aspirations, for his activity during this particularly difficult time. On the basis of those aspirations, the buddhas praised him as being like a white lotus, the most pure, or valued, among all lotuses, because his aspiration to help beings at this very difficult time was superior to all other bodhisattvas' aspirations for this aeon. It is said that through the force of his very positive aspiration, merely hearing the name of Buddha Shakyamuni gradually leads one to the state of "no turning back" on the path away from samsara.

Another example of the aspirations of bodhisattvas bringing results comes from another day and age in Nepal. A chicken farmer and her four sons built the main Boudhanath Stupa. When they were finishing the very top of the stupa, her sons made aspirations. One wished to take rebirth in the form of a king, in order to be the patron of the buddhadharma. Another aspired to be born miraculously and to be able to take all humans, gods, and demons under his control. A third wished to be the abbot of a great foundation of the Buddha's teaching. The fourth wished to bring the other three together. In one of the sutras, the *Reply to the Questions of the Pure Goddess*, the Buddha predicted that the buddhadharma would spread from India in the northern direction. It did spread from India to Nepal, from Nepal to Tibet, and from Tibet to Mongolia and other northern regions. The buddhadharma spread in Tibet due to the abbot Shantarakshita, the master Padmasambhava, and the king Trisong Deutsen.

When King Trisong Deutsen was a young man in his late teens or very early twenties, he looked at the papers left by his father and his predecessors back to the time of Songtsen Gompo, the first king of Tibet to follow the Buddha's teachings. They all had made the wish for the dharma to spread through the country. King Trisong Deutsen decided that one of his activities as king should be to encourage the spread of the buddhadharma in Tibet. Because a temple was necessary for dharma practice, he decided to establish a temple at a site called Samye, an inconceivable place.

He started the construction of the temple, but whatever was done during the day was mysteriously destroyed during the night. He decided to invite a master from India to consecrate the ground, because he thought that then the temple could be completed. He invited Shantarakshita (Tib. Khenpo Bodhisattva) to Tibet to consecrate Samye, who did so with the thought of great compassion. They resumed the construction, but once again, whatever they built during the day, they found in ruins the next morning. The king asked Shantarakshita, "What's going wrong?" Shantarakshita said, "I've blessed the ground out of compassion, but you need more forceful, wrathful activity in order to bring the gods and demons of Tibet under control. I suggest you invite the great master Padmasambhava from India to come here and consecrate this work." The king said, "That's impossible. We'll never be able to bring such a sublime master here. He'll never come."

At that point, Shantarakshita related the story of the four sons in Nepal. He said, "Padmasambhava will come to Tibet because previously he made this aspiration to come." So a messenger, Nanang Dorje Dudjom, and a few companions were sent to India to invite Guru Rinpoche to come to Tibet. Shantarakshita said, "Nanang Dorje Dudjom is the man to send to invite Guru Rinpoche because he also has a previous connection and aspiration." (Nanang Dorje Dudjom was the reborn fourth son.)

Guru Rinpoche already knew they were coming. He went as far, perhaps, as Pharping, Nepal, to meet them. He agreed to come to Tibet and told them to return, that he would be following. He came, and on his way, the gods and demons created many apparent obstacles, like lightning and so forth, to block his way, but through his miraculous power, he overcame all the malevolent forces. Through his view, or his meditation, he forced them to protect all dharma practitioners and not harm any. Thanks to Guru Rinpoche, many groups of gods and demons are now dharma protectors, such as the twelve *tenma* goddesses, the twelve *yama* gods, Tseringma and her sisters, and so forth. They were brought to the dharma by Guru Rinpoche at that time, and Tibet became filled with dharma protectors.

When Guru Rinpoche met these gods and demons, he said, "I'm not asking a whole lot of you. You must confess, or acknowledge, your negative acts of the past, promise not to harm any sentient beings from now on, and protect the dharma teachings." He placed his vajra on their heads, gave them nectar to drink, and gave them this vow. Until this day, they remain our protectors. At the end of many of our rituals, we make offerings of *tormas* that we throw outside, such as offerings to the twelve tenma goddesses, because Guru Rinpoche ordered them to help all dharma practitioners who make torma offerings. These goddess protectors have become companions to meditators.

Perhaps you have heard of the Nechung Oracle. When the Dalai Lama has questions that he can't answer himself, questions are asked of this oracle. The Nechung Oracle was once a very terrible, very negative demon called King Pehar. Guru Rinpoche overcame his negativity, placed his vajra on his head, gave him nectar to drink, and said, "All right. From now on, you must not harm any sentient being. If you break your vows, your body will split into hundreds of thousands of pieces." He installed this demon as one of the guardians of Samye Monastery. King Pehar became the personal protector of the great Fifth Dalai Lama. Up to the present day, the Nechung Oracle, when possessed by this protector, responds to questions from the Dalai Lama or others. This protector, like so many others in the Tibetan world, originate from the activity of Guru Rinpoche.

To continue our story, Guru Rinpoche, Shantarakshita, and King Trisong Deutsen (who were the reborn incarnations of the first three sons) finally met each other in Tibet. Thanks to that meeting and their activity, the buddhadharma became firmly established in Tibet. As mentioned in the life story of the translator Vairochana, Guru Rinpoche foretold that Vairochana would be the great translator for that era. Vairochana and the other translators translated everything from the Shravakayana tradition up to and including all the luminous Dzogchen teachings into Tibetan. From that time, thanks to the aspirations of the abbot, the master, and the king, the buddhadharma shone like the sun in the Tibetan region.

In the same way that the abbot, the master, and the king were able to act for the benefit of all sentient beings thanks to their previous aspirations, those of us who follow in their footsteps should make aspirations. Through the force of the truth of these aspirations, they will come to fruition.

## Meditation on Vajrasattva

To meditate on Vajrasattva, we begin in our own form, not changing the impression of our own body. Immediately above our head, we envision a thousand-petaled open lotus. On top of the lotus is a flat disk of the moon, very pure and white, and above that is our root teacher, be it Dudjom Rinpoche, Thinley Norbu Rinpoche, or whoever, in the form of Vajrasattva. The essence is the same, but the appearance aspect is different. When we are meditating on refuge, on developing the mind of awakening, and on mandala offerings, we imagine Guru Rinpoche in the sky before us, facing us; in this case, Vajrasattva faces the same way as us, outward. Vajrasattva rests one cubit (the distance from the elbow to the tip of the middle finger) above the crown of the head, whatever distance feels comfortable.

Vajrasattva is youthful, brilliantly white, completely pure, incomparably radiant like the sun. In his right hand, he holds a golden five-pointed vajra at his heart, and a bell in his left hand. He sits in vajra posture, or full-lotus position. His hair is blue-black in color, piled up on the crown of his head, and adorned with jewels. He wears five articles of silk clothing: an upper garment, a lower garment, multicolored ribbons on his crown, a long silk scarf that looks like a *kata*, and a jacket, or a shawl, on the upper part of his body. We try as much as possible to create this visualization. Vajrasattva (and most peaceful deities in sambhogakaya form) wears eight jeweled ornaments: a crown, earrings, one necklace just around the neck, one midway to the chest, one down to the navel, bracelets and armlets, anklets, and a belt.

Vajrasattva embraces his consort, Nyemma Karmo (Vajratopa), who is also white in color and looks like a sixteen-year-old girl, stunningly beautiful. She is wearing five kinds of jewelry, which represent her possession, or that she is the epitome, of the five wisdoms of enlightenment. At the crown of her head are wheel ornaments representing her wisdom of the sphere of totality. Her earrings (women's earrings are longer than men's) represent her embodiment of the wisdom of discrimination, or discernment. Her necklaces represent her wisdom of equanimity. Her belt represents her all-accomplishing wisdom. And her bracelets and anklets represent mirrorlike wisdom. In her right hand, she holds a cutting knife with a semicircular blade and a vajra handle. With this, she has her arm around the back of the neck of Vajrasattva. In her left hand, up fairly high, she holds a skull-cup. She is sitting in the lotus posture, with her legs around the body of Vajrasattva.

Vajrasattva and his consort appear with the nine aspects of peaceful deities in union—delicate, flexible, intertwined, graceful, youthful, light, shining, glorious, and radiant. The forms of deities in sexual union are part of the special teachings of the highest tantras. They represent the inseparable union of appearance and emptiness. More particularly, the appearance aspect of inseparable emptiness and great exaltation is Vajrasattva in sexual union. The forms of deities in sexual union are symbols of the nature of all sentient beings' minds. The nature of the mind is the inseparable union of great exaltation (or great bliss) and emptiness. In order to have a reference point and focus for meditation, to see some symbol of the nature of our mind, we have these various forms. It's not as if Vajrasattva and his consort have fallen in love or are making love in a very ordinary way. In our practice of tantra, the appearance of deities in sexual union, representing appearance and emptiness, allows us to realize the wisdom of great exaltation and emptiness.

In the heart of Vajrasattva, at the very center of his chest, we imagine the flat disk of the full moon. Standing on the disk is a five-pointed crystal vajra, in the central sphere of which stands a white syllable *hung* encircled by the one hundred syllables of the Vajrasattva mantra. The arrangement of the syllables of the hundred-syllable mantra is as follows: Take a piece of paper with writing on it and curl it with the syllables facing outward. They start in front and go around toward the left, counterclockwise. But to be read, they must turn clockwise. Generally, it is this way with male deities. For most female deities, you would curl the paper with the syllables on the inside, arranged to the right, clockwise, but turning counterclockwise.

This is just a general rule. Some female deities' mantras face outward, and some male deities' mantras face inward. For example, in the meditation on the peaceful and wrathful deities, we say, "Male deities turning right, female deities turning left." As we gain stability and skill in meditation on the mandala of the peaceful and wrathful deities, we can imagine many hundreds of deities with the male deities' mantras turning clockwise and the female deities' mantras turning counterclockwise, all at the same time. We begin with the peaceful deities, maybe adding males first and then females, then the wrathful deities, males first and then females, in whatever order, but we work in stages.

Try to imagine each of the mantra syllables as finely drawn as possible. The finer, the better, for meditation practice. If you can't do it so fine, imagine something coarser.

In the empty space of the central sphere of the crystal vajra is the syllable *hung* surrounded by the mantra. In commentaries, the *hung* is said to be facing either outward or sideways. In any phase of creation meditation, the point is for the practitioner to meditate however it is easiest to develop clarity in meditation. Sometimes it says, "Begin with the syllable facing outward, and if you can really meditate clearly, meditate with the central syllable sideways." There is no real difference. It depends on which way allows you a clearer meditation.

The first syllable of the hundred-syllable mantra is *om*. Thinley Norbu Rinpoche refers to *om* as "supreme praise." In the *Secret Essence Tantra*, *om* indicates auspiciousness and blessing, so it begins almost every mantra. We can think of it as praise to Vajra-sattva or to all buddhas.

The second series of syllables is *vajra sattva samaya*. *Vajrasattva* means "mind warrior" and *samaya* means "tantric commitment." *Vajra* refers here to the nondual nature of everything. *Mind* refers to the nondual experience. *Warrior* refers to remaining in the state of nondual experience of the nature of everything. This is the ultimate meaning of the name *Vajrasattva*. The form of the deity Vajrasattva is the manifest display, or symbol, of this state. The tantric commitment means the connection between the ultimate and the display. Vajrasattva's commitment is the nondual essence of everything, and our commitment is to realize this.

Then, *manu palaya vajra sattva* is a cry, or plea, to Vajrasattva to protect, or nurture, us. One way to express this is "Please grant your protection, Vajrasattva."

Then, *tenopa tit'hra dridho mebhawa*: We ask Vajrasattva to remain firm, remain stable within. Once our negative karma and obscurations have been cleared away, we request that his body, speech, and mind qualities remain firmly within us.

*Suto khayo mebhawa*: "Make me totally satisfied." Satisfaction means to be granted both temporary and permanent accomplishment.

*Supo khayo mebhawa*: "Increase the positive within me" refers to all the qualities of the bodies and wisdoms of enlightenment, the experience of buddha nature. We ask that these be increased in our experience.

*Anu rakto mebhawa*: This literally means "Have passion toward me" or "Be loving toward me." This is tantric language. It means "Have compassion for me."

*Sarwa siddhi me pra yatsa*: "Bestow all the accomplishments." The accomplishments here are the ordinary accomplishments of pacifying, enhancing, magnetizing, and overpowering activities and the ultimate accomplishment of enlightenment.

*Sarwa karma su tsa me*: This asks for the achievement of all activities to be bestowed.

*Tsittam shri yam kuru*: "Make my mind virtuous" means that once our negative karma, obscurations, and negative emotions are cleared away, our mind turns entirely to the path of enlightenment.

*Hung*: This represents the vitality, or the life force, of the heart of Vajrasattva. The syllable *hung* is inseparable from Vajrasattva— Vajrasattva is the syllable *hung*; the syllable *hung* is Vajrasattva. All the other syllables of Vajrasattva's mantra are supplementary or auxiliary. This is the main syllable. It can be considered the causal syllable, or the vital heart, of Vajrasattva.

*Ha ha ha ha*: These represent the four immeasurables (love, compassion, sympathetic joy, and equanimity), the four joys (joy; supreme joy; coemergent, or special, joy; and joyless joy), the four empowerments (the vase empowerment, the secret empowerment, the knowledge and wisdom empowerment, and the precious word empowerment), and the four bodies of enlightenment (the ultimate body of enlightenment, the body of enlightenment's perfect splendor, the manifest body of enlightenment, and the essential body of enlightenment).

*Ho*: This is the sound of Vajrasattva's joyous laughter as he benefits sentient beings, or it's the laughter of the realization of the nature of reality.

*Bhagawan sarwa ta t'hagata*: "Victorious One who embodies all the tathagatas." *Bhagawan* is "conqueror" and *ta t'hagata* is "transcendent ones," which refers to the buddhas, they who pass beyond, go beyond, or come from beyond. It refers to the five main buddha families of enlightenment.

Next is *vajra ma me muntsa*: "Vajrasattva, don't abandon me!" but purify all my faults and broken tantric commitments and, ultimately, guide me to full and complete enlightenment.

*Vajri bhawa*: "I pray that I may become a vajra holder." In fact, it is asking Vajrasattva to make us exactly like he is: "However you are, help me become exactly like that."

All of the above represents Vajrasattva's commitments.

*Maha samaya sattva*: "Bestow the empowerment or accomplishment" or "Don't abandon me" or "Satisfy my mind."

The *ah* at the end is to enter into union with Vajrasattva in a state of enlightenment.

## The Four Forces

The complete visualization of all the aspects of Vajrasattva and his consort, with all their clothing and ornaments, together with the Vajrasattva mantra comprises the "force of support" in Vajrasattva meditation, the first of four such forces.

We give our attention fully to Vajrasattva at the crown of our head. We consider Vajrasattva to be our root lama, as well as the union, or epitome, of the buddhas of the past, present, and future. We consider that we have had many lifetimes in the past among all the six realms of beings and during this time we have acted negatively. We have committed many of the nonvirtues. We turn our mind fully to Vajrasattva. We have full confidence and faith in Vajrasattva, not from our mouth but from the bottom of our heart. With great regret for any nonvirtuous, or negative, things that we might have done in the past, we pray for all our negative karma and obscurations to be cleared away through his blessing. This is the second force, the "force of turning away," or the "force of changing one's way," sometimes called the "force of regret" or the "force of remorse."

We acknowledge all our negative karma and obscurations of the past. Among these are the five acts of immediate retribution that create the cause for rebirth in the lowest of the hells, the hell of suffering without respite, the worst of all acts one could commit: to kill one's father, to kill one's mother, to kill an arhat, to cause a buddha to bleed, and to split the practitioner, or monastic, community. Whether in this life (remembered or not), or in any of our previous lifetimes, we acknowledge that we have committed these acts.

The acts close to immediate retribution are the five other extremely serious acts: to have sexual intercourse with one's mother or with a female arhat, to kill a bodhisattva, to kill someone who is on the higher stages of development to become an arhat, to steal any of the possessions of the monastic community, and to destroy a stupa. Even if we have no memory of having committed seriously negative acts, we still acknowledge that in previous lifetimes we may have done so.

We acknowledge, as well, having broken the vows of personal liberation (the novice vows or full monk, or nun, vows), the layperson vows, the vows of bodhisattva training, and any of the tantric commitments, regardless of the level. From our heart, we think, "From now on, even if I lose my life, I won't commit these acts again."

Then, we recite the hundred-syllable mantra of Vajrasattva. At this point, we imagine that from the vajra in the center of Vajrasattva's heart and the circle of mantra syllables, pure white nectar fills the body of Vajrasattva and his consort, descends through the point of their sexual union down the stem of the lotus into our body through the crown of the head, and causes all sickness, mental disturbances, negative karma, and obscurations to pass out of our body. We imagine that this is expelled through the anus, the path of urine, and all our pores. All the heaviness, the solidity of our past acts and negative karma, passes out of our body entirely and descends to the depths below in the earth. We imagine that in those depths are the lords of our karmic debts. There is no distinction between singular and plural in Tibetan, so it can be one, two, or many. Each one can be male or female. Whether we are aware of these karmic debts or not, if we don't repay them, they will come back later in this life or in future lives. For instance, having beaten or struck other persons can cause great sickness and physical discomfort; having killed many beings can cause a short life span; having stolen can cause poverty. So we imagine that all our negative karma and obscurations leave our body, go down very deep into the earth, and enter the mouth of the lords of our karmic debts, causing them great joy and pleasure. We repay our karmic debts in this way.

Through meditating on the lama as Vajrasattva, we should develop confidence that whatever negative acts we have done in the past are purified. However many or few, however great or minor, all negative acts can be purified through the four forces of Vajrasattva meditation. However, the key words here are "the *four* forces." One must have all four forces together. It's not just naturally that negative karma and obscurations will be purified. We must bring the four forces to this meditation.

Through the force of absorbing the nectar from Vajrasattva, our body turns radiantly pure and luminous like crystal, filled with great bliss and exaltation. This is the third force, the "force of remedial activity," or the "force of the antidote." We are counteracting our previous acts by a different act.

We begin the meditation with the development of faith and devotion to Vajrasattva, the force of the support represented by our visualization. We continue with great regret in relation to our past karma and obscurations, the force of turning away from our past. As we recite the hundred-syllable mantra, we continue both the meditation of faith and devotion to Vajrasattva, as well as regret for past karma, and we meditate that our body becomes luminous like crystal and filled with great exaltation. This is the force of remedial action. We maintain this meditation, and then, at the end, through the acknowledgment of our faults and through this meditation, we imagine that Vajrasattva is extremely pleased with us. He smiles at us and reassures us that all our bad karma and obscurations have been completely cleared away.

After receiving Vajrasattva's reassurance that all our negative karma and obscurations are definitively purified, Vajrasattva dissolves into light and is absorbed into our body, which transforms into the form of Vajrasattva. We have melded inseparably with Vajrasattva, holding a vajra in our right hand and a bell in our left. At our heart, there is the seed syllable of Vajrasattva, *hung*, surrounded by the six syllables of the short mantra of Vajrasattva (*om vajrasattva hung*). We imagine that light radiates from these syllables and fills the infinity of space, transforming the outer world into Vajrasattva's pure land (Truly Joyful) and transforming all sentient beings into deities of the mandala of Vajrasattva.

We continue to meditate that all appearances are the pure land and celestial palace of Vajrasattva, all sentient beings are Vajrasattva, and the whole world vibrates with the very pleasant sound of Vajrasattva's mantra, *om vajrasattva hung*. We imagine that this sound arises everywhere. We continue to meditate and recite the mantra for as long as we wish. Finally, at the end of our meditation, we imagine that the outer world and all sentient beings dissolve into us as Vajrasattva. Our body, as Vajrasattva, dissolves into the seed syllable *hung* at our heart. And gradually, from the bottom of this seed syllable, each part of it dissolves into the part above it: the *shabchu* dissolves into the *achung*, the *achung* into the *ha*, the *ha* into the crescent (the *chandra*), the crescent into the *bindu* (Tib. *thigle*), and the *bindu* finally into the finest point of light at the very tip (the *nanda*). This dissolves into clear, luminous emptiness. We rest our mind in radiant emptiness for as long as we wish. This is "the force of healing," or "the force of having reversed all negative acts," the fourth of the four forces.*

## The Meaning of Vajrasattva

Our meditation on Vajrasattva as above us, with the nectar falling and clearing away our negative karma and obscurations, is one way of purifying ourselves. However, resting the mind in radiant emptiness is an equally effective way of purifying negative karma and obscurations. Resting our mind in radiant emptiness is meditating on the ultimate, certain meaning of primordial Vajrasattva. The nature of our own mind is primordial Vajrasattva. This is really what Vajrasattva is.

We can relate the levels of Vajrasattva to the three bodies of enlightenment: the Vajrasattva that we meditate on as a form can be viewed as either the form of the body of enlightenment's perfect splendor, or the manifest body of enlightenment, or both. Meditation on the nature of mind as radiant emptiness is Vajrasattva as the ultimate body of enlightenment.

---

*The four forces can be summarized as refuge, remorse, resolve, and remediation, an easy mnemonic.

Dudjom Rinpoche said,

Self-awareness is from the beginning unchanging
   as the manifestation of dharmakaya.
In the freshness of this present awareness,
The uncontrived practitioner who abides naturally
Will find their own mind to be Vajrasattva.

When we relax naturally in our primordially unchanging natural awareness, this display of the ultimate body of enlightenment, our present awareness, without any changing, or artificial, activity, in a spontaneous, or immediate, placing of the mind, we can realize Vajrasattva within. This could also be called "the view of Dzogchen." This is how we allow our mind to rest at the end of the Vajrasattva meditation.

Once we have finished resting in the view, when we arise from that meditation, we make prayers of dedication. We wish in every lifetime to be reborn in the vajra family of enlightenment, to be a teacher of the Secret Mantra of Vajrasattva. We wish to be reborn with compassion, with devotion to the teacher, lifetime after lifetime. We wish, in all our lifetimes, to be holders of the vajra and bell, to be capable of learning profound instructions, and to work for the benefit of sentient beings. In other words, we wish, in all our lifetimes, to follow the example of Vajrasattva, to be like Vajrasattva. We dedicate whatever merit was done through this practice to all sentient beings, whose numbers are infinite. We don't just think, "My own bad karma and obscurations are purified. That's great! I'm going to attain enlightenment." We recall that all sentient beings at one time or another have been our parents. They all have their own negative karma and obscurations. We dedicate the merit of our practice to all sentient beings, wishing that they attain supreme transcendence, the state of Vajrasattva. We wish for every single sentient being without exception to attain exactly this state.

Thinley Norbu Rinpoche mentions that the dedication prayer is the vajra speech of our sublime masters. Vajra words don't just refer to a smart person who has written something good. They are either a mind treasure or the words of the great awareness holders of the past—Guru Rinpoche, Longchenpa, Mipham Rinpoche, Dudjom Lingpa, Dudjom Rinpoche, or others. Vajra speech has blessings and value. It does not come from an ordinary person with good thoughts who writes a prayer, or composition, that begins one way and finishes in a contradictory way. There is never a contradiction in the vajra words from the mind treasures or the great awareness holders of the past.

The Nyingma tradition recognizes one hundred tertons, the past, present, and future revealers of mind treasures and treasures from under the earth. Generally, these treasures were written down by Guru Rinpoche, Yeshe Tsogyal, or Vairochana and then concealed. Though the tertons are different individuals, the treasures are almost entirely the speech of Guru Rinpoche, so there is no difference in the quality of the teachings. We can have confidence in that.

We practice according to the empowerments and reading transmissions we have received. We can practice the New Treasures of Dudjom Rinpoche, the Longchen Nyingtik (Innermost Essence of Longchenpa), the teachings of Lerab Lingpa, Ratna Lingpa, or any of the tertons. It is not correct to hold one treasure teaching above any other. If it is a question of empowerments or reading transmissions you haven't received, of course, don't do those practices. Each person should practice as they wish, with the full knowledge and confidence that there is no difference in quality between any of the practices.

All deities share the same essence. If we are doing Tröma practice, it's perfectly okay to do that sometimes and the Khandro Thugtik at other times. They have exactly the same essence. Or we can choose to do just one, and then all the forms of the dakinis are gathered into that one deity. It depends entirely on you. There is no difference between them in the same way that there is no difference between enlightened beings. It doesn't show a very high understanding of enlightenment or the buddhas to say, "I will meditate on this buddha, but that other buddha is lesser." Preference is fine, but judgment is wrong.

It would be absurd to think of Shakyamuni being upset or jealous about someone doing Amitabha practice instead of meditating on Shakyamuni! Seeing a difference between specific buddhas is just a thought sentient beings have. Buddhas don't have that experience. If we think that doing one protector practice means that we are going to miss out on another, perhaps among worldly protectors, then honoring, or venerating, one protector would make another jealous. But for wisdom deities, doing one wisdom protector practice is doing the essence of all the protectors.

In the same way, Vajrasattva and Buddha Ever Excellent, Samantabhadra, share the same essence. Rongzompa said that just as the nature of all form is space, all appearances and experiences are in essence the enlightenment of Vajrasattva. This is the ultimate meaning of Vajrasattva.

Ever Excellent's name points out that everything has the nature of enlightenment within the mind of awakening, that this is the ultimate mind of enlightenment. In Tibetan, Samantabhadra is Kuntuzangpo. Rongzompa said that the first syllable, *Kun*, refers to all things and experiences of samsara or nirvana not being mixed together; they are distinct and complete. Being distinct, they appear as multiplicity, but they all share the same nondual nature. So there is nothing about samsara to be rejected, and nothing about nirvana to be gained. This is the significance of the third syllable, *zangpo*, which means "excellent." The shared nature of everything is the excellence in which there is nothing to be grasped or rejected. Rather than the common translation of Samantabhadra as "Ever Excellent," perhaps it should be "All Excellent." Rejecting samsara and seizing on the experiences of transcendence wouldn't be Kuntuzangpo, Ever Excellent, or All Excellent. It would be Half-Excellent. Kuntuzangpo is not Half-Excellent!

This Buddha Ever Excellent, Samantabhadra, is the essence of everything. To understand this, think of space. If I ask you if there is space in an apple, of course, there is space within the apple. There is also space outside the apple. Everything is pervaded by space. It is what provides the opportunity for things to exist. Just so, the nature of all things, both samsara and transcendent states, are equally Samantabhadra. He is also equal to the sphere of totality, the field, or expanse, of everything, dharmadhatu. If there were two, or many, spheres of totality, many natures of reality, then there would be different buddhas for different natures. However, because they are all one, all these forms of enlightenment represent the same ultimate nature.

This is not just a perspective that some people dreamed up. This represents the nature of reality. It is how things are: they have one single nature. We don't say that buddhas share the same essence because people like some buddhas and combine them (for example, Guru Rinpoche and Shakyamuni). It reflects the single nature of reality.

The nature or reality of fire is heat. In the same way, when we talk about the nature of reality, it isn't just a teaching. It's not just a meditation or an invention that we create with our mind. We are identifying how things are. The sphere of totality is the nature of reality.

There are many traditions and teachings about worldly life. To the extent that they correspond to the way things are, these teachings, or traditions, are true. When they depart from what is true, what is real, then they are false, misleading, or misguided. Our teaching and our meditation must correspond to reality, both in temporary circumstances and ultimately.

For example, how we relate to the nature of fire, air, water, and earth must correspond to their reality. It is not only a question of emptiness being the nature of things. Our teachings must also correspond in all the details to the nature of reality. This is a very critical issue when we practice. How we decide what is true and what is false must correspond to the way things are. Each object has its own nature in a temporary way, and it has an ultimate nature of emptiness. Our teaching must correspond to both. It must be able to describe these accurately.

If we think of sunlight, does it or does it not illuminate and clear away darkness? Honey is sweet. Anybody who claims the opposite is giving a contradictory teaching. That is the nature of these things. The point is when you judge teachings, don't judge according to how the teaching sounds. Ask yourself, "Does this correspond to the nature of my experience, to the nature of samsara, to the nature of reality, to the nature of transcendent states?"

The path we follow must be in accord with the basis, or the ground. If the basis, or ground, reflects the nature of reality, then the path must also reflect the nature of the basis. We must practice, in the same way, the nonduality of appearance and emptiness. This is the path in accord with the basis. Our practice must reflect the basis.

The result must arise from the path and reflect the exact nature of the ground or the basis, which in turn reflects the nature of reality. Our result must be the actualization in every respect of the ground or the nature of reality.

When we speak of the path, all three parts (view, meditation, and action) must correspond in every detail to the nature. The view is the mind that sees the nature of the mind, the nature of reality, as it is (for example, emptiness and appearance). If the mind perceives something that is not the correct nature of reality, then the view is incorrect. Based on this view that sees the nature of reality, we can meditate. Without the recognition of the nature of reality that has been pointed out to us, our meditation is not effective. It is confused. As Mipham Rinpoche said, our meditation must correspond to our view. If it does not, then our meditation and conduct will be equally confused. If, through meditation, we get familiar with, and maintain, the view, our action, or conduct, in turn will correspond to our view and meditation. This is the correct, or genuine, view, meditation, and action. All of these find their source in the nature.

Traditions, or habits, such as nihilism and eternalism have misguided, or wrong, views because their view does not correspond to the nature of reality. When the view does not correspond to the nature of reality, then meditation and conduct are equally as misguided.

The nature is really important.

# CHAPTER 7

# Guru Yoga

Although all the sections of the foundational practices that we have discussed—the four thoughts that turn the mind to enlightenment, taking refuge, developing the mind of awakening, mandala offering, and the meditation of Vajrasattva—are indispensable preparations for Dzogchen teachings, Guru Yoga is really the main subject. Guru Yoga is the very heart of the path into Dzogchen.

First, we must define Guru Yoga. *Lamai naljor* in Tibetan means "to join with the state of mind (or the natural state) of the ultimate lama." The first aspect of the natural state of the ultimate lama is the inconceivable appearance of the nature of reality: Kuntuzangpo, Ever Excellent, Buddha Samantabhadra. However, this inconceivable appearance of the nature of reality, the skillful means aspect of the lama, is not the only aspect. The essence of all appearances is great emptiness: the female Buddha Ever Excellent, Samantabhadri, Kuntuzangmo, transcendent knowledge—emptiness that does not change in the past, present, or future, an eternal presence that never gets lost in thought or falls into any extreme. The ultimate lama is the union of these two aspects: skillful means (the appearance of the nature of reality) and its essence, emptiness.

The union of the appearance and emptiness of everything, skillful means and transcendent knowledge, male Samantabhadra and female Samantabhadri, is the basis upon which all enlightenment, all forms of buddha, appear. The eternal union of the appearance and emptiness of the nature of reality is often portrayed as Vajradhara (Dorje Chang), which means "holder of the vajra." Vajradhara, in this sense, is the basis of the appearance, or manifestation, of all buddhas.

The lama (*lamai* in *lamai naljor*) is the indivisibility of appearances and emptiness, the primordial nature of reality. We can call this Samantabhadra and Samantabhadri. We can call it Buddha Vajradhara. The resultant three bodies of enlightenment are also the lama. Whatever appears from the original basis, or the primordial nature, arising as the resultant three bodies of enlightenment, is the lama. The lama we see and hear in ordinary reality is any manifestation of the lama in the world from the primordial nature, the original indivisibility of appearance and emptiness, the configuration of Samantabhadra and Samantabhadri. In Guru Yoga practice, this is what we mean by the guru.

*Yoga* (*naljor*) means to "join with" that ultimate nature of mind. In the Tibetan term *naljor*, *nal* refers to the natural state of mind and *jor* refers to union. The Guru Yoga practitioner experiences entering into union with the natural, ultimate state of mind.

As Guru Yoga practitioners, we do not create a new state of mind, change the mind, or enter into an unusual state, some state that does not already exist naturally. We enter into the state of the nature of reality, which is why we use this specific name for the practice and why we explain it this way. The original state of mind is the lama. The ultimate master is the primordial state. As practitioners, we enter into, or unite with, that original state, so we say *lamai naljor*. Guru Yoga is not found just in the Dudjom Tersar Ngöndro. Every tantric practice in both the creation and completion stage is a way to enrich the union with the ultimate master.

In Mahayana (we might say "greater Mahayana"), there are two basic contexts for practice. One is the causal way of the transcendent perfections and the other is the resultant way of the tantras. If we compare these two contexts, we find that the same nature is identified in both of them: both contexts talk about buddha nature and ways of realizing it.

However, in the tantras, buddha nature is more clearly explained and practiced, there is no delusion or lack of clarity, and the path is relatively easy. The path of the transcendent perfections requires great effort over long periods of many lifetimes, even aeons. The tantras are taught for those of a more acute level of mind, and it is said that, in this very body and during this very lifetime, or, possibly, in three lifetimes, we can arrive at enlightenment. Further, the tantras say that ordinary persons like ourselves can see the nature of reality, while the path of the transcendent perfections says that only after achieving a high level of development is sight of the nature of reality possible. For all these reasons, we say that the tantric path is superior to the path of the transcendent perfections.

## The Four Reliances

On this subject of the superiority of the tantras or the luminous Dzogchen teachings, the Buddha described the context of tantric teachings by listing "the four reliances." First, "Do not rely on the teacher but on the teaching." Regardless of how a teacher may appear—it doesn't matter if they are poor or even seem foolish—we have to focus on the teaching, not the outer form. Many great teachers have appeared as beggars or simpletons. A great teacher from the past said, "Even if a fool has repeated very profound teachings, the wise should practice those teachings." In the same way, even if a teacher is rich and famous and has great titles, we must again rely not on the individual but on the teaching. Is it in accord with the Buddha's teaching? Is it beneficial to us? We must look at that. If, on the other hand, we rely on the person rather than the teaching, this will not be useful for us.

The second reliance is "Do not rely on the words but on the meaning." In Tibet, people would often get very familiar with the words of teachings. They would train for many years in the words, but somewhere along the way, they would lose the sense of the real meaning. In their hearts, they didn't develop disengagement from fixation in samsara. When they took refuge, they repeated the refuge prayer and understood all about refuge, but they didn't develop faith. When they practiced developing the mind of awakening, the words and understanding were all there, but they didn't develop compassion. It is not enough to be capable in words. One must pay full attention to the meaning.

Milarepa said that, during his time, in eastern Tibet, people were interested in developing a good outer appearance; in central Tibet, they were mainly interested in debate; and in western Tibet, they were interested only in the conventional truth rather than the certain meaning of the teachings. They had a great understanding of the words, but they weren't interested in meditative practice—Dzogchen or Mahamudra. Milarepa told Rechungpa, "You should aim for the certain, or absolute, meaning of the teachings."

We waste the opportunity of our study if we give our attention to the teacher rather than to the teaching, or if we give our attention to the words rather than the meaning. When we make these mistakes, we lose the purity of the buddhadharma.

The third reliance is "Do not rely on the conventional meaning but on the absolute meaning." Literally, the conventional meaning is "the meaning that leads sentient beings." The Buddha often taught on the conventional level to lead beings on the path. For example, to say that the hell realms are located a certain distance below Mount Kailash or that the main residence of the starving spirits lies below Rajgir or Bodhgaya is a teaching given for certain sentient beings' minds. The description of the universe with the supreme mountain, Mount Meru, and the four continents around it or the Buddha's teachings on the aggregates, the different elements of our mind, are conventional teachings to lead toward an experience of the nature of reality. Hearing at the very outset, "Everything is empty; all experience is simply the appearance of our habitual tendencies," may not be relatable or acceptable. So other teachings are given to lead beings toward that truth. However, if we study only conventional truth, we miss the ultimate truth. Our attention should be given to where the teachings lead, to the ultimate, absolute truth.

One story tells of a time when the Buddha's family was in a war. While his whole family and kingdom were being wiped out, the Buddha said he had a headache and backache. This is what the Buddha claimed, but it was just to instill faith, or confidence, in the listener in karma, and cause and effect—even the Buddha could experience the result of past karma. He made that statement to lead persons to a certain conclusion, but it didn't reflect reality. The Buddha didn't actually have a headache or a backache.

The fourth reliance is "Do not rely on ordinary consciousness, or what lies within the domain of our ordinary consciousness, but on the domain of wisdom." Ordinary consciousness means what we can see, hear, taste, touch, smell, or think about with our ordinary minds.

In Tibet, people often did not rely on wisdom but on their ordinary consciousness. Tibetans can be very comfortable in the realm of logic. They can approach emptiness intellectually and be very happy with that study and that level of experience; but to consider emptiness that goes beyond ordinary consciousness, emptiness that goes beyond the bounds of ordinary mind, can make people feel uncomfortable.

In the past, many people made the sphere of totality, the three bodies of enlightenment, part of the domain of ordinary consciousness. They took what is part of wisdom back into the realm of ordinary mind. So their study, or experience, of the three bodies of enlightenment, the sphere of totality, and the qualities of enlightenment remained within their ordinary consciousness. And they were very happy with that. Going beyond the bounds of ordinary consciousness was not understood, appreciated, or comfortable. That's the way it was.

When Dzogchen and Mahamudra were presented in Tibet as being beyond the bounds of ordinary mind, many found themselves in discord with those teachings. They considered them to be negative teachings. They saw emptiness, or the sphere of totality, as a kind of nonexistence. They took the three bodies of enlightenment down so it was within the bounds of ordinary consciousness, within intellectual bounds. This is not going beyond our ordinary mind. It put enlightenment into the realm of concepts, or thought, almost as if it were another part of the material world. It became another object. When there is no sense that enlightenment, the three bodies of enlightenment, the sphere of totality, or emptiness exceeds the bounds of our ordinary thought, concepts, and intellect, then the buddhadharma is reduced to nothing special.

We have to rely on wisdom rather than on ordinary consciousness. We have to rely on wisdom's domain of the three bodies of enlightenment, the various mandalas, or configurations, of enlightenment. This is where we must pay attention. In the realm of our ordinary mind are the four extremes of existence, nonexistence, both, and neither, and all our ordinary ways of dealing with the world. Thanks to our reliance on ordinary consciousness, we have continued to be reborn lifetime after lifetime. If we wish to attain enlightenment, we have to go beyond the bounds of ordinary mind, beyond those four extremes, and enter the domain of wisdom.

The teaching of the four reliances was given by the Buddha. If, in all circumstances, we rely on these principles, we will not stray from our path. Otherwise, we might think that there are contradictions between various teachings given by the Buddha. If we use this focus, we see that some of his teachings are just conventional teachings, but he pointed us in the direction of wisdom. When we take these four reliances to heart, when our practice is not within the bounds of our ordinary consciousness (because that isn't really the point of practice), when we practice in the domain of wisdom, we arrive at the very peak of the Buddha's teaching, the luminous Dzogchen teachings.

There are many different dharma activities: building temples or monasteries; taking different levels of vows; practicing rituals; the creation phase; the completion phase; and many different forms of meditation. The point of all dharma practice can be reduced to view, meditation, and action. Of these three, the main point is the view of the nature of reality. This is what we're meant to focus on. Everything else, any other dharma activity, is a supporting practice. The critical point is this identification of the nature of reality, the view.

Many Tibetan monks used to think that it was enough to be a monk and to have entered into that lifestyle, without paying attention to the view. Taking vows, building stupas, all these different forms of practice, are, of course, virtuous and beneficial. But if they become the main concern and we leave aside the nature of the mind, then we are relying on ordinary consciousness, not wisdom, whereas in fact, it should be the other way around. What is really critical is the domain of wisdom. Any other dharma activity is an auxiliary practice. If we take vows, build monasteries, make stupas, play instruments, or do rituals, we must do so in order to realize the nature of mind. If we miss the purpose of auxiliary practices, it is like looking at the footprints of an elephant and thinking that the footprints are more important than the elephant. The main point is to rely on wisdom, to understand the nature of mind. Empowerments, preparation for empowerments, making paintings, and other beautiful activities are all beneficial supportive practices when they are done while holding the view. When we understand the nature of mind, we enter the domain of wisdom. We become the sovereign of all experience, gaining control over everything whatsoever. This is very wonderful. There's no point to the eighty-four thousand teachings of the Buddha other than serving as means to realize the nature of mind. When the four reliances are complete, we have entered the realm of Dzogchen.

In the *Treasury of the Supreme Way of Spiritual Development*, Longchenpa said that all paths in the buddhadharma that include a focus for ordinary consciousness explain the basis, the path, and the result in relation to the ordinary mind. This is true for any level of practice apart from the luminous Dzogchen teachings. Because they explain the development of realization in relation to the ordinary mind, they don't really get to the vital point of the teachings. For example, in the practice of Mahamudra, we look at the mind and find, "This is what the mind is when it's resting. This is what the mind is when it's moving. This is the awareness of mind." We meditate using the mind. This is fine, but it leaves us in the realm of the ordinary mind. However, in the Dzogchen teachings, we have the immediate pointing-out instruction of the nature of awareness, and we have the basis of wisdom, the path of wisdom, and the result of wisdom. This is a different approach from every other way of dharma practice. This is the special quality of Dzogchen teachings. This wisdom is not covered up by dualistic experience. It is not covered up by ordinary thought. Wisdom is not covered up, or concealed, by either samsara or nirvana. Naked wisdom itself is pointed out.

In lower Mahayana, we take the example of a pillar, or a house, and analyze it in terms of existence, nonexistence, both, and neither. We continually explore, using the mind, what emptiness is. It is said that, after one incalculable aeon of this type of meditation, we arrive at the conclusion and directly see wisdom. It takes such a long time because we remain in the domain of our ordinary mind.

In Kalachakra practice, the highest level of tantra in the New Schools, we begin with extensive practice with the energy-winds (Skt. *prana*). We meditate on the three main channels in the body. We do *bep* (falling practice), an extreme form of Tibetan yoga. These practices undo the knots in our channels. Then we enter retreat in a completely dark place, where we see empty forms and have many experiences. We use this gradually to develop. After perhaps six, seven, or eight years of this kind of practice, it is said that the nature of mind can arise. It is a very long and arduous approach. There is nothing in these teachings about how, at the very beginning, the nature of mind can be pointed out directly.

Even in the three inner tantras of the Nyingma tradition, for example, in the *Secret Essence Tantra*, in Mahayoga and Anuyoga tantra, we work with much of the material used in Kalachakra. All of this practice, whether for an incalculable aeon or for a period of years, whether it consists of analytical meditation, yoga practices, or visualizations, is useful to approach the wisdom of the nature of mind. However, in Dzogchen teachings, the nature of mind can be directly pointed out without our having to spend all that time or face other difficulties.

In Dzogchen teachings, it is said that not only wisdom but also enlightenment is possible in six months, three years, five years, six years, and, in any case, within one lifetime. Wisdom is pointed out right from the very beginning. For those with the highest acumen, if they practice trekchöd and thögal, they can arrive at enlightenment during this lifetime. For those at the middle level, it is possible to arrive at liberation at the time after death or before the next life. At the very least, one has the assurance of rebirth in the pure realms of the manifest body of enlightenment.

Why is it that in other traditions enlightenment is so difficult and takes a longer time to attain? It's because they expect to find enlightenment within the ordinary mind, the source of samsara. This is a mistake at the very basis of their approach. But Dzogchen is based in wisdom. From this basis of wisdom, we expect the result to be wisdom.

When we think enlightenment comes from the ordinary mind and use that as the basis and the path, the mistake is that ordinary mind has dualistic experience. If we expect to find enlightenment within the bounds of our ordinary mind, our enlightenment will also have this dualistic quality. Also, our ordinary mind includes all our habitual tendencies, all our karma. If we consider the ordinary mind and dualistic experience to be the basis of enlightenment, our habitual tendencies, our karma, will be part of the experience of enlightenment. However, our ordinary mind, our experience of our habitual tendencies, and our karma are part of the experiences, or appearances, of confusion and are not part of the experience of enlightenment.

Someone might ask, "If there is no ordinary mind, how can there be enlightenment?" The reply is that enlightenment does not depend on the presence or absence of the ordinary mind. It depends on the presence or absence of the wisdom of the ultimate body of enlightenment. It depends on the pointing-out instruction of wisdom. It depends on the path of familiarization, or meditation, on wisdom. And it depends on the result of the actualization of wisdom. Without the presence of wisdom having been pointed out, there is no basis of wisdom, no path of wisdom, and no result of wisdom. The bottom line is the presence of wisdom.

Everything encompassed by samsara and transcendent states appears within the wisdom of Dzogchen and shares the same nature as Dzogchen. All aspects and experiences of enlightenment appear within the wisdom of Dzogchen. Anything liberated is liberated within the sphere of the wisdom of Dzogchen. Anything of samsara or transcendent states, whether it is created or has origination; whether it rests, remains, or abides; or whether it disappears or ceases, has nowhere to exist in or to cease in other than the wisdom of Dzogchen. If only nirvana or enlightenment had the nature of Dzogchen but not samsara, this would not be Dzogchen. That's why we call it "Dzogchen." *Dzog* means "perfect" or "complete." *Chen* means "great" (beyond any measure or comparison). Everything is included within its sphere.

We will discuss in more detail below the subject of the basis, path, and result of Dzogchen. Briefly, we recognize the basis of Dzogchen as the nature of everything in samsara and transcendent states; we recognize the path of Dzogchen as the nature of everything in samsara and transcendent states; and we recognize the result of Dzogchen as the nature of everything in samsara and transcendent states. Since wisdom is the nature of its basis, path, and result, because it is totally inclusive, we can say that it is Dzogchen, "great perfection."

## The Importance of Guru Yoga in Dzogchen

All the tantras of Dzogchen say that the development of the wisdom of Dzogchen depends upon your relationship to your teacher. Wisdom is developed in Dzogchen by meditating on the lama above your head or in the sky above, beseeching your lama to receive the four empowerments, and joining your mind with the mind of the lama dissolved into your heart. It doesn't matter which master you meditate on. It is important that it be your root teacher and that you have great faith in this person. It could be Dudjom Rinpoche, Thinley Norbu Rinpoche, or any one of many different teachers that you accept as your principal teacher.

In Dzogchen, we consider the lineage of enlightened masters, each of whom has complete realization, to be like the Buddha himself. This lineage is like a thread of pure gold without any of the impurities that come from breaking the relationship of tantric commitments. It includes your root teacher, whom you can imagine as Guru Rinpoche. You develop intense faith and devotion toward the lineage teachers and, more specifically, toward your root teacher, thinking, "May you know me." You pray to your teacher with intense devotion and openness. Then you join your mind with your teacher's mind. And through the thought of your teacher, your prayers, and the dissolution, which mixes your mind and your teacher's, the blessing of the influence of your teacher comes into your mind and the realization of Dzogchen arises in your experience.

It is not essential to receive teachings directly from a master who is alive right now. Jigme Lingpa was a great master who lived hundreds of years after Longchenpa. He went into retreat and for four or five years he meditated on, and prayed to, Longchenpa. After this, he received the blessing of Longchenpa; all Longchenpa's realization poured into the mind of Jigme Lingpa. Thanks to that, we have the mind-treasure teachings of Jigme Lingpa, the Innermost Essence of Longchenpa (Longchen Nyingtik). This is not Longchenpa's writing; it is Jigme Lingpa's, but it represents the nature of the mind of Longchenpa. Through intense devotion and prayer, realization welled up within Jigme Lingpa's mind.

It is possible even these days, if you have faith, to pray to Longchenpa, Jigme Lingpa, Mipham Rinpoche, or Dudjom Rinpoche, and through a relationship of faith and devotion, through the practice of Guru Yoga, to receive the blessing, or realization, of Dzogchen. It is possible when you study teachings that you've received to gain some understanding, but then you can meditate on Guru Rinpoche or any lama with faith and devotion, praying, "Please know me," in a very open and lucid state of mind. Returning to the same teachings, you may understand them better than before. Or while looking at notes from teachings you've attended, you can do the same Guru Yoga practice—pray to Guru Rinpoche, pray to your lama—and then return to the notes and find that you understand what you didn't understand before.

Here's an example from the life of my own root teacher, enlightened master Khenpo Jigme Phuntsok Rinpoche: There is a four-page instruction on the nature of mind written by Mipham Rinpoche (who lived in the twentieth century). Right from the beginning, Jigme Phuntsok Rinpoche understood all the words of the commentary. There wasn't anything he didn't understand. But he recited a four-line prayer (which I also recite at the beginning of my classes) to Mipham Rinpoche about four million times. And he recited this four-page commentary about ten thousand times. One day, as he was reciting the prayer and repeating the commentary, his understanding of the commentary from the perspective of the three classes of Dzogchen teachings (the mind class, the spatial class, and the direct-instruction class) became clearer and clearer. It was as if the mind-realization of Mipham Rinpoche transferred to the mind of Jigme Phuntsok Rinpoche; he could then compose songs and write texts from the Dzogchen view. He could compose rituals of offering or meditations on Mipham Rinpoche. He could sing songs of realization and write long commentaries on this original short commentary. He had really gained realization. He wrote four long commentaries on this short text. Thanks to his practice and devotion, he received this blessing directly from the mind of Mipham Rinpoche. This is not just a story from the past. It happens in the present day. It is the force of the blessing of the lama's mind that comes into our mind.

Longchenpa commented that it is not possible to reach liberation just by practicing the phases of creation or completion. Practicing either of these by themselves, without the Dzogchen view, will not lead to liberation. They are forms of either activity or the enrichment of experience but are not themselves the wisdom of Dzogchen. On the other hand, Guru Yoga is a practice complete in itself. By praying to the root lama, by praying for blessings, the realization of the wisdom of Dzogchen can arise in your mind and you can reach liberation. Therefore, the path of Guru Yoga is more profound than any other path.

We shouldn't think that the foundational practices are to be given up for a later practice. We shouldn't believe that later practices are deeper, more profound, or more important. In *Words of My Perfect Teacher*, Patrul Rinpoche said that we can call them "preliminary practices," but, in fact, they are the main practice.

Guru Yoga practice is the point of departure for all the more "advanced" practices. This is what we should give our attention to without thinking, "There is something greater, more important, and more central to my practice later on." The practices of the phases of creation or completion can enrich Guru Yoga practice. Other instructions that you receive in Dzogchen will all be based on Guru Yoga practice. If you have done the Guru Yoga practice, you can recognize Dzogchen wisdom and develop it. We say this is the one bridge that crosses one hundred rivers.

Thinley Norbu Rinpoche and the teachers of the past all say the same thing: Guru Yoga practice is the most important practice. My enlightened master Khenpo Jigme Phuntsok Rinpoche didn't advise anything else as essential besides Guru Yoga practice. He didn't place undue emphasis on the phases of creation or completion. In the Nyingma tradition, we have nine ways of development, but the heart of all of them is Dzogchen practice. And the heart of that practice, the way to access it, is the practice of Guru Yoga.

Our tradition is extremely vast and profound. Many texts contain the teachings of the Buddha, and even more contain the commentaries of great masters of the past, such as Nagarjuna and other Indian masters, or Longchenpa and other Tibetan masters. However, when it comes down to us, who want to put the teachings into practice, we need to be able to apply those teachings to our immediate situation. If we have only knowledge of the teachings, but we don't know how to apply them or put them into practice, then however vast and profound they might be, they are of no use to us. We may lose heart and get upset with all the various thoughts that arise in our mind. We may get filled with hope or apprehension toward our practice. We may anticipate our practice instead of just doing our practice. We may hesitate and put off our practice for another day. If we do not learn how to condense and apply the teachings to ourselves, the time for liberation, the time for freedom, will never come. We will not have the opportunity. One way to join all the elements of the teachings and apply them is the practice of Guru Yoga.

The foundational practices, and especially Guru Yoga practice, are the way that we can grasp the essence of the different levels of development in the Nyingma tradition and, particularly, in Dzogchen. What's more, in Guru Yoga, the most important point is the development of devotion and appreciation. If we can grasp that the foundational practices and Guru Yoga, in particular, are the central point of our practice, and that the development of devotion, appreciation, and cherished reverence toward the sublime master is the vital point of Guru Yoga, then even if we were to die at this very moment, we would not fall into the ravine of the three lower realms. We would not suffer at the time of death. We would have no question about where we would be reborn in our next life. This is the essence of our practice.

Nagarjuna said that some people climb to the very top of the mountain and think, "I'm not going to fall off the mountain," but then they do. But if you have received teachings and make this connection with the master, then even if you think, "I'm not going to attain enlightenment," you do! Even if you think, "I don't want to be liberated," or you don't develop that intention, still you will.

In the discourses and tantras, the teacher is praised as the epitome, or the personification, of the three jewels. If we can integrate the master's blessing into our life, the result is the attainment of enlightenment. There is nothing greater than this to strive for.

## The Three Lineages

We define the lama as the holder of three lineages that start with Buddha Samantabhadra and continue down to the present day, ending with one's principal teacher.

The first lineage is the mind-to-mind lineage between buddhas. It begins with Buddha Samantabhadra: his mind and the mind of Vajrasattva are a single mind-stream. What was in one mind arose within the other's mind. There is no separation between the mind, or realization, of Buddha Samantabhadra and that of Vajrasattva. It is not as if what was in one person's mind was transferred to another, and then the second person somehow improved and came to a higher level. Rather, there is absolutely no difference between one mind and the other.

The second lineage is transmitted through symbols or gestures between awareness holders. In the symbolic lineage, teachings are transmitted through a finger snap or a gesture—for example, in the fourth, or precious word, empowerment, sometimes the lama shows a crystal ball. The first member of this lineage is Garab Dorje, who was born in Oddiyana. He met Buddha Vajrasattva directly and through Vajrasattva's gestures, or symbols, received the transmission. This was passed from Garab Dorje to Manjushrimitra to Shri Singha to Guru Rinpoche Padmasambhava.

The third lineage is the aural (or oral) lineage. For example, from Guru Rinpoche, it went to the king Trisong Deutsen, the subject Vairochana, and the companion Yeshe Tsogyal. This lineage includes all members of the circle of Guru Rinpoche's disciples, but in this case we stress these three. From the time of Trisong Deutsen, Vairochana, and Yeshe Tsogyal down to the present day, this lineage has usually been transmitted through oral instructions.

For example, the Dudjom Tersar teachings have been received through the series of previous incarnations of Dudjom Rinpoche. He was one of Guru Rinpoche's twenty-five main disciples, then known as Drokben Lotsawa. Later he reincarnated as Dudul Lingpa, then Traktung Dudjom Lingpa, and then Dudjom Rinpoche.

These lineages have been passed down from the very beginning, from Buddha Ever Excellent down to the present day through a series of masters. We consider our own principal teacher to be the union of all the minds of all the buddhas and masters of the past. It is not right to consider the mind-to-mind transmission as exclusive to buddhas, the lineage passed through symbols as only the domain of awareness holders, and the aural lineage as only between ordinary human beings. The different appearances of buddhas, awareness holders, and ordinary human beings are all equally manifestations of enlightenment without any hierarchy among them. It is wrong to see any hierarchy in the realization of the various holders of the lineage and, particularly, to see our own teacher as an ordinary human being. The teacher holds the blessings of the three lineages and embodies the lineages' realization from the beginning to the present day.

One tantra says that if we have contempt for, or look down upon, a future vajradhara (vajra holder), our own enlightened activity will deteriorate or be broken. Therefore, we must see the present holder of the lineage, who is a future vajradhara, as a representative of the enlightenment of all members of the lineage.

Buddha Vajradhara said, "In the future, I will appear in the form of a teacher, and it is that person who will receive offerings. If you please the master, you will receive my blessings and you will purify your obscurations."

A commentary by Dudjom Rinpoche on the foundational practices says that if you don't have devotion and faithful appreciation toward the teacher, even if you meditated on the deities of the six tantras for a very long time, it would be impossible to attain supreme accomplishment. Even if you tried to attain ordinary accomplishment—for example, long life, better health, riches, or magnetizing what you want, you wouldn't gain them. Even if it were possible to attain some small accomplishment, it would be an extremely arduous process. This points out the fault of not having devotion or appreciation.

In Guru Yoga practice, we develop incontrovertible faith in Guru Rinpoche as our root master or our root teacher in the form of Guru Rinpoche. We pray to Guru Rinpoche, receive the four empowerments, and join our mind with Guru Rinpoche's mind. At that point, we don't have to entertain any doubts about our practice or our mind. We remain in the state of our mind being inseparable from the mind of Guru Rinpoche. This is the heart of the practice. This is how to clear away any obstacles and improve our meditative experience.

All Vajrayana practices, including Dzogchen, require transmission from teacher to student. There are three lineages specific to transmission; these are distinguished from the three lineages discussed above. The first is when a master receives the inheritance of a particular teaching or lineage through a prophecy. For example, when Guru Rinpoche or a deity predicts that at a certain time and place a master will appear and a certain teaching will be useful, this teaching becomes the property of that master, who inherits that particular teaching, or transmission, through its having been foretold. The second lineage of transmission is empowerment through aspiration; a realized being develops the aspiration to appear at a certain time for particular beings. The third is known as "the seal of the dakinis"; Guru Rinpoche concealed treasures throughout Tibet for particular times and for specific individuals who would appear when these teachings would be important. He gave the dakinis orders to reveal the treasures or to allow specific individuals to receive the treasures at those specific times.

## Guru Yoga Practice

Now we come to the main practice of Guru Yoga. First, we imagine ourselves as Vajrayogini (Tib. Dorje Naljor).

Who or what is Vajrayogini? On the level of the ultimate body of enlightenment, in Vajrayogini, *vajra* (Tib. *dorje*) represents emptiness, or the ultimate nature of reality, and *yogini* (Tib. *naljorma*) represents the enlightened female in unity with the vajra; so it is often said that Vajrayogini is "the absolute vajra space of emptiness." Vajra symbolizes what cannot be divided, or split, by anything but what can overcome everything. No dualistic thinking, no part of samsara, no ordinary thought, no obscuring emotions can overcome the vajra, but the vajra of the ultimate nature can overcome everything else. It is the inexpressible, inconceivable nature that has never come into being, doesn't remain, and will never cease. It is great emptiness, which is the essence of space. It is natural wisdom, the mother of all buddhas. All the profound discourses and tantras speak about the vajra sphere of emptiness that is the ultimate body of enlightenment and the wisdom of the dakini who is the mother of the buddhas of the past, present, and future.

The ultimate body of enlightenment's unimpeded luminosity is the body of enlightenment's perfect splendor. It appears as the forms of Vajrayogini of the five buddha families, and in the highest pure land as the female buddhas: Sangye Chenma, Mamaki, Gokarmo, Damtshig Drolma, and Ying Chugma.

The radiance from the unimpeded appearance of the Vajrayogini of the ultimate body of enlightenment creates the different forms and pure lands of the body of enlightenment's perfect splendor. They appear in the six realms of existence, manifesting as various forms of dakinis in all walks of life. These are Vajrayogini as the manifest body of enlightenment. Forms of Vajrayogini can appear in various worldly places. In the context of tantra, forms of Vajrayogini appear as women with all the signs of a tantric practitioner or as women whose tantric practice has arrived at the stage of Vajrayogini. There are also vajrayoginis of coemergent wisdom—women who have developed realization of the nature of mind. We can recognize forms of Vajrayogini who take rebirth in the context of tantric practice or as a vajrayogini of coemergent wisdom because they appear in a buddhadharma context and as practitioners. But Vajrayogini does not appear only in the context of tantric practice or as a consort of a lama; she appears everywhere to help sentient beings. She can appear in passionate forms, in peaceful forms, or in any way that leads sentient beings to enlightenment and relieves their suffering. We may not immediately recognize her as such.

There are limitless forms of Vajrayogini in the ultimate body of enlightenment, the body of enlightenment's perfect splendor, and the manifest body of enlightenment. All these together in one form are personified in the dakini Yeshe Tsogyal.

In Thinley Norbu Rinpoche's text, there is a prayer, or song, to Yeshe Tsogyal written by Mipham Rinpoche: the *Song of the Yearning of Faith to Yeshe Tsogyal*. She is described as Vajrayogini of the ultimate body of enlightenment, the mother of all buddhas; as the embodiment of Saraswati (literally "the melodious one who is the master of all forms of speech or song"); as Tara, she who compassionately works for the liberation of all sentient beings;

and the dakini who has shown particular kindness to Tibetans, because so much of the treasure teachings, the basic instructions, and the Dzogchen instructions have depended on her activity, her kindness. She ensured the preservation and continuation of buddhadharma teachings in Tibet. When Guru Rinpoche was in Tibet, it was mainly Yeshe Tsogyal who requested and wrote down his teachings. She would fervently entreat Guru Rinpoche (sometimes using the phrase *kuchi kuchi*, or "pretty please") to say what was going to happen in the future. He would explain, and based on his prediction, she would make a request: "Please give a teaching that will be useful to help people at that time." When tertons find teachings written on yellow parchment that Guru Rinpoche had concealed for discovery in the future, most often they are in Yeshe Tsogyal's handwriting. So we consider Yeshe Tsogyal to be the central figure through whose activity the teachings of Guru Rinpoche were preserved for generations of Tibetans (and now for all of us).

This is just the briefest mention of Yeshe Tsogyal's activity.* If we went into detail, we would never finish talking about how Yeshe Tsogyal has been central to the development and preservation of Vajrayana. You can read her biography or autobiography, and if you check the treasure teachings, in most of them, at the end, you will see that it was Yeshe Tsogyal who originally asked for those teachings. They were concealed and centuries later revealed by a treasure revealer. It is true that some treasure teachings were requested by King Trisong Deutsen, but the great majority were requested and written down by Yeshe Tsogyal.

This song is part of a longer prayer, the *Longing Melody of Faith*, a wonderful, profound text by Mipham Rinpoche, which Thinley Norbu Rinpoche quotes in his book. It feels like a child calling to its mother.

The practice of the dakinis is very important. With other forms of practice, one can encounter obstacles. But the practice of the dakinis prevents all obstacles. In each cycle of treasure teachings

---

*Appendix 3 describes Yeshe Tsogyal's qualities and activities in more detail.

(for example, the New Treasures of Dudjom Rinpoche, Longchen Nyingtik, Khandro Thugtik, Lerab Lingpa's Heart Practice of Yeshe Tsogyal), there is a practice of Yeshe Tsogyal. Each is considered critical to prevent obstacles. Because there are no obstacles in the practice, it has great influence. There is no practice with quicker or more efficient results than the practice of Guru Rinpoche and Yeshe Tsogyal because their activity was particularly focused on this dark and difficult time in history. Their intent was to help this age and time. Their influence is especially strong now.

If you read the biographies or autobiographies of Yeshe Tsogyal, you will begin to understand her special qualities. You will be able to see that she was a great practitioner, extremely kind to people, and the supreme embodiment of compassion. And every time you look at the colophon of a treasure teaching, you will see her name, that she was responsible for these treasure teachings. Gradually, looking at her story and looking at the presence of her activity, you will be able to really understand her kindness, her compassion, her enlightened activity, and her blessing.

Sometimes before we do the Shower of Blessings practice, we recite a four-line prayer by the Fifteenth Karmapa, Kakyab Dorje. He prays to Yeshe Tsogyal, saying, "She is the mother who has given birth to all buddhas. She is the female form of Buddha Ever Excellent, Samantabhadri, the sphere of totality. She is the sole mother who gives refuge to all Tibetans and to all beings, an extremely kind woman. Yeshe Tsogyal is she who bestows supreme accomplishment. She is the central dakini of all dakinis of great exaltation. To Yeshe Tsogyal, I pray."

Mipham Rinpoche, Kakyab Dorje, and many of the great lamas of the *terma* (treasure) tradition wrote heartfelt prayers to Yeshe Tsogyal. Thinley Norbu Rinpoche explains that Yeshe Tsogyal is the nature of everything, the sphere of totality, and the female form of Ever Excellent, and her appearance has all the signs and marks of enlightenment, the manifest form of the sphere of totality. This is the dakini Yeshe Tsogyal.

This introduces the idea that, in the context of Guru Yoga practice, there is a connection between visualizing our body as Yeshe Tsogyal and the realization that will appear in our mind. This is what the great masters of the past have taught. To quickly receive the blessings of Yeshe Tsogyal and Guru Rinpoche when we do the Guru Yoga practice, we don't think of our body as ordinary, a solid physical form, but as, in essence, the dakini Yeshe Tsogyal, the essence of the three bodies of enlightenment, appearing as Vajrayogini. By thinking that our body is free from all obscurations, we become a proper receptacle, which allows us to very quickly and efficiently receive empowerment from Guru Rinpoche.

By imagining our body as, in essence, Yeshe Tsogyal and, in appearance, Vajrayogini, we take the result as our path. The basis is exactly the result that we are aiming for. We are not doing something that will produce an effect only later on. We start with the result. There is a connection because, in the same way that Guru Rinpoche bestowed ordinary and supreme accomplishment on Yeshe Tsogyal, here we take the form of Vajrayogini (in essence, Yeshe Tsogyal) and imagine Guru Rinpoche before us. We imagine our root lama as Guru Rinpoche. In the same way that Guru Rinpoche bestowed accomplishment on Yeshe Tsogyal, we begin our practice. This is the auspicious connection.

We begin by imagining our present environment not as an ordinary appearance but as the highest pure land of Lotus Light. There, in the center of a celestial palace, we imagine, as a symbol of freedom from desire, a lotus. As a symbol of freedom from the darkness of ignorance, we imagine the flat disk of the sun on this lotus. As a symbol of freedom from all thought of self, we imagine a human corpse. This is the seat: a lotus, a sun, and a corpse.

On this seat, we imagine ourselves in the form of Vajrayogini. Our form is a very radiant red. Our face is both peaceful and wrathful; our mouth is smiling, but our eyes show wrath. We have a very passionate attitude. As Vajrayogini, our teeth are white, very bright. Two of our three eyes represent the two form bodies of enlightenment, the body of enlightenment's perfect splendor and the manifest body of enlightenment. The third eye, in the center of our forehead, represents the ultimate body of enlightenment. With these three eyes, as Vajrayogini, we look with great joy and a great sense of connection into the sky, into space, into the eyes and heart of Guru Rinpoche.

Vajrayogini's right hand holds a cutting blade, symbol of having cut through the web, or net, of negative emotions, and the left hand holds a skull-cup, symbol of the bestowal of supreme and ordinary accomplishment. The skull-cup is filled with sublime nectar.

Our two feet are on the ground. The right leg is straight down and the left leg is somewhat extended. There are several ways Vajrayogini or Yeshe Tsogyal is represented in thangkas. Sometimes her legs are completely straight, both together. In this case, the left leg is slightly extended to the side.

Our hair is up in a topknot with a wish-fulfilling jewel at the very crown of the hair. Half of the hair is drawn up and the other half falls down in tresses on our back. A crown of jewels, as well as flowers that never wilt, adorn our hair.

We have a wheel ornament on our head and earrings of wheels with tiny bells attached. All of these ornaments, as well as our armlets and bracelets, which also have small bells attached, are made of gold.

We have a wheel on our head, earrings, bracelets or armlets, anklets, and a belt. These are the five *mudras* (ornaments, in this context) that Vajrayogini wears.

We imagine ourselves wearing great long necklaces of lapis, rubies, diamonds, pearls, and so forth, all different forms of jewels. We have silk ribbons that fall from our crown. We imagine our form as irresistible and surrounded by a brilliant five-colored light. We imagine ourselves supremely beautiful, yet only as appearance without the slightest solidity, as if our form were like a rainbow. We imagine our body as both clear and pure, appearance without substantiality.

This meditation comes from the highest level of tantra. It represents the view. When we have the view of great infinite purity and equanimity, our attitude and conduct rise to that level. When we have a very limited view, our conduct is very, very limited. For example, on the level of the Middle Way we cannot meditate like this; even in the lower tantras, we do not meditate like this, let alone at the Shravakayana level.

The object of Vajrayogini's meditation is, of course, Guru Rinpoche. Guru Rinpoche's life was predicted by Buddha Shakyamuni in four lines of the text *Reciting the Names of Manjushri* that say he is the glorious and illustrious buddha born from a lotus, the holder of the treasury of omniscient wisdom. *Wisdom* can refer to the five wisdoms of the five transcendent buddhas or the three wisdoms of enlightenment (the essence, nature, and all-pervasive compassion, or energy, of mind). In any case, Guru Rinpoche holds the treasury of these wisdoms. He is the king of miraculous appearances who takes various forms; this refers to the eight forms of Guru Rinpoche, as well as the other forms that he presented during his appearance in the world. He is the one who upholds tantric practice; if we look at the history, it is really Guru Rinpoche who spread Secret Mantra teachings throughout India and Tibet.

Buddha Shakyamuni predicted that a person superior to himself would appear. This doesn't mean that Guru Rinpoche's realization was higher or greater but simply that the Buddha taught the discourses and Guru Rinpoche taught tantra and Dzogchen. From the perspective of their essence, there is no difference between Guru Rinpoche and Buddha Shakyamuni. In relation to their activity, Guru Rinpoche was more focused toward beings of this very dark and difficult time, as a teacher of tantras as the means to attain freedom during this age, than was Buddha Shakyamuni.

In a treasure text that gives advice to the Tibetan people, Yeshe Tsogyal said that, in the future, all Tibetans will have Guru Rinpoche as their lama. It is their fortune that their connection to the dharma will be through the master Guru Rinpoche. She advised everyone to be diligent in the practice of Guru Yoga. In that practice, she said, regardless of one's own master, one imagines the essence to be one's master but the form to be Guru Rinpoche. There was no better, quicker, or more efficient way of receiving the blessings of the dharma master.

In each series, or cycle, of treasure teachings that the one hundred tertons have revealed, we find a heart practice of Guru Rinpoche. Yeshe Tsogyal advised that whether one does an extensive or a short version of a heart practice of Guru Rinpoche, the instructions should be followed as given. "If you do this," she said, "I swear that you will attain enlightenment during one lifetime." In the New Treasures of Dudjom Rinpoche, the heart practice of Guru Rinpoche is Lake-Born Vajra. In the practice of Chokgyur Dechen Lingpa's termas, it is Clearing Away All Obstacles (Barche Kunsel). In Lerab Lingpa's termas, it is the Common Form of the Jewels. In Ratna Lingpa's extensive form of the heart practice of Guru Rinpoche, you practice each of the eight forms of Guru Rinpoche. These are just examples. Each of the tertons revealed one heart practice, one heart meditation, of Guru Rinpoche.

Guru Rinpoche's own adamantine speech promised that if someone with faith in him and a karmic connection to him prayed with great yearning, in times of happiness, sorrow, or suffering, no buddha's compassionate blessing would be swifter than that of Guru Rinpoche, due to his aspirations and the connections of cause and effect.

Mipham Rinpoche commented that however strong the negative emotions become or however deep and difficult beings' situations get, Guru Rinpoche's activity would increase. He said that, during the degenerate time, peoples' negative emotions increase, the length of their lives decreases, their busyness increases, and the parts of their lives that create suffering increase. But at that time, in the same way as when the sky gets darker, the moon gets brighter, the activity of Guru Rinpoche will increase as things get more difficult.

One of Ratna Lingpa's treasures is the practice of Sangwa Dupa (the Union of Mysteries). In that text, Guru Rinpoche says, "If you practice me, you will accomplish all buddhas. If you see me, you see all buddhas. I am the union, the epitome, of all buddhas." This is the adamantine speech, the true words, the promise of Guru Rinpoche.

There are a number of ways to meditate on Guru Rinpoche. For example, we can imagine Guru Rinpoche, and above his head sit the series of lineage masters, one above the other, until Buddha Ever Excellent. We can imagine Guru Rinpoche surrounded by the three jewels and the three roots, as if in a crowded marketplace. Or we can imagine that all these objects of refuge are joined in the single form of Guru Rinpoche; this is "the single jewel" style. It is fine to practice any of these styles, whatever style of meditation feels right to you.

Guru Rinpoche said that in the pure land of Great Bliss resides Buddha Amitabha. On Mount Potala lives the protector Chenrezig. And Guru Rinpoche himself was born on Lake Danakosha, as Padmasambhava. These three forms represent the three bodies of enlightenment, but in fact they are inseparable. There is no difference in essence between Amitabha, Chenrezig, and Padmasambhava. Further, in relation to the three bodies of enlightenment, in the sphere of totality, there is Buddha Ever Excellent, Samantabhadra. On the level of the body of enlightenment's perfect splendor, in the pure land of Dense Design (or Rich Design), there is Buddha Vajradhara. At the Vajra Seat, Bodhgaya, there is Buddha Shakyamuni, the manifest body of enlightenment. But these three bodies of enlightenment are inseparable from Guru Rinpoche himself. Guru Rinpoche said, "Therefore you should pray continually to me." So with very sincere belief and confidence, we can practice imagining all three bodies of enlightenment, all forms of enlightenment, gathered into one form—Guru Rinpoche.

Thinley Norbu Rinpoche includes here a description of Guru Rinpoche taken from a commentary to the Khandro Nyingtik (Innermost Essence of the Dakinis). We imagine in the sky before us, directly in front and slightly elevated, in a tent encircled by rainbows, a throne supported by eight lions. Upon the throne are many silk or brocade cloths, on top of which is a one-hundred-thousand-petaled lotus, upon which are the flat disks of the sun and the moon.

Upon the moon disk we imagine our root lama in the form of Guru Rinpoche. Guru Rinpoche's color is white with a red complexion, as if translucent red paint were put on a conch shell, with both the white and red color coming through. He appears as a youth, eight years old, with all the signs and marks of the physical perfection of enlightenment in a very radiant form. It is almost unbearable to look at him. Guru Rinpoche is at the same time both peaceful and wrathful. He is smiling. His eyes look at us very directly with a very loving gaze, looking to us as Vajrayogini.

His right hand makes the gesture (*mudra*) of conquering everything, holding a five-pointed golden vajra above his heart. His left hand in his lap holds a skull-cup (*kapala*) filled with wisdom nectar, in which is a vase of the nectar of immortality, ornamented with the sprig of a wish-fulfilling tree. Leaning against his left shoulder is his wooden trident staff (*katvanga*), which is a concealed form of his consort Mandarava. On it is a crossed vajra, above which is a vase. Above that are three skulls. Above the skulls is a trident. Hanging on the trident are nine links of a chain. There are silk ribbons, a skull drum (*damaru*), and bells hanging down.

The inner, secret vajra layer of Guru Rinpoche's clothing is white. Over that is the tantric practitioner's garment, dark blue, and over that are the monk's robes, red with gold designs. A cape covers all these layers. Sometimes Guru Rinpoche is completely encircled by the cape. The cape's red color is the color of power.

Guru Rinpoche's hat is "the lotus hat that brings liberation on sight." His legs are in the position of "royal ease." His body is extremely brilliant. His body, with all the marks and signs of the physical perfection of buddhas, radiates pure light. His speech is equally as brilliant, or radiant, with the sixty qualities of buddhas' speech. His mind is brilliantly clear with the nondual wisdom of knowledge, love, and capability. To the right of Guru Rinpoche (to our left as we face him) is Mandarava, his consort when he attained the state of awareness holder of longevity. She holds the arrow of longevity, the force of long life.

We do not have to imagine Guru Rinpoche's body as enormous, but the nature of his body pervades all the pure lands of the buddhas (that is to say, his body remains in this one nature yet manifests everywhere in the pure lands and the ten directions). Each pore of his body holds infinitely many pure lands. We think of the body of

Guru Rinpoche not as substantial flesh and blood but as if it were a magical display. His form is the essence of all refuges.

When we meditate on Guru Rinpoche in this way, we should meditate so that all our ordinary common appearances are blocked by the attention given to Guru Rinpoche.

There are a series of phrases that describe the brilliance of Guru Rinpoche's body, speech, and mind. First, the brilliance, or the radiance, of his body refers to his body being not a substantial material body but like the appearance of the reflection of the moon on water. This is the clarity, or the radiance, of Guru Rinpoche on the physical level: *lhamed* in Tibetan.

The next term, *lha nge wa*, refers to the qualities of Guru Rinpoche's enlightened speech, which is without any obscuration, fault, or hesitation. It is limpidly clear.

The qualities of Guru Rinpoche's mind are gathered in the term *lhen nge wa*. This radiant, or luminous, mind refers to Guru Rinpoche's mind not having any of the agitation or depression that ordinary sentient beings have. His mind doesn't go out and get grabbed by outer appearances. Neither does it sink inside. Ordinarily, sentient beings have elation or depression. Guru Rinpoche's mind has neither, no extremes. The text says that his mind is like the radiance of a wish-fulfilling jewel. Guru Rinpoche's mind never strays from the sphere of totality.

We can consider Guru Rinpoche to be the union of the three bodies of enlightenment or to be the union of the three "mysteries" (of body, speech, and mind) of enlightenment. There is no contradiction between these two. Guru Rinpoche appears to sentient beings in ways that are appropriate to guide them.

We've set up our meditation; we imagine ourselves as Vajrayogini, and we imagine Guru Rinpoche in the sky before us. Now we do the invitation practice. Up to this point, we have practiced the visualization; this is our creation, clear within our mind, but now we invite Guru Rinpoche to really appear.

As Vajrayogini, from our heart an inconceivable amount of multicolored light radiates to the Palace of Lotus Light in Guru Rinpoche's pure land, the Copper-Colored Mountain. When the light touches the heart of Guru Rinpoche, he becomes aware that the time has come for him to appear before us, to bless us. Surrounded by hundreds of thousands of awareness holders and dakinis, he comes into the sky before us.

Once Guru Rinpoche, the awareness holders, and the dakinis arrive in the sky before us, the visualizations that reflect our commitment, the *samayasattvas* (commitment deities), and the deities who appear from the pure land, the *jnanasattvas* (wisdom deities), dissolve inseparably into one another: Guru Rinpoche and the awareness holders dissolve into the form of Guru Rinpoche, and the form of Vajrayogini, who has come with Guru Rinpoche from the Copper-Colored Mountain, dissolves into us. Instead of being in the presence of our own mental projections, we now develop confidence that we are Vajrayogini and that the Guru Rinpoche seated in the sky before us is exactly the Guru Rinpoche of the Copper-Colored Mountain.

We can do this elaborate invitation process; or, if we have very deep confidence and stable faith in the visualization, simply by recalling the symbols, signs, and meanings described above, the commitment deities and the wisdom deities can be immediately made inseparable. If that is the case, we do not have to invite the wisdom deities from the pure land. We can be confident that if we have stable faith, just doing this immediate visualization will be effective for us to receive the blessing.

How is this possible? Even in the sutras, it is said that the Buddha stands directly before whoever brings the Buddha to mind. Whoever keeps the Buddha in mind will continually receive his blessing and be freed from all faults. This applies to Guru Rinpoche as well.

Guru Rinpoche himself said, "A form of me will appear before any person who has faith in me." So we don't have to think of Guru Rinpoche as being far away in the Copper-Colored Mountain; with faith and devotion, Guru Rinpoche will appear directly before us. Thinley Norbu Rinpoche comments that each of us has to judge according to our own needs and time available which visualization to do, elaborate or brief.

## The Seven-Branch Prayer

Other foundational practices often include at this point a prayer to cultivate seven positive attitudes, popularly known as the Seven-Branch Prayer. In the Dudjom Tersar's very brief foundational practice, we have only a four-line prayer, but the meaning of the Seven-Branch Prayer is gathered in these four lines:

> The complete embodiment of all buddhas of the three times,
> Supreme root lama, I pray to you.
> In this life, the next lives, and between lives, hold me with
> your compassion.
> May your blessings flow unceasingly throughout the three
> times.

The first two lines say in effect, "Guru Rinpoche and the root lama are the union of all the buddhas of the past, present, and future. And to my root teacher I pray." In the next line, we ask Guru Rinpoche to protect and nurture us with his compassion. "In this life" means whether we're happy or suffering from sickness or psychological disturbances, regardless of our situation, we ask for Guru Rinpoche's attention to make our lives work, be successful, help clear away obstacles on our path to enlightenment, and at the very best increase our experience and realization so that we can attain enlightenment during this lifetime. We ask for his compassion, attention, and nourishment during this lifetime. We ask particularly for Guru Rinpoche's aid in clearing away all obstacles to our progress, most particularly for the development of the realization, or recognition, of the Dzogchen view.

We ask, as well, for Guru Rinpoche's compassionate attention for the benefit of our future lives. We wish to be reborn among human beings, to regain all the aspects of the precious human birth, to meet a qualified master, to have all our obstacles and impediments to realization cleared away, to be happy in body, speech, and mind, and most particularly, to have the opportunity to receive the teachings of luminous Dzogchen. We also ask for Guru Rinpoche's compassion and attention between lives (during the intermediate state, the *bardo*). There are several different kinds of bardo, discussed at length below. There is the bardo of the moment of death, and we ask Guru Rinpoche's attention that we be free from fear and suffering. In the next moment, the bardo of the nature of reality, we ask Guru Rinpoche that we be able to recognize the nature of reality. If we do not recognize the nature of reality, we enter the bardo of becoming, or existence. At that time, we ask to be freed from any fearful or other kind of appearance whatsoever, regardless of what our experience is. Between the time of death and our future life, we ask that Guru Rinpoche watch over us.

Next in Thinley Norbu Rinpoche's text is a description of the seven branches of the Seven-Branch Prayer. The first is the remedy to pride: to render homage to Guru Rinpoche. Pride can take the form of disrespecting those who are above, such as the three jewels, our teacher, our very kind parents, or any persons who are worthy of respect. Or we may have contempt for persons who are inferior to us. When we have pride, we are not attractive to anybody during this lifetime and in future lifetimes we take rebirth among very arrogant people. To defeat pride, we must develop selfless devotion toward the three jewels, our very kind master, and the community of practitioners. And we should develop respect for our parents, ancestors, elders, and anybody who has good qualities. Toward all others we should develop a great loving, affectionate attitude. Shantideva said that we shouldn't regard any sentient being with angry eyes. Sentient beings enable us to attain enlightenment because they give us the opportunity to develop the mind of awakening by practicing patience.

Physically, we pay homage by doing prostrations if the body is capable. (Recall, we can do prostrations as part of the refuge prayer.) Our hands join in the form of a lotus bud. Touching the forehead symbolizes purification of our physical obscurations; touching the throat symbolizes purification of verbal obscurations; and touching the heart, the purification of mental obscurations. Then we touch forehead, palms, and knees to the ground. This is the prevailing custom. In the tantric tradition, we also have long prostrations; you go completely face down, flat on the floor, with hands outstretched. Lamas of the past said that long prostrations are more effective for purification of obscurations because they are more difficult. When accumulating one hundred thousand prostrations, you can do either the short prostration or the long prostration. There's no real need to do one rather than the other. What matters is your intention.

The benefits of doing prostrations are mentioned in a text. It is said that in future lives you will have a good complexion, will be beautiful, will have noble speech, will dominate one's surroundings, will be loved by gods and human beings, will be befriended by holy persons, will be very brilliant or luminous, and will attain the riches of the higher realms (that is to say, liberation).

The second of the seven branches is the remedy to greed—to make offerings. To overcome our greed, we fill the sky with offerings in the same way as the bodhisattva Samantabhadra; he emanated one hundred forms of himself from his heart. These in turn emanated many forms of himself, each of whom made tremendous offerings (flowers, incense, perfumed water, lamps, music, and so on) to the buddhas and bodhisattvas. Following this example, we fill all space with offerings carried by male and female bodhisattvas. Making these offerings enables us to experience the happiness of being a god or a human being until we attain enlightenment. And we come to be regarded as venerable to others.

The third branch is the acknowledgment of faults, the remedy to anger. We acknowledge our faults and the faults of all sentient beings before Guru Rinpoche with great regret and with the four forces (refuge, remorse, resolve, and remediation) that were described in the teaching on Vajrasattva. Once we have acknowledged our faults before Guru Rinpoche and have been purified, we don't do any negative acts that can cause us to be reborn in the lower realms.

The fourth branch is to rejoice in the merit of others, the antidote to jealousy. When we consider the good situation, happiness, or possessions of others, rather than envying them, we rejoice and wish for them to be even happier, to have more of the same. A text says that if on hearing of someone's virtue we don't feel jealousy or any other negative attitude but sincerely rejoice in the other person's enjoyment, then the power of our joy is enough to receive the same merit.

The fifth branch is the request for the wheel of the dharma to be turned, the remedy for ignorance. As we gradually learn, we begin to recognize our suffering and its causes. We become conscious of our situation and the possibility of freedom and enlightenment.

A solitary sage of the Shravakayana has received teachings in a previous lifetime, but in their current lifetime they do not receive more teachings. But coming upon a human skull, the solitary sage reflects, "Why is this skull here? Because a death occurred. Where did death come from? It came from old age. Where did old age come from? It came from birth. Why is someone born?" The solitary sage reflects on the causes of birth, how consciousness comes into the mother's womb, and where consciousness comes from by retracing the stages of the development of consciousness to its source, ignorance. Without ignorance, there would be no aggregate of volition; and without volition, no consciousness; and without consciousness, no desire or sensation, and so on, to lead to eventual birth, old age, and death. Thus, the solitary sage understands the process of interdependent causation that produces death. By returning to the source that is ignorance, ignorance is undone and the state of arhat is achieved. However, the solitary sage does not reflect on the true nature of reality, so from the point of view of Dzogchen they remain in a state of ignorance. Sentient beings need to receive teachings to do away with their ignorance completely.

Generally, sentient beings don't understand that happiness comes from virtuous acts, suffering arises from negative acts, and they are caught in the trap of samsara. They don't know how to free themselves from the three realms of existence. We call this "ignorance."

Therefore we must encourage the buddhas and bodhisattvas to teach.

At this stage in the seven-part service, we make mental offerings to the buddhas, bodhisattvas, and our teacher, offering all our possessions and including everything wonderful that can be offered. We ask them to teach sentient beings according to their needs. This is the same kind of act as when, after the Buddha attained enlightenment, the gods offered him a conch, a wheel, and other offerings, and asked him to teach. Requesting teachings purifies the obscuration of having abandoned practice or teachings and allows us to develop knowledge and wisdom. We will hold the teaching and eventually attain enlightenment.

The sixth branch is the request to the buddhas, bodhisattvas, and our own teacher not to pass into nirvana; this is the antidote for wrong views. We tell them, "Please don't think that because you have spent years or aeons working for the benefit of sentient beings that it is time to pass on." We ask them to remain in samsara until all sentient beings are freed and attain liberation. Making this request purifies the negative karma that might have shortened our life or produced an untimely death, so we attain longevity.

When we ask our teacher or any buddha or bodhisattva not to pass into nirvana, it does not mean that we don't want them to transcend suffering. The Tibetan word for "nirvana" literally means "to transcend suffering." But here we are simply using an honorific way of asking them to remain with us so they can teach.

The seventh branch is the dedication of merit, the antidote to doubt. Whatever virtuous actions we do, whether relatively minor (such as doing circumambulations of stupas, statues, and so forth), or major (such as working with the view, meditation, and action, or serving sentient beings), we must dedicate all our merit so that we and all sentient beings attain the essence of awakening, the heart of enlightenment.

Of course, any virtuous act will ripen, will produce positive effects, or will give us a certain power over our mind, but when we separate our virtuous acts from enlightenment, they ripen one time and then dissipate. But if we place our virtuous, or positive, acts in the context of the path to enlightenment, there is some accumulation of the effect of our virtue and our dedication helps to keep our focus on awakening rather than doubting.

It is vital that we dedicate our merit to awakening. An example from the discourses of the Buddha is found in his answer to questions from the bodhisattva Lodro Gyatso. The Buddha said to him, "If you spit on sand, your spit will quickly evaporate. But if you spit in the ocean, your spit will remain until that ocean goes dry." In the same way, whatever virtuous act we do, if we don't think about it at all, if we do it with a selfish or malicious intent, if we regret what we have done, or if we dedicate it in an inferior or misguided way, the act will eventually dissipate. But if we dedicate merit within the great ocean of the wisdom of enlightenment, the merit of our virtuous act remains as long as the ocean of wisdom. This joins our virtuous acts and merit with the wishes, positive intentions, and dedication of all buddhas and bodhisattvas.

In another discourse, the Buddha remarked that just as many rivers join from different directions, feed into the ocean, and become of one taste with the ocean, so too when people dedicate merit to supreme awakening, their virtue becomes of one taste with supreme awakening.

Thinley Norbu Rinpoche mentions that Longchenpa clarified the difference between the act of dedication and the act of aspiration (or prayer). When we dedicate merit, we do so because we have finished a virtuous act. In an aspiration or a prayer, there isn't a specific virtuous act to dedicate, rather we pray that in the future may such and such an event happen, may I do such and such, or may all beings attain the heart of enlightenment.

Continuing with the four-line prayer of the Guru Yoga practice: "All buddhas of the three times" refers, first, to the three buddhas who appeared in this aeon and world before Buddha Shakyamuni— the Buddha of Lamps, the Buddha Who Destroys Samsara, and Golden Sage. In the present time, we live in the era of Buddha Shakyamuni. In the future, there will be 996 buddhas, beginning with Buddha Maitreya and ending with a buddha named Devotion. When we address our root lama as the embodiment of the buddhas of the three times, we are speaking of all buddhas past, present, and future.

Speaking of the buddhas of the past, present, and future in this way is to take a slice of time in just one aeon. But we can also go further in the past, or, in the period of Buddha Shakyamuni's teaching, we can identify a past, present, and future. When we think of our root lama as the personification, or epitome, of the buddhas of the past, present, and future, we can include the twelve teachers of the Dzogchen tradition, who go back to the very beginning of beginningless time. Further, there are the lamas of the lineage of the mind-to-mind transmission, the transmission through symbols, and the aural lineage. In the Nyingma tradition, there are the five king tertons, the one hundred great tertons, and the one thousand lesser tertons. Of the one hundred great tertons, the three supreme emanations are considered to be particularly like wish-fulfilling jewels, the greatest and the best. We have many teachers of our tradition, and we imagine all these buddhas of the past, present, and future joined in the one person of our root teacher.

We address our root lama as our principal, root, or source master (Tib. *tsawe*). To help define *tsawe*, consider that the "general teacher" is venerated by persons of all traditions; the "master who guides us" leads us on the path to the happy results of future rebirths as gods and humans, and guides us on the path to freedom, or liberation; and the "master with whom we have connection through empowerment and tantric commitments" is a teacher from whom we've received empowerment into a tantra and with whom we have therefore taken tantric commitments related to specific deities. These three can be considered as our lama, but really our root lama is the one who has given us empowerment into the highest levels of tantra (in the Nyingma tradition, these are the three inner tantras), has explained the tantric path, and particularly has given the direct, naked, pointing-out instructions of awareness (*rigpa*) and thereby places us on the direct path to enlightenment. This is our real root teacher. The kindness or love this person has shown us is far greater than that of any other. There is nothing higher than that.

In the Ngöndro prayer, we say, "My root teacher, to you I pray." Physically, we render homage with great respect; verbally, we pray with great devotion; and mentally, we give our faith wholeheartedly and single-mindedly to our root teacher with great reverence.

## The Intermediate States

The next line in the Ngöndro prayer is "In this life, the next lives, and between lives, hold me with your compassion." We have come to the subject of the intermediate states (the bardos). The time from the moment of birth to the moment we begin the process of death is usually called "the natural bardo." In English, the phrase "natural bardo" is confusing. In Tibetan, it is very clear that after you die there is the "bardo of the nature of reality." It is possible for us to mistake those two phrases. So instead, I will call the natural bardo "the bardo of life," which is the intermediate state after having been born.

In some Dzogchen texts, four bardos are listed. In our text, Thinley Norbu Rinpoche identifies two other bardos during this lifetime. We can count them as separate or include them in our ordinary state of life, this bardo of life. One is the bardo of meditation, which lasts from the moment we sit down to meditate until we enter the postmeditative state. It applies to any sort of meditation practice such as calming the mind, insight meditation, and so on. Another bardo that is part of our experience of life is dreaming. When we have a lucid dream (that is, when we recognize we are dreaming) and can transform appearances, manifest them, and eventually purify our experience while dreaming into the luminosity of mind—clear light—this is the bardo of dream. These two can be included in the intermediate state of life.

The bardo of dream depends entirely on a person's practice. It appears only to practitioners who can enter the dream state and can either multiply, emanate, or transform appearances or purify them entirely into the state of luminous awareness. There are commentaries about the intermediate state of dream that explain how to recognize we are dreaming, how to purify appearances or train in the dream, how to multiply or transform appearances, how to go to pure lands (such as Padmasambhava's Copper-Colored Mountain), and how to purify entirely any impure appearance in a dream and rest in the luminous state of wisdom, or awareness, at the time of sleep. For others, the dream state is just part of the bardo of life.

After the bardo of life comes the bardo of the time of death, which lasts from when the signs of death first begin to appear until you have taken your last breath. You are still alive, but you are checking out. Whatever happens during that time, whatever fear, suffering, or experience, practicing the transference of consciousness or other instructions, checkout time is an intermediate state all in itself.

During the process of dying, on an inner level, the elements dissolve, one into another: earth into water, water into fire, fire into wind, and so forth, and there are different experiences: your mouth gets dry, you can't hear sounds distinctly, your vision clouds. In your mind, at the moment when your breathing ends, the wisdom of the ultimate body of enlightenment, pure primordial awareness, appears like a pure sky, if you recognize it. To use the image of the sky, it is not obscured by bright sunlight (as the sky might seem less clear in bright sun). There is no darkness, clouds, wind, or anything else that obscures the sky. This direct pure awareness is without any obscuration, whether from thoughts, the aggregates, or any mental creation.

Rigdzin Jigme Lingpa said that at the time of death, the white element of our body, which is from our father, descends from our head to our heart, and the red element, which is from our mother, ascends from our navel to our heart. At the time of death, they join at our heart, and at that moment we fall into unconsciousness; our ordinary mind dissolves and the original nature manifests. As practitioners, we try to recognize it. Whether we name it "buddha nature," "primordial nature of mind," "wisdom," or "the basis," it appears clearly to us at that moment. This is the moment for recognition of the primordial nature of mind.

It is like the autumn sky, without any obscuration. It is direct awareness without any complication or pollution. If we recognize this state, we are liberated into the expanse of the ultimate body of enlightenment, and after that there is no more bardo. That is the end of the story. We come to the end of the line right there. When we arrive at liberation within the ultimate body of enlightenment, the impulse, or momentum, the force behind our karma, obscurations, and negative emotions that would have had the effect of propelling us into future lifetimes ceases entirely. There is no more energy pushing us to take rebirth. Then we are free to fill the whole world with emanations in pure and impure situations to lead all sentient beings to enlightenment through the force of great compassion and wisdom.

At the time of death, the teacher or a lama or even companions in practice should speak in the ear of the dead person and remind them that everything that appears should be recognized as an appearance of their own mind. Whatever happens, happiness or suffering, is all an appearance of mind. Remember that. It is a little message to take into the intermediate state. It is a very helpful reminder, a very strong reminder, that whatever appears is entirely the deceased's own experience. We have to remind them, "Whatever you see, don't be afraid. Don't have any apprehension. You're just seeing your own home movies. This is your own experience." This reminder not to be afraid and to recognize that all the appearances that arise are the person's own experience is critical for the person who has just entered into the state of death. It is very similar to a lucid dream. When you understand you are dreaming, you can get carried away by water, fall off a cliff, or do anything you want. You recognize that everything is just a dream as it is happening. There is no fear. You relax in the middle of whatever is happening. But if you don't realize you are dreaming, then falling into a strong river or off a cliff provokes tremendous anxiety. This happens when we enter the intermediate state thinking that our experiences reflect reality when they are just our own experience, like a dream.

If, at that time, we don't recognize that nature, that primordial mind, that direct awareness, we pass on to the next stage, the bardo of the nature of reality (*dharmata*). At this time, the natural display of the nature of reality takes the form of the peaceful deities (the buddhas Vairochana, Ratnasambhava, Akshobhya, Amitabha, and Amoghasiddhi) and the wrathful deities. However, these appearances depend upon Dzogchen practice during the bardo of life. All sentient beings will have these appearances, but unless we have trained in awareness, they will appear for only an instant. If we can remain in awareness for fifteen minutes during this lifetime, these appearances will remain for fifteen minutes during this intermediate state. If we can rest in the nature of reality without moving for an hour, in the intermediate state the appearances will remain for a long time and we will be able to come to some recognition. For an ordinary sentient being, the length of time will be very, very small, hardly enough for a flash of recognition; appearance and disappearance happen almost simultaneously, like a shooting star. There is just a moment to recognize that something has happened, but we don't recognize it as the nature of reality, so we go directly to the next stage.

For Dzogchen practitioners, when appearances arise, such as Vairochana or Vajrasattva, we recognize them as our own appearance or as having arisen through the nature of our mind. They are not experienced as "other." If Buddha Vairochana appears, it is recognized as the appearance of the nature of reality or of the nature of mind, and that recognition brings liberation into the state of Buddha Vairochana. If we recognize Vajrasattva, we are liberated into the essence of Buddha Vajrasattva.

The peaceful and wrathful deities are not appearances from outer space or from outside ourselves, not something to which we have no natural relationship. The appearance of the peaceful and wrathful deities relates to the nature of our own mind. Specifically, the forty-two peaceful deities relate to the channels at our heart and the fifty-eight wrathful deities relate to the channels in our brain. At the time of death, the pure aspects of the channels appear to us. They are the primordial, or pure, appearance of our own nature that appear directly before us; first the peaceful deities and then the wrathful deities.

Right now, our experience of the nature of reality, the nature of our mind, is obscured by our body, speech, and mind. At the point of death, we separate from our body, our speech, and the greater part of our mind. Then the nature of reality, the nature of our mind, appears directly to us. That is a very critical, very powerful, moment. At that stage, a Dzogchen practitioner rests in awareness, in the nature of mind, but now, in our present waking state, it isn't as vivid or clear as it might be. For example, compared to our waking state, it is far clearer during the time of dreaming. We can enter into the clear light, the luminous state during the time of dream because our ordinary senses are blocked during sleep. So the appearance of the nature of mind can be more vivid and complete at the time of sleep or dream. It is even more vivid and clear during the bardo of the nature of reality, for a Dzogchen practitioner.

Upon death, all ordinary thoughts of anger, desire, and ignorance (eighty in all) are naturally blocked. We no longer have the psychophysical aggregates for the support of these thoughts. It is not through our practice that they are blocked; it is just that naturally there is no longer any support for them. In the absence of these thoughts, the nature of reality, the nature of mind, appears completely clear. In the same way, when clouds leave the sky, we see the clear blue sky or the sun. This is like the experience of the time after we die. Everything appears very clearly. But the duration of clarity depends on our Dzogchen practice.

As Dzogchen practitioners, when we are in this intermediate state seeing pure lands, deities, or any pure appearance, peaceful or wrathful, we immediately recognize that these have not appeared from something else but are appearances of the nature of our own mind. The image we use is that of a child who, without reflecting, crawls into its mother's lap. Our awareness and the appearances join as one, and we are liberated in the appearances of the nature of reality. This is "liberation into the body of enlightenment's perfect splendor." It comes after the first stage in which only the original purity of mind appeared, and we could have been liberated into the ultimate body of enlightenment. If we had been liberated at that point, none of the other appearances of the intermediate state would have continued. We wouldn't have entered into further experience in the bardo.

To recognize the appearances of the nature of reality, it is vital for us to have received pointing-out instructions of trekchöd from our teacher. We can talk about recognizing awareness, rigpa, and we will have a certain idea of what that is, but through direct pointing-out instructions, we can recognize awareness and rest within it. Once we have the recognition of awareness, our experience during the bardo is very easy. It is the same recognition that we were introduced to during the pointing-out instructions.

Let's say we meet for the first time. Before that, I didn't know you; I couldn't recognize you. The next time we meet, since we've already been introduced, we may know one another a bit. The more often we meet, the more familiar I get with you. I get to know who you are. In the same way, if we haven't been introduced to the nature of our mind, we don't recognize it. But once we've been introduced through pointing-out instructions and once we have become familiar with the nature of our own mind, when we encounter this same nature in the bardo state, it is very easy. Without the first introduction, the pointing-out and recognition that we familiarized ourselves with during this lifetime, it is really, really difficult for us to understand the meaning when experiences arise during the bardo.

In fact, in the bardo, it is far easier to arrive at complete liberation. We don't have to pass through all sorts of different stages and paths. At the moment of recognition, there is liberation because after death the eighty natural thoughts of anger, desire, and ignorance cease entirely so there is nothing else besides this recognition and liberation.

Our practice during this lifetime is really a preparation. Perhaps we are going to arrive at liberation during this lifetime, perhaps during the bardo, or perhaps during a future life. After we have chosen a place to live, prepared the land, and built a home, when we enter the home we feel safe and sound because we have made all the arrangements. In the same way, we are preparing for liberation in this life, in the bardo, or in the next life.

The critical issue is recognition of the view. When we study bardo teachings, sometimes we spend lots of time studying all the appearances we will experience, but what is most important in the bardo teachings is recognition of the Dzogchen view. It is no different from recognition of the Dzogchen view during this lifetime. Different appearances arise during this lifetime or during the bardo, but to remain unseparated from the view presented in trekchöd teachings carries us through this life, the bardo, and the next life. The particular appearances are not really all that significant. If they appear, that is fine. If they don't appear, that is fine. What is critical is to remain within the view.

To see the peaceful or wrathful deities as a positive experience and the appearance of the six realms of beings as a negative one is not of very much benefit, if one's attention is given to these various appearances. That is all unprofitable. The real teachings of the bardo come down to the point of recognition and remaining in the recognition of the Dzogchen view.

In talking about recognition, we have to use certain words such as "we recognize the nature of reality," but it is not a dualistic experience. We can recognize something without the dualistic experience of subject and object. In Dzogchen practice, we become familiar with nondualistic recognition of the nature of mind.

Now we come to the bardo of becoming. When practitioners of Dzogchen enter the bardo of the nature of reality, the peaceful and wrathful deities appear. A practitioner who recognizes them as the appearance, or display, of their own awareness reaches liberation. There is no longer any impulse, impetus, or need to take rebirth in samsara. However, if these appearances are seen as the manifestation of a dualistic mind and fear, then apprehension, or another dualistic experience, arises; the bardo of the nature of reality ends and the bardo of becoming begins. Habitual tendencies create the impression of a body that is similar to the body of our lifetime.

Because we have not recognized the peaceful and wrathful deities as the display of our own awareness and think of them as other, instead of this solid body we create a mental body. It is very similar to our experience of a dream. When we dream, we experience walking, sitting, and talking. We are involved in the world, but it is entirely a creation of our own mind. In the same way, during the bardo of becoming, we create this mental impression of a body and we hold it as real. While we have the mental body, we no longer eat, of course, as we do now. There is nothing solid, but in this intermediate state we nourish ourselves with smells. Beings in the bardo of becoming are called "smell eaters who surround." There are practices done for a person who has died and burned offerings of food are made to help them. Burned food isn't delicious or attractive to anybody except beings in this bardo. They gather and are nourished by the smell.

Now what do we do in the bardo of becoming? We have come back to ourselves, and we're back at our ordinary state with our habitual tendencies and our ordinary experience. At this time, when we wake up to ourselves, we can pray. We pray to our meditation deity, to our lama, to Guru Rinpoche. We pray wholeheartedly once we have realized where we are. Thanks to our prayers, we can be reborn in a pure land. Or thanks to our prayers, we can be reborn with a precious human body and the opportunity to again encounter the teachings. Here, in the bardo of becoming, we open our mind to our teachers and pray wholeheartedly.

If through our prayers we are reborn with a precious human body, then, through the force of truth of our practice of Dzogchen during this lifetime, it is said that if we encounter the teachings of Dzogchen by the time we are twenty years old or so, we will be liberated.

During this lifetime, in the Dzogchen tradition, we receive pointing-out instructions and recognize the nature of mind, or awareness. These teachings can lead us to enlightenment or to liberation in this lifetime. However, we might wonder, "What if I don't reach liberation during this lifetime?" In that case, during the bardo of the time of death, the appearance of the basis of mind arises. Through resting in the view, we can recognize the nature of mind as it appears at the moment of death. If we don't recognize it, then we enter into the bardo of the nature of reality. Again, we have certain teachings to recognize appearances at that point. If that doesn't work, there are additional teachings. If that doesn't work, we have at least the opportunity of meeting Dzogchen teachings and arriving at liberation in our next life. This all depends on Dzogchen teachings. Other traditions have some bardo teachings, but when we go into the details of the appearances that arise in the intermediate states, this is the domain of the Dzogchen tradition.

In Dzogchen, we are working with exactly how the mind is, through all its different stages, during this lifetime and at death. In other levels of Vajrayana, such as the *Kalachakra Tantra* or the *Secret Essence Tantra*, how to attain liberation in the intermediate states is not described in any of the detail given in Dzogchen. This is because in Dzogchen, we try to describe exactly the nature of mind.

During this lifetime, we must prepare ourselves well for our future journeys. When we are going somewhere new, we buy a travel guide, look at maps, and try to understand our destination so that we have a good time and don't get lost along the way. We should study the intermediate states with the same mentality. We know that we are going on this trip, and we have to prepare ourselves. We have to understand what happens at the time of death, how to prepare ourselves for the bardo of the nature of reality and the bardo of becoming, what will happen then, how to face that inevitable journey.

At the time of death, it is important not to have many thoughts. Don't fuss about your family, possessions, anything. Try to prepare your mind for the time of death. The best preparation is to have a mind at ease in the Dzogchen view, the recognition of awareness. Second best is to die within the feeling that your mind and your lama's mind, Guru Rinpoche's mind, are inseparable. This is the highest and most sovereign of all practices of transference of consciousness (which is discussed below).

Teachings about what to do at the time of death are described in detail in such practices as the peaceful and wrathful deities practice (such as Karling Shitro). It is not possible for us to go into great detail about these practices, but we have discussed the essence of what must be done at that time—to recognize all appearances as one's own subjective experience and to rest the mind in the view.

The *Prayer to Buddha Ever Excellent* (*Kunzang monlam*) says that the basis of all things and all reality is noncomposite. It is the inexpressible, self-manifest expanse. Within this, there is neither the basis of all things and appearances nor the basis of our mind. There is neither the name of samsara nor of nirvana. When we wake to this, it is enlightenment. Whether now, during this bardo of living, at the time of death, during the bardo of the nature of reality, during the bardo of becoming, or at any point, we must recognize the nature of mind. At that point there is no longer any experience of intermediate states. We have attained enlightenment.

When we can rest unmoving, as do all buddhas in the ultimate body of enlightenment, no matter what appears, we do not enter confusion. No matter what appears during any intermediate state, because we rest unmoving within the ultimate body of enlightenment of awareness, no confusion can arise. Ordinarily, our mind moves. We have many thoughts, positive and negative. We have many reactions to appearances. Our confusion arises. But when awareness remains within its own nature, when we remain within the ultimate body of enlightenment, we don't label samsara as negative and the transcendent state of nirvana as positive. We remain in that state and no matter what appears, nothing changes our awareness. Any appearance whatsoever is entirely the same because the mind never moves from its own nature.

Thinley Norbu Rinpoche comments that upon recognition of the primordial basis of mind, which can occur during any one of the intermediate states, samsara and transcendent states cease to exist for us. This is not the nihilist view that, at death, our senses and our consciousness dissolve and nothing continues. When we have gone beyond all concepts, all labeling, all ideas of existence and nonexistence, we've gone beyond the nihilist and eternalist views. When our consciousness, or our awareness, dissolves into the appearance of the primordial basis, we transcend even the name of samsara and transcendent states.

In the fourth line of the four-line prayer, we ask for our master's blessing continuously in the past, present, and future. This begs the question, what is time? Regarding future time, present time, and past time, Thinley Norbu Rinpoche quotes again from Rong-zompa: in the same way that our experience of the outer world and space is the appearance of confusion, our experience of time is also a creation of our confused mind. When we go to sleep, we might dream about a period of one hundred years in an instant. Time is as relative as space. Our ordinary experience of time as past, present, and future is only an appearance of our lack of understanding of the nature of reality. If we take appearances to be other, we experience self and other. This is the first moment of dualistic experience. When we enter samsara and dualistic experience, all changes happen in the context of our experience of space and time.

There is an appearance of a continuous progression of past, present, and future. But apart from this appearance, there isn't a fundamental reality. Previously, I gave the example of a dream about setting out to go to Tibet. If I found myself halfway, in Hong Kong, I would think, "I have now come as far as Hong Kong. Previously I was in the States. In the future, I am going to Tibet." But those experiences of past, present, and future are only in relation to dream appearances. In fact, the whole experience of time was relative to a particular creation of mind that had no reality. This is what happens in a dream. But in our ordinary waking situation as well, we have the impression of having been born at one time, abiding in life for a certain amount of time, and then passing away. This, as well, is a creation of the confused mind; we think about events as occurring to us. Without dualistic mind, there is no time. Whatever division of time we invent is all a creation. The impression of time passing is a creation of our mind. We have seconds, minutes, hours, days, months, years, and aeons, each related to one another. When we begin to look at time and examine it closely, in the same way that we can analyze space and objects, we see that the basis of time is emptiness.

Asking Guru Rinpoche to bless us throughout the three times means asking him to bless us with his compassion as long as we wander within this confused impression of past, present, and future.

At the level of enlightenment, there is no time, no division between past, present, and future. We call this "the fourth time" or "the time of equanimity." We call the level of enlightenment "the supreme enemy of time" because time cannot enter that sphere of totality. We pray to Guru Rinpoche to physically, verbally, and mentally bless us until we've arrived at that state. We pray to Guru Rinpoche wholeheartedly and single-mindedly. The image for being single-minded is a dagger. The mind is sharp, clear, intense, and focused. We bring this intensity to our prayer to Guru Rinpoche.

Speaking of the fourth time is speaking of the nature of reality, the sphere of totality that is "beyond all atoms." It means we don't see anything solid in the outside world, within our negative emotions or within time. There is not even the finest particle of anything substantial within mind, the outside world or time. It is primordial time or the time of original purity. The sphere of totality is completely free from even the finest substantiality. In primordial or original purity, there is no hope for transcendence, nor any fear of falling into the lower realms or samsara. There is neither happiness nor suffering in relation to samsara and nirvana. This freedom from any complexity of mind is supreme happiness. It goes far beyond the ordinary, temporary happiness that changes into suffering or creates a cause for suffering.

Thinley Norbu Rinpoche's text includes Mipham Rinpoche's *Praise to Manjushri*. It says that, among all peaceful deities, Manjushri is the most peaceful. The first syllable of the Tibetan word for Manjushri, *jam*, means "gentle" or "soft," because through purification and clearing away all impurities of mind, the mind becomes extremely soft, gentle, or tender. The second syllable, *pal*, means "illustrious" or "glorious." This refers to his mind's many qualities that have manifested. Manjushri is said to have the form of great compassion that pervades space. He appears in the form of a sixteen-year-old youth.

The *Praise to Manjushri* continues by saying that of all the wrathful deities, he is the most wrathful! He is the one who overcomes, or defeats, everything. He is the slayer of the lord of death. He consumes all existence and nirvana into the sphere of totality. He is the great enemy of time (which is why we have this praise here). When sentient beings suffer from entrapment within the impression of the solidity of time, Manjushri liberates them to the fourth time, the time of equanimity, the time without time.

## The Four Empowerments

Until now, we have recited prayers to Guru Rinpoche that our mind be filled with the experience of the energy and realization of the nature of mind, that we be free from suffering and samsara, and that we attain both temporary happiness and the permanent happiness of enlightenment. After having prayed to Guru Rinpoche, we receive the blessings and the qualities of Guru Rinpoche's body, speech, and mind. To draw his blessings to us very efficiently and quickly, we take the four empowerments. This is how we practice Guru Yoga in the tantras. Tantric practice depends upon receiving empowerment; then we can receive instruction in tantra and direct instruction in meditation. It's not possible to practice tantra without empowerment in the same way that it's not possible to row a boat without oars.

Because empowerment sets the stage for our practice, the first tantric empowerment we receive directly from our master is "the empowerment of the basis." Later, when we imagine Guru Rinpoche in the sky before us and receive empowerments during Guru Yoga visualization, these are "the empowerments of the path." Finally, when the wisdom of the empowerment fully manifests to us, when we perceive directly the three bodies of enlightenment, it is "the empowerment of the result."

There are an incredible number of different empowerments in the tantras related to the basis, the path, and the result. However, there is nothing greater than the visualization we do in Guru Yoga practice; we develop intense devotion and appreciation toward our root teacher, receive blessings from his body, speech, and mind to our body, speech, and mind, and in this way we receive the blessing that his wisdom joins inseparably with our mind. In the Dzogchen tradition, there is nothing higher or better than that form of empowerment.

Once we finish the prayers to Guru Rinpoche, we receive the four empowerments. We begin by imagining that at Guru Rinpoche's forehead stands a white syllable *om*, clear and radiant. From it, pure and clear white light radiates and touches our forehead, which bestows the first of the four empowerments, the "vase empowerment." In our body of fully ripened karma, the obscurations of our inner channels are purified and our body becomes the display of the body of enlightenment. We receive in our mind the fortune of attaining the manifest body of enlightenment.

Second, we imagine a red syllable *ah* at Guru Rinpoche's throat. Red light from the syllable *ah* streams into our throat, bestowing the second empowerment—the "secret empowerment" and the blessing of Guru Rinpoche's speech. We imagine that our voice is blessed by his; in the same way that our speech is related to our breathing, or our energy, this empowerment at the level of our throat removes the obscurations of the energy-winds throughout our body. We receive the fortune to attain the body of enlightenment's perfect splendor.

Then we imagine a dark blue syllable *hung* at Guru Rinpoche's heart. From it, dark blue light streams and dissolves into our heart, bestowing upon us the third empowerment—the "wisdom empowerment." It purifies the obscurations of our mind and the vital essence (*thigle*) of our body. We imagine that our mind is blessed by the enlightened mind of Guru Rinpoche. The blue light places in our mind the fortune to attain the ultimate body of enlightenment.

Then from Guru Rinpoche's heart comes a sphere of five-colored light, the essence of freedom from ordinary thought. This clear globe of light dissolves into our heart. It removes our habitual tendencies and the two obscurations (the obscuring emotions and our lack of understanding). It bestows upon us the fourth empowerment, the "precious word empowerment." We are blessed with inseparability from the qualities and the enlightened activity of all buddhas. The fourth empowerment places in our mind the fortune to attain all these qualities in one place and one time, without being mixed up, called "the essence-body of enlightenment" (svabhavikakaya).

The lights from Guru Rinpoche have removed four levels of obscurations. They have bestowed the four empowerments and placed in our mind the fortune to attain the four bodies of enlightenment. We receive five aspects of the blessing of Guru Rinpoche: his enlightened body, speech, mind, qualities, and activity.

## The Vajra Guru Mantra

Depending on which foundational practice or commentary one reads, at this point we might recite the twelve-syllable mantra of Guru Rinpoche—*om ah hung benzar guru pema siddhi hung*. According to some foundational practices, it is recited before the empowerments. Sometimes it is recited after the empowerments. Here is the meaning of the mantra according to the New Treasures of Dudjom Rinpoche:

*Om, ah,* and *hung* are the seed syllables of the three vajras—the body, speech, and mind of all buddhas or of Guru Rinpoche.

*Benzar* is a Tibetan "mispronunciation" of the word *vajra.* Phonetically, it should be pronounced *vajra,* but it has been pronounced for so long as *benzar* that there is as much blessing in mispronouncing it as in pronouncing it properly. Only recently has it been pronounced properly. Many awareness holders and great masters of the past have attained accomplishment by saying *benzar.* Without a doubt some of them recited *vajra,* but most recited *benzar.* If you recite *om ah hung benzar guru pema siddhi hung,* you shouldn't have any doubt that this will lead you to accomplishment.

Benzar (Skt. *vajra*) in this case is a weapon that cannot be defeated and can overcome, or split, anything in its path. As related to our practice, vajra is the symbol of awareness and emptiness, which cannot be divided by any complications of dualistic experience or ordinary thought. Awareness and emptiness cannot be overcome by any thoughts of solid reality. Awareness and emptiness refer to the empty and clear nature of our mind that cannot be overcome by any thing, by any ordinary thought. This is vajra, the nature of our own mind. Vajra is the nature of reality, or the sphere of totality, beyond any characteristics. In this case, it is the ultimate body of enlightenment.

*Guru* literally means "heavy" in Sanskrit, because the lama is heavy with all the qualities of the seven aspects of the body of enlightenment's perfect splendor (which were mentioned in the discussion of refuge). The lama endowed with the weighty qualities of the pure land of enlightenment is related to the body of enlightenment's perfect splendor.

*Pema* (or *padma*) evokes the lotus family of enlightenment, the wisdom of discernment, and great exaltation. All forms of Guru Rinpoche belong to the lotus family of enlightenment and all were born miraculously. The Lake-Born Vajra, the eight forms of Guru Rinpoche, and so forth are all miraculous manifestations of enlightenment in the world. *Pema* refers to Guru Rinpoche as the manifest body of enlightenment. The master from Oddiyana, the great Vajradhara, Guru Rinpoche, embodies all three bodies of enlightenment. In the perceptions of ordinary sentient beings, a distinction exists between the ultimate body of enlightenment, the body of enlightenment's perfect splendor, and the manifest body of enlightenment. For Guru Rinpoche, these three bodies are inseparable, indivisible, without distinction. The body of enlightenment's perfect splendor is the display of the ultimate body. The manifest body is the display of the body of enlightenment's perfect splendor. They are one, although it doesn't appear this way to ordinary beings.

Recalling the enlightened qualities of Guru Rinpoche, we recite the mantra as a prayer, with complete openness and simplicity of mind, without any complications or elaborations. We allow our mind to be completely open as we recite. Reciting the mantra in that way, we receive Guru Rinpoche's blessing and accomplishment.

Accomplishment is the meaning of the next two syllables, *siddhi*. We receive both supreme and ordinary accomplishments.

In brief, the first three syllables of the mantra *om ah hung benzar guru pema siddhi hung* relate to the body, speech, and mind of all buddhas. *Benzar guru pema* relates to the ultimate body of enlightenment, the body of enlightenment's perfect splendor, and the manifest body of enlightenment. *Siddhi* means "accomplishment." We finish the mantra with the syllable *hung*, which here means "Give me this right now!" We remember the meaning of the mantra as we recite and think to ourselves, "Body, speech, and mind of Guru Rinpoche's three bodies of enlightenment, give me blessing right now!"

Guru Rinpoche takes many forms. His eight different manifestations are only some of his forms. In fact, he appears in an inconceivable number of forms. This mantra is, in fact, a form of Guru Rinpoche. Guru Rinpoche is inseparable from this mantra. Mipham Rinpoche's commentary to the *Secret Essence Tantra*, the *Essence of Luminosity*, states that the deities and their mantras are one and the same. He explains in detail how it is possible for manifestations of enlightenment to take many different forms including that of a mantra, and how the essence of the deity appears directly in the mantra. We don't have the fortune at this time to see or encounter his human form, the manifest body of enlightenment, as people did in the eighth century. However, this mantra helps us arrive at the experience, or realization, of the mind of Guru Rinpoche.

If there were no presence of Guru Rinpoche, reciting countless numbers of mantras would have no effect. It would be like doing something completely impossible. But we can receive, or attain, supreme and ordinary accomplishments through reciting the mantra. It invokes the presence of Guru Rinpoche. No matter how much ordinary talk we engage in, we won't receive the blessings of the buddha of the three times, Guru Rinpoche's blessing. However, reciting this mantra does attract his blessing.

When reciting the Guru Rinpoche mantra, maintain very strong faith and devotion to Guru Rinpoche who appears in the sky before you. Imagine that the mantra is the manifest form of Guru Rinpoche. Keep Guru Rinpoche in your speech, in your mind, and in your imagined sight of him in the sky before you. You imagine seeing the nature of your own mind as Guru Rinpoche. If you continue to recite the mantra with that attitude, imagination will manifest as reality and there is a very great danger that you might attain enlightenment!

## Accomplishments

As explained above, Guru Yoga yields accomplishments (*siddhis*). We receive both supreme and ordinary accomplishments. With this mantra, in the category of ordinary accomplishments, we request eight major accomplishments and twelve forms of enlightened activity, which can be synthesized into four enlightened activities. First, pacifying enlightened activity calms any sickness, mental suffering, or obstacles, everything causing disharmony in our life, everything unwanted.

Second, the activity of enhancement increases the positive side of our experience—our longevity, merit, and the wisdom and qualities on the stages and paths of awakening.

Third, magnetizing activity brings our own appearances under control and prevents loss of self-control. Once we bring our own experience under control, we can, literally, overpower others' appearances. Ordinarily, our attention gets lost in outer appearances. This causes suffering. But in the mind of a practitioner, 100 percent of attention stays in the person's experience. We no longer lose our mind, our attention, or our control to outer appearances.

Guru Rinpoche had complete control over his own appearances. He was able to experience everything as a magical display, or a dream. No matter what the appearance, whether of gods or demons, it evoked no fear, or apprehension, in his mind. Similarly, when we have control over our own appearances, we don't lose our attention to happiness or sadness. No matter how happy or pleasant the outside world is, we don't get attached to it. We are self-contained.

Our attention doesn't get lost in whatever seemingly positive or negative appearances arise. In addition, it is possible through magnetizing activity to overpower others' experience, or appearances. For example, when Guru Rinpoche or any yogi of realization enters a specific environment, they are seen as very important persons. When Guru Rinpoche went to Tibet, all the gods and demons who formerly had assumed important places for themselves became humble. They helped Guru Rinpoche with his work. They experienced Guru Rinpoche as a powerful individual. We, too, might have the experience of coming before a yogi and being unable to speak, think, or act in the way we ordinarily do. This is an effect of their experience creating an environment and transforming those who encounter them. With time, and as our practice progresses, this will happen.

The fourth accomplishment is wrathful activity. In the case of spirits or beings who greatly harm the teachings and many beings and who are unable to be tamed by peaceful means, an end to their activities can be accomplished forcefully—not through anger but through the great compassion of wrathful activity. Recall the example of wrathful activity described above, the story from a past life of the Buddha, when he was on a ship carrying five hundred bodhisattvas and knew that one person was planning to kill them all. The Buddha considered the effects this would have: five hundred people would die and their killer would be reborn in the lower realms. To save these five hundred lives and prevent the person from falling into the lower realms, the Buddha killed him. It is said that one who has great compassion has permission to kill someone who is harming great numbers of sentient beings.

By reciting the mantra, we can also attain supreme accomplishment—the four bodies and five wisdoms of enlightenment.

Near the beginning of this commentary, I mentioned the spontaneous appearance from the primordial basis. Recognition of the appearance from the basis produces enlightenment. Lack of recognition is our state as sentient beings. Within the appearance of the basis, the essence of our mind is empty; this is the ultimate body of enlightenment. Its nature is clarity; this is the body of enlightenment's perfect splendor. Its energy is all-pervasive; this is the manifest body of enlightenment. These are the three bodies of enlightenment as they exist within each and every sentient being's mind at the basis. Without recognition, the basic nature of the three bodies of enlightenment goes latent, shrouded by ordinary thought, habitual tendencies, and negative emotions.

The lack of recognition of our basic nature has its own energy, its own display. When we have not recognized our basic nature, we experience this display, like clouds that appear out of space and block our sight of the sun. In the same way, out of the sphere of totality, incidental, or transitory, appearances of separation arise. We begin to experience ourselves through the mode of ordinary thought, subject and object, and this experience gets denser, thicker, more solid. We generate the three basic negative emotions of anger, desire, and ignorance. They grow coarser and coarser and lead us to the experience of self and other, to attraction and aversion. Eventually, they grow so strong that they create karma, which in turn creates the aggregates, senses, and our physical form, and we enter into the experience of samsara, the outer world, ourselves, and other sentient beings.

At the present time, because we have continued in the lack of recognition of our basic nature, our experience is very solid and very real. It seems evident and natural to experience the world through our ordinary thinking, through dualistic experience. We have great attachment to self and appearances. We must begin to change this situation with ordinary thinking about objective experience and gradually loosen up and make less solid the subject-object play of our experience. When we recognize and are aware of the nature of mind, eventually what we experience now as ordinary thought, or dualistic experience, becomes the display of wisdom. On the path to enlightenment, all our experience is transformed directly into the experience of the bodies and wisdoms of enlightenment. We have the experience of the three bodies of enlightenment as the path.

At the beginningless beginning, we didn't recognize the nature of our mind. We didn't recognize the empty essence, the clear nature, and the all-pervasive energy of our mind. We entered the confused state of a sentient being. At that same beginningless beginning, Buddha Ever Excellent, Samantabhadra, recognized this nature and was primordially liberated. Then, the difference between a sentient being and a buddha was lack of awareness or awareness. Today, right now, the difference between a sentient being and a buddha is exactly the same. When we are aware of the essence, or nature, of our mind, we are liberated; by not recognizing the nature of our mind, we remain a sentient being. There is no difference between the original point and right now. We can't say, "I failed to recognize the nature of mind countless lifetimes ago, but now, the situation is somewhat different." It is exactly the same. We are at the same point we were at any time in the past. The only difference between enlightenment and a sentient being is awareness or lack of awareness of the nature of mind. This must be pointed out through Dzogchen practice on the level of trekchöd.

Although the pointing-out instruction of the nature of mind is, strictly speaking, the domain of trekchöd, by reciting the twelve-syllable mantra, even without having received the instructions of trekchöd, we can receive empowerment directly from Guru Rinpoche. Through this visualization and recitation of the mantra, we can receive the blessing of his mind and have the realization of the nature of mind as the ultimate body of enlightenment arise within our mind. Through practice on the path, we can have the experience of appearances as the three bodies of enlightenment. There is no difference between that experience and the experience we gain through trekchöd practice. We can call it "the blessing of Guru Rinpoche" or "the view of trekchöd" that has arisen in our mind precisely as it is in the teaching.

## Effects of the Four Empowerments

As signs of reversing our continuation in samsara, we have experiences of exaltation, clarity, and nonconceptuality on the path. There are other signs of blessing as well. The vase empowerment, received on the level of our body, is the blessing of Guru Rinpoche's body. The outer sign that this empowerment is becoming effective is that our attachment to place, our body, our possessions, our position, and all things related to our surroundings diminishes. Our negative emotions relating to our basic attachment, which can be summed up as desire, also diminish.

The inner sign of having received the vase empowerment is that our attachment to the solidity of the elements of earth and water in our body is purified. On the level of our body, the element of earth is our flesh and the element of water is our blood. Based on the diminishing attachment at the physical level to our own body, we experience the outer elements of earth and water as being less substantial.

Gradually, as the process continues, the outer and inner elements (that is, the outer elements are the outside world and the inner elements are in one's body) progressively purify and lighten. This is the process of our dualistic experience moving toward nonduality. The effect on the level of body is that our experience of pain lessens. In duality, the more solid and real we experience water and earth, the more we experience pain and suffering. We are threatened by this solidity. As the outer and inner elements of earth and water get progressively purified and lighten and we experience nonduality, we are less subject to pain. Bodhisattvas also experience pain and suffering, but with a difference: ordinary sentient beings have strong dualistic clinging, so their pain and suffering are experienced as coarse, real, and solid; bodhisattvas have less experience of pain as it becomes purified, or diminished. Their suffering is far less real, or solid, far less intense. At the level of enlightenment, there is no dualistic experience whatsoever. There is no pain, no suffering, nothing to create pain, and no one to experience pain. This is the nature of reality. This is the experience of enlightenment.

The positive experience of the vase empowerment is a development of the eyes of transcendent knowledge. Distant objects can be seen very clearly. Physically, the great exaltation and emptiness of the manifest body of enlightenment is felt. It is as the great Indian master Indrabhuti said, "The wisdom of great exaltation is permanent." He pointed out that great exaltation is part of the nature of reality, the nature of mind, the nature of everything. The experience of exaltation, or happiness, in our lives as sentient beings is impermanent; it's not great exaltation because we are happy one day, but the next day it fades. In enlightenment, the experience of enlightenment doesn't change. There is no apprehension that "Tomorrow this will all be over and I will fall into samsara. This will change into something else. I'm going to lose this." The experience of the nature of mind, the nature of reality, the nature of the sphere of totality, is great exaltation because it does not change.

One of the eight tantras of the Secret Essence cycle says that the nature of great exaltation is neither material nor nonmaterial. Neither is it somewhere in between the two.

The effect of receiving the vase empowerment is that when we practice the path of inseparable exaltation and emptiness, it leads to the manifest body of enlightenment. All ordinary thoughts and experience are exhausted, or emptied, into the experience of great exaltation, the form of enlightenment of appearance and emptiness. All appearances arise without any substantiality. This is the meaning of visualizing white light streaming from the *om* at Guru Rinpoche's forehead to our forehead; we receive his blessing, the fortune to attain the manifest body of enlightenment.

In the second empowerment, red light, like the rays of light at sunrise, streams from the *ah* at Guru Rinpoche's throat to our throat. It bestows upon us the secret empowerment that purifies our inner energy-winds and our acts of speech, whether important or just gossip. Our speech rides on our inner energy, which is purified. Further, this empowerment purifies anger. The sign of its effectiveness is that in our body, the elements of fire and wind are purified. In the same way that the vase empowerment relates to earth and water, the secret empowerment relates to fire and wind. We become less attached to them as substantial, or material.

We have to receive our empowerment with the thought that we really do receive it. As we practice regularly, it becomes more of a reality. We receive empowerment continually, until gradually we can recognize self-manifest awareness. This is the path to receiving the blessing of the lama's body, speech, and mind.

The elements fire and wind are related, of course, to our bodily heat and our breath. The inner process affects our experience of the outer elements. Gradually, our attachment to the outer elements of fire and wind as solid, or real, diminishes. We come to the point where we no longer distinguish between our inner elements of heat and breath and the outer experiences of fire and wind, and for those who have realization, ordinary sound arises naturally as the sound of teachings. For example, when Dzogchen master Khenpo Jigme Phuntsok Rinpoche was staying in New Delhi, India, there was an overhead fan in his room. Ordinary persons heard the fan and the air moving, but for one hour he heard a four-line prayer repeated again and again. This is really what he heard. He wrote it down. He and others recited it. For Milarepa as well, all appearances became like a text of realization. He was able to read in mere ordinary appearances the words of teachings.

In the vase empowerment, we worked with appearance and emptiness. With the second empowerment, we work with sound and emptiness, sound without origin. We begin to have the ability to hear sounds from a very long distance. In our speech, we have the experience of great clarity. Before we had exaltation, on the level of body. Here it is the experience of clarity, at the level of speech.

In the vase empowerment, we had the intense experience of exaltation that became the path of emptiness and exaltation, the path of the manifest body of enlightenment. In the secret empowerment, the experience that arises is clarity of speech. We enter the path of clarity and emptiness, the experience of the body of enlightenment's perfect splendor.

As we practice clarity and emptiness, the body of enlightenment's perfect splendor, without attachment, the result we attain is the same as the Buddha's. When the Buddha taught one instruction, that one teaching satisfied the minds of countless beings. For example, persons at the listener level would receive the teaching and think, "The Buddha taught us the Four Noble Truths." The bodhi-sattvas would listen to the same teaching and say, "The Buddha taught us the subject of emptiness." Those on the level of tantra would say, "The Buddha taught us Mahayoga." And those on the level of Dzogchen would hear a Dzogchen instruction. All of these levels come through one teaching of the Buddha, which is appropriate to, and touches the mind of, every sentient being in ways that guide those beings. That is the outer explanation. The inner explanation is that the Buddha teaches within total nonelaboration, complete peace. His speech comes from the complete stillness and freedom from all complexity within his mind.

In one discourse, the Buddha commented that from the time he attained enlightenment to the time he passed away into nirvana, he never taught any words of instruction. From the view of the ultimate body of enlightenment, there is no word, no teaching, and no experience of the teaching. The Buddha said that even though he did not teach one word of instruction to any being, beings experienced him teaching in an inconceivable number of ways, according to their needs, intentions, or wishes. These teachings were not the result of any ordinary thought or intention of the Buddha, who had no such thing.

All appearances of the Buddha in this world—that he was born in India, grew up to become a king, got married, had children, renounced his home and went to meditate, did ascetic practices, eventually attained enlightenment, and later taught, up to the time when he passed away—are appearances to sentient beings in this world, according to their needs. In the Buddha's own experience, there was no need for any of these events. They were merely the way sentient beings could be guided to enlightenment. The Buddha himself never moved from the ultimate body of enlightenment.

Take, for example, the eight forms of Guru Rinpoche. The life story of Guru Rinpoche seems very strange to us because he appears sometimes as Dorje Drolod (Wild Wrathful Vajra), riding on a tigress; sometimes as Tsokye Dorje (Lake-Born Vajra); some-times as Senge Dradrok (Lion's Roar); sometimes as a fully ordained monk, Shakya Senge; sometimes as Lodon Chokse (Wise Seer of the Sublime); sometimes as Nyima Ozer (Rays of the Sun); sometimes as Pema Gyalpo (Lotus King); and sometimes as Padmasambhava (Lotus Born). He appears in these forms according to the needs of sentient beings. For those who need to be guided through forceful, or wrathful, means, he appears with forceful, or wrathful, forms. For those who need to be guided by a fully ordained monk, he appears as Shakya Senge. For the dakinis or the spirits, he appears as Guru Rinpoche. Guru Rinpoche does not need to appear at all; he does not move from the state of complete enlightenment.

You can read these stories about Guru Rinpoche in detail in the translation of the life story of Guru Rinpoche, the *Life and Liberation of Padmasambhava*. This is a treasure text revealed by Orgyen Lingpa. There, we can see how Guru Rinpoche manifested in relation to the needs of different sentient beings.

We can see that in the Buddha's experience, there is no teaching, yet in the experience of sentient beings there are an inconceivable number of teachings. Through our practice and by receiving the secret empowerment, the empowerment on the level of speech, we enter that path. That is the result we are heading toward. The essence of the speech of enlightenment is the inexpressible sphere, the source of all grammar, words, meaning, and sounds yet transcending all language and all expression. It is inconceivable.

There is a quote in Thinley Norbu Rinpoche's text from the *Secret Essence Tantra* that begins, "How marvelous, how wonderful this thing that appears is." What is this thing that appears? It is the speech of perfect enlightenment that transcends all sounds, words, and terms. The essences of words, grammar, sound, and terms all find their source in emptiness. Yet from this emptiness all sounds flow.

When I speak, in fact there is nothing. I make sound. There are words. Yet where are these words? They are not on my tongue. They are not on my teeth. They are not on the bottom of my mouth or the upper part of my mouth. They cannot be found in my throat. They don't really exist anywhere. They are empty, yet at the same time they appear. Any sound in the world has its source in emptiness. It appears, but at the same time it is empty. All sounds find their source in the nature of reality.

The essence of the speech of enlightenment, the speech of the buddhas, is a single speech, a single quality. It pervades, in all its branches, all sounds because all sounds have emptiness as their nature. No sound has ever been created. The single essence of the speech of enlightenment pervades all sounds. The essence of all sounds is emptiness. They have no other essence than emptiness. They are nothing besides emptiness. The essence of sound is the speech of enlightenment.

Because the essence of sound is emptiness, sounds and names and words can appear. In the same way, if we hold a small crystal ball up to some scenery, we may see a huge mountain clearly within the crystal. It is because the crystal is empty that we can see a clear appearance within it. Because the reflection of the mountain is emptiness, it can appear within the empty crystal. If it were solid, it would be impossible for the mountain to come within the crystal. In the same way, because the nature of sound is empty, sounds can appear. It is the same for forms: because forms are empty at the moment they appear, they can appear. Because at the very moment sounds appear, their essence is inexpressible, sounds can appear as the essence of the speech of enlightenment. We say that all sounds appear as the Great Symbol of the speech of enlightenment.

One of the tantras says that the highest pure land, which is inconceivable, is the sphere in which our dualistic experience and all appearances of dualistic experience have set. Within the great expanse of equanimity, beyond all partiality, the mandala of the speech of enlightenment appears spontaneously.

In conclusion, when we receive the secret empowerment, the blessing of the speech of Guru Rinpoche, we gain mastery of the facets of the speech of enlightenment. As a result, we attain the body of enlightenment's perfect splendor.

The next empowerment is that of transcendent knowledge and wisdom. In our visualization, blue light streams from the *hung* at Guru Rinpoche's heart and dissolves into our heart. As a sign that

this empowerment is received, our thoughts of defeating our enemies and nurturing our friends, our various thoughts relating to
our ordinary situation, diminish. In particular, our happiness and
suffering, our hopes and fears, and what we accept and what we
reject in any context of our life in samsara diminish. We've reached
the transcendent knowledge and wisdom empowerment.

This empowerment purifies the obscurations of our mind and the
vital essence of the body. It purifies the negative emotion of ignorance. Recall, the vase empowerment purifies desire, and the secret
empowerment purifies anger. The sign that our ignorance is being
purified is that our inner clinging dissipates. The effect is that the
outer experience of the element of space is purified. Seeing the outer
element of space as empty joins with our inner spatial element, our
awareness. We lose track of the distinction between outer space and
inner awareness. They merge into the eternal expanse of the great
sphere. At that point, our dualistic experience of clinging to self
and other, subject and object, ordinary consciousness, is purified.

At the beginning of our work on this text, I described how beings
get confused. Through mistaken experience, the five lights of the
basis are experienced as the five elements. Now, through the process of empowerment, we see how the five elements are purified
into their basic nature. Here, we've come to the outer element of
space, which we see as empty. Our dualistic mind is purified into
awareness and emptiness.

The effect of this empowerment and the purification of our ordinary dualistic consciousness is that we have no obscuration in our
sight, outside or inside. We have direct, penetrating sight. We attain
"the eyes of the nature of reality." As we approach the attainment
of the eyes of the nature of reality, we no longer get lost in thought.
From the vase empowerment, we have the experience of exaltation;
from the secret empowerment, we have the experience of clarity.
Here the experience is to rest without being lost in thought. At this
stage, we can rest in the view for twenty-four hours, or a week or
more, without interruption from any ordinary thought whatsoever.
Our mind is completely clear. Nothing distracts us or comes in the
way of our experience of the view.

Abiding without dualistic experience, without subject and object, without ordinary thought, is the path of the ultimate body of enlightenment. If we maintain the wisdom without concept, if we have no attachment to that experience, if we remain in the view, the result is the attainment of the ultimate body of enlightenment.

In the discourses, the Buddha said that the enlightened mind of the buddhas is inconceivable. Enlightened mind has no ordinary mind, intellect, or consciousness. However, it remains always in meditative absorption. We call this "the inconceivable mystery of the enlightened mind of the Buddha." By making a path of the practice of the ultimate body of enlightenment, we actualize the result, the ultimate body of enlightenment.

Finally, on receiving the precious word empowerment, we receive the blessing of the body, speech, mind, qualities, and activities of enlightenment at one place and time, indivisibly, the benefits of which are inconceivably vast and inexpressible.

We must continually and regularly practice receiving the four empowerments from Guru Rinpoche. As we continue to practice, signs and experiences will definitely arise.*

We may hear it said, "I only meditate on my own true nature so I don't need to relate to any outer manifestation such as Guru Rinpoche." Until we undoubtedly realize our true nature, visualizing Guru Rinpoche in his outer manifestation has the power to keep us out of an arrogant ego trap, thinking, "I have buddha nature but others don't," as well as the opposite ego trap of thinking recognition of our true nature will never occur. Such attitudes can prevent us from developing the appreciation, devotion, and gratitude we so sorely need. Although it may seem that we, as Vajrayogini, are separate from Guru Rinpoche, when we receive the blessings and empowerments, dissolve Guru Rinpoche's mind into our mind, and behold the ultimate lama in a state of nonduality, the appreciation and gratitude we have developed yield extraordinary benefits.

---

*See appendix 4 for a summary of the four empowerments and their effects.

# CHAPTER 8

# Dzogchen

Other magnificent works, including those by Traktung Dudjom Lingpa and Dudjom Rinpoche, describe Dzogchen. But yielding to fervent requests, Thinley Norbu Rinpoche thought it was appropriate to include some details about Dzogchen at the end of his section on Guru Yoga rather than write a separate text on the subject.

In the Guru Yoga practice, as explained above, we imagine ourselves as Vajrayogini. We imagine that Guru Rinpoche, our root teacher, appears in the sky before us. We receive the four empowerments and the blessings of his body, speech, mind, qualities, and activity. Following this visualization, we imagine that our lama, Guru Rinpoche, in great joy, dissolves into light. We imagine that from the seat of Guru Rinpoche upward and from the crown of his head downward, he dissolves into a ball of five-colored light that dissolves into us. At this point, we think that we have become completely inseparable from Guru Rinpoche.

## The Ultimate Lama

In the foundational practice text, we recite, "The lama dissolves into light and is absorbed into oneself." The second line is "Abide in indivisible awareness and emptiness, which is the face of the absolute lama." Guru Rinpoche as imagined in the sky before us is the lama on the relative level. This is a form and a labeling of the lama. But when we rest within clarity and emptiness, within the nature of mind, within the Dzogchen view, this is the ultimate lama.

That's the short story. Now we'll describe the details. When we imagine the lama dissolving into us, we consider that our mind and the lama's mind become inseparable. When you pour water into water, you can no longer distinguish between the water you pour in and the water that was there before. They become entirely indistinguishable. In the same way, when we do this visualization, our mind and the lama's mind become inseparable, indivisible, indistinguishable one from the other, beyond all joining or separation.

The nature of the lama's mind is primordial freedom from any elaboration, from any thoughts. Our mind has the same nature. When we do this visualization, our mind and the lama's mind become inseparable, and we rest our mind in the awareness of this inseparability. This is the enlightened mind of the lama, the mind of all buddhas. This is the Dzogchen view. This is the nature of our mind. At this point, there is a blending between the nature of our mind, the enlightened mind of the lama, and our view of Dzogchen. The three blend inseparably. There is only one meaning to these three. We recognize it for what it is. It is the nature of our mind. It is the lama's mind. And it is the Dzogchen view. We rest in this recognition.

Another translation of these lines says "inseparable within one's own state of being." In Tibetan, this is *ngang*, which in ordinary Tibetan speech often means simply "within" in reference to a person's basic character, or personality. If one person is characteristically short-tempered and another person is characteristically very patient, that is a description of their *ngang*. In this case, however, after we've done the visualization and the lama's mind and our mind rest inseparably, we have to identify the character of that. This isn't to say that we change, like changing from a short-tempered to a patient person. We're not improving ourselves. We're identifying our own nature, or the nature of the mind beyond a point of origin, abiding, or cessation. Once the lama's mind and our mind become inseparable, we consider our true nature to be the inner character of our mind. It goes beyond any consideration of ordinary character.

At this point, we rest as long as possible within that character of the nature of our mind. We try to maintain it for as long as possible. We come face to face with the ultimate teacher, the ultimate lama. This is the nature of our mind. This is the nature of the lama's mind. This is the nature of Guru Rinpoche.

When a teacher appears before us, either as a human being teaching the dharma or as a visualization of the lama in the sky, it is the lama on the relative level; it is not the ultimate lama. When we have done this visualization and the lama has dissolved into us, that is the ultimate, true, real lama, the real teacher, the real buddha. When we look at the face of the lama, it is not like looking at an individual outside of us. When we're looking directly at the face of the nature of our mind, we are not looking in the ordinary way; we're abiding in the Dzogchen view, in which the viewer and what is seen are indivisible, not two. We call this "looking at the face of the ultimate lama."

Where does the lama who appears outside appear from? When we imagine Guru Rinpoche in the sky before us and then he dissolves into us, it is the display of the nature of our mind dissolving into the nature of our mind. It is not as if Guru Rinpoche comes from outside and is absorbed into us. It is the display of the pure aspect of our own mind that is absorbed into the nature of mind.

## Rigpa

The next line says that we look at the face of the ultimate lama, awareness and emptiness. In Tibetan, the first word is *rigpa* (awareness). There is awareness (*rig*), and there is our ordinary mind (*sem*). Ordinary mind begins with the relation between a subject and an object, which provokes desire, anger, ignorance, and other thoughts and negative emotions. It creates karma. Once this mind is present, we experience samsara. Rigpa isn't dualistic mind. Awareness is not the root of samsara. When we can see the nature of the subject-object experience for what it is, and when it is purified, resting in clarity and emptiness is rigpa.

The Dzogchen tantras say that both the ordinary mind and awareness have clarity. Ordinary mind and rigpa are not distinguished from that perspective. The difference is that the ordinary mind follows what appears to be; there is clarity and an understanding, but in the connection between it and what appears to be, there is dualistic experience. No matter what the mind experiences with clarity, there will be a connection, through thought or emotion, between it and everything else. For example, we either analyze the past, anticipate the future, or, in the present moment, are lost in thought. That is the ordinary mind. Rigpa, on the other hand, is clarity with recognition of its own nature. There is no ordinary thought or experience in rigpa. Rigpa has no connection with an object. There is no reliving, or remembering, the past; no anticipation of the future. And in the present, there is no ordinary seeing of an object, no ordinary objective experience. When we say "rigpa," we can mean the nature of mind as emptiness or the nature of mind as clarity. When we say the essence of mind is rigpa, clarity, or emptiness, these are all synonyms for the same essence.

Garab Dorje, who was Vajrasattva in human form, was the first human of the Dzogchen lineage. After Garab Dorje, the lineage went to Manjushrimitra, Vimalamitra, Shri Singha, and then to Guru Rinpoche Padmasambhava. Actually, two great traditions of the Dzogchen teachings originated with Garab Dorje, but later they separated, although their meaning is the same. One came down through Vimalamitra and the other through Guru Rinpoche.

Garab Dorje declared that mind is originally pure. The significance of this to us is, at this point of the visualization practice, when we imagine that the lama has dissolved into us and we rest gazing at the face of the ultimate teacher (that is, abiding in emptiness-awareness), it is not a new mind or a new rigpa we've created. This is originally, primordially, the nature of our mind. Garab Dorje then stated that we rest in the sphere of rigpa. The sphere of rigpa is like space, space that we cannot describe but at the same time is everywhere. When we describe the nature of our awareness, everything in samsara and everything of transcendence appear in our awareness.

Awareness is very wide, open. Everything appears in it, everything rests in it, and when things and experiences dissolve, they dissolve into it. This is the sphere of awareness. Inconceivable and inexpressible, it is the nature of our mind, and everything appears within it. It is the all-englobing sphere, in the same way that all things appear in, remain in, and dissolve back into space.

Metaphorically, everything in this or any other universe appears within the sphere of space; space embraces everything, and we can't somehow put all space into a container. In the same way, everything in the perceived outer universe and in our inner experience is encompassed by rigpa. Whatever we do, wherever we go, we always remain within the sphere of rigpa. When we go to sleep at night, we dream. Dreams take us to faraway times and places, but whatever we dream, whatever we experience in our dream, we never go beyond our bed. In the same way, we rest always in the space of awareness. From awareness comes mind, which produces various experiences of samsara and nirvana. But regardless of what we experience, we remain in the space of awareness.

Our experience begins with the recognition or lack of recognition of awareness. Recognition of awareness produces enlightenment, and the lack of recognition of awareness produces the experience of a sentient being. However, regardless of our experience, we have nowhere else to go. Whether we have a positive experience, the appearances of enlightenment, or a negative experience of a sentient being, all appear in the space of awareness.

## Ultimate Bodhichitta

Within rigpa there are no faults. None of our faults (specifically conceptual thought, negative emotions, karma, and suffering) have ever been experienced by our awareness. They are experienced by ordinary mind. There is no downside to awareness. At the same time, the qualities of enlightenment are found naturally within awareness without being created anew. They are primordially, naturally, there. They are not created by anything whatsoever. Within rigpa are the three or five wisdoms, the five bodies of enlightenment, and the essence, nature, and all-pervading energy of mind. These positive qualities within rigpa are naturally present, so we say that within rigpa the sufferings of samsara are completely purified and all the qualities of enlightenment are naturally present. These two qualities of rigpa—the purification of all suffering and the presence of the qualities of enlightenment—are signified by the two aspects of the Tibetan word for bodhichitta (*jangchub kyisem*). This is a special use of the word *bodhichitta*, the mind of awakening. We call it "rigpa." We call it "buddha mind." We call it "wisdom." This is the part of our mind that has never experienced samsara, the part of our mind in which all qualities of enlightenment are naturally present.

Thinley Norbu Rinpoche distinguishes between *jangchub kyisem* as used in the Dzogchen context and as used in the context of the causal vehicle of the transcendent perfections. Bodhichitta, the "development of the intention to attain enlightenment for the benefit of all sentient beings" or the "mind of awakening" in the context of Mahayana, is relative bodhichitta, the relative mind's intention to attain awakening. But in Dzogchen, *jangchub kyisem* means the nature of our mind, our buddha nature, the wisdom of enlightenment.

In Dzogchen, the nature of mind, or awareness, is seen to be primordially without origin. Awareness did not come into being at any particular time; it just is—original mind. When there is no separate subject (that is, no self) but just awareness, there is no object. In the same way, sentient beings are not said to be real. They do not exist in the realms of the hells, the starving spirits, the animals, the humans, the gods, or the demigods. We do not see their sufferings as real, or existent, in the way it is explained in the Mahayana. Because awareness is the subject, all things are seen as appearances in a dream. This is the nondual wisdom of the mind of enlightenment. As bodhisattvas meditate, they do not experience sentient beings or themselves. They have no dualistic experience. They remain within the mind of enlightenment, buddha mind, in which there is neither a bodhisattva nor a sentient being. Then, apart from that, they manifest compassion toward sentient beings who mistake illusion, or a magical display, for reality.

One might worry that without the dualistic experience of self and other, of bodhisattvas and sentient beings, compassion will come to an end. Thinley Norbu Rinpoche says that we don't have to worry about that. He refers to Rongzompa, who taught that realizing the nondual nature of everything, the equanimity of nonduality, is not an obstacle to the development of great compassion. The buddhas and bodhisattvas have no dualistic experience, yet their compassion is limitless and their activity for the benefit of sentient beings is inconceivably vast. On the other hand, if you really hold to things as real and hold to self and other as existent, your compassion will be limited. Shravakayana practitioners and ordinary sentient beings have a very strong idea of self and other. This strong dualistic experience doesn't increase their compassion at all. In fact, quite the opposite is true.

The compassion of buddhas and bodhisattvas is based on their seeing that sentient beings have never had true confusion, but they experience confusion; they have never had suffering, but they experience suffering; they experience what has never existed as being truly existent. The basis of sentient beings is the same as the enlightened basis of buddhas, but sentient beings are confused in their experience. Buddhas and bodhisattvas see that this does not reflect the true nature of sentient beings. From this basis, buddhas and bodhisattvas express compassion toward all sentient beings to remove their confusion. They can't help having this response. If we saw a sleeping person suffering violently from a nightmare, we would naturally take action to wake up the person. In a similar way, buddhas and bodhisattvas help sentient beings wake up from the experience of all the appearances of confusion. Shravakayana practitioners and ordinary persons may think to themselves, "I want to be free from this suffering. I want to attain enlightenment. I want to be happy one way or another." But they don't think of all sentient beings as having enlightened nature and that they are simply confused.

One of the tantras says, "I develop the wish to see this primordial nature and, based on this, to help all sentient beings see their true primordial nature. Because sentient beings do not see their own primordial enlightened nature, for their benefit, I develop the mind of awakening."

## The Path of Trekchöd

In the practice of trekchöd, through symbols, words, or directly from mind to mind, the realization, or awareness, of the teacher is transferred to the student. One way or another, we recognize awareness. Through pointing-out instructions, we cut directly through all our ordinary thoughts, negative emotions, and suffering, as if with a knife, or sword, we cut a piece off a solid table. We meditate with an emphasis on the nature of the mind, the wisdom of emptiness. All sentient beings have the wisdom of emptiness. Nothing exists in reality as solid or real, but this is the essence of our mind. In ordinary Mahayana terminology, it is buddha nature. In the terminology of Dzogchen, they are the primordial wisdoms of mind—essence, nature, and energy. Nothing is impeded at the level of the primordial basis, and it can appear as the various peaceful and wrathful deities.

If there were no primordial basis, then there could be no enlightenment. In the observed universe, if there were no sun, no moon, no stars, no lamps, no electricity or any form of light, then the world would be plunged into total darkness. Likewise, if the primordial basis did not exist, then there would be no possibility of liberation or a moment for liberation. There would be no enlightenment. There would be only ignorance. There would be only negative emotions, karma, and suffering.

Because these three primordial wisdoms of mind are fundamental, they provide the possibility for the nature of our mind to be pointed out, for the appearance of enlightenment in the world, for enlightenment to take the forms of the peaceful and wrathful deities, and for the ultimate body of enlightenment to be recognized.

When the pointing-out instruction is given, the nature of mind is introduced directly, unconcealed. If I told you that behind me I was hiding a pot of gold, you probably wouldn't believe me. But if I took it out and showed you, you'd say, "Yes, there it is." That is the pointing-out instruction. This is the style that Guru Rinpoche used to point out the nature of mind. In one text, Yeshe Tsogyal asked questions of, and received answers from, Guru Rinpoche. She asked how awareness should be pointed out to all sentient beings. Guru Rinpoche answered that it is through introduction to the essence, nature, and pervasive energy of mind. There are other styles of pointing-out. For example, there is another pointing-out instruction called the "four direct placings of the mind": the view is like a mountain; the meditation is like an ocean; the action, or conduct, is appearances; and the result is awareness. Then there is Garab Dorje's style, the *Three Words That Strike the Essence*. The essence is pointed out directly, and one arrives at a single decisiveness and then confidence in liberation.

Regardless of the style of pointing-out instruction, the same thing is pointed out: the nature of mind. This all falls under the category of trekchöd. Through the pointing-out instructions, we have direct access to the nature of mind. Then through thögal, one sees all appearances in infinite purity. These are the two sides of the very special teachings of Dzogchen practice. There is nothing more than that. We must begin, however, with pointing-out instruction and seeing the nature of mind.

However, it is not enough for awareness to be merely recognized or understood. It must be matured. The Tibetan term for this means, literally, "to perfect the energy of awareness," which means that after one recognizes primordially existent awareness, one tries to maintain and extend the time that one rests in that recognition. Just as a child goes through different stages of development until it reaches adulthood, having recognized our awareness, we must get more and more familiar with it.

Right now our ordinary mind has tremendous power and capability. Our ordinary mind is lost in thought, feels very strong emotions, and has created the whole experience of samsara. But gradually, as we get more familiar with the nature of mind, our ordinary mind begins to lose power, and we rest more and more in awareness. Eventually we can no longer function with desire, anger, ignorance, and the appearances of confusion as we did in the past; the ordinary mind is cut like a snake (from deadly to dead with one swift slash) naturally through the power of recognition of awareness. This is called "arriving at stability within the practice of rigpa."

On all levels of buddhadharma, we talk of samsara and transcendence. Samsara is suffering and nirvana is fun. But in Dzogchen we go straight to the experience. We can show, "This is the mind that creates samsara. This is suffering. And this is the experience of transcendence of suffering." There is less talk. The experience is pointed out directly.

The process of maturation of awareness has two stages. First, as we recognize the nature of mind and can rest in recognition more and more, our ordinary thoughts, emotions, suffering, and experience of samsara diminish. They are overpowered by the appearance of nondual wisdom. We develop experience of the nature of mind, experience of awareness. These increase with stability.

The second stage is when the nondual experience of awareness has gained so much power that no ordinary thoughts, emotions, or suffering occur. The dualistic mind is completely overpowered by the experience of wisdom. This is called "gaining stability" or "capturing the citadel of awakening." At this point, we no longer have any hope, or expectation, of attaining enlightenment, or any fear, or apprehension, of descending into samsara, or the lower realms. There is no enlightenment and no process of enlightenment apart from this.

The process of recognition of awareness is not created by anyone. It is returning to the recognition of our own nature. Appearances of confusion arose from the basis of mind, and we have returned to the basis rather than remaining connected to the appearances. We return to the basis through the recognition and maturation of awareness.

A related subject is the distinction between rigpa and *osel* (clear light, luminosity, or radiance). In their essence, there is no distinction whatsoever between rigpa and clear light, but in describing them, we can make a distinction. Thinley Norbu Rinpoche states that rigpa is the undeluded wisdom aspect of the mind, unobscured by thoughts, negative emotions, or lack of understanding. Clear light shares the same essence as rigpa, direct knowledge of the nature of mind. It is the luminous, clear radiance of the nature of mind. It doesn't mean ordinary and impermanent lights or lamps, which are the results of causes and conditions. We can call the whole play of our senses and sense consciousnesses "clarity," but it is not the same clarity as the clear light of the nature of our mind.

Thinley Norbu Rinpoche says that even when we say somebody is very sharp, aware, or bright in ordinary, worldly language, that is not what we mean by clarity, or radiance, in relation to wisdom mind. When we go beyond the bounds of dualistic experience, when we talk about the appearance of wisdom and the recognition of the nature of mind, or of enlightenment, that is clear light, luminosity, beyond all bounds. It is the radiant nature of mind beyond any dualistic experience of clarity, or luminosity.

We can say that clear light is "luminosity that transcends the limits of our ordinary mind." We can infer something about the domain of luminosity within awareness, within the nature of mind, within wisdom. We have to take notes. We have to read or listen to teachings. We have to try to understand the domain of radiant awareness. However, the experience of the radiance, or luminosity, of awareness is gained through Dzogchen pointing-out instructions. Then it can be experienced directly.

If you tried to introduce chiles to somebody who had never eaten them, they might ask, "Do they taste like honey?" "No, they don't taste like honey." "Do they taste salty?" "Not really." You could explain, "They taste really spicy hot." But they might not get it until that first taste. Then the person would understand what chiles are all about. In the same way, when we use the phrase "radiant wisdom that transcends the bounds of our ordinary mind," we're trying to understand the words in order to infer the experience. But it is far more critical, once we have understood the words, to have the experience. Through Dzogchen, we can have that experience. Then we will know the domain of wisdom and radiance.

Clear light, or luminosity, as we have described, is the radiant aspect of awareness, yet it is inseparable from awareness. The Buddha's first words after attaining enlightenment were that he had realized a "profound, peaceful, still state free from elaboration—noncomposite luminosity." "Profound" means that he transcended the state of an ordinary sentient being. "Peaceful" means that he was free from all ordinary thought processes. "Free from elaboration" means that he was free from dualistic experience. The luminous state's being "noncomposite" means that it is not part of the collection of causes and conditions and does not come about through causes and conditions. The state the Buddha said he had attained was like drinking nectar.

The great Indian master Chandrakirti said that luminosity was free from (or had cut through) all the nets of ordinary thought. "Ordinary thought" here refers to thinking "This is emptiness" or "This is not emptiness," "This is pure" or "This is impure." Any thought related to things is part of the net of ordinary thought. In luminosity, such nets are completely cleared away.

The personification of the state of enlightenment is Kuntuzangpo. In the Mahayana, it is understood as the bodhisattva Samantabhadra, and in Dzogchen, as Buddha Ever Excellent, Samantabhadra. He is identified as the master of both the "profound" and "vast" forms of enlightenment. "Profound" means emptiness beyond all extremes, beyond all limits. "Vast" refers to the infinite purity of everything. We call him "luminosity that radiates everywhere." Luminosity here is natural wisdom, naturally manifest awareness, part of the nature of all sentient beings' minds. However, just as a lamp placed inside an opaque vase doesn't shine to the outside, so too the luminous wisdom that all sentient beings' minds have as their basic nature doesn't appear, or manifest, without recognition and maturation of this luminous nature. With pointing-out instruction, the vase is broken. Through the view and meditation, we manifest the luminous nature of mind.

We identify Buddha Ever Excellent, Samantabhadra, who represents our inner enlightened nature, as having "radiance that manifests (or emanates)." To "manifest" or "emanate" indicates that enlightened nature is primordial, not new or brought in from outside. How is it possible that enlightenment flows, or radiates, from within us? It is because it is already there. In the same way, if there weren't a lamp or light inside a vase, when we break the vase, light wouldn't radiate outward. If we did not have buddha nature, nothing would flow from our inner state. We always identify buddha nature as noncomposite. It is not created through causes and conditions. Because it is noncomposite, it is natural. It is not created or produced anew. "Radiance" is the same as "luminosity" that was discussed above.

One of the texts of the Prajnaparamita sutras defines the nature of mind and the nature of luminosity. It says that within the mind, the mind does not exist. This means that, in the essence of the mind, ordinary mind has no foundation and is beyond all substantiality and nonsubstantiality. Its essence is emptiness. The wisdom of emptiness is the ultimate body of enlightenment. However, this emptiness, the essence of mind, is not just empty. Its nature is clarity, or luminosity; its appearance aspect is the bodies and wisdoms of enlightenment. This is why we identify the nature of mind as clarity, or luminosity. The essence of emptiness and the appearance aspect of emptiness (which is luminosity) are inseparable.

The "wisdom" part of self-manifest wisdom refers to unobstructed, unceasing luminosity. Our basic nature is the self-manifest nature of all sentient beings and all enlightenment, natural wisdom. Just as the sun does not have to be created in the sky when clouds obstruct it, so too luminosity is always present. Clarity is always present. It doesn't have to be created. It is self-manifest, or natural, wisdom. Recall that in Tibetan, the word for "wisdom" is *yeshe. Ye* means "primordial" and *she* means "consciousness." It is primordial consciousness, primordial luminosity, or primordial mind. It is consciousness beyond dualistic experience.

*Conscious luminosity*, *luminous mind*, and *buddha mind* are all terms for natural, or self-manifest, wisdom. Natural wisdom is the great union of awareness, emptiness, and luminosity. Awareness and emptiness, and clarity and emptiness, in union does not mean that there are two separate things joined, like threads twisted together. They are not two things that cannot be torn apart; they are one and the same. Rigpa is not separate from emptiness. Nor can we talk about emptiness as separate from awareness. Awareness and emptiness, from the very origins of time, from the primordial moment, have never experienced any separation. The essence of our awareness is emptiness. Awareness and emptiness are always and primordially inseparable.

The empty aspect of rigpa is the ultimate body of enlightenment. Its appearance aspect is the form bodies of enlightenment. However, the emptiness and appearance aspects, as well, are inseparable, always indivisibly in union. We can say awareness and emptiness, appearance and emptiness, clarity and emptiness, exaltation and emptiness, the bodies and wisdoms of enlightenment, and the bodies and pure lands of enlightenment are all inseparably united. This is the great noncomposite state of union.

These forms of inseparability, or union, are different terms relating to the same basic reality. Mahayana talks about the union of appearance and emptiness. In Mahayoga, we have clarity and emptiness. Anuyoga is based on the experience of exaltation and emptiness. In Dzogchen it is the union of awareness and emptiness. But they all point to the same fundamental reality.

We can also relate these forms of union to the body, speech, and mind of enlightenment. The body of Guru Rinpoche is the union of appearance and emptiness. His speech is the union of clarity and emptiness. His mind is the union of exaltation and emptiness. We call this "the great noncomposite state of union." Union, in meditation, relates to appearance and emptiness. At first, we meditate on emptiness, and then within emptiness, we meditate on form. In Tibetan, *union* is *zung juk*. *Zung* means "a pair," or "two." *Juk* means "to enter." So we're entering into union. We could meditate on this by first meditating on emptiness, then meditating on appearance, and then meditating on the two together, seeing that they arise at the same time. Through that meditation, we see the nature of reality.

The fundamental tantra of Dzogchen, the original Dzogchen tantra spoken by the ultimate body of enlightenment, Buddha Vajradhara, is the *Sound That Reverberates from the Nature of Reality* (*Dra talgyur*). It is the source tantra of the seventeen tantras of Dzogchen. This tantra says that a jeweled palace stands at the heart. What we keep in our heart, the essence of emotions, love, or any positive feeling, is original purity. It is the form of emptiness and clarity together. In an ordinary sentient being, this nature is like a vase containing a spontaneously present ball of light. The essence is primordially pure, and the nature is a ball of light. This describes our basic nature, what we have in our heart. We do not claim that there is actually light of some sort in our heart, but it is the nature of what we keep in our heart. When that nature is pointed out, the light from inside appears outside in the form of both compassion and energy. Each form, or color, of light appears on the outside.

We have this basic nature in our heart, but at the moment its luminosity is blocked by our habit of getting lost in thought. Thinley Norbu Rinpoche states that when we enter into recognition of awareness, these distinct colors manifest. Of course, colors will not come streaming out of your heart. What manifests are the primordially existing wisdoms—the wisdom of equanimity, all-accomplishing wisdom, the wisdom of totality, mirrorlike wisdom, and the wisdom of discernment. These wisdoms are part of our nature but are now blocked. The luminosity does not appear outwardly; when we recognize awareness, the vase is broken and the wisdoms manifest.

We've returned to ideas from the beginning of this text, the primordial basis and the appearance from the primordial basis. For sentient beings, our nature is only inner luminosity, inner appearance. When inner luminosity appears outside, that is enlightenment, like a crystal ball that has the potential to produce rainbow light but must be struck by sunlight for rainbow light to appear outwardly. The potential is the inner luminosity. With recognition of our basic nature, and with practice, the five wisdoms appear on the outside.

I understand that some people look at the words and don't understand the meaning. They think Dzogchen teaches that a form of buddha, in a particular position and holding various objects, resides in the heart. This is because they haven't had an explanation from a lineage-holding lama. The words say one thing, but you have to understand the meaning. Some scholars in Tibet criticized Dzogchen, saying, "Dzogchen teaches that there is a buddha at the heart. But if you look carefully, in fact, there isn't a buddha at the heart." They criticized Dzogchen on that basis, because they didn't understand the correct meaning of words like this.

## Thögal

In the practice of Guru Yoga, what is essential in looking at the face of the ultimate lama is the teaching on trekchöd: recognizing and maintaining awareness of the nature of mind. Thinley Norbu Rinpoche says we might think that if this is really the essential point of Guru Yoga, there is no point in discussing the subject of thögal, which seems to be extraneous to Guru Yoga. However, he says that is not the case.

In trekchöd practice, we meditate with an emphasis on the nature of the mind, *the wisdom of emptiness*. The other aspect of Dzogchen is thögal practice, which can be translated as "passing over." At this stage, we meditate with an emphasis on the *wisdom of appearances*. Here a certain amount of diligence is necessary. There are some very strange postures that one takes, unlike other forms of Tibetan yoga. One looks up into space or one looks down. One looks at the sun. One looks at a lamp. One looks at the moon. All these postures and gazes are useful in purifying one's experience of all appearances. The trekchöd part of Dzogchen purifies the mind, and the thögal side purifies all appearances. Once these are finished, there is nothing else to do.

In trekchöd practice, we change our ordinary thoughts, negative emotions, and suffering into wisdom. We have the *basis* of the three bodies of enlightenment. In thögal practice, the *appearances* of the three bodies of enlightenment are brought onto the path. All appearances, including one's own body, are transformed into bodies of light.

Thinley Norbu Rinpoche does not go into great detail on thögal— for example, he doesn't describe the "four lamps" and the "four visions"* in detail. But he says enough about thögal to teach the basis of thögal practice, to present the fact that all sentient beings have the basis for the arising of the appearances of thögal. Also, for those who practice thögal, the following will explain the relationship between original purity, which is great emptiness (trekchöd), and spontaneous luminosity (thögal): how these two are connected and how they must be connected on the path of thögal.

Thinley Norbu Rinpoche reminds us that recognition of the nature of mind, the view of trekchöd, and the appearances that arise in thögal, the luminous display of that inner, intrinsic aware-ness, are emptiness and appearance inseparable. To meditate on the appearances of thögal without grounding in trekchöd is, as Mi-pham Rinpoche said, no more meaningful than children looking at rainbows. With the proper relationship between the inner view of trekchöd and the outer appearance of thögal, it is possible for our practice of both to improve at the same time. Since the outer and the inner have the proper relationship, one goes directly to the great transference of the rainbow body. Even for persons who are not doing thögal practice, the teaching that emptiness and clarity aren't separate from one another, that in one's trekchöd practice the clarity that arises will be used in thögal, can be very reassuring.

The teaching that the wisdom of emptiness and the wisdom of appearance are one in essence can be very meaningful if it brings out the point that these two practices must be understood in union. We

---

*Orgyen Chowang Rinpoche has indicated that "visions" can be a misleading trans-lation of the Tibetan term *nangwa*, as it may imply something supernatural. He has not determined the right translation yet, although "experiences" is a possibility.

must keep in our awareness that, in trekchöd practice, the appearance aspect is thögal, and that, in thögal, we must be rooted in the emptiness aspect in order to work with appearances.

In thögal, we meditate on the same appearances that arise during the bardo of the nature of reality. There is the bardo of living, then the bardo of the time of death, and then we enter the bardo of the nature of reality. The appearances we meditate on in thögal are the very same as the appearances of the bardo of the nature of reality. We call the practice "thögal" because we are crossing over, or leaping over, to the appearances of that bardo. Ordinarily, we must die before we have this experience.

The great Dzogchen masters of the past stated that if we have not recognized our intrinsic awareness through trekchöd practice, meditation on the appearances of thögal practice causes further confusion in samsara. To regard the appearances of thögal as truly existent and to have attachment to them, to use these appearances without recognition of intrinsic awareness, causes confusion. If we stay anchored in our intrinsic awareness when we see the appearances that arise in thögal practice, we recognize them as the display of intrinsic awareness. Otherwise, there's no point whatsoever.

Whatever appears to us, whether in the mind or outwardly, must be seen through "the view of the three doors of liberation"— emptiness, beyond characteristics, and wishlessness. This is true for the appearance of exaltation, clarity, or nonconceptuality in our meditation. It is true for any activity we do with our body, speech, or mind. And it is true for the appearances we might experience in thögal. All appearances, whatever we do, must be experienced through this view. So it's critical in thögal practice to recognize all appearances as the luminosity, or brilliance, that arises from rigpa and to recognize that these appearances do not have fundamental existence.

Thinley Norbu Rinpoche advises us to remember what Tilopa said to Naropa: "You are not bound by appearances. You are bound by your attachment to appearances." Nothing we experience is solid, or real. Our attachment to appearances as real must diminish. Thinley Norbu Rinpoche says to remember this and feel inclined to that perspective.

Just as, in trekchöd practice, an ordinary sentient being can have awareness pointed out directly, in thögal practice, the bodies and realms of enlightenment are pointed out directly, manifestly, to ordinary beings. This special quality of Dzogchen is not found in any other teaching. Having had both the emptiness aspect of our nature and the luminous nature of appearances pointed out, all appearances can be seen in their pure form.

In thögal practice, we talk about the inner channels—both ordinary channels and wisdom channels. We work with the channel running from the heart to the brain to the eyes. Through thögal practice, anybody who has received these teachings can directly see the appearance of outer luminosity. It is an inconceivably wonderful and profound practice. In brief, on the path of Dzogchen, for all the inner qualities that are part of inner luminosity to appear and manifest on the outside, we practice thögal. In thögal practice, whatever we have in our heart (as described here), we see directly with our eyes.

Thögal practice uses "the four lamps," which produce, or help us to experience, "the four visions." In the text *Chanting the Names of Manjushri*, it is said that the appearance, or vision, of wisdom is clear and apparent, the wisdom lamp is within all beings, and its garland of brilliance is very beautiful. That's a completely obscure text, but on one level, "the vision of wisdom is clear" refers to the lamp of the pure sphere. (We're just going through the names here.) "The wisdom lamp is within all beings" refers to the lamp of the sphere of emptiness. "Its garland of brilliance is very beautiful" refers to the vajra brilliance of awareness. The first lamp refers to the empty essence of mind. The second lamp refers to the nature of clarity of mind. The third lamp refers to the all-pervasive energy of mind.

The four visions increase our experience of the bodies and wisdoms of enlightenment. The target in thögal meditation is the rainbow body. The idea of the rainbow body really only comes into practice in thögal. Right now, we experience our body as being solid—flesh, blood, and bones. But through thögal practice, we experience our body as a rainbow body. Thögal practice begins by developing visions of spheres (another use of *thigle*). Through the practice of working with the four lamps, the channels, and the four visions, one starts seeing thigles—spheres of light. In the beginning, they are like little zeroes. Gradually they grow as big as the lid of a cup, then as big as one's arm span, and then progressively larger so as to include all space. Finally, everything appears as a great sphere of luminosity. Then attention turns to the body. Progressively, in the same way that the nature of all appearances arises as luminous wisdom, one's body arises as luminous wisdom, like a rainbow, as a sphere of light. Eventually one's body is seen as a rainbow body by others. This is the domain of thögal practice.

In Kalachakra and Mahamudra teachings, even though we might recognize that all beings have the potential of attaining a rainbow body, the teachings don't lead us to that state. Only in thögal is that potential recognized; the practice brings out the potential and enables the practitioner to arrive at that state. Even in the practice of trekchöd, we attain "the body beyond atoms," but still we don't arrive at a rainbow body. In trekchöd practice, we work more with the empty aspect of awareness; we don't meditate (or very rarely) on the spheres of light and the four lamps. In thögal, both emptiness and appearance are utilized. This practice led such great masters as Guru Rinpoche, Vimalamitra, and others to "the great transference" of the rainbow body.

In thögal practice, the sun, the moon, and the flame of a lamp are used as supports for the practice. Looking at sunlight is the support for the ultimate body of enlightenment. Looking at moonlight is the support for the body of enlightenment's perfect splendor. Looking at the flame of a lamp is the support for the manifest body of enlightenment. But it is not a case of thinking, "This flame from a lamp is the three jewels; we bow to this lamp." There is nothing sacred about these sources of light; rather, they are supports for our practice.

Through thögal practice, one progresses through the four visions: (1) the vision of manifest reality, (2) the intensification of experience, (3) the full measure of awareness, and (4) the exhaustion of everything in the nature of reality (briefly described below). At that point, there is no sunlight; there is no darkness; there is no one looking; there is no viewer of the sunlight. Everything dualistic has been exhausted into wisdom. There is no sun, no moon, no one looking at the sun and moon. All the paths and stages of awakening to wisdom have been traversed.

## The Four Visions and the Four Awareness Holders

Of the four visions of thögal, the first is the "vision of manifest reality," the direct seeing. It is the unconcealed, unhidden, direct seeing of the mind's essence, nature, and all-pervasive energy. One sees this nature of mind directly.

As one gets more and more familiar with the vision of manifest reality, then one's experience, both within oneself and of the nature of appearance, increases. The outer elements and the movement of the energy-wind inside are progressively purified, and one experiences the spheres of the five wisdoms. Within that experience, one sees the different aspects of pure vision, pure lands, or pure appearances. This is the second vision, "the vision of the intensification of experience." The experience within meditation is increasing. This intensification of experience has two aspects. Inwardly, one transcends the limits of ordinary thought. Outwardly, the experiences gradually increase in purity.

In the third vision, as one's experience increases more and more, all appearances appear as spheres of light, as radiant forms, as male and female buddhas. Male and female bodhisattvas appear as celestial palaces, as pure as pure lands, as inconceivable pure appearances. That stage is the "vision of the full measure of awareness." Awareness has arrived at its limit. Of course, thögal practice deals with appearances as things arise outside. However, at the same time, there is one's inner experience of the wisdoms.

The visions within thögal practice are really extraordinary. In thögal practice, one can understand and have the great transference of the rainbow body. Before that, when we hear about the rainbow body, we think, "We have this ordinary body of flesh and blood. What is a rainbow body?" In thögal, one can understand, and gain confidence in, such things as the rainbow body. One can understand how it is possible. Thögal is much more exalted than trekchöd practice. In trekchöd practice, though the rainbow body is mentioned, it is the "small rainbow body." Only thögal practice has the great transference of the rainbow body. Other levels of practice—Mahayana, Mahayoga, the Secret Essence Tantra, Kalachakra, Mahamudra—don't even have the name or the concept of the rainbow body. Only in thögal does it really become a reality.

In the fourth vision, one arrives at the rainbow body. Even with the thought "There won't be any arrival there," arrival occurs. The fourth vision occurs when the energy-winds of the five elements dissolve entirely into the sphere of the five wisdoms and the ordinary energy-winds are completely emptied into the sphere of wisdom. At that point, there is no longer any designation of appearance or nonappearance. There is no thought of the appearance of ordinary reality or the appearance of pure forms (buddhas and bodhisattvas). There is no ordinary thought of samsara or the transcendence of samsara. There is only the nature of reality, like the autumn sky without any clouds. (In Tibet, the autumn sky is a very, very deep blue without any clouds, without any embellishment.)

This fourth vision is the "exhaustion of everything into the nature of reality." Mipham Rinpoche said that there are two ways of understanding the word *exhaustion*. We can say that one's ordinary subjective experience has completely emptied into the nature of reality. Or we can say that the subjective experience, completely perfected, has completely embraced all reality. It comes down to the same thing. The subjective experience has disappeared or it has become entirely of one essence.

Progress through the four visions provides the means to attain the levels of the four awareness holders. In Dzogchen practice, we don't talk about the ten stages of awakening; we talk about the levels of an awareness holder (Skt. *vidyadhara*, Tib. *rigdzin*), which refers to someone who has seen the nature of mind, awareness, directly and unmistakenly. *Rig* means "awareness" and *dzin* means "holder—to maintain this within the mind, to hold or grasp."

The four levels of an awareness holder are mentioned in all three levels of the inner tantras (Mahayoga, Anuyoga, and Atiyoga). The four states are usually described in the following way: The first state is the "completely ripened awareness holder." This refers to one's body being the complete ripening of previous karma. We call the body "the completely ripened body." Even though one is not free from the "seal" of the body, the mind is completely purified, and one has the experience of the body of the deities.

The second level of an awareness holder is the "awareness holder of long life" or the "awareness holder of the control of longevity." At this stage, even though one has not abandoned this body, it is transformed into a pure form. When we say that one has not abandoned the body, we mean that one doesn't die, but the body is transformed into a pure form, and one is able to use the pure form to go to enlightenment. For example, a person who is one hundred years old can transform their body into the body of a sixteen-year-old. The body becomes an eternal support for the attainment of enlightenment.

The third level of an awareness holder is the "awareness holder of Mahamudra." One can transform one's form into any divine form, such as Vajrakilaya, Manjushri, or any other form at all.

The fourth level of an awareness holder is the "spontaneous awareness holder." One has realized all that can be realized. That is the general context of the four levels of an awareness holder.

The first two visions, the vision of manifest reality and the vision of the intensification of experience, are related to the first level of an awareness holder, the completely ripened awareness holder. The third vision, the full measure of awareness, is related to the second level of an awareness holder, the control of longevity awareness holder. The fourth vision, exhaustion of everything in the nature of reality, is the experience of the Mahamudra awareness holder. When one has completed all the levels and arrives at enlightenment, that is the spontaneous awareness holder.

## Defusing Criticisms of Thögal Practice

Most Dzogchen texts are practically impossible to understand when you just look at the words. The meanings of the words differ from those of other teachings. Without direct teaching from a lineage holder, the words themselves don't point us in the right direction. Many Dzogchen texts are in a secret, or concealed, language. For example, one Dzogchen text mentions a channel that connects the jewel and the ocean. It doesn't appear to mean anything at all. How do we connect these two? We need a lineage holder to tell us, "The jewel is your heart. The ocean is your eyes. This refers to the meridian connecting your heart and your eyes." If we receive instructions, or if we pray wholeheartedly to Guru Rinpoche, then maybe we will understand.

Some who have read and considered certain Dzogchen texts but have no experience or real understanding criticize Dzogchen practice, thögal in particular. They say, "This is a nondharma practice; these practitioners are just sun gazers." Some monasteries in Tibet did not stress practice; instead of practicing Dzogchen or Mahamudra, they were interested mainly in debating concepts. They spent their time thinking, "How will I defeat somebody in debate tomorrow?" Approaching the profound teaching of Dzogchen with this type of argumentative mind does not give access to the teachings. Since they had not received the direct instructions of a Dzogchen teacher, the Dzogchen teachings didn't seem consistent with their opinions. For many Tibetans who had thought about dharma, it was enough for them to enter the monastery, take monks' vows, develop skill in debate, and pass their lives without thinking of actual practice. If you practice Mahamudra or Dzogchen, your aim is to be liberated from the suffering of samsara for the benefit of all beings. But their attention was in joining the monastery team, being part of an institution, and furthering the institution. At the end of their life, they became gray on the outside and empty on the inside. They had to face the end of their life without ever having really practiced.

Since they didn't understand trekchöd or thögal, they didn't try to practice them. Even with the new tantras such as *Kalachakra*, people would take the initiation, but if you went to the monastery and asked them about it, they would say, "Later for that." They would receive the empowerment, but they would put off practice for another day.

Concerning the criticism of thögal practitioners as sun gazers, it is not only thögal that mentions the sun. Buddhas and bodhisattvas are often compared to the sun or the moon. The image of enlightenment as being like the sun is not strange. Tantric practices of all schools often include visualizations of deities sitting on flat disks of the sun and moon. So looking at sunlight or moonlight in thögal practice doesn't seem to be contradictory. If meditating using light from the sun or the moon is somehow nondharma, imagining deities sitting on the sun or the moon would also be nondharma. There is only one sun and moon. There isn't a dharma sun and a nondharma sun, or a dharma moon and a nondharma moon. Those nondharma believers who gaze at the sun or the moon consider them to be gods, and they make prostrations and offerings to them. This is not the case in thögal practice. Rest reassured.

The tantras prior to Dzogchen use the inner channels, the energy-winds, and the vital essence of the body to produce the experience of wisdom, so there seems to be no reason why we can't use sunlight, moonlight, and lamplight for the same purpose. They are all being used as supports for the development of wisdom, not as objects to worship. If it were true that looking at the sun or moon or lamps was a nondharma practice, we could say the same thing about practice using the channels, winds, and the vital essence of the body.

When we encounter a philosophy or practice based on wisdom, then worldly, or even buddhadharma, philosophies based on ordinary consciousness, no matter how subtly or finely they are expressed, defeat themselves through their own logic. If we take the materialist Shravakayana philosophy to its extreme, we see that their proposition that atoms are indivisible doesn't hold up. The Mind Only school believes that the objects of clinging do not exist, yet there is inward clinging. Middle Way philosophy contends that there is ultimate truth but, on the relative level, things exist; this also doesn't hold up. When ordinary consciousness meets wisdom, consciousness self-destructs.

A scientific viewpoint provides an initial understanding; we appreciate scientific observation and everything that science can produce, and we enter the materialist philosophy. From there, we enter the Mind Only and then the Middle Way. As we increase our intellectual understanding, we begin to appreciate tantra. We appreciate working with the channels, energy-winds, and vital essence. We appreciate the tantric idea of infinite purity. But when we arrive at Dzogchen and see the nature of reality directly, then suddenly everything that we've looked at before seems minor. Our attachment to any philosophy based on ordinary consciousness disappears. My case was the same as for any of us. At the beginning, when I was first studying, I really appreciated the Mind Only school. Then I appreciated the Middle Way school. Later, there was nothing better than the tantras. Then finally I got to Dzogchen. Everything else—any attachments to philosophy or anything based on ordinary consciousness—disappeared entirely. When we directly see the nature of reality, philosophies based on ordinary consciousness just don't do it anymore.

It's not that Dzogchen debates with or puts down the other philosophies or other ways of practice. When we understand, or see, philosophies or practices based on wisdom or the experience of wisdom, anything else seems to be merely a creation of ordinary thought. The Dzogchen experience is not judgmental; it is "Wow!"

## Emptiness

In discussing gazing at the face of the ultimate lama, awareness and emptiness, I commented on the first word, *rigpa* (awareness); the distinction between ordinary mind and rigpa; and the relationship between luminosity (*osel*) and rigpa. I have also talked about trek-chöd and thögal practice. Now we come to the next word in that line, *tong* (emptiness).

We could say that emptiness is the essence of awareness. For one person, simply to say that directly is enough. For another, whose mind may not grasp awareness or emptiness directly, we must make distinctions, such as that within awareness there is no past, present, or future; no time, no direction, no color; nothing substantial or insubstantial. There is neither existence nor nonexistence, neither both, nor neither. This is the empty essence of the nature of mind. Mipham Rinpoche said that just as one can look directly into space (not into the sky as an object but directly into all-pervasive space) and see nothing whatsoever (no color, no form, and so forth) and realize that it has always been that way, without a moment when space came into being, it is essential to look directly into the mind to see and develop firm certainty that the mind is the same; it has no color, form, size, or any other characteristic, and it has never existed.

It is possible that if you look into the mind and see that it is empty, gradually you will be able to understand the luminous, or clear, aspect of the mind at the same time that it is empty. After you see that the mind has no color, location, time—nothing substantial— and recognize its nature as such with complete certainty, you recognize the nature of mind for what it is beyond all causes and conditions. If you aren't firmly decided, then anger, jealousy, pride, and other negative emotions continue to arise, and you experience them as you would in a dream. These appearances come from the manifestation, or display, of not realizing emptiness. Everything comes back to lack of recognition of one's own nature.

With certainty in recognition of the empty essence of mind, the reality of emptiness, there is no longer any possibility of creating happiness or suffering. The basic causes and conditions for the creation of happiness and suffering, our experience in samsara, naturally cease.

There are numerous ways to reach the experience of the empty essence of mind. Some persons go directly to the experience of nondual wisdom. Others must approach it through emptiness and later develop the experience of clarity. Others work with the clarity, or luminous nature of mind, to arrive at the experience of emptiness. At first we may need to understand emptiness conceptually. Later we develop direct experience and certainty in the practice, so that we are 100 percent convinced that the essence of mind is emptiness.

By looking directly within the essence of mind, we can see that we have never been lost in thought. From the perspective of the essence of mind, desire, anger, and ignorance have never been part of our experience. It's our attachment to them that makes them seem real. Within the essence of mind, they have never arisen. If you look now directly into the essence of your mind, you will see that desire, anger, and ignorance don't exist. Just look now, directly.

Well?

The mind is empty like space. Within the essence of mind, nothing at all exists. As Mipham Rinpoche said, "You look directly into space, and you understand space directly before you. There is no form, no color, nothing that exists within empty space. Mind is exactly the same as this empty space." We have a body with a brain and a heart. Mind does not exist in the heart or the brain. The impression of the mind being in the heart or brain is only an appearance of confusion. It may appear like that, but it is not a reality. It is merely an apparent existence.

To look into the nature, or the essence, of our mind and see that the mind is empty is the ultimate body of enlightenment.

However, although looking into empty space is useful for recognizing emptiness, our mind isn't really empty like empty space. It is not indefinite like space. Rather, the mind is the union of both emptiness and appearance.

We mentioned the essence of mind as emptiness and the nature of mind as clarity, or luminosity. The inseparability of these two is its all-pervasive energy (*thugje*). However, we can also identify the essence of mind (emptiness) as the ultimate body of enlightenment; its nature (clarity or luminosity) as the body of enlightenment's perfect splendor; and its all-pervasive energy (the union of the two) as the manifest body of enlightenment. We call the energy "all-pervasive" because it is the mind of all buddhas and sentient beings. The literal translation of *thugje* is "compassion," which is not other than what the word really points to: the mind of all buddhas and the true nature of all sentient beings.

We must understand that these aspects of mind—the three bodies of enlightenment and mind's essence, nature, and energy—are inseparable. Although we have names for all three, they are one and the same.

Mind's essence is wisdom, its nature is wisdom, and its all-pervasive energy could also be called "wisdom"; but on the level of words, this may not seem to aid understanding. But there is the essence, the nature, and if you understand that third aspect as wisdom, that is really what it is. If you identify the inseparability of emptiness and luminosity as wisdom, you've got it.

## The Inseparability of Basis and Result

Ordinarily, when we study the teachings, understanding the primordial basis is our point of departure. Then we have a path. From following the path, we arrive at a result that is related to the basis and the path. In order to understand the basis, path, and result, we have a relationship with the three bodies of enlightenment, the lama. However, in this case, when we talk about the absolute, or ultimate, lama, we speak in terms of the basis and the result being inseparable. This is the ultimate master: we see the basis and the result together.

In Dzogchen, there is no difference between the basis and the result. The basis is the primordial purity of mind of all sentient beings, and the result is its complete actualization. We don't start with primordial purity and go elsewhere with it. Mipham Rinpoche said that, in your mind, you might divide the space in a room into a lower, middle, and upper space, but that is only conceptual; there is no difference between the upper and lower space in space itself. In the same way, the distinction between the basis, the path, and the result is conceptual, consisting of temporary, or incidental, obscurations. In Dzogchen, there is no difference between the basis and the result.

Thinley Norbu Rinpoche quotes from a prayer that accompanies the Dudjom Tersar Ngöndro in which Dudjom Rinpoche identifies the ultimate lama. First, he says it is clarity of mind without any sense of specific location. There is clarity without saying, "This is my mind. This is my clarity. This exists. That doesn't exist." There is clarity without any focal point or ordinary thought. He says, "It is awareness and emptiness, which is naked." The word *naked* is important in Dzogchen practice: we look into naked awareness and emptiness. Just as we are naked when we take off our clothes, awareness is naked when the clothes of the mind—ordinary thoughts—are removed. In clarity, there is awareness without any ordinary thought. The mind is completely unclothed—unsullied, unpolluted, and untouched by ordinary thought. The clarity, awareness, and emptiness are direct. Nothing comes between us and this experience. Clarity, emptiness, and awareness, Dudjom Rinpoche says, are the ultimate lama, who is Yeshe Dorje (Wisdom Vajra), the name of Dudjom Rinpoche. We recognize this as the ultimate Yeshe Dorje, the ultimate Dudjom Rinpoche. It is the clarity, emptiness, and awareness of our own mind. It is direct; when we look into the nature of mind, awareness and emptiness, clarity without concept, that is the ultimate lama.

The next words of the practice text say, "Gaze at the face of the ultimate lama." What does it mean to gaze at the face of the ultimate lama? It may sound like looking at an object, but the ultimate lama is not like anything we might identify in the outer world. Nor is it gazing as it is done in tantric meditations where we imagine being the commitment deity and we gaze at the wisdom deity in the sky before us. Gazing at the ultimate lama doesn't involve subject and object, self and other.

Then what is it? First, the viewer and what is seen are nondual. There is no distinction between them. What is being looked at is what is looking. This is awareness. This is the great thigle, the great vital essence, the great zero, without any center, corners, or sides. This is the great sphere of awareness. Whatever we create as a subject and whatever we experience as an object are completely exhausted. We regard directly the nonduality between our awareness and the sphere of totality. This is the direct, "naked" gaze into our own nature.

When we look into awareness and emptiness, we do not see anything. It is "the great sight of not-seeing" or "the great not-seeing sight." We look directly into the mind: we see awareness and emptiness and we see nothing at all. It is "the naked sight of, or gaze at, the ultimate lama." So gazing at the face of the ultimate lama refers to the view of awareness and emptiness.

We look into the essence of awareness and we look into the essence of emptiness. They are exactly the same thing. We look and there is neither viewer nor something to view in the gaze. If there were an object of sight in gazing at the ultimate lama, it would be part of our experience of samsara. There would be attachment to some thing we had seen. But in this gaze, there is no subject or object; the viewer and what is seen are inseparable, empty awareness. As we gain more experience in this gaze, ordinary thoughts, negative emotions, and so on are liberated into the space of awareness-emptiness.

The *Secret Essence Tantra* states that awareness is not in front of, or behind, or at any particular place in a buddha. This naked awareness is entirely pervasive, without any direction or localization. This refers to Buddha Ever Excellent, Samantabhadra. We call this "the ultimate lama of awareness and emptiness." We can also say it is the lama of wisdom because the ultimate lama is not polluted, or touched, by the obscurations of ordinary thought. It is the state of noncomposite luminosity, which is the primordial nature. The awareness that rests within the primordial nature is wisdom. This is the wisdom lama.

## The Four Ways of Liberation

When we rest within awareness and emptiness, whatever arises, whether negative thoughts of anger, desire, or ignorance, or positive thoughts of faith, compassion, or the mind of awakening, as well as all the appearances of samsara and nirvana, arises as the ornaments, the play, or the display (we use all three words for this) of awareness. Since no basis for restriction exists, it is called "primordial liberation," the first of the "four ways of liberation."

Just as the sun, moon, and stars are the ornaments of space, or the sky, all these experiences, things, and events are the ornaments of awareness. Just as rays of light come naturally from the sun, positive and negative thoughts, or appearances, arise naturally from awareness. Everything arising from rigpa is the display of rigpa. The sun, moon, stars, and planets, this world and everything that exists in this world, appear within space. There is nowhere we can go that is not within the bounds of space; we can't go outside space no matter how far we go. Everything that appears within space, whether the positive, pure appearance of transcendent states or the impure appearance of samsara, is the display, or play, of space. Likewise, since there is no experience that is not pervaded by awareness, all experience is part of the play, or display, of awareness.

Because an ordinary sentient being does not recognize the self's true nature, the manifestation, or energy, of awareness is not recognized for what it is and is experienced as an object. That energy actually provokes dualistic experience. A Dzogchen adept who remains in awareness recognizes anger, desire, ignorance, faith, compassion, and the mind of awakening—any appearance of samsara or nirvana—as the manifestation, or energy, of awareness. Such a Dzogchen practitioner also recognizes that within awareness there was never any clinging to begin with and there is no need for a new liberation. So liberation is primordial.

The second way of liberation is "natural, intrinsic liberation." For a Dzogchen practitioner, there is no need to push negative experiences away or embrace positive experiences. In the sutra tradition, we look at desire, anger, and ignorance as tough, poisonous enemies. We apply antidotes to these poisons; for example, we counteract anger with patience. However, in Dzogchen, anger does not escape from the sphere of awareness, and for a practitioner who sees that anger's nature is awareness, it naturally dissolves within the sphere of awareness. No matter what positive or negative appearances arise, nothing must be rejected and nothing must be accepted, or encouraged. Everything is seen in its own nature.

Third is "direct liberation," which refers to the knowledge aspect of mind being not concealed, not hidden from us. It is direct. It is manifest. We can stare directly into the nature of mind. We can look directly at the nature of anything. When a Dzogchen practitioner looks directly at desire, anger, or ignorance, at any appearance or experience, it is directly liberated by that sight. This is not lazy sight; it is direct seeing with awareness. Whatever is seen is directly liberated.

The fourth way of liberation is "complete liberation." In the *Treasury of the Sphere of Totality*, Longchenpa said that everything is liberated within awareness from the beginning. Having been completely liberated, whatever appears doesn't have to be liberated again. The world of samsara is originally pure, therefore it is liberated. The nature of samsara is the three bodies of enlightenment. The nature of nirvana is originally pure, therefore it is liberated. In transcendent states, the bodies and wisdoms of enlightenment are spontaneously present. It is not necessary to recreate enlightenment or accomplish the ultimate body of enlightenment, the forms of enlightenment, or the wisdoms of enlightenment. They are spontaneously present in the transcendent states. Therefore liberation is complete.

Dzogchen practitioners reach liberation through confidence in these four styles of liberation. Patrul Rinpoche said that what appears to a Dzogchen practitioner is exactly what appears to all sentient beings. After the recognition of awareness, what appears continues to be exactly the same. There is no difference. But the Dzogchen practitioner attains liberation through these four styles of liberation in relation to what appears.

## Dzogchen Practice

Dzogchen is the summit of the nine vehicles of development. Patrul Rinpoche stated that it is the peak of the vajra, beyond effort, beyond the sphere of the intellect, or the ordinary mind, and that through these teachings one attains enlightenment without meditation. Awareness and emptiness are experienced nakedly. Therefore, without meditation, one remains within awareness and emptiness. This path is without any work involved in the creation phase, the completion phase, study, or whatever it is that characterizes the other stages of buddhadharma practice. At this stage, the nature of mind is presented and recognized. So all this effort is unnecessary.

So now you know! In Dzogchen, making distinctions between meditation and postmeditative states, or between various kinds of mental pacification and insight meditations, or making our practice very complicated, is not advised. Nor is it advised to formulate a sense of different stages, or paths, in our development. All that is necessary is to rest within the great sphere of awareness and emptiness and come to certainty about this state. Just that is enough.

Thus, it is often said in such discourses as the *Changeless Nature* and the *Ornament of Realization* (both by the bodhisattva Maitreya), and in the tantras,

> There is nothing to be cleared away; there is nothing
>     to be added.
> Nothing whatsoever.
> One sees the true nature by the true nature.
> When one sees that true nature, one arrives at liberation.

From the Dzogchen perspective, "There is nothing to be cleared away; there is nothing to be added" refers to awareness and emptiness, to the basis. Seeing without making a distinction between the seer and what is seen is the path. As we gain familiarization and our true nature manifests, this is the result, liberation. Within these four lines are basis, path, and liberation. Dzogchen master Jigme Phuntsok Rinpoche, my root teacher, taught extensively on this. Mipham Rinpoche made it even more succinct by saying, "When you see this nature to which nothing needs to be added or taken away, you arrive at liberation."

There are some very complicated meditations to calm the mind, such as the nine ways to place the mind. There are also many ways to meditate on insight. But meditations on tranquillity and insight are complete within the essence of awareness, the Dzogchen view. Within the view, the presence of the primordial nature is natural meditation, or natural calm. And natural clarity, or luminosity, within that nature is the insight aspect.

Thus, by remaining in the Dzogchen view, both tranquillity and insight are naturally complete. The tranquillity part of the view is the empty essence of awareness that doesn't change throughout the past, present, and future and is always present and free from any ordinary thought. That basic nature, the essence of awareness, is totally peaceful. That is tranquillity. Then, within empty essence, awareness is not only emptiness; there is also an aspect of knowledge in awareness. That knowledge aspect, in which all the bodies and wisdoms of enlightenment are naturally present, is the insight aspect of the view. One experiences these two as inseparable. This is the infinite expanse of a buddha's realization.

Thinley Norbu Rinpoche's text quotes from Longchenpa's *Treasury of the Sphere of Totality*:

> Profound openness, profound openness, in the
>     nature of profound great openness,
> Longchen Rabjam* is abiding in the expanse of
>     profound light.

The first words are "profound openness," which can also be expressed as "vast expanse." "Openness," or "expanse," in this first phrase refers to everything that appears or occurs outwardly. It is like the sphere of space without a center or a border. It is all appearances because there is no center or limit to what appears or occurs. "Profound" or "vast" refers to the recognition that it is

---

*Longchenpa is a shortened version of Longchen Rabjam (infinite, vast expanse of space).

without a basis and primordially empty. To see the nature of all appearances and occurrences is the profundity, or vastness, of the openness. There is no point where we can say, "It is that" or "It is one thing." It is the opposite of being very dense, or concentrated, in a particular locale. Seeing that everything is primordially empty creates a very wide, or open, expanse.

The second two words in this line are the same as the first two. While the first two words refer to everything that appears or occurs outwardly, the second two refer to the open inner expanse. In one's inner nature, thoughts and emotions are beyond all arising and liberation. In the same way that a bird's footprints do not appear in the sky, all thoughts and emotions, all inner experiences, exist in this wide-open expanse.

The last words in this line, "in the nature of profound great openness," refer not to the outer expanse (the first two words) or the inner expanse (the second two words) but to the secret expanse, the expanse of inseparable awareness and emptiness, unceasing naked awareness and emptiness. This is the profound great openness of awareness.

The outer, inner, and secret expanse were nakedly realized by the Dzogchen practitioner Omniscient Longchenpa. He realized that it is unnecessary to renounce samsara because it is primordially pure. It is unnecessary to accomplish nirvana, or transcendent states, because they are spontaneously present. So Longchenpa experienced primordial purity (*kadag*) and spontaneous presence (*lhundrup*) within the three spheres (outer, inner, and secret). He realized that both samsara and nirvana were one within awareness. Both arise in the expanse of awareness, so one is not better and the other is not worse. Because he realized that they both exist within the sphere of awareness, they are nondual. Then he realized this within the coil of great exaltation. Another of Longchenpa's names is Natsok Rangdrol (the natural, intrinsic liberation of many things). He arrived at the exhaustion of everything into the nature of reality. Because he had arrived at the end, the perfection of the increase of his experience, he arrived at the state of Buddha Samantabhadra, the permanent state of enlightenment.

Longchenpa realized the emptiness of the outer, wide expanse of everything. He realized the natural purity of the inner expanse of his mind. He realized awareness and emptiness as the secret expanse. Thanks to that, whatever appeared in his mind was naturally liberated into the nature of reality. In one lifetime, he arrived at the state of the ultimate body of enlightenment. Then for the benefit of future generations of Dzogchen practitioners, he wrote the instructions to arrive at the same liberation, or realization. He advised us to look at the instructions of the lineage from the time of Buddha Samantabhadra down to the present day, to receive instructions from our teacher, and to read his various writings. By doing so, and by entering the great expanse of Dzogchen practice, he said that we will arrive at the state of Buddha Samantabhadra.

When we discern the nature of our own mind, we see that samsara and nirvana are equal in emptiness, so we enter the equanimity of the nature of mind, called, in this case, "discerning one's own nature." We discern the nature of our own mind and see it is awakening, it is enlightenment. We see that the nature of the three realms (desire, form, and formless) too is enlightenment. The nature of all sentient beings is enlightenment. When the mind enters confusion, that is samsara. When the mind is free from confusion, that is transcendence, or awakening. It is the Dzogchen view, but in fact, from the Mahayana on up, it is the view in buddhadharma practice.

In the special teachings of Dzogchen, the nature of reality doesn't change, no matter whether confusion is present or absent. Everything from the very beginning reflects the energy, or manifestation, or display, of enlightenment, or rigpa. There isn't a difference between pure and impure, between nirvana and samsara, because, from the very beginning, everything is the reflection of awareness, or awakening. The difference lies in whether we recognize the nature of reality or not. It is not that reality itself is impure and later becomes pure, or that reality is confused and later is perfected by confusion being cleared away. The nature of reality is primordial purity. That is the special teaching of Dzogchen, and mature Dzogchen practitioners realize that everything is the reflection of awareness and arises out of the energy, the manifestation, of awareness. If there were some things that arose out of confusion, there would be a contradiction between this realization and the nature of reality. But the Dzogchen practitioner is seeing reality for what it is. Nowhere and at no time has anything resulted from confusion. To know and remain within the essence of appearing reality, of what appears but doesn't actually come into being, of what seems to remain but does not remain, of what seems to cease but does not cease, is awakening.

The teachings of the Mahayana or even the Middle Way tend to see appearances and events, our objective experience as well as our negative emotions, as great enemies. We battle with them. We arm ourselves against outward experiences, as well as against the inner phenomena of anger, desire, ignorance, jealousy, and pride. This gives them more energy, and they get even stronger. This is not the Dzogchen attitude. In Dzogchen, we never consider our negative emotions to be enemies, and we never consider any outer experience to be threatening. If a huge army riding across the plain is known to be illusory or like a dream, there is no need to be afraid. If we see a river in a mirage or an optical illusion, there is no need to worry about being carried away by the water; we see that it is just a mirage, a magic show, a dream. Dzogchen's attitude toward everything, whether objective or subjective, remains within the equanimity of the illusory nature of everything. Rongzompa said that many levels of dharma philosophy talk about things being like a magic show, a dream, an illusion, a mirage, or an optical illusion, but only in Dzogchen do we learn how to use this idea in order to attain realization.

One of the sutras states that it is possible to completely abandon desire, anger, and ignorance and to attain liberation, but this style of liberation is for those who have a very strong sense of self, because clinging to a self solidifies our experience of desire, anger, and ignorance. When we feel the solid presence of these three poisons, we must fight with them, bring an antidote to the negative emotions. But for those who are free from this sense of self, desire, anger, and ignorance are naturally liberated. It is not necessary to renounce them. Dzogchen practitioners see either that the essence of desire, anger, and ignorance is like an appearance in a dream, or a magical display, or that, in their essence, there is no moment that they actually come into existence, so they are naturally liberated.

The early stage of knowing that desire, anger, and ignorance lack a solid nature, like a magic display or a dream, isn't exclusively the Dzogchen view, still that experience is extremely helpful in getting to know the nature of everything. When we enter the Dzogchen view, we see not only that all things lack a fundamental nature but also that samsara and nirvana are a reflection of enlightened awareness.

When we look directly into the nature, or essence, of anger, desire, or any other negative emotion, even when anger is like a pot of boiling water or desire is like an intense flame, we see that there is no point when they come into existence, no point when they abide somewhere, and no point when they cease. Even in the most intense experience of anger or desire, when we look into the essence, we see that they have never ever come into being. To see their nature exactly as they are, to know their nature, enables us to see them as the display of wisdom.

The sutras say, in the context of the idea of emptiness, that the entirety of samsara and nirvana have the nature of awakening. But it doesn't really move us because the ideas remain on the level of a teaching. The tantras, particularly the Mahayoga tantra, describe the experiences of sentient beings and a buddha's experiences and join them so we see their relation. By studying and practicing the tantras, we arrive at some certainty because it is explained through reason, through proof. But it is only when we practice Dzogchen that we can actually gain that experience. Then it is not a teaching; it is not just an intellectual certainty. It is direct experience of the nature of both samsara and nirvana being one and the same.

When we practice Dzogchen, entering this experience, or realization, we let go of all complications of ordinary virtuous practice, such as circumambulations, prayer wheels, and so on. Ordinary virtuous practice is outside the view of Dzogchen. We put ordinary virtuous practice aside. We set aside reciting prayers. We set aside meditation on deities. During Dzogchen practice, we enter only the experience of the view of Dzogchen. The *Union of Secrets Tantra* states that if we wish to attain supreme awakening, we need not read books or circumambulate stupas, and if that's all we do, we won't reach awakening. Instead, we just need to remain within the view.

Longchenpa's *Treasury of the Sphere of Totality* says that all experiences, events, and things of samsara and transcendent states, all ordinary thoughts and experiences of sentient beings, are primordially liberated. It is not necessary for them to be liberated anew. This is not just a teaching. We discussed the four forms of liberation: primordial liberation, natural liberation, direct liberation, and complete liberation. We can add to those: liberation on arising and single liberation. This is the experience of Dzogchen. The experience of Dzogchen is the primordial liberation of everything. So it is unnecessary to bring energy or effort, apart from resting in the view. We can either understand primordial liberation or experience it. Even just understanding it is very beneficial. To experience it through Dzogchen practice is extremely beneficial.

Longchenpa continued, saying emphatically, "Don't watch, don't watch, don't watch what occurs in the contrived mind." This means that we must recognize the Dzogchen view and remain within it. But, at that point, thoughts such as "My mind is empty," "My mind is not empty," "My mind is clear," "My mind is not clear," "I'm getting it," and "I'm not getting it," are ordinary mental experiences. Instead, in Dzogchen, we rest in recognition of the view and don't continue to check on our mind. We don't create this state with our intellect.

In Dzogchen, we recognize the view and remain only within the view. To think, "Things are not going very well; I've just had lots of thoughts; I've got to get rid of those thoughts," and then to think, "Now I've got rid of the thoughts; things are going well; I'm making some progress"—this kind of thinking concern, creating meditative states with one's mind, is not the Dzogchen view.

There is no work other than to remain in the recognition of the view. Even such thoughts that come from one's study, such as "My mind is really empty; the nature of my mind is emptiness," must not contaminate our view. We remain only in the view. There is nothing else to do.

Longchenpa continued, saying, "Don't meditate, don't meditate, don't meditate on the occurrences of the contrived mind." This applies to any form of meditation, such as the creation phase, the completion phase, trying to intellectually create the state of Dzogchen, and other forms of meditation. Meditation in Dzogchen is simply to extend the time in maintaining recognition of the view. We begin by recognizing the view, and then we relax within this view. Nothing else is needed. In Dzogchen, there is no difference between the view and meditation. The view is just recognition of the view. To maintain this recognition or get more and more familiar with it is meditation. There is nothing apart from that.

Longchenpa next said, "Don't examine, don't examine, don't examine subject and object." This refers to analysis as it is practiced in the Middle Way tradition. We look at what occurs in our mind and try to arrive, through analytic meditation, at some certainty, some conclusion, that things are empty. Then we see that these empty things come from the mind. We give our attention to the mind and analyze it. We see that the mind itself is empty. This gradual analytic meditation is not needed in Dzogchen, and in fact, it can be detrimental to the view. We remain in the Dzogchen view, and there is no place for analyzing the mind by asking, "Is it empty?" "Is it not empty?" "Does it have a color?" "Does it have a form?" "Is it existent, nonexistent, both, or neither?" Dzogchen goes directly to the conclusion without passing through all these stages.

Longchenpa then said, "Don't accomplish, don't accomplish, don't accomplish the result of hope and fear." This refers to thinking that your practice is getting somewhere and hoping to attain some particular state that goes beyond the bounds of samsara, or to looking at samsara and trying to accomplish freedom from the fear of falling into that cycle. This is not Dzogchen practice. Because we see the equanimity of samsara and transcendent states within the view, there is no need to entertain all these hopes and fears or to follow them in the context of our practice. Whatever appearances arise, we remain in an impartial state, in great equanimity. If we rest in great equanimity, this is the greatest, or supreme, form of keeping our tantric commitments, our samaya.

Longchenpa said that awareness is changeless and without any elaboration. That is just one very brief way to describe, or point to, awareness. No experience of samsara or nirvana, when seen from the perspective of rigpa, has ever been created, has ever come into existence. When resting within rigpa, all that arises has arisen primordially but has never had existence. This is called "as things arise, they are liberated" or "liberation upon arising." Seen through the eyes of rigpa, nothing really exists. The essence of everything is empty.

Even though things appear to arise, like space, there is no point when they actually come into being, no point when they stay, and no point when they reach liberation. When seen through the eyes of rigpa, there is nothing in the essence of anything except liberation on arising, liberation on abiding, and the primordial liberation of all things. Longchenpa explained that this includes all negative experiences such as desire, anger, and ignorance, and all positive experiences such as faith and compassion. Everything is seen in its essence as empty.

As sentient beings, we only see something arise, rest, or be liberated if we see it actually come into being and we experience it as an object. We make a connection between our mind and an object, and we create karma. But if we see the arising of everything through the eyes of rigpa, we see its empty essence. No attachment occurs, so there is no possibility of creating karma.

The process of immediate liberation at the moment of arising, of seeing everything through the eyes of rigpa, is continual. It is a great stream of liberation: at no point does one grasp anything as real. There is only the continual stream of arising and the liberation of everything.

Because there is no longer the creation of karma, the continuity of our negative karma, which could send us to the lower realms, is cut, and no positive karma can send us to the higher realms. When we are free in this way of the impulse that carries us into the six realms, Longchenpa said, there is no possibility of a mistake in our meditation. We have this sort of experience during our practice in Dzogchen of "the space class" and "the direct instruction class" of teachings. We must receive pointing-out instructions in intrinsic awareness, and due to these instructions and our recognition of intrinsic awareness, we will have this experience of everything. However, not everyone will understand the pointing-out instructions.

Through Dzogchen, we can clearly see the difference between a sentient being and an enlightened being. Other forms of buddhadharma discuss enlightenment, but it seems incredibly distant from our experience, resulting only after a great amount of time and effort spent accumulating causes and conditions. Dzogchen makes enlightenment very close to us. Dzogchen lets us see the difference between sentient beings and buddhas as being like the back and the front of a hand. They are that close. The difference is the recognition or the lack of recognition of awareness (rigpa and marigpa). If we can recognize awareness and the nature of everything seen through awareness, this is enlightenment. If we have dualistic experience of subject and object and take the object of experience as being real, this is the state of a sentient being. The difference is no more than that. We don't have to think about many different persons or all sentient beings. Take me, for example. If at any moment I have dualistic experience—subject and object, and all the thoughts and emotions that come in that framework—I am a sentient being. If I recognize intrinsic awareness and rest within that, I am enlightened.

Intrinsic awareness is primordial and never changes, without center or limit. It is the nature of mind, the nature of reality. It is emptiness and awareness. This is the expanse of Buddha Ever Excellent, Samantabhadra. Its nature is unceasing and unimpeded luminosity that takes the form of the different bodies and wisdoms of enlightenment. It is without any change, deathless. Longchenpa said that this is also Buddha Vajrasattva. The expanse of Buddha Ever Excellent and Buddha Vajrasattva are always inseparable.

This inseparability of emptiness and awareness is natural, or intrinsic, awareness or the nature of reality. It is important for us to recognize, in talking about the expanse of Buddha Ever Excellent or Buddha Vajrasattva, that we are speaking of them not as buddhas of form but as the ultimate body of enlightenment without form. There is an image of Ever Excellent, blue in color and in the pure exaltation of sexual union with his consort, who is white. That is the form of Ever Excellent that appears in the minds of sentient beings. Here we are talking about Ever Excellent as the nature of everything. Similarly, we can think about Vajrasattva as white in color, holding a vajra at his heart and a bell, and embraced by his consort, but this again is just the form that appears in the minds of sentient beings.

It is important for us to be sensitive to the context in which words are used. In the context of the words *ultimate lama*, we mean the nature of mind, the nature of reality. We can talk about Buddha Ever Excellent or Buddha Vajrasattva in terms of form or as representing the nature of our own mind and the nature of reality. We have to understand what we mean when we say "buddha" or when we say "enlightenment." We can think of the buddha as Buddha Shakyamuni, gold in color, holding a begging bowl, and pointing downward with his right hand. We can think of buddhas in pure realms in various forms. But these attitudes reflect confusion. *Buddha* or *enlightenment* means the unmistaken recognition of the nature of reality, the nature of our own mind. That, and that alone, is buddha.

At this point, you might wonder how we act in body, speech, and mind to maintain the recognition of intrinsic awareness. For those beginning the practice of Dzogchen, normally karmic energy is very strong, and as Thinley Norbu Rinpoche says, we must dissolve karmic energy into the central channel. Karmic energy is our habit of getting lost in thought, and the central channel is the sphere of wisdom. Ordinary thought must dissolve into the sphere of wisdom. However you understand it, the meaning is the same.

For beginners, when we sit down to practice, it is recommended that we keep the body straight, which keeps the channels straight, allowing the energy-wind inside the body to circulate as it should. When the energy-wind circulates properly through straight channels, the mind becomes very calm and clear. Otherwise the mind is in danger of losing its clarity. If we lean forward with our head, we will fall asleep; if we lean backward, it stimulates our thoughts. We try to create the physical environment for a clear mind that doesn't go out toward objects.

Thinley Norbu Rinpoche's text describes the seven-point posture of Vairochana. If possible, our legs are in the vajra posture, in what we call "full lotus" or at least with the legs crossed. The hands are relaxed on our knees or cupped, one in the other. The stomach is drawn in a little. The chin is drawn in just a little bit as well. The shoulders are drawn up slightly. The tongue touches the roof of the mouth. The eyes look directly in space, slightly downward. The posture of Vairochana creates the physical environment for meditation experience.

On the level of speech we do vajra recitation. When we inhale, we think *om*. At the moment before we breathe out, we think *ah*, and as we breathe out we think *hung*. It is not a verbal recitation. It is a mental recitation coordinated with our breathing. It is advised here to do this at the beginning of sitting meditation, although Dzogchen practitioners of the past also did it before they were about to finish their period of meditation. There are many benefits of doing this practice. It purifies our body, speech, and mind, and we gain control of the experience of tranquillity and insight meditation.

On the level of mind, many different meditations are done as preparatory practices to Dzogchen to enrich our meditative experience. For example, in the practice of "destroying the small house of mind," we imagine the syllable *hung* in front of us. It flies away, far away, all over the place, and then it flies off into space and dissolves. Or we can imagine and focus on many *hung*s on a stick placed before us. We can do other meditations that cause the mind's focus to go out or return. Even though these meditations are important to enrich our meditative experience as part of preparing for Dzogchen practice, the best form of meditation is simply the recognition of intrinsic awareness.

These forms of meditation practice are included in the special tradition of Dzogchen. But all the foregoing "rules" about placing the body, speech, and mind in the right place for meditation should be considered in light of Guru Rinpoche's advice to Yeshe Tsogyal. He said that we can take many different postures during meditation, but the very best is to rest precisely in the posture that is most comfortable, or natural. Of all the vital points on posture, this is the most important, and this, in itself, is enough. Simply place the body in the most comfortable position. He said that many teachings are given about what to do on the level of speech. For example, we can work with the energy-winds in vase breathing. We take a breath, force it down, bring up the lower breath, and hold it very strongly like a vase in our body. There are teachings such as this, and there are countless mantras to recite. But among all the teachings on speech and the energy-winds, the best is to rest without any verbal expression, as if we were mute. In the same way that relaxing the body naturally gathers the vital points of all the teachings on posture, so resting without talking, as if we were mute, gathers all the vital teachings on working with energy-winds and speech.

And the most important, vital point about how to work with the mind is to allow it to rest in its natural state, to have nothing artificial about your mind. This holds true for positive thoughts as well as negative thoughts. There is no need to think that your own mind, exactly the way it is, has to be changed. You don't have to add thoughts of faith, development of the mind of awakening, or compassion. You don't have to create negative thoughts of desire, anger, or ignorance. Just leave your mind exactly as it is, like a mirror, completely natural, reflecting exactly what is there. If you put something blue behind a crystal, you see blue; if you put something red, you see red. In this way, you can see the nature of the crystal. Allow the mind to rest in natural relaxation exactly like it is, without any artifice. Let the mind rest in its natural state. If we arrive at certainty within the single sphere of awareness and can guard the recognition of intrinsic awareness, then any form that appears, any object of our five senses or any mental experience, is seen as the three bodies of enlightenment, or the nature of our own mind. At that point, for the Dzogchen practitioner who guards intrinsic awareness, there is no thought of something to be rejected or wisdom to be gained. Body, speech, and mind rest in their natural state. The definition of the relaxed natural state is when we no longer think about pushing anything away or gaining anything. Everything is seen as the display of the three bodies of enlightenment, or the nature of our own mind. Whatever arises is liberated into the sphere of intrinsic awareness.

These instructions in the vital points of body, speech, and mind are preparatory to Dzogchen meditation. When we begin like this, it creates the proper environment for Dzogchen so we can go directly to it.

The great, omniscient master Longchenpa said in the *Treasury of the Sphere of Totality* that we meditate in the place where the mind is happy, and there we allow the body and mind to relax. Here we are talking about where we sit as well as how we sit. It can be in retreat or in isolation, but it has to be a place where the mind is happy. Guru Rinpoche said that we could meditate in the center of a city if that's where we are comfortable.

In the place where we are happy, we relax physically and mentally. Relaxing physically means to sit down and relax. Relaxing mentally means not to think that this happened and then that happened, or I've got to do this and then do that; it means not to clutter the mind with lots of mental events.

Our basic consciousness, or basic mind, at that point should be relaxed and open. Longchenpa used the example of someone who has just finished their job. They come home and sigh, "Whew . . . finished." They just relax. They feel fine, and they are done; they don't have to think about it anymore. It's five o'clock. It's over. Go home and relax. Our mind should feel like a person who has just finished a day of hard but not exhausting work. We should be very comfortable in body and mind, not overly tight or overly relaxed. Longchenpa's text says,

> However one stays, stay in one's pure nature.
> However one abides, abide in one's pure nature.
> However one goes, go in one's pure nature.
> In the space of enlightenment, there is naturally
>     no going or coming.

In a dream, we can have the impression of coming, going, or resting. However, there is no fundamental reality to that impression. It is just appearance. In the same way, we have the experience of coming, going, and resting, living the events that make up our life, but all experience exists within the sphere of awareness. This awareness in which there is no coming or going is the body of the buddhas.

Longchenpa continued by saying that whatever we say, however we speak, however we express ourselves, these different forms of expression take place within the sphere of awareness. We may experience sound, or verbal expression, in a dream, but in fact it exists only in the context of the dream. In the same way, within the sphere of awareness, no verbal expression really exists. It appears, but it does not have existence within the sphere of awareness. This sphere is the speech of all the buddhas.

In the same way, whatever we think, whatever turns in the mind, also appears within the sphere of awareness. Within the mind of awakening, there are never any ordinary thoughts or reflections. Within awareness, they primordially do not exist. The primordial freedom from thought is the mind of all the buddhas.

Within our intrinsic awareness are the three bodies of enlightenment. Its empty essence, in which nothing has fundamental existence, is the ultimate body of enlightenment. That anything whatsoever can appear clearly within awareness is its nature of clarity, luminous wisdom. That these two, emptiness and luminosity, are inseparable and can take any form whatsoever, is the manifest body of enlightenment. So the three bodies of enlightenment abide within intrinsic awareness. This is the mind of every sentient being. This is the mind of every buddha. The only distinction between them is that sentient beings lack recognition and buddhas do not. Apart from that, there is no difference.

## The Five Great States of Dzogchen

Thinley Norbu Rinpoche says that the essence of the wisdom of Dzogchen is explained through the ways of placing the mind in five states of greatness. When we keep these five qualities in mind, it is possible, in this one lifetime, without difficulty, to gain mastery of the citadel of the primordial protector.

The first great state of Dzogchen is how enlightenment is actualized. In contrast to the sutras, where enlightenment is presented as being on the far side of three incalculable aeons in which one clears away obscurations and cultivates merit and wisdom, in Dzogchen, any sentient being, however ordinary, lacking any special qualities and who is not an exalted being, can have pointed out to them and can recognize the ultimate body of enlightenment. Resting within recognition of their nature during this very lifetime, this ordinary sentient being can actualize enlightenment. This special quality overcomes, or overpowers, all lower views.

The second great state is that enlightenment is attained in "the great personification" or "the great epitome," which means that in reaching enlightenment through Dzogchen, one gains control of, or independence from, all the experiences of samsara and nirvana. The great Indian master Saraha said that both ordinary existence and transcendent states arise through the nature of our mind, through awareness. All ordinary and extraordinary accomplishments arise through our awareness. It is the wish-fulfilling jewel that underlies all our experience. Recognition that the nature of mind underlies all enlightenment and all sentient experience overcomes the view of nihilism.

The third great state is that enlightenment is attained within the sphere of totality, beyond all dualistic experience, and not in the fundamental consciousness of our ordinary thought. Therefore, enlightenment is not impeded by any appearance. This quality of Dzogchen overcomes the view of materialism.

The fourth great state of Dzogchen is that the recognition of awareness as enlightenment is itself recognized as enlightenment. It is a special quality of Dzogchen teaching that we have confidence in intrinsic awareness as enlightenment. When awareness is recognized as enlightenment, we realize that there is nothing else besides this awareness and that enlightenment is found there. This overcomes all doubts.

The fifth great state of Dzogchen practice is that everything is recognized as enlightenment. Literally, there is nothing that is not part of enlightenment. In Dzogchen practice, we see our intrinsic awareness, in its essence, is primordially pure, the ultimate body of enlightenment. We see that all the experiences of samsara arise from the energy, or as the manifestation, of intrinsic awareness. We also see that all the experiences of transcendent states arise from the manifestation of our intrinsic awareness.

In Mahayana, sentient beings and buddhas are treated as completely separate. Sentient beings begin as sentient beings through ignorance and all the various forms of negative emotions and continue ceaselessly. Buddhas, on the other hand, have traveled the path to enlightenment and have achieved all the enlightened qualities. In Dzogchen, both are seen as the concurrent display, or manifestation, of intrinsic awareness. Even when the things of samsara appear, it is not necessarily considered an experience of confusion because all these appearances are simply the manifestation of intrinsic awareness, exactly as is the case with all the manifestations, or appearances, of enlightenment. That is why we say that everything partakes of enlightenment or that there is nothing that is not part of enlightenment.

Dzogchen has a view of primordial purity. *Purity* in Dzogchen means that at the very moment that samsara appears, it is never covered, or obscured. This enlightenment, this intrinsic nature, this intrinsic awareness never, from the moment that it appears, ever really exists. So there is nothing to purify, as if it were once dirty and then becomes pure. Rather, this is primordial purity. At the very moment of appearance, samsara has never come into being and has never really existed. Primordial purity is the emptiness aspect of our experience, the emptiness aspect of reality. Neither samsara nor nirvana ever comes into substantial existence; there is no underlying, fundamental existence, or substantial reality, to these appearances. They are primordially pure. They are appearance only.

In Dzogchen practice, we see everything as the manifestation, or display, of intrinsic awareness. Remaining within the recognition of the nature of everything is called "the enlightenment of two purities" or "buddhahood with two purities." One purity is the intrinsic nature of awareness, intrinsic enlightenment. The second is recognition of everything as the display of intrinsic awareness.

We can come to a conclusion about this. We can really decide this today. We experience a dream, but a dream, like ourselves (within our essence), is just a dream. There are experiences, but within ourselves, when we come back to ourselves, there is no confusion. In the same way, sentient beings experience the six realms of existence, yet within our essence, there is no confusion whatsoever. There is no moment when, within our intrinsic awareness, there is confusion. There are only the appearances of confusion, which don't have their own nature, which don't really exist. For example, you can see a huge building in a mirror. It appears very clearly. There is no mistake. But the building has never been inside the mirror. It is just a reflective surface. In the same way, many experiences, or appearances, appear on the surface of intrinsic awareness, but intrinsic awareness has never ever experienced confusion.

Just as samsara is primordially pure, so too nirvana is primordially pure. Because there has never been any confusion within intrinsic awareness, there is nothing that is the opposite of confusion (that is, nirvana). Therefore, nirvana can also be recognized as having the nature of appearance without any substantial existence. In the same way that samsara is a reflection of intrinsic awareness, so too nirvana is a reflection of intrinsic awareness without any substantial existence.

Within our natural, intrinsic awareness, which is primordially and spontaneously present, there has been no liberation, there is no liberation, and there will be no liberation. None of the buddhas of the past were ever liberated. Buddha Shakyamuni was never liberated. The other 996 buddhas of this aeon will not arrive at liberation either. Why is this the case? The appearance of Buddha Shakyamuni in this world, his enlightenment in Bodhgaya, and his attainment of liberation are only appearances of liberation. However, Buddha Shakyamuni and others are primordially pure. Talk about liberation assumes that there is first binding and then liberation from the binding. If the buddhas have primordial purity, there is nothing to be liberated from. Their nature is already liberation. It doesn't have to be liberated anew.

The *Secret Essence Tantra* says that nothing binds the enlightened nature; that would be like trying to tie a knot in space, an impossibility. Such a knot doesn't have to be untied; it simply doesn't exist. All the buddhas of the past, present, and future primordially transcend liberation. They merely appear before sentient beings, appearing to become liberated. However, in their essence, they transcend even primordial liberation.

Both *samsara* and *nirvana* are just names that we give to certain appearances. But nobody has actually experienced liberation, and nobody will actually experience liberation, because there has never been any binding, anything to be liberated from. Both samsara and nirvana partake of the same nature, which is like open space, completely pure. There is no division, or locality, in open space. There is neither a distinction between samsara and nirvana nor a distinction between being bound and being liberated. The open space of intrinsic awareness is primordially pure. There is total liberation because there has never been any binding. This is primordial, or original, purity.

Longchenpa's conclusion is that enlightenment, or buddha, is not something an ordinary person can hope to attain in another realm, somewhere else, as if the buddha were a great and noble person in another realm that we can aspire to attain. In Dzogchen, enlightenment is the primordial nature of all samsara and nirvana. The last of the five great states of Dzogchen is that enlightenment is everywhere, that all existence partakes of enlightened nature. Each of these great states of Dzogchen counteracts views from other parts of the buddhadharma or other kinds of practice, such as the idea of bringing lots of exertion and effort to our practice, as if we were going to somehow extract ourselves from something and go somewhere else. When we see that all samsara has the nature of enlightenment, we give up the idea of enlightenment, or buddha-hood, as being outside of ourselves or our circumstances.

Rongzompa remarked that we call these "the great states of Dzogchen" because they overcome all other views, in particular the views of the eight lesser yanas, which are based on clinging. These other views are not larger or smaller, but the Dzogchen perspective is considered the great one because it goes beyond all reference points, all comparisons. If we compare large and small, we never come to the end of something larger. However, transcending all our intellectual boundaries is what we call "large." It is not large in a comparative way; it is the ultimate view.

The view of Dzogchen is beyond views of meditation or non-meditation. It is simply resting within that view. It is beyond any consideration of action or lack of action. It is beyond consideration of emptiness or nonemptiness. It is beyond the extremes of existence and nonexistence.

Within the recognition of awareness, which is beyond all expression and conception, there is no attachment to awareness. The nature of awareness is simply recognized for what it is. This recognition neither increases nor decreases with time. Once naked awareness is recognized, it continues to be exactly the same.

Thinley Norbu Rinpoche comments that we should arrive at some conclusion about exactly how this experience, or this awareness, is described in the vajra words of Buddha Ever Excellent, Samantabhadra.

## The Benefits of Guru Yoga in Dzogchen

In Dzogchen, Guru Yoga is probably the most critical, or most important, practice we do. It's very important for us to understand, to visualize receiving the four empowerments, to do the dissolution, and to gaze at the face of the ultimate lama. Thinley Norbu Rinpoche says that Guru Yoga is really central to all Dzogchen practice. Doing Guru Yoga practice, either we can receive mind-to-mind the realization of the lama and have this well up within our mind-stream through receiving their blessing, or we can practice ngöndro and receive direct teachings from our teacher. We can take either path in Dzogchen practice. However, both depend upon Guru Yoga.

In the practice of Guru Yoga, we must develop extraordinary, or special, faith. We can describe faith in three different aspects: (1) inspired, or lucid, faith, (2) the faith of wishing, and (3) the faith of trust. For example, when we see or hear of Guru Rinpoche, great inspiration or "lucid faith" can arise in our mind; then we can wish, or aspire, to unite our mind with the mind of Guru Rinpoche. As well, we can develop total trust, or confidence, in Guru Rinpoche by recognizing that all the teachings of Dzogchen have come to us through Guru Rinpoche and that all the wonderful and profound teachings are brought to us in the person of Guru Rinpoche.

Even though Guru Rinpoche appeared in this world over a thousand years ago, we can still understand and have direct access to the qualities of Guru Rinpoche. Through our study, through our practice, we can recognize that Guru Rinpoche was an authentic master and a holy person.

In our visualizations, our practice, and our prayers to Guru Rinpoche, whom we visualize in the sky before us, our success depends on our devotion and faith. With clear faith and devotion, we effortlessly receive the blessings of Guru Rinpoche.

When we talk about faith, though, we do not mean blind faith, or surrendering to faith without proof. Our faith must be grounded in recognizing and understanding the qualities of Guru Rinpoche. All these teachings represent the wisdom and enlightened activity of the body, speech, and mind of Guru Rinpoche. Based on our appreciation of his qualities, we develop faith. Some persons can be attracted by looking at the image of Guru Rinpoche, but now, having received these teachings, we can really understand his qualities.

Now that we've had the opportunity to meet the Dzogchen teachings—authentic teachings from the authentic teacher, Guru Rinpoche—where else are we going to place our trust or our confidence? If we have no trust or confidence in Guru Rinpoche, then it is unlikely that we are going to have trust or confidence in anyone.

Every teaching we have received relates to the qualities of the enlightened mind of Guru Rinpoche. These teachings have come through him. Therefore, the more we understand, or recognize, these qualities and have trust, confidence, and faith in them, the more this brings devotion. The more we have faith and devotion, the more blessings we will receive from Guru Rinpoche and the more experience and realization will arise in our mind. We will identify with those enlightened qualities, and our identification with ordinary qualities, such as our emotions and sense of self, will diminish.

We should reflect to ourselves that, in fact, there has been nothing foolish about the words or the meanings presented here. Everything has been reasonable. Everything has been in accord with ordinary logic and ordinary reason, as well as in accord with enlightened mind. We should develop the faith and confidence that by keeping Guru Rinpoche and Yeshe Tsogyal in mind, by keeping them as our refuge, they will be able to help and protect us, in this life, at the time of death, in the intermediate state, and in future lives. Our friends and family, even the most powerful person in the world, will not be able to do that.

If we understand the teachings and pray to Guru Rinpoche with special faith, trust, and devotion, then this life, the time of death, and the next life will be extremely happy. If our life goes pleasantly, we will be happy. Even if our life has suffering, this won't have a very great influence on our mind. We will be happy inside. This is the effect of our understanding and faith in Guru Rinpoche. It will change our lives. It will change the ways our mind works. It will bring us a very extraordinary experience of happiness.

At the time of death as well, our faith and confidence and practice of these teachings will be of great benefit. We will die happy. At the time of death, nothing else will be helpful to us, such as medicine or others' advice. If we die having strength of mind from having developed faith and confidence, from having practiced these teachings, then we will know very well, "There is nothing else I need right now. I have exactly what I need to face death. Guru Rinpoche is there as a refuge for me after death, just as he has been a refuge for me during this lifetime." We will know that this strength comes from the practice of the Dzogchen teachings. If at the time of death we enter, or to stay within, the view of Dzogchen, if we imagine facing Guru Rinpoche, then we will die completely happy. There won't be the sufferings of death.

If we face death without the Dzogchen view and without this refuge, then we will experience a lot of pain and confusion. We will be racked with anxiety and doubt about where we are going, what is going to happen. We might feel very afraid. Maybe there is a future life; maybe not. Maybe we will see our parents or loved ones; maybe not. We have no certainty about what will happen after death. As much as our friends and family try to hold on to us, there is nothing to hold on to. As much as we try to hold on to our possessions, there is nothing to hold on to.

We practice Guru Yoga to develop faith, confidence, and devotion in Guru Rinpoche not for Guru Rinpoche's benefit but for our own benefit because we need this refuge.

With faith and confidence in Guru Rinpoche, we don't even need to talk about future lifetimes. Through these teachings and through our faith and devotion in Guru Rinpoche, we have the possibility of inconceivable happiness during this lifetime. When this happens in this lifetime, we will have no fear about what awaits us in the future.

Another benefit of the Dzogchen view and of faith and devotion in Guru Rinpoche is that we will feel great happiness wherever we go, in one country or another, in the wilds or the city, by oneself or with friends, whatever our circumstances.

In this practice of Guru Yoga, we continually pray to Guru Rinpoche with faith and devotion, and then we receive the four empowerments. Then Guru Rinpoche dissolves into light, is absorbed into us, and we rest while gazing at the face of the ultimate lama, which means abiding in intrinsic awareness and emptiness. We rest in the state of our mind and Guru Rinpoche's mind being inseparable. We can rest for one minute, three minutes, however long we wish. When our ordinary thoughts begin to return, then we can do a dedication prayer or we can practice the transference of consciousness (discussed in the next chapter). We can do the whole Ngöndro, just the Guru Yoga practice, or we can do a practice like Mipham Rinpoche's practice, the Shower of Blessings, based on the famous Seven-Line Prayer to Guru Rinpoche, thinking that our mind and Guru Rinpoche's mind are inseparable, and we can practice within that experience. Whatever the case, we should spend as much time as we can thinking of our mind and Guru Rinpoche's mind as being inseparable, resting within the state of gazing at the face of the ultimate lama, awareness and emptiness, and then following that with the dedication of merit.

# CHAPTER 9

# Phowa: The Transference of Consciousness

*Phowa*, called the "transference of consciousness," literally means "to move." We can move from Tibet to here or from here to New York, or lose attachment to one place and get attached to another place. At the time of death, phowa refers to the movement, or transference, of consciousness between this life and the pure land of a buddha. In the practice of the transference of consciousness, we transfer our ordinary consciousness to the sphere of totality, or to the heart of, for example, Buddha Amitabha. The meaning of these two is the same.

When we recognize our intrinsic awareness and mature that experience, gaining great confidence in our recognition of intrinsic awareness, then we recognize that the unborn nature of awareness is the ultimate body of enlightenment, that its being unimpeded is the body of enlightenment's perfect splendor, and that its not resting, or abiding, in any one place is the manifest body of enlightenment. When we have recognized and gained confidence in the nondual experience of our intrinsic awareness, we go beyond the experience of what is transferred or what moves, the place where it moves, and the action of movement. We recognize intrinsic awareness as changeless, beyond all birth and death. At that point, there is no more transference of consciousness, or movement of consciousness, that occurs between one lifetime and another, and these instructions are not necessary. However, as long as we remain within dualistic experience and experience birth and death, or beginning and ending, do not have enough confidence about where we will be reborn, or continue to have physical and mental experiences of suffering, we need these instructions.

A Dzogchen tantra says that because, in our ordinary mind, we experience passing time, we have also the experience of past, present, and future lives. It is all due to the presence of dualistic experience. If our mind-stream moves from one body to another, going from this life to another life (and thus changing), we experience entering a mother's womb and taking birth again. The experience of birth and death depends physically upon our mind going through transformative changes. Our mind goes from one body, or one lifetime, to the next. The ordinary mind that changes and transfers from one lifetime to the next creates the experience of sickness, happiness, and suffering. This mind experiences the maturation of karma within samsara.

A Mahayana sutra says that the nature of everything is like open, endless space, in that nobody comes into being and nobody dies; so within the nature of reality, there is no transference, no movement from one world to another. However, there is the appearance of birth and death. Even though it is similar to the appearance of a dream, and in essence appearances are empty, we who are unfamiliar with the nature of mind still take outward appearances to be real, holding to a self and to everything in experience. There is no greater foolishness or ignorance than that.

One of the Prajnaparamita sutras says that with understanding and experience of the nature of mind, the psychophysical aggregates (for example, consciousness) do not move or transfer to another lifetime. The present consciousness no longer connects to a future consciousness (or future life).

It is essential to begin with the realization of the lack of creation of all things, that things do not come into being to begin with. We enter the equanimity of past, present, and future, where there are no solid characteristics or anything substantial, no substantial existent reality related to ordinary thoughts. When we enter the great luminosity of intrinsic awareness, beyond past, present, and future (which is equanimity in relation to all sense of time), then who or what is going to die and be transferred to something else? There is no continuity anymore within past, present, and future.

Longchenpa commented that, within the nature of mind, the mind of awakening, or the mind of intrinsic awareness, there is no presence of past, present, or future. There is no presence of the three poisons of desire, anger, or ignorance. The nature of mind transcends all such distinctions. Like space, it has no birth, no death, no happiness, no suffering. In the *Treasury of the Sphere of Totality*, Longchenpa said,

> The nature of enlightened mind
> Is like stainless sky, so it has no birth, death, happiness,
>     or suffering.

Thinley Norbu Rinpoche has repeated these two lines out loud very often. He has said that he read this treasury many times. He advised me and others, "Even if you don't read the whole thing every day, at least read one chapter every day." Unfortunately for those who don't speak or read Tibetan, these lines sound much more beautiful in Tibetan than in English. These lines mean that when you think about the nature of mind, doesn't that make you happy from the inside? When we expect being entertained to make us happy from the outside, one day or another that is going to pass away. But as we reflect on these lines and take them into our heart, the outer world loses much of its heavy, or serious, quality and the mind is uplifted and inspired.

When we have understood these teachings, then everything we experience helps us. Experience becomes a companion. Whether we are watching a movie, visiting friends, or even if somebody is making life really difficult for us, these teachings allow us to accept whatever is happening as help for our direct understanding of awareness.

If we are in a quiet place away from busy activities, we may not have a lot of experiences or sensations. We may not have a lot of happiness or suffering. We may be happy all by ourselves and nothing much is happening. We meditate and feel that it will be helpful ultimately, but we may not be sure if our Dzogchen practice is really helpful in our immediate circumstances. Life is so easy when we don't have any tests. But when we go into the everyday world, these teachings prove to be very effective. They really help us an awful lot. Without practice, all of these different sensations strike against the mind and cause us pain, confusion, and suffering. But for us Dzogchen practitioners, no matter how much stimulation or sensation we feel, it is all an aid to the experience of Dzogchen. With understanding of these teachings, everything feeds the fire of the experience of the nature of mind.

Thinley Norbu Rinpoche quotes from Dudjom Rinpoche's *Unending Manifestation of the Song and Dance of Sublime Aspirations*. It begins with *Ah ho ye!* (How marvelous!) Then, "In the sacred, pure land of Great Bliss (Dewachen) resides the guru of the ultimate body of enlightenment, Amitabha. 'Look upon me, your son who prays to you, with your compassionate wisdom. Grant blessings and confer empowerment.'" Then Dudjom Rinpoche says, "This awareness that is empty radiance, free from edge and center, Lord, is this not your wisdom mind?" Almost as if he were struggling with the idea that Amitabha is something separate, he keeps asking Buddha Amitabha, Isn't this basic nature your mind as well as mine? Dudjom Rinpoche then answers his own question: "I have never been separate from this, not even for an instant."

Dudjom Rinpoche continues, saying that he was never so separated, but he didn't recognize this nature of mind; now that he has recognized this as his own intrinsic nature, the idea of Amitabha as something separate, something to which his mind will be transferred, has fallen to pieces, completely destroyed. The idea that this pure land of Great Bliss is elsewhere has completely disappeared. Dudjom Rinpoche has recognized everything as being the pure land of Buddha Amitabha and his own mind as being Amitabha.

Dudjom Rinpoche says that his mind has entered the wisdom mind that is beyond any coming into being. Within the mind of Dudjom Rinpoche, everything is recognized as exaltation and emptiness, the play of awareness. There are no dualistic thoughts or experiences to upset, or cause any turmoil in, the mind. The mind rests in awareness, the unity of exaltation and emptiness.

Whatever experiences arise within awareness are part of the great expanse of the ultimate body of enlightenment. In that experience, the thought of a pure land elsewhere is deceptive, nonsense.

The next line of the prayer says that the limits of all appearances are not outside but are within. Another way of interpreting this line is that one of the names of Buddha Amitabha is Unchanging Light, and this light is not outside of ourselves but inside. We don't need to look for Buddha Amitabha or Dewachen outside. It is very much like you've gotten rid of Buddha Amitabha or Dewachen by having recognized the nature of your own mind.

The last lines say, "Having found that the ultimate body of enlightenment comes from myself is the great satisfaction. This is the wonder of unceasing tranquillity. *Emaho!* How completely marvelous!" Ordinarily, when we feel happy, it is a very temporary experience. But the experience of understanding, or realizing, the ultimate body of enlightenment, as Dudjom Rinpoche says here, is a continual experience. This happiness remains continually. How marvelous!

In our ordinary lives, our happiness is temporary. We can be happy for a moment, but sometimes the same things that make us happy also make us very, very sad. Nothing is particularly certain about our experience of happiness in this life. But when we gain this realization, there is no time that doesn't make us extremely happy. Sometimes we are happy to go to a restaurant, see a movie, or see friends; but who knows the outcome of that happiness or those encounters? This is not like that. This is continual, uninterrupted, unconditional happiness.

Through the experience, or the energy, of our view and meditation, sometimes it is impossible not to sing. As with Milarepa, Longchenpa, and Dudjom Rinpoche, when the experience of the energy of the view and meditation overflows, we can't help but sing a song like this prayer.

Dudjom Rinpoche's song has the same meaning as the line in our foundational practice about gazing at the face of the ultimate lama of awareness and emptiness. When we recognize awareness and emptiness, all the movement of our karmic energy-winds is completely exhausted into the ultimate body of enlightenment.

The tantras refer to a buddha as an enlightened being "who has no breath." This means that in enlightenment, there is no movement of the energy-wind of karma. All habitual tendencies and ordinary thoughts are completely exhausted into the deathless state of wisdom. The dissolution of our karmic energy-wind into wisdom, or the deathless state beyond what moves from one lifetime to another, is the highest phowa, the highest form of the transference of consciousness.

For those who have not yet gained mastery of wisdom energy, those who are progressing gradually through the stages of the path, we begin with refuge and progress through development of the mind of awakening, mandala offering, Vajrasattva, and Guru Yoga, and then we come to the practice of phowa. We start the prayer in the Ngöndro text, "I pray to the protector, Amitabha, Buddha of Boundless Light."

In the Dudjom Tersar practice, Guru Rinpoche is the union and manifestation of all the buddhas of the past, present, and future. The basis for his manifestation in the world is Buddha Amitabha. The very famous prayer *The Spontaneous Fulfillment of Our Wishes* begins, "In the pure land of Great Bliss, Amitabha's compassion stirred and took the form of Guru Rinpoche within the world."

In this practice, we imagine that, in essence, Guru Rinpoche is Amitabha. In form, he appears as Amitabha. We imagine Amitabha in the western pure land of Great Bliss. We imagine that this pure land appears before us as it is described in many prayers.

We pray to Buddha Amitabha for rebirth in that pure land. We think to ourselves that wherever we are born in the six realms of existence, we won't transcend suffering, so we develop engagement toward disillusionment or disengagement toward rebirth in the six realms, and we develop the wish to be reborn in Amitabha's pure land.

We began this commentary on the Dudjom Tersar Ngöndro with the four thoughts to turn the mind. At the beginning, perhaps those ideas were very vague and we didn't have much interest in them. Now, coming back to these ideas of the precious human birth; death and impermanence; the inevitability of the relations between karma and cause and effect; and the suffering of the six classes of existence, they are far more meaningful to us than they were then. We are more and more attracted to the more "elementary" teachings (such as refuge and development of the mind of awakening) when we know from the perspective of Dzogchen that they really are useful and true.

Now we think, "From time without beginning until the present, I have been circling within samsara. I have been going from humans to gods, gods to the hell realm, and again to the human realms. This has been going on for an awfully long time. May I develop disillusionment in relation to this cycle of birth and death."

If we think to ourselves, "I am not going to do anything that causes me to be reborn in the lower realms. I want to create the karma to be reborn in the human realm," that is possible. But if we do that, we will still continually experience the sufferings of birth, old age, sickness, and death each time we are reborn in the human realm. Just consider how much suffering is possible, physically or mentally, in the course of a lifetime.

Particularly in this dark and degenerate time, there are lots of obstacles in our life. The happiness we might experience as a god or a human being is like eating poisoned fruit. It tastes very good, but it causes sickness or death. Our experience as human beings is like that. So we pray to not have the slightest bit of desire in relation to our human life. We wish to develop the desire for liberation, or freedom.

All the enjoyments, possessions, friends, and family who are close to us are impermanent like a magical display, like appearances in a dream. We pray to not have the slightest amount of attachment toward any of them.

Wherever we live, whatever home we live in, is like a home appearing in a dream. It has no substantial, fundamental reality. We pray to know its lack of fundamental existence.

When we find liberation from the prison of samsara and go to Amitabha's pure land, we pray to go there without ever looking back. In the same way that we would run away after escaping from prison, we don't look back over our shoulder.

When we are about to practice transference of consciousness, we keep all of this in mind. Of course, we are not going to wish to be reborn in the three lower realms. Even rebirth as a human or a god is not what we wish for from the depth of our heart. In our ordinary consciousness, we aim for the pure land of Buddha Amitabha.

Then we say the prayer found in the practice text, "May you bless me to accomplish the profound path of transference."

## Five Types of Transference

Transference of consciousness can take several forms. The first is the transference of consciousness into the ultimate body of enlightenment. We discussed this above, when we talked about the different stages of bardo. At the time when our breath finally stops, we have three mental experiences called "appearance," "spreading," and "attainment." Finally, we pass into complete unconsciousness. At that point, our perception becomes extremely clear, like the cloudless, very deep blue autumn sky.

This moment of clarity and emptiness is sure to appear. At that moment, if we can remain within original, or primordial, purity, the sphere beyond ordinary thought or mind, that state is called (perhaps misleadingly) "ordinary consciousness." The phrase *ordinary consciousness* can be used in three ways. The first one refers to the ordinary consciousness of persons in the domain of ordinary, or confused, thought, the common experience or common mind. The second refers to the ordinary consciousness of practitioners who get lost in thought but recognize when that happens in meditation practice. The third is the ordinary consciousness of realization, which refers to mind without any artificial additives—we haven't changed our mind; we aren't falling into the extremes of samsara or any transcendent states; we're not making any effort. We are not adding any practice to our mind; we look directly, with nothing artificial whatsoever added, into the nature of mind. This type of ordinary consciousness is the nature of our mind and of all sentient beings' minds. It is the three bodies of enlightenment. We are trying to practice and realize this form of ordinary consciousness. If we can recognize and remain stable within this mind, then we gain liberation into the original sphere, the original, or primordial, basis. In the instant that we recognize this mind or these appearances as our ordinary consciousness, we enter the state of Buddha Ever Excellent, Samantabhadra.

Recognizing and entering the state of the ultimate body of enlightenment is the highest form of the transference of consciousness. For a person of a high level of Dzogchen practice, any other practice of transference (such as meditating on the vital essence in the heart, saying *hrih* many times, and ejecting it from our body into space or the pure land of Amitabha, which is discussed below) is unnecessary. A person arrives at enlightenment directly through this first form of the transference of consciousness.

The second type of transference is the transference of consciousness of the body of enlightenment's perfect splendor. It is "the transference of consciousness of the union of luminosity," and it is for those who have achieved some stability in the practice of the creation and completion phases of meditation. In the bardo of the nature of reality, the appearances of the peaceful and wrathful deities arise within sound, luminosity, and light. When these appearances are recognized as manifestations of mind, liberation is attained in the body of enlightenment's perfect splendor.

Guru Rinpoche said that when we experience sounds, rainbow lights, and the forms of the peaceful and wrathful deities during this intermediate state, we should recognize them as the brilliance of our own innate awareness. We should not have any doubts about this. The mind is so sensitive at that moment that doubt separates us from what we see, which sends us into the ordinary thoughts of samsara.

Ordinary thoughts and doubts are really ignorance. Appearances of the primordial basis appear before us, but once again we take them to be other instead of being appearances of our own innate awareness, so we enter dualistic experience. If we recognize them as our innate awareness and rest within this clarity and emptiness, then we enter the three bodies of enlightenment. At that point, there is no cause for returning to samsara.

If an individual does not succeed at these first two levels of the intermediate state but has received empowerments, teachings, oral instructions, and blessings from a teacher during their lifetime, then during the next intermediate state (the bardo of becoming), if they do not get confused but turn their mind to a pure land, then this is the third type of transference, "the transference of consciousness of the manifest body of enlightenment." It is to enter the pure land of Amitabha (Dewachen) or Guru Rinpoche's Copper-Colored Mountain.

The fourth transference is the transference of consciousness with "three perceptions." In brief, in the center of our body, we imagine a central channel, straight and about the width of an arrow. It is open at the top of the head, "the aperture of Brahma." At the heart, our consciousness takes the form of the syllable *hrih*. We imagine the central channel as a road, or a path, the consciousness at our heart as a traveler, and the pure land in Amitabha's heart as our destination—these are the "three perceptions." The transference of consciousness for the ordinary person is when our consciousness as *hrih* is ejected from our body and travels up to the pure land.

This form of transference of consciousness is very strongly advised for those who have finished the foundational practices but have not begun the main practice of Dzogchen and for those who are practicing Dzogchen but have not yet arrived at stability in their practice. Once stability is gained in the practice of Dzogchen, this form of transference of consciousness is no longer necessary.

The fifth form of transference of consciousness is the "transference of consciousness of the hook of compassion." It refers to the performance of phowa by a realized practitioner on somebody who has died. Through the hook of compassion, they grab the consciousness of that person and fling them to a pure land. Whoever performs this practice, such as a realized lama, must be able to draw in the consciousness of the person who has died. It is not as if the lama doesn't know exactly where this person who has died has gone, thinking "Where is he now?" The lama knows exactly where the consciousness is and can draw it in and send it directly to a pure land.

One of the tantras says that this last type of transference of consciousness should be done at the time of death or immediately following the time of death when the stages of dissolution of consciousness have just begun. Anybody can do it for someone when their consciousness is still in the body, but once the person has died, then a realized lama must do the visualization because the consciousness has entered the intermediate state. The tantra says that this practice for the time of death is done through sound, the *hrih* sound or the *phat* sound, which ejects consciousness into a ball of light.

We do this form of transference of consciousness only for ordinary persons, never for realized beings. A lot of people thought of doing phowa for Dudjom Rinpoche when he passed away. No matter how good a practitioner you may be, you never ever do phowa for your root teacher. You don't even do all those special forty-nine-day ceremonies for your teacher. Why not? Because your teacher is a buddha, inseparable from Vajradhara. In Tibet, India, and elsewhere, many people misunderstand this. They do all these ceremonies and think about their teacher almost as an ordinary person who has died. (The Vajrasattva practices often done after the passing of a teacher are for the benefit of practitioners, during a time when the teacher's blessings are especially accessible; they are not for the benefit of the teacher.)

When the lama is alive, you must follow them. When your teacher dies, don't put yourself in their position and then imagine that they need to be drawn from samsara with phowa. That is stupid. Really dumb.

Thinley Norbu Rinpoche includes this advice because not everybody who lived in Tibet understood buddhadharma. People made a lot of mistakes and accumulated negative karma through this misunderstanding. They mixed their dharma practice with politics or other considerations, with ordinary worldly life. He wrote this for them.

There's a story in *Words of My Perfect Teacher* about a lama who was doing a lot of prayers and practices for a very high lama who had died. People asked, "This is a very great lama. Why are you doing these sorts of practices, as if for an ordinary person?" He said, "Yes, this person had a very high level of realization in the stages of the bodhisattvas, but at a certain point in his lifetime, he received offerings in order to do prayers for a dead person, but he didn't do them." This was causing him obstacles after death. Except for the case of someone having insight into the status of a consciousness after death, these sorts of prayers, or aid, are not necessary or appropriate for higher beings.

At this time in our life, we should receive teachings in phowa from a qualified teacher and practice until we achieve the signs (for example, pus comes out of the top of the head and the lama can put a blade of *kusha* grass in the hole that has formed there). At this time, what we are doing in this practice of phowa is training. We're not actually doing it. We practice until we get the signs. But we are not actually transferring our consciousness and saying goodbye. It is like practicing kung fu. We practice all the movements so that when the time comes to meet our enemy, then we can beat the hell out of them. But the time of training is not the time to beat the hell out of anybody. In the same way, when we're doing phowa, we're training until we get the signs, and then, at the actual time of practice, we beat the hell out of our body and leave at the time of death.

We train until we get the signs, and then we stop until the actual time of death has definitely arrived. There is a danger of making this practice into a form of suicide. When the right time has come, then you can do phowa. If you do it at the wrong time, the tantra says that you are killing deities—your body's sacred, or divine, nature. You respect that this body's channels, winds, and vital energy are the nature of the deities.

The master who performs phowa for somebody else or who gives us instruction must, in the best case, recognize the nature of reality, and, at the very least, be very familiar with the practices of the creation and completion phases of meditation.

When do we actually beat the hell out of our body? When we see the signs of death's approach, either directly or in a dream. In Dzogchen, many dream signs are explained, and we can see, "This is death approaching." Or we practice phowa when the doctors have given up, because there is nothing more they can do on a medical level, and it is certain that we are going to die.

When the signs of death have appeared, then we know it is time to put our kung fu into practice. We imagine that our consciousness is a ball of light, with the syllable *hrih*, in our heart; our mind and *hrih* are one, inseparable. This ball of light is very unstable; it is moving around, vibrating, shaking, ready to go. We imagine that underneath it a lot of energy collects. When we say the forceful sound *hic!* then it ejects very easily. We send it out of our body, without having it drop back down, to the heart of Buddha Amitabha or Guru Rinpoche in the sky above us. At the time of death, we continually send the consciousness out without having it return. If we do this, we will be reborn in the pure land.

Thinley Norbu Rinpoche says that this practice of the transference of consciousness is more difficult for a young person than for an older person. A younger person's inner channels, energy-winds, and vital essence are very strong. The example he uses is that a younger person is like fruit on a tree in the spring, when it's difficult to get them to drop from the tree. When a person is older and the channels, energy-winds, and vital essence of the body turn old or ripen, then it is very much like fruit on a tree in autumn. You just shake the tree, and they all fall off.

Even if we haven't come to the time that we put phowa into practice, at any time we can still maintain the thought "I wish to be reborn in Amitabha's pure land," or "I wish to be reborn in the Copper-Colored Mountain," or "Tomorrow or the next day, when I die, this is the place I want my consciousness to go."

When you arrive at the time of death, if you haven't got your travel plans very set in your mind, you may think of transferring your consciousness but may not be really sure where you want to go or exactly where you're aiming for. You should really have it very clearly in mind beforehand, "This is what I want to do." Have very great confidence, "This is where I want to go after death." You can think in terms of the transference of consciousness to the pure land or, if you have Dzogchen teachings, you can aim for one of the three bodies of enlightenment as explained above. Whatever the case, you should make these plans before the time of death. When the time of death comes and the time for phowa has arrived, that is the time to do the practice in the framework of what you're aiming for. Have that very clearly in your mind, and be confident in it well in advance.

Dzogchen master Jigme Phuntsok Rinpoche encouraged us all to make prayers and think of going to the pure land of Dewachen. He said himself that he was going to Dewachen. So we recited prayers together at the Five-Peaked Mountain of Manjushri in China and the other places that we went together. I have already got my travel plans made.

## Longevity Practice

If we wish to help both sentient beings and the buddhadharma teachings and wish to arrive at the limits of our life span and practice, then we should do the longevity practice.

The longevity practice considers the vital essence of our body. On a relative level, when it is undamaged, then our health and complexion are good and we have a very good presence, or recollection, of mind. The ultimate vital essence of the body is our innate awareness. This should be recognized and guarded. It is the support for the bodies of wisdoms of enlightenment. The energy-winds of the five elements move in our body. When the coarse energy-winds have been purified into wisdom energy in our body, or, we can say, when the coarse, relative vital essence of our body and the ultimate vital essence of our body are joined in the purity of nondual union, then we attain unending, or unconquerable, longevity. For example, in the case of Guru Rinpoche, all the coarse elements of his body and all the subtle thoughts of his mind dissolved into wisdom energy, the natural state of intrinsic awareness. Due to this, he basks in the state of an awareness holder of infinite life.

There are numerous longevity practices. One practice associated with Amitabha is the longevity practice of Amitayus (Buddha of Boundless Life), the sambhogakaya aspect of Amitabha, which is part of Jigme Lingpa's Innermost Essence of Longchenpa (Longchen Nyingtik). Of course, we should practice according to the empowerments and reading transmissions we have received.

# CHAPTER 10

# Chöd and the Dedication of Merit

The last lines of the Dudjom Tersar Ngöndro state, "Now my body, wealth, and the root of my virtue of all my lives I give without clinging to all sentient beings, who have all been my mother. May great waves of benefit be accomplished without obstacle for all sentient beings."

In our innumerable past lives, we have been hell beings, starving spirits, animals, human beings, demigods, and gods. During these innumerable lives, we haven't managed to come to any stable happiness or to attain the unconditional happiness of enlightenment. Nothing we have done with our self or body has provided any lasting benefit. But now we have the opportunity to create benefit; in order to make use of this very precious body, this body that we are very attached to, we should use it to make inexhaustible offerings in this lifetime.

Though it is not mentioned in Thinley Norbu Rinpoche's text, these lines provide a very brief reference to the practice of chöd, offering one's body to "the four guests." (*Chöd* literally means "to cut through.") The three jewels are the first set of guests. We imagine the lamas, yidams, and dakinis in the sky before us. We then do the following visualization, which you will see is a form of "tantric cooking." Imagine that, by using the meditation of the transference of consciousness, we eject our consciousness from our body up into space, and our mind takes the form of the wrathful dakini Tröma Nagmo. You may have seen images of her; *tröma* means "wrathful woman" and *nagmo* means "black."

As Tröma Nagmo, using the cutting knife in our right hand, we slice off the top of the skull of what used to be our body. The skull morphs into a very, very vast container. We put it down. We throw the rest of the body into this vast container. Underneath this large skull containing the body, wind moves and a fire starts to cook what is inside the skull. All that is impure in the body overflows from the skull. What's left inside is nectar (*dudtsi*). Our body is now nectar inside the large skull-cup. Then the steam rising from the skull becomes many offerings of sight, touch, taste, smell, sound, and even more—flowers, incense, lamps, perfumed water—whatever is pleasing to any of the five senses. All the nectar is offered in this form to the three jewels.

Our second set of guests is the group of seventy-two protectors, who appear in the sky below the three jewels. There are groups of protectors related to different lineages. There is Ekajati. There is Damchen Dorje Legpa. The whole gang is there. We make offerings to the protectors in whatever way that pleases them. We think that, through this offering, we cultivate merit and wisdom and clear away all obscurations. By making offerings to the protectors, we think that through these offerings, the protectors perform whatever enlightened activity we want to accomplish.

We make offerings upward to those above, to the three jewels and the protectors. Then we give downward, which is like making a charitable donation, to the beings of the six realms (the third set of guests) and to the beings to whom we have karmic debts (the fourth set). They could be spirits, ghouls, demons, and whatnot, or simply persons with whom we have karmic debts from the past; then we think that all our karmic debts are paid off.

We have made the skull-cup full of nectar and have offered it upward and given it downward. We have thereby cultivated merit and wisdom and have cleared away obscurations. After this rather elaborate visualization, we rest within the primordial purity of the luminosity of Dzogchen, without thinking of the objects of offering or the acts of offering and giving. We return to the state of the primordial purity of Dzogchen. We practice this in order to clear away the sicknesses, mental disturbances, and whatever hindrances, or obstacles, we are experiencing, on a temporary level. We also do this in order to cultivate merit and wisdom and clear away all our obscurations, not only those in our current situation but also those that may arise at any other time.

We began this visualization by offering our body. At this point, we also imagine offering all our possessions and all our virtue from the past, present, and future, for the benefit of all sentient beings. Our body, our possessions, and our virtue are three things that we hold dear. We give them without holding anything back, without any clinging or regret. We wish for this gift to be of benefit to all beings, that it be effective. We wish that all sentient beings attain the state of being a human beings or a god, which is the support for the eventual attainment of enlightenment. We wish that they be able to enter and find teachings in the path of awakening in relation to their needs and wishes. Ultimately, we wish for all sentient beings to arrive at the state of full and complete enlightenment. Having made this prayer, we ask the blessing of the buddhas and bodhisattvas to help us create the positive and favorable conditions for these prayers to become a reality.

We come now to the dedication of merit to all sentient beings without any attachment, to the limits of space. To do so, we don't think of sentient beings or ourselves as existent; we imagine that we and all others are one in the state of a dream, like a magical display. Without thought of self, others, or the action of dedication, we dedicate all merit to the sphere of totality, which is the nature of space.

In the same way that space is without a point of origin, beyond all center and limits, when we recognize our merit as emptiness and dedicate it to this state of emptiness, our merit grows as large and as all-embracing as space, utterly limitless. When we have done this dedication of merit, we allow our mind to rest within the sphere of totality.

# Dream Practice

Although there is nothing in Thinley Norbu Rinpoche's text about the practice of dreams and sleep, it's appropriate to say something about it. After all, we might as well make use of our sleep time.

One suggested practice is this: when going to bed at night, imagine a red lotus of either four or eight petals at your heart. Seated on the lotus is Guru Rinpoche in union with his consort. They sit within the essence of great exaltation. Without any tightness of mind, relax and keep your mind on that image and go to sleep.

Why do we do this practice? First, we won't fall asleep in an ordinary fashion with ordinary appearances. Second, we won't have bad dreams or negative experiences during sleep. Third, we create the conditions we need to have the experience of clear light, or luminosity, as we sleep. Fourth, we will recognize our dreams (we will have lucid dreams).

Even if we don't do the visualization or if it is not possible to visualize clearly, the most critical point is to think that Guru Rinpoche is in our heart and to fall asleep with that impression. This is the path to the experience of the state of clear light during sleep.

When we go to sleep, instead of being distracted by sensory input from the play of the six senses that get drawn into our consciousness, we should bring that attention within the inner luminosity of awareness. This may sound like there is outer attention and inner attention, outer mind and inner mind, but that is not how we should understand it. The mind is not gathered inward, but we have entered the state of recognition of intrinsic awareness, the nature of reality.

For an ordinary sentient being, the play of our senses is drawn in at the time of sleep. We are confused during the day and then we are confused during the night with dreams that reflect our outward attention. For Dzogchen practitioners who have received the pointing-out instructions and recognized their radiant wisdom, when they go to sleep, the play of the six senses is brought inward, and through their visualization practice, the experience of radiant wisdom arises. Their sleep is a reflection of their daytime practice. Then there is no confusion during the day and no confusion at night.

A second kind of dissolution that is without ignorance or dullness is the ultimate form of the dissolution of the senses into the nature of reality. We don't go completely senseless. Instead, the ordinary senses dissolve into the nature of mind, into the ultimate, inner luminosity, in which the bodies and wisdoms of enlightenment reside.

In order to recognize the state of radiant wisdom, or clear light, during sleep, during the day, wherever we are and whatever we're doing, we think, "This is only a dream. I'm dreaming right now." By coming back to this thought repeatedly during the day, when we go to sleep at night and dream, we remember, "Oh yes, this is just a dream." Through the force of visualizing and repeating to ourselves that this is just a dream, at night when dreams arise, our mind remains in a state in which, as we are dreaming, we recognize that we are, in fact, dreaming.

The great awareness holders of the past said that if through practice we recognize that we are dreaming as it is happening, then when we enter the intermediate state after our death, we will again be able to recognize that those appearances too are just projections that have arisen in our mind in the same way. The great masters of the past said that the practice of recognizing dreams as they are happening is very useful, because if we develop enough of a habit of doing this, if we can do it just seven times, then we will be able to recognize the appearances of the intermediate state in the same way.

The experience of the luminous stage, or clear light, as we sleep is "the child luminosity." At the time of the intermediate state, it is the luminosity of the basis; it is not a meditation experience. It is "the mother luminosity." The child recognizes the mother and crawls into her lap. This is why, with continued recognition of the luminous state during sleep, after the time of death, that state is very recognizable.

At this point in our practice, during daytime, when dreaming, or in deep sleep, we have a very partial and slight recognition of luminosity, the nature of reality. At the time of death, we have a very strong experience of the luminous nature of reality, because then, all our ordinary thoughts are completely cleared away though the impact of having died; but we need to recognize the luminosity as the nature of reality. So during this life, our daytime practice, our dream practice, and our practice of the luminous state during sleep will help us recognize great luminosity after death. Our practice enables us to be liberated with the recognition of mother luminosity at the time of death, or we can be assured of a rebirth in the Copper-Colored Mountain, the pure land of Guru Rinpoche, after death.

When we wake up after seemingly negative dreams, we shouldn't think all sorts of thoughts about the experience, such as "That was a terrible dream! What does it mean?" Instead we should remember Guru Rinpoche and his consort. Place the mind within intrinsic awareness; remember that, within awareness, all appearances, including dreams, have no substantial reality. When we awake from good dreams, like meeting deities, lamas, buddhas, friends, or whatever, we should think of making inconceivable offerings to the three jewels. Even if we experience a very intense sensation of joy and happiness, in that sensation we should again recognize and maintain recognition of intrinsic awareness. We should recognize the nature of this awareness, this exaltation and this emptiness, as Vajrasattva.

By placing the mind within its awareness, gradually our positive and negative habitual tendencies will cease, because just as we can't sow seeds in space, so we can't create new habitual tendencies in awareness. During the day or during the night, in waking or in dreaming, whatever we're doing, the critical point is to recognize, and maintain the recognition of, intrinsic awareness. When we maintain intrinsic awareness, then everything dissolves into the sphere of intrinsic awareness.

Right now we are targets for positive and negative experiences that strike our heart and provoke emotions, both positive and negative. Nice things happen. Negative things happen. We are like a walking open wound. This causes reactions, sometimes positive and sometimes negative. When we have recognized intrinsic awareness and maintain recognition, things no longer touch us in the same way. Everything, whether positive, negative, or neutral, dissolves within through the eyes of intrinsic awareness. Just as we can't strike space with a hammer, in the same way, whatever arises in our mind, whatever happens in the outer world, dissolves rather than strikes our heart. When we recognize and guard awareness, they have nowhere to strike.

If we can guard awareness, then our sleep gets progressively finer, or more subtle. There are some great Dzogchen practitioners who can stay conscious of all the sounds, sights, and activities of their surroundings even during sleep. They have what we call "higher perception" or "direct perception." With our own practice, maintaining the state of naked awareness has an influence on our ordinary mind. Our ordinary mind with its thoughts and emotions, which is normally very heavy, very serious, very solid, very dense, gradually gets lighter, more purified. Our ordinary mind and our ordinary way of dealing with reality lose strength and capability. Our mind becomes finer and finer, subtler and subtler. In turn, it influences the degree of density, or thickness, of our sleep. Lightness of mind is a portent of our intrinsic awareness dissolving into the sphere of luminous wisdom. As we develop more recognition of intrinsic awareness, we naturally develop new capabilities—for example, to be conscious of our surroundings in extraordinary ways, to recognize the luminous state at night, and to have lucid dreams.

All our mind and aspects of our consciousness have arisen from the state of intrinsic awareness, from luminous wisdom, and all will again return to luminous wisdom. In the same way that even very thick clouds that have arisen out of the sky will eventually dissolve back into the sky, all the various aspects of the mind, no matter how heavy or solid they appear to be, through recognition of intrinsic awareness, will again dissolve back into their source. In the same way that sunlight penetrates and disperses diminishing clouds, as we meditate and recognize intrinsic awareness, gradually the luminous nature, the luminous wisdom of mind, penetrates and disperses the clouds of our ordinary consciousness.

As we get more and more familiar with intrinsic awareness, with the luminous nature of mind, and as we arrive at great confidence in the practice, whatever appears during the day or at night in dreams or the luminous state, whatever appears from past lives or future lives or this life, whatever appears in our ordinary thoughts, becomes completely purified into the experience of infinite luminosity. This is the state of enlightenment.

There is much we can do during the day to develop intrinsic awareness. When we are eating, we offer our food to the three jewels. Then there won't be any obscuration from having eaten this food through it having been offered to us by anybody else. Through this offering, we will cultivate merit. When we get dressed, especially in new clothes, we offer whatever we have to the three jewels as well. This helps us to avoid attachment to our clothing in the same way that we don't have attachment to our food. Whether we are sleeping, eating, moving around, or watching television, whatever we are doing, we try to develop pure vision toward all our acts. We try to bring all our acts to our awareness. The point is to try to make our human life meaningful. Up to now, we have had many, many lifetimes and they haven't really been brilliant in their meaning. So we try our hardest to make everything that happens in this life meaningful, to bring it to our experience of intrinsic awareness.

In the same way, as we approach sleep at night, it is very important not to think about things that were going on during the day, about anything that has to do with your ordinary life. Give your mental focus to your deity or to your teacher, or remain within the luminous ultimate body of enlightenment, the intrinsic awareness that has been pointed out to you by your teacher.

# Conclusion

Thinley Norbu Rinpoche says that those who are intelligent should read *Words of My Perfect Teacher* as well as the very extensive ngöndro commentary written by his father, Dudjom Rinpoche. For those with a fairly developed intellect or who are working gradually through the stages and paths of enlightenment, Thinley Norbu Rinpoche thought to write a text that discussed in detail the different forms of calming the mind and insight meditation, the various ways the meditative and postmeditative states are related, the relationship between clearing away the obstacles, or hindrances, on the path of meditation and enrichment, and all the different paths and stages of enlightenment. He included all these details in his text because he was writing for persons who are interested in, or find themselves in the middle of, a very gradual progression through the stages of awakening. Many of these details are in the very long section on the transcendent perfection of meditation, which begins with meditation from the perspective of Mahayana and then examines it from the perspectives of Mahayoga, Anuyoga, Atiyoga, trekchöd, and thögal. We discussed all these different stages from the perspective of calming the mind, insight meditation, postmeditative states, and so forth.

Patrul Rinpoche commented that the thought to help others and particularly the thought to help them in their practice are two qualities of really sacred teachings. Such teachings do not need elevated grammar or poetry or very high language. The style of bodhisattvas is to teach directly in the language of the people, in the very ordinary language of the village. For example, the *Kalachakra Tantra* says that sentient beings have to understand the buddhadharma teachings, so the teachings have to be presented in words and language that are accessible to ordinary persons.

Thinley Norbu Rinpoche says that he kept this in mind and hoped to write a book in the style that Patrul Rinpoche mentions. He didn't have a very complicated outline for the book. He didn't use "window dressing" of the type that Tibetan books often use—for example, lots of fancy poetry and things like that. He gave up all that and just wrote whatever came into his mind, whatever seemed to be useful.

Many treasure teachings, the termas, are like that. They reflect what arose in the mind of a treasure revealer and were written down without editing, without thinking, "This is good; this is bad." Dzogchen master Jigme Phuntsok Rinpoche said that this style of direct writing or teaching is from the space of intrinsic awareness. It is the overflow from the expanse of awareness. It is written directly without consideration of anything except what arises directly in the mind of the writer. Jigme Phuntsok Rinpoche said that one of the special qualities of the Nyingma lineage and the lineage of awareness holders is that the writing comes straight out of awareness and emptiness.

The text mentions that I asked Thinley Norbu Rinpoche on many occasions to write a commentary on Dzogchen. I knew that he was writing a commentary on the foundational practices and asked him to write a text on Dzogchen as well. He said, "Dudjom Rinpoche wrote a text on Dzogchen. So did Dudjom Lingpa. Those are enough." Still I insisted, so at the point in the text where the lama dissolves into light, becomes inseparable from us, and we gaze at the face of the ultimate lama, awareness and emptiness, he included the teachings on Dzogchen that I had requested. He said that the teachings in the Guru Yoga section, after we begin to gaze at the face of the ultimate lama, were written for those who do not develop gradually through stages of practice but who go directly to Dzogchen without any intermediate thoughts.

Whether from these teachings or elsewhere, it is essential for us to receive pointing-out instructions. We can receive them from a teacher who has great confidence within the view and who has received the blessings of the lineage of enlightenment. One should receive the pointing-out instructions from this sort of teacher.

Why do we need pointing-out instructions of our intrinsic awareness? The nature of our mind is primordial purity. If we do not recognize it, we can try for countless years or aeons to accomplish enlightenment outside of our basic nature, but we are not going to succeed.

In the past, during countless lifetimes, we have been caught in our dualistic experience. The habitual tendency of dualistic experience has grown very strong. What is, in fact, very easy to realize (intrinsic awareness, the nature of mind) has become extremely difficult to realize—it is secret, hidden, or concealed.

This is just our own mind; it is not something else. For that reason, it is actually very easy to realize intrinsic awareness. If we want to find enlightenment somewhere else, it might take us aeons of time and cause us a lot of difficulty to do. But this is really just our own mind. Because of our habitual tendencies, we don't understand, or we can't see, our mind's nature. However, if we have direct instructions from our master, it makes the realization of the nature of mind very easy.

The oral, or direct, instructions from a master facilitate our recognition of intrinsic awareness, our enlightenment. When we consider going from San Francisco to New York City, we could walk or take a car, but it will be very difficult. On the other hand, if we take a plane, we can be in New York very quickly. This is like direct instruction. It is really up to us. There is no difference with enlightenment. We can't say that because someone really made a headache out of the whole process of attaining enlightenment for three incalculable aeons, it is big enlightenment and Dzogchen is a small enlightenment. The destination is exactly the same. It is just like going to New York City: if you go by plane, you get to the same city as when you go by foot. This is the quality of the direct instructions of Dzogchen.

Rongzompa said that the words of Dzogchen are very large and

gross, but their meaning, what they point out, is very fine and subtle, like the element of space. In the lower levels of buddhadharma,
the words are fine, subtle, and elegant, but what they point to is
fairly coarse, like a heap of sand or rock. He is not criticizing lower
levels of practice. He is just describing what they point out through
their teachings and saying that it is not particularly subtle, from a
Dzogchen perspective.

Take, for example, Dzogchen vocabulary: *primordial purity,
spontaneous presence, intrinsic awareness*. On the level of vocabulary, these words are fairly plain in Tibetan, but thinking about
the meanings brings great peace, great openness of mind. These
ideas are subtle like space. If you really look at Middle Way teachings about nonelaboration, being free from all extremes, and the
various discussions of emptiness, they are like a traffic jam. There
are many things being put together: existence, nonexistence, both,
and neither. The Middle Way also uses many different analogies for
buddha nature: gold under the ground, a lamp, a vase. The collection
of elaborate explanations is large and looks very beautiful, but it
never comes down to pointing out exactly what this buddha nature
is. The finger of the teaching doesn't point directly to buddha nature.

The Dzogchen teachings are not outstanding from the point of
view of grammar or logic. People attached to teachings that are
very elegant from the perspective of grammar, reasoning, or logic,
see Dzogchen teachings as really awful because they don't look as
beautiful as their own philosophies. But that is just the perspective
of pride of those who like the teachings of the abhidharma or others.
Rongzompa said that it is not a correct view that those attached to
their philosophies because they are very beautiful from the perspective of grammar or logic reject Dzogchen because it doesn't have
the same beauty on the level of words or reasoning. He says that
Dzogchen does hold up to reason and that one enters Dzogchen
through faith. To do otherwise, to analyze it from the perspective
of grammar or logic, is a wrong view.

Thinley Norbu Rinpoche's text quotes from the great Indian master Vasubandhu about those who write texts following the tradition

of buddhadharma, without any thought of worldly benefits—that is, without thinking of their own fame or fortune. (Literally he says "without any distraction," meaning any worldly thought.) Vasubandhu says, "When anyone writes a text with the desire for liberation for themselves or others, when it is written in harmony with the path to liberation, I think of these texts as the speech of the Sage [the Buddha], and I place them on the crown of my head."

Thinley Norbu Rinpoche comments that his own teaching is not up to the standard of being written in accord with the path to liberation or without any other thought. But he quotes Patrul Rinpoche who says that if a very ordinary, common person, who has one hundred faults, has one single quality of knowledge or understanding, then don't think of those hundred faults but think of that one quality. Tibetans believe that there is a certain kind of swan that is able to drink milk and water mixed together and take only the milk and leave the water behind. Thinley Norbu Rinpoche says that we should be like the swan and not think of his one hundred faults but think of that one quality. He says he is trying to follow that example of having at least one quality among his hundreds of faults. This finishes the concluding virtue of our text.

Although Thinley Norbu Rinpoche quotes extensively from the Buddha, Longchenpa, and Rongzompa, much of the text has been Thinley Norbu Rinpoche's own experience. He was one of the most outstanding masters of view and meditation in Dzogchen.

So much of what I have taught is based on this text. Any good qualities you see in these teachings come from Thinley Norbu Rinpoche and Dzogchen master Jigme Phuntsok Rinpoche, from my spending time with them and receiving instruction and their lineage from them. I've said an awful lot and undoubtedly mixed these pure teachings with my own ordinary thoughts.

If you read this and think, "This is not really right," any faults come from myself.* Any good qualities in these teachings are from Jigme Phuntsok Rinpoche and Thinley Norbu Rinpoche. I myself

---

*Or from the editor's mistaken understanding of the meaning.

have not the slightest quality of learning or realization. If you find any benefit in these teachings, something that really seems true to you, it is because I have been repeating the words that I heard from my teachers. My teachers are buddhas, and I am an ordinary person. When I add details and make mistakes, please be sensitive to that. Also be sensitive to so much that is true and authentic and beneficial in these teachings. If there is the presence of these teachings, it is because I have been able to repeat the words of my teachers.

I spent nine years with my enlightened teacher Jigme Phuntsok Rinpoche. From the very beginning through to the end, I did not have one moment of thinking of my teacher as an ordinary individual. I always considered him to be an enlightened being. Here, I am just being a messenger between Jigme Phuntsok Rinpoche and you; a mail carrier.

Khenpo Jigme Phuntsok Rinpoche and Thinley Norbu Rinpoche are really and truly the buddha. Teachings like this, if they can be translated or given directly, are perfect. It is only when we start explaining them that we lose our way by adding things, mistaking things, and making what is very clear and perfect, unclear and imperfect. I apologize to the three roots and protectors. Whatever has been good about these teachings is an offering to them and to all of you.

These teachings, as you have seen, from beginning to end, have special qualities. Particularly, they are based in logic and reasoning and are accessible. If dharma practitioners have reasonably open and honest minds, then when they hear these teachings, they can understand. These teachings have gone into detail in order to really explain why and how we should practice on the path to awakening. These teachings have explained very clearly why sentient beings suffer, how it is that they become sentient beings, how they become enlightened, the situation of sentient beings, the state of enlightenment, and the recognition of the awakened state and ultimate nature. All of this has been presented in detail. Also, there are many teachings on Dzogchen that have been presented from the perspective of ordinary reasoning as well as from the direct instructions of the vajra master.

It is my hope and expectation that, by reading or hearing these teachings, you will then have some basis for understanding the qualities of enlightenment, the Buddha, Guru Rinpoche, and the teachings. With an appreciation of the qualities of enlightenment, you can approach your practice and not be discouraged, because your practice will be grounded in having seen the qualities of enlightenment. From the beginning of your practice, it is really critical to have appreciation for the qualities of enlightenment. If you have appreciation, you can practice for a long time without any regret, and you can be stable and unchanging in your relationship to the teachings. Otherwise, without a clear grounding in understanding the qualities of enlightenment and the teachings, you end up feeling a lot of regret for all the time and energy spent in practice.

After reading or hearing these teachings, hopefully you've reflected on them. You must take one step further and put them into practice. You must meditate. Why meditate? Don't meditate for anyone else's benefit. It is for your own good. You are trying to put the teachings into practice in order to make your life happy during this life, make the time of your death happy, and make your future life happy. The teachings should be able to help you gain that happiness. By understanding the nature of reality, by understanding the nature of appearances, by understanding the nature of your mind, this life should become a happy circumstance. These teachings are not just for the future. They should make your present life happy.

Then, based on these teachings, you will also develop great compassion for others, compassion for so many sentient beings who don't understand these kinds of profound teachings. They don't have access to this understanding. Perhaps you will become like Longchenpa or Milarepa. They looked at how people lived, the lifestyles of people in their own day and age (and it is the same in this day and age). Going into town, thinking about these teachings, or sometimes looking at others would make them laugh. Sometimes it would make them cry—to think of the teachings and look at the lives of people who didn't understand.

I advise you very strongly to continue your foundational practices and to finish them. Once you have finished them, ask for and receive teachings in Dzogchen. You can ask for teachings based on Thinley Norbu Rinpoche's text, or there are many other texts of Dzogchen teachings. This book, my teaching on his text, is a consolidation of three months of oral teachings given at Pema Osel Ling, the center for Vajrayana teachings and practice founded by Lama Tharchin Rinpoche. I very much appreciate the effort of all the students who attended these teachings, that they dedicated so much time to coming there and listening to the teachings. Because of this, I have been giving the teachings out of appreciation for their effort and out of very pure motivation.

# The Consequences of the Nonrecognition of the Wisdom Lights

As sentient beings, we experience our mind and the outer world when we fail to recognize naturally manifest awareness (the "wisdom lights") as being our own appearance.

| Wisdom light | Body of enlightenment | Element | Inner level | Aggregate level | Secret level |
|---|---|---|---|---|---|
| white | dharmakaya | space | vital essence | mental states | ignorance |
| green | sambhogakaya | air | breath | perception | envy |
| red | sambhogakaya | fire | bodily heat | karma (tendencies) | desire |
| blue | nirmanakaya | water | blood | consciousness | anger |
| yellow | nirmanakaya | earth | flesh | sensation | pride |

# The Three Kayas

| Dharmakaya | Sambhogakaya | Nirmanakaya |
|---|---|---|
| ultimate body of enlightenment | body of enlightenment's perfect splendor | manifest body of enlightenment |
| essence | nature | display |
| empty essence of mind | clarity and unobstructed nature of mind | all-pervading energy of mind |
| awareness and emptiness | clarity and emptiness | bliss and emptiness |
| eternal because of its essence | eternal because of its continuity | eternal because it never ceases |
| the five wisdoms | the seven aspects (including the five certainties) | the five uncertainties |

# Yeshe Tsogyal's Great Qualities, Activities, and Appellations

- conqueror of supreme knowledge, compassion, and power*
- consort who pleases the enlightened mind of the Lotus Born (Padmasambhava)
- constant protector
- deceitless compassionate one
- dispeller of suffering†
- glorious one who fulfills all wishes
- her benefit for others reaches the far bounds of existence‡
- holder of profound treasures
- the manifestation of power§
- mother of skillful means, who compassionately manifests whatever form is necessary to subdue beings
- the one who accomplishes the hopes of beings
- the one whose blessings enter quickly
- queen of dakinis

*These are the three qualities of the Buddha.

†This refers to the physical suffering or the unhappiness of mind that arises in ordinary, temporary circumstances, which she relieves.

‡Yeshe Tsogyal ensures the continuation of the buddhadharma through the existing teachings and the treasures yet to be revealed and the long life of our teachers.

§This refers to her control of many manifestations of enlightenment.

- · radiant one of blue light*
- · sole consort of the Lotus Guru
- · sole mother and only refuge of the people of Tibet
- · sole mother lineage holder†
- · the source of the profound secret Vajrayana teachings
- · supreme guide of beings
- · vidyadhara (awareness holder) accomplished in the supreme attainment of immortality
- · wish-fulfilling jewel
- · yogini who has perfected all the stages and paths‡

*Intense Blue Light is the name of Yeshe Tsogyal when she is with Guru Rinpoche at his pure land, the Copper-Colored Mountain.

†Yeshe Tsogyal is the lineage holder of Guru Rinpoche's teachings.

‡Yeshe Tsogyal has arrived at the thirteenth stage, complete enlightenment, and among the five paths she has arrived at the path beyond training, the final path, enlightenment.

# The Four Empowerments of Guru Yoga

| Empowerment | What is blessed | What is purified | Outer elements | Inner elements | Body of enlightenment | Mode of emptiness |
|---|---|---|---|---|---|---|
| vase | body | desire | earth water | flesh blood | nirmanakaya | exaltation |
| secret | speech | anger | fire wind | bodily heat breath | sambhogakaya | clarity |
| wisdom | mind | ignorance | space | vital essence | dharmakaya | awareness |
| precious word | all the qualities and activities of the three kayas at one place and time, indivisibly | | | | svabhavikakaya | |

# Aspiration

ALAK ZENKAR RINPOCHE

Treasury of millions of instructions from vidyadharas of the
    threefold transmission,
Supreme master of the great secret teachings of the Ancient
    Translations,
Longchen Rabjam Drimé Özer,
To your dance-like emanation, I pray.

With your great stores of *fearless* confidence naturally released,
You are a *master of life*, a crown ornament of a hundred adepts,
And supreme Dharma lord whose *activity* is boundless as space—
If you are not the unique *jewel* that this world requires, who is?

Now that the activity of your three secrets has concluded,
I pray that this abundance of Dharma, a relic of dharmakaya,
Which you have bequeathed as a gift to fortunate heirs,
May benefit beings on a scale equal to the vastness of space!

*Upon the publication of a work by the supreme Dungsé Thinley
Norbu, crown ornament of a hundred adepts and emanation of the
primordial protector, the great omniscient one in human form, I,
a vagabond from Minyak called Tudeng Nima, put my palms and
ten fingers together at my heart and offered these words out of joy,
reverence, and faith, from an island in the East on the third day of
the first month of the year 2024.*

NOTE: Tudeng Nima, known to many as Alak Zenkar Rinpoche, wrote this benedic-
tion to mark the publication of this work by Orgyen Chowang Rinpoche and honor
the author of the original text, Kyabje Thinley Norbu Rinpoche.

# Index